Rick

PROVENCE &
THE FRENCH RIVIERA

2005

Rick Steves & Steve Smith

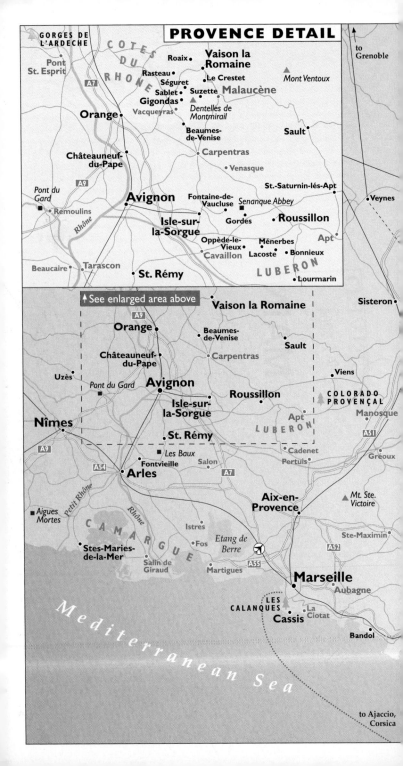

PROVENCE & THE FRENCH RIVIERA

A7	Freeway/Autoroute
	Rail Line
	Bus Line
	Ferry Line
✈	Airport
Cassis	Recommended location*
Toulon	Just passing through**
🌲	National Park/Natural Wonder
■	Ruin, Museum, other Point of Interest

* Black locations are places of interest to tourists, sized by importance. Many are covered in this guidebook.

** Gray locations are places of little or no interest to tourists and are sized by population.

Les Deux-Alpes

Briançon

L'Argentière-la-Bessée

Guillestre

Embrun

Gap • Savines-le-Lac

Le Lauzet-Ubaye • Barcelonnette

FRANCE

ITALY

Digne-les-Bains

Verdon

Var

Entrevaux

Castellane

Moustiers-Ste-Marie

Riez • Lac de St-Croix • Aiguines • D-71

GORGES DU LOUP

Tourrettes-sur-Loup

La Turbie

Ventimiglia

A8

Menton

Gourdon • Vence

Eze

Beaulieu

MONACO

GRAND CANYON DU VERDON

Comps

Le Bar-sur-Loup

St-Paul-de-Vence

Villefranche

Cap Ferrat

Aups • D-956

Grasse

Nice

Cagnes

Draguignan

Antibes

to Bastia, Corsica

Cannes

Les Arcs • A8

Fréjus

Scenic drive

R
I
V
I
E
R
A

C
Ô
T
E

D'
A
Z
U
R

to L'Isle Rousse, Corsica

St-Raphaël

Ste. Maxime

A57

Grimaud • St-Tropez

Hyéres • Le Lavandou

Toulon

Iles d'Hyères

0 km		25 km

0 miles		15 miles

Rick Steves'

PROVENCE &
THE FRENCH RIVIERA

2005

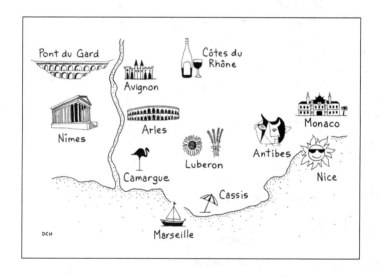

AVALON
TRAVEL

CONTENTS

Top Destinations
in Provence & the French Riviera

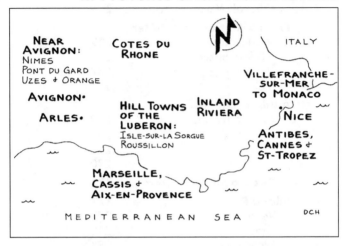

INTRODUCTION

Provence and the French Riviera make an intoxicating bouillabaisse of enjoyable cities, warm stone villages, Roman ruins, contemporary art, and breathtaking coastlines steaming with sunshine and stirred by the wind. There's something about the play of light in this region, where natural and manmade beauty mingle to dazzle the senses and nourish the soul. It all adds up to *une magnifique* vacation.

Provence and the Riviera stretch along France's southeast Mediterranean coast from the Camargue (south of Arles) to Monaco, and ramble north along the Rhône Valley into the Alps. The region is about the same size as Massachusetts—you can take a train or drive from one end to the other in just three hours—yet it contains more sightseeing opportunities and let's-retire-here villages than anywhere else in France. Marseille and Nice, the country's third and fifth largest cities, lend good transportation and an urban perspective to this otherwise relaxed region, where every day feels like Saturday.

In Provence, gnarled sycamore-lined roads twist their way through stone towns and oceans of vineyards. France's Riviera is about the sea and money, populated by a yacht-happy crowd wondering where the next "scene" will be. While Provence feels older and *muy español* (with paella on menus and bullfights on Sundays), the Riviera feels downright Italian—with fresh-Parmesan-topped pasta and red-orange pastel-colored buildings. For every Roman ruin in Provence, there's a modern-art museum in the Riviera. Provence is famous for its wines and wind, while the bikini and ravioli were invented on the Riviera.

Throughout 16 years of guiding tours and writing France guidebooks together, Rick Steves and Francophile Steve Smith have worked hard to discover the most interesting destinations in Provence and the Riviera, giving you tips on how to use your time

Provence & the French Riviera

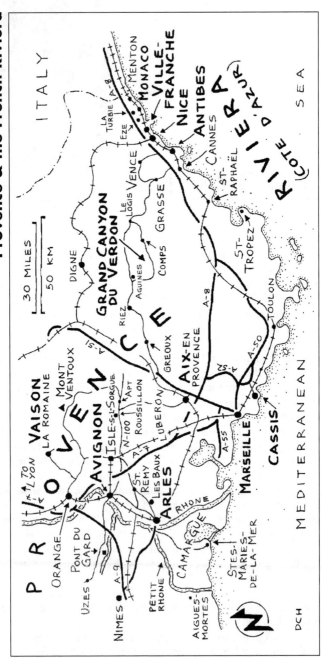

and money most efficiently. Each of our recommended destinations is like a glass of fine wine—and this book provides instructions on how to enjoy the full bouquet.

This book covers the predictable biggies and mixes in a healthy dose of Back Door intimacy—from jet-setting beach resorts to lost canyons. Along with the Pont du Gard, Nice, and Avignon, we'll introduce you to our favorite villages. You'll stop by wineries and see untouristy Roman ruins. You'll marvel at ancient monuments, take a canoe trip down the lazy Sorgue River, and settle into a shaded café on a small square. Discover the ideal beach to call home. At day's end, dive headfirst into a Provençal sunset from a hill-town perch. You'll try tasty-yet-affordable wines while feasting on a healthy cuisine heavy on olives, tomatoes, and spices. Just as important, you'll meet the intriguing people who run your hotel or the nearby bistro.

Rick Steves' Provence & the French Riviera is a tour guide in your pocket—actually, two tour guides in your pocket. We've been selective, including only the most exciting sights and romantic villages. There are *beaucoup* Provençal hill towns...but we cover only the most enchanting. And while there are dozens of beach towns on the Riviera, we recommend the top three.

The best is, of course, only our opinion. But after more than 25 busy years between us of travel writing, lecturing, guiding tours, and satisfying our Francophilia, we've developed a sixth sense for what touches the traveler's imagination.

This Information is Accurate and Up-to-Date

This book is completely updated every year. Most publishers of guidebooks that cover a region from top to bottom can afford an update only every two or three years, and even then, the research is often by letter or e-mail. Since this book is selective, covering only the places we think make the top two weeks of sightseeing in Provence and the French Riviera, we can update it in person each summer. Of course, even with an annual update, things change. But if you're traveling with the current edition of this book, we guarantee you're using the most up-to-date information available in print. For the latest, visit www.ricksteves.com/update. Also at our Web site, check our Graffiti Wall (select "Rick Steves' Guidebooks," then "Provence and the French Riviera") for a list of reports and experiences—good and bad—from fellow travelers.

This book will help you have an inexpensive, hassle-free trip. Use this year's edition. People who try to save a few bucks by traveling with an old book are not smart. They learn the seriousness of their mistake...in France. Your trip costs at least $10 per waking hour. Your time is valuable. This guidebook will save you lots of time.

About This Book

This book consists of two obvious parts—Provence and the Riviera (although almost everything covered in this book is officially considered part of the "Provence–Alpes–Côte d'Azur region" by the French government).

The Provence half focuses on Arles, Avignon, and their daytrip destinations; the photogenic hill towns of the Côtes du Rhône and Luberon; and the coastal towns of Marseille and Cassis and nearby Aix-en-Provence. On the high-rolling French Riviera, we cover the waterfront destinations of Nice, Villefranche-sur-Mer, Monaco, Antibes, Cannes, and St-Tropez—plus the best of the inland hill towns and the amazing Grand Canyon du Verdon.

The book is organized in the following way:

Planning Your Time, with suggested schedules in the Provence and Riviera introductions, offers ideas on how best to use your limited time. We've also included a day-by-day description of our favorite two-week trip by car (page 26) or by train and bus (page 16).

Orientation material for all key destinations, including tourist information, city transportation, and easy-to-read maps, is designed to make the text clear and your arrival smooth.

Sleeping and **Eating,** offering a great range of good-value accommodations and restaurants, covers everything from homey, affordable places to worth-the-splurge experiences. The best trips are a blend of both.

Sights, described in detail, are rated: ▲▲▲—Don't miss; ▲▲—Try hard to see; ▲—Worthwhile if you can make it; No rating—Worth knowing about.

Self-Guided Tours include a walk through Old Nice, the Chagall Museum, and Antibes' Picasso Museum. We also cover self-guided **driving tours** of our favorite trips, allowing you to explore the Côtes du Rhône wine road, two Luberon hill-town routes, the Grand Canyon du Verdon, and inland hill towns of the Riviera with the knowledge of a local.

Transportation Connections has specifics on linking destinations by train, plus route tips for drivers.

Traveling with Children offers general tips and destination-specific advice, like kid-friendly hotels and restaurants. Your authors have kids (from 3–16 years old), and we've used our substantial experience traveling with children to improve this book. Our kids have enriched our travels, and we hope the same will be true for you.

Shopping has suggestions for this region's best souvenirs and bargains. Steve's wife, who had a business importing French products to the United States, contributed her shopping-savvy advice.

A handy **appendix** with telephone tips and useful phone numbers, a climate chart, and a festival calendar.

Browse through this book, choose your favorite places, and

organize your trip. You'll travel like a temporary local and get the absolute most out of every mile, minute, and euro. You won't waste time on mediocre sights because, unlike other guidebooks, we cover only the best. Since your major financial pitfall can be lousy, expensive hotels, we've worked hard to assemble the top accommodation values for each stop. As you visit places we know and love, we're happy you'll be meeting our favorite French people.

PLANNING

Trip Costs

Five components make up your total trip cost: airfare, surface transportation, room and board, sightseeing/entertainment, and shopping/miscellany.

Airfare: Don't try to sort through the mess. Find and use a good travel agent. Nice is the handiest airport for Provence and the Riviera. A basic round-trip United States-to-Nice (or Paris) flight costs $700–1,300 (cheaper in winter), depending on where you fly from and when. (Smaller budget airlines now provide bargain service to cities such as Avignon and Montpellier; see "Cheap Flights" on page 305 for details.) Always consider saving time and money in Europe by flying "open jaw"—into one city and out of another. Flying into Nice and out of Paris costs roughly the same as flying round-trip to Paris.

Surface Transportation: Allow $20 per day per person for public transportation (trains, buses, and taxis), or $30 per day for a rental car (based on two people sharing) for rental fees, tolls, gas, and insurance. Car rental is cheapest if arranged from the United States. Train passes only make sense if you are traveling to regions beyond Provence and the Riviera, as distances within this region are short and point-to-point fares are reasonable. Remember that married couples, seniors, students, and families can benefit from discounts (*réduction,* ray-duke-see-own). Railpasses are normally available only outside of Europe (see "Transportation," page 20, for more details on car rental, rail trips, and bus travel).

Room and Board: You can thrive in Provence and the Riviera on $90 a day per person for room and board. A $90-a-day budget allows $8 for breakfast, $12 for lunch, $25 for dinner, and $45 for lodging (based on two people splitting the cost of a $90 double room). That's definitely doable. Students and tightwads do it on $45 a day ($25 per bed, $20 for meals and snacks). But budget sleeping and eating requires the skills and information covered later in this chapter (and in much greater depth in *Rick Steves' Europe Through the Back Door*).

Sightseeing and Entertainment: Allow about $5–10 per major sight (Arles' Roman Arena-$5, Nice's Chagall Museum-$7, Pont du Gard combo-ticket-$11), $4 for minor ones (climbing church towers), $12 for guided walks, and $25 for splurge experiences (e.g., bullfights or concerts). Arles, Avignon, and the Riviera region each offer a money-saving museum pass (details listed in this book). An overall average of $15 a day works for most. Don't skimp here. After all, this category directly powers most of the experiences all the other expenses are designed to make possible.

Shopping and Miscellany: Figure $3 per ice cream cone, coffee, or soft drink. Shopping can vary in cost from nearly nothing to a small fortune (to stretch your euro the furthest, see the Shopping chapter, page 293). Good budget travelers find that this category has little to do with assembling a trip full of lifelong and wonderful memories.

When to Go

With more than 300 days of sunshine per year, Provence and the Riviera enjoy France's sunniest weather. Spring and fall are best, with generally comfortable weather—though crowds can be a problem if you're not careful, particularly during holiday weekends (see below). April can be damp, and any month can be windy.

Summer means festivals, lavender, steamy weather, long hours at sights, and longer lines of cars along the Riviera. Europeans vacation in July and August, jamming the Riviera, the Gorges du Verdon, and Ardèche (worst during July 15–Aug 20), but leaving the rest of this region relatively calm. While many French businesses close in August, the traveler hardly notices.

September brings the grape harvest, when private wineries are off-limits to taste-seeking travelers (for information on wine tasting, see page 52). Late fall delivers beautiful foliage and a return to tranquility in normally crowded places.

While you can find mild, sunny weather in any season, Provence is famous for its bone-chilling winters when the wind blows. Winter travel is okay in Nice and Avignon, but you'll find smaller cities and villages buttoned up tight. Sights and tourist-information offices keep shorter hours, and some tourist activities (like English-language castle tours) vanish altogether. To get the latest weather forecast in English, dial 08 99 70 11 11, then press 1. Also see the climate chart in the appendix.

Thanks to Provence's temperate climate, fields of flowers greet the traveler much of the year:

April–May: Wild red poppies *(coquelicots)* start sprouting.

June: Lavender begins to bloom in the hills of Provence, generally during the last week of the month.

July: Lavender is in full swing in Provence, and sunflowers are awakening. Cities, towns, and villages everywhere overflow with carefully tended flowers.

Le Mistral

Provence lives with its vicious mistral winds, which blow 30–60 miles per hour, about 100 days out of the year. Locals say it blows in multiples of threes: three, six, or nine days in a row. *Le mistral* clears people off the streets and turns lively cities into virtual ghost towns. You'll likely spend a few hours taking refuge—or searching for cover.

When *le mistral* blows, it's everywhere, and you can't escape. Peter Mayle said it could blow the ears off a donkey. Locals say it ruins crops, shutters, and roofs (look for the stones holding tiles in place on many homes). They'll also tell you that this pernicious wind has driven many crazy (including young Vincent van Gogh). A weak version of the wind is called a *mistralet*.

The mistral starts above the Alps and Massif Central Mountains and gathers steam as it heads south, gaining momentum as it screams over the Rhône Valley (which acts like a funnel between the Alps and Pyrénées) before exhausting itself as it hits the Mediterranean. While this wind rattles shutters throughout the Riviera and Provence, it's strongest over the Rhône Valley...so Avignon, Arles, and the Côtes du Rhône villages bear its brunt. While wiping the dust from your eyes, remember the good news: The mistral brings clear skies.

August–September: Sunflowers flourish.

October: In the latter half of the month, the countryside glistens with fall colors (since most trees are deciduous). Vineyards go for the gold.

Sightseeing Priorities

Depending on the length of your trip, here are our recommended priorities:

5 days:	Arles, Avignon, Les Baux, Pont du Gard, and Nice/Monaco.
8 days, add:	Cassis, Orange, and Côtes du Rhône.
11 days, add:	Luberon, Grand Canyon du Verdon, and Antibes.
14 days, add:	Nîmes, Marseille, Aix-en-Provence, and Camargue.

For details, refer to the daily itineraries of our favorite two-week trip by car (see page 26) or public transportation (see page 16).

RESOURCES

French Tourist Offices in the United States

France's national tourist offices are a wealth of information. Before your trip, request any specific information you may want (such as

Rick Steves' Guidebooks

Rick Steves' Europe Through the Back Door
Rick Steves' Best European City Walks & Museums
Rick Steves' Easy Access Europe

Country Guides

Rick Steves' Best of Europe
Rick Steves' Best of Eastern Europe
Rick Steves' France
Rick Steves' Germany & Austria
Rick Steves' Great Britain
Rick Steves' Ireland
Rick Steves' Italy
Rick Steves' Portugal
Rick Steves' Scandinavia
Rick Steves' Spain
Rick Steves' Switzerland

City and Regional Guides

Rick Steves' Amsterdam, Bruges & Brussels
Rick Steves' Florence & Tuscany
Rick Steves' London
Rick Steves' Paris
Rick Steves' Prague & the Czech Republic*
Rick Steves' Provence & the French Riviera
Rick Steves' Rome
Rick Steves' Venice

*New in 2005

(Avalon Travel Publishing)

city maps and schedules of upcoming festivals). For questions and brochures, call 410/286-8310. Ask for the France Guide. Materials delivered in 4–6 weeks are free; there's a $4 shipping fee for information delivered in 5–10 days. Their Web site is www.franceguide.com, their e-mail is info@franceguide.com, and their offices are in:

New York: 444 Madison Ave., 16th floor, New York, NY 10022, tel. 212/838-7800, fax 212/838-7855, Mon–Fri 10:00–16:00, closed Sat–Sun.

California: 9454 Wilshire Blvd. #310, Beverly Hills, CA 90212, tel. 310/271-6665, fax 310/276-2835, Mon–Fri 9:00–13:00 & 14:00–17:00, closed Sat–Sun.

Rick Steves' Books and Public Television Shows

Rick Steves' Europe Through the Back Door 2005 gives you budget travel skills on minimizing jet lag, packing light, planning your itinerary, traveling by car or train, finding budget beds, changing money, avoiding rip-offs, hurdling the language barrier, staying healthy, using your bidet, and much more. The book also includes chapters on 38 of Rick's favorite "Back Doors," including one on Paris.

Rick Steves' Country Guides, an annually updated series that covers Europe, offer you the latest on the top sights and destinations, with tips on how to make your trip efficient and fun.

Provence & the French Riviera 2005 is one of our **City and Regional Guides.** Updated every year, these focus on Europe's most compelling destinations. Along with specifics on sights, restaurants, hotels, and nightlife, you'll get self-guided, illustrated tours of the outstanding museums and most characteristic neighborhoods.

Rick Steves' Easy Access Europe, written for travelers with limited mobility, covers London, Paris, Bruges, Amsterdam, and the Rhine River.

Rick Steves' Europe 101: History and Art for the Traveler (with Gene Openshaw) gives you the story of Europe's people, history, and art. Written for smart people who were sleeping in their history and art classes before they knew they were going to Europe, *101* helps Europe's sights come alive.

Rick Steves' Best European City Walks & Museums (with Gene Openshaw) gives you self-guided tours of the major museums and historic neighborhoods in Paris, London, Amsterdam, Rome, Florence, Venice, and Madrid.

Rick Steves' French Phrase Book helps you meet the people and stretch your budget. It's written by a monoglot who, for 25 years, has fumbled through France struggling with all the other phrase books. This handy book has everything you'll need, including a menu decoder, conversation starters for connecting with locals, and an easy-to-follow telephone template for making hotel reservations.

Our public television series, *Rick Steves' Europe,* keeps churning out shows. Several of the 95 episodes, including two new shows from the latest series (as well as past shows from *Travels in Europe with Rick Steves*), feature the sights covered in this book.

Rick Steves' Postcards from Europe, Rick's autobiographical book, packs 25 years of travel anecdotes and insights into the ultimate 2,000-mile European adventure.

Other Guidebooks

For most travelers, this book is all you need. But if you're traveling beyond our recommended destinations, consider some supplemental information. Considering the improvements they'll make in your $3,000 vacation, $25 or $35 for extra maps and books is money well spent. One simple budget tip can easily save the price of an extra guidebook.

Of the several guidebooks on Provence and the Riviera, many

Trouble In Paradise: Population Growth in Provence and the Riviera

From the snazzy beaches of the Riviera to the cozy villages of Provence to the rugged alpine interior, there are big differences among the people living in southeast France. But two troubling growth-related issues face them all.

The first issue is the number of northern Europeans choosing to relocate to this sunny climate. Cheap flights from Paris, England, and the Netherlands and lightning-fast train service have enabled many to experience the south of France as a weekend getaway. Relatively inexpensive homes (with pools) have added fuel to this southern migration. As local homes are picked off by wealthy northerners, prices are inflated, and few options remain for the average Jean. On every trip to this region, I hear more and more complaints of traffic jams, higher property taxes, and less open space brought on by heat-seeking northern Europeans.

The second issue is immigration, particularly from North Africa. With native French birth rates below replacement levels and a historic loss of able-bodied men from two world wars, France has looked across the Mediterranean to its old colonies for cheap sources

are high on facts and low on opinion, guts, or personality. Most try to cover too much, thus diluting their information as well as their ability to update every year. For well-researched (though not annually updated) background information, try the Cadogan guide to Southern France. Serious learners prefer the Knopf guides to the Eyewitness guides' pretty pictures. The popular, skinny, green Michelin guides are dry but informative, especially for drivers. They're known for their city and sightseeing maps and for their succinct, helpful information on all major sights. English editions, covering most of the regions you'll want to visit, are sold in France for about €14 (or $20 in the United States).

Recommended Books and Movies

To get a feel for France in general, and specifically for Provence and the French Riviera, consider reading some of these books or seeing these films:

Books: To better understand the French, read *French or Foe* (by Polly Platt). To understand village life in Provence, read *A Year in Provence* and *Toujours Provence* (by Peter Mayle). *The Course of French History* (by Pierre Goubert) provides a succinct, readable summary of French history. Ina Caro's *The Road from the Past* is filled with enjoyable essays on her travels through France with an accent on history. *A Goose in Toulouse* offers keen insights to rural France through its focus on cuisine (Mort Rosenblum). Other good of manual labor. As these workers came, they brought their families, who stayed in France and had large families of their own, which steadily increased their numbers.

Today, five million North Africans legally reside in France (about 8 percent of the population)—and many more live here illegally. More than 100,000 illegal immigrants arrive in France each year, about half of whom are North African. Most live in the south (a quarter of Marseille's population is North African). This concentration of immigrants among a very Catholic French population, combined with high unemployment (14.5 percent compared to a national average of 10 percent), has led to the rise of racist politics. This anti-immigrant movement has been spearheaded by the Front National party, which wants to keep "France for the French." Its leader, Jean-Marie Le Pen, has referred to the increasing numbers of North Africans in France as "the silent invasion." The Front National received almost 30 percent of this region's vote in a recent election, and four key cities elected mayors from this party. You'll see signs and billboards on both sides of this issue ("F. N." means Front National).

non-fiction books include *Travelers' Tales: France* (edited by James O'Reilly); *Portraits of France* (by Robert Daley); *Holy Blood, Holy Grail* (by Michael Baigent, Richard Leigh, and Henry Lincoln); *At Home in France* (by Ann Barry); *Postcards from France* (by Megan McNeill Libby); *A Distant Mirror* (by Barbara W. Tuchman); *Adapter Kit France: A Traveler's Tools for Living Like a Local* (by Terry Link); and *Culture Shock: France* (by Sally A. Taylor). Also see the list of books recommended for children, which many adults could enjoy, on page 290.

Flicks: *Les Misérables, French Kiss, To Catch A Thief, Jean de Florette, ...And God Created Woman, My Mother's Castle, My Father's Glory, Manon of the Spring, Mr. Hulot's Holiday, The Horseman on the Roof,* and *Lust for Life.*

Maps

The black-and-white maps in this book, drawn by Dave Hoerlein, are concise and simple. Dave, who is well-traveled in France, designed the maps to help you locate recommended places and reach TIs, where you'll find more in-depth (and often free) maps of cities or regions. Better maps are sold at newsstands—take a look before you buy to be sure the map has the level of detail you want.

My *Rick Steves' France Planning Map* is geared for the traveler and shows sightseeing destinations prominently. Michelin maps are available throughout France at bookstores, newsstands, and gas

Begin Your Trip at www.ricksteves.com

At ricksteves.com you'll find a wealth of **free information** on destinations covered in this book, including fresh European travel and tour news every month and helpful "Graffiti Wall" tips from thousands of fellow travelers.

While you're there, Rick Steves' **online Travel Store** is a great place to save money on travel bags and accessories specially designed by Rick Steves to help you travel smarter and lighter. These include Rick's popular carry-on bags (wheeled and rucksack versions), money belts, day bags, totes, toiletries kits, packing cubes, clotheslines, locks, clocks, sleep sacks, adapters, and a wide selection of guidebooks, planning maps, and *Rick Steves' Europe* DVDs.

Traveling through Europe by rail is a breeze, but choosing the right railpass for your trip (amidst hundreds of options) can drive you nutty. At ricksteves.com you'll find **Rick Steves' Annual Guide to European Railpasses**—your best way to convert chaos into pure travel energy. Buy your railpass from Rick, and you'll get a bunch of free extras to boot.

Travel agents will tell you about mainstream tours of Europe, but they won't tell you about **Rick Steves' tours.** Rick Steves' Europe Through the Back Door travel company offers more than two dozen itineraries and 250-plus departures reaching the best destinations in this book...and beyond. You'll enjoy the services of a great guide, a fun bunch of travel partners (with group sizes in the mid-20s), and plenty of room to spread out in a big, comfy bus. You'll find tours to fit every vacation size, from weeklong city getaways (Paris, London, Venice, Florence, Rome), to 12–18 day country tours, to three-week "Best of Europe" adventures. For details, visit www.ricksteves.com or call 425/771-8303 ext 217.

stations (about €5 each, half the U.S. price). Train travelers can do fine with Michelin's #989 France map (1:1,000,000). For better detail, pick up the yellow Michelin Local series maps as you travel (we've listed the map number when pertinent). Drivers going beyond Provence and the Riviera should consider the soft-cover Michelin France atlas (the entire country at 1:200,000, well-organized in a €20 book with an index and maps of major cities). Spend a few minutes learning the Michelin key to get the most sightseeing value out of these maps.

PRACTICALITIES

Red Tape: You need a passport, but no visa or shots, to travel in France. It's a good idea to bring photocopies of your identity papers if the originals are lost or stolen. You are required to have proof of identity on you at all times in France.

Time: In France—and in this book—you'll use the 24-hour clock. It's the same through 12:00 noon, then keep going: 13:00, 14:00, and so on. For anything over 12, subtract 12 and add p.m. (14:00 is 2:00 p.m.).

Business Hours: You'll find much of rural France closed weekdays from noon to 14:00 (lunch is sacred). Sundays and holidays have pros and cons, as they do for travelers in the United States (special events and weekly markets, limited hours, shops and banks closed, limited public transportation, no rush hours). On Sunday, most businesses are closed (family is sacred), though small stores such as *boulangeries* (bakeries) are open until noon, and museums are open all day. On Monday, many businesses are closed until 14:00 or even all day. Smaller towns are often quiet and downright boring on Sundays and Mondays, unless it's market day. Saturdays are like weekdays. Note that on any day, sights stop admitting people 30–60 minutes before they close. Beware of strikes *(grèves)*, which seem more common in the south and can bring trains, flights, and freeways to a halt.

Shopping: Shoppers interested in customs regulations and VAT refunds (the tax refunded on large purchases made by non-EU residents) can refer to page 298.

Discounts: While discounts for sights and transportation generally are not listed in this book, seniors (60 and over) and students (with International Student Identification Cards; contact STA Travel, below) may get discounts—but only by asking. Those under 18 nearly always receive generous discounts. Teachers with an International Teacher ID Card might be given discounts or free admission to some sights. To get a Teacher or Student ID Card, contact STA Travel (U.S. tel. 800/777-0112, www.statravel.com) or the International Student Travel Confederation (www.isic.org).

Watt's up? If you're bringing electrical gear, you'll need a two-prong adapter plug and a converter. Travel appliances often have convenient, built-in converters; look for a voltage switch marked 120V (U.S.) and 240V (Europe).

MONEY

Exchange Rate

We've priced things throughout this book in the local currency: the euro.

1 euro (€) = about $1.20

To convert prices in euros to dollars, add 20 percent: €20 = about $24, €45 = about $50. Just like the dollar, the euro is broken down into 100 cents *(centimes)*. You'll find coins ranging from €0.01 to €2, and bills from €5 to €500.

Banking

Bring a debit card (or ATM card) and a credit card, along with a couple hundred dollars in cash as a backup. Traveler's checks are a waste of your time and money.

The best and easiest way to get cash in euros is to use the omnipresent French bank machines (always open, low fees, and quick processing). You'll need a PIN code—numbers only, no letters—to use with your Visa or MasterCard. "Cash machines" in French are signed *point d'argent* or *distributeur des billets;* the French call these *D.A.B.* (day ah bay).

Before you go, verify with your bank that your card will work and alert them that you'll be making withdrawals in Europe; otherwise, the bank may not approve transactions if it perceives unusual spending patterns. Bring two cards in case one gets damaged.

Just like at home, credit or debit cards work easily at larger hotels, restaurants, and shops. Visa and MasterCard are more commonly accepted than American Express. Smaller businesses prefer payment in local currency. Smart travelers function with hard cash and plastic.

Keep your credit and debit cards and most of your money hidden away in a money belt (a cloth pouch worn around your waist and tucked under your clothes). Thieves target tourists. A money belt provides peace of mind and allows you to carry lots of cash safely. Don't be petty about changing money. Change a week's worth of money, stuff it in your money belt, and travel!

TRAVEL SMART

Your trip to France is like a complex play—easier to follow and really appreciate on a second viewing. While no one does the same trip twice to gain that advantage, reading this book in its entirety before your trip accomplishes much the same thing.

Reread this book as you travel, and visit local tourist information offices. Upon arrival in a new town, lay the groundwork for a smooth departure; write down the schedule for the train or bus you'll take when you depart.

If you're using public transportation, read up on the tips for trains and buses, both listed later in this chapter. If you're driving, be sure to peruse our driving tips and study the examples of road signs (see page 23).

Slow down and ask questions. Most locals are eager to tell you about their town's history and point you in their idea of the right direction. Buy a phone card or mobile phone and use it for

Damage Control for Lost or Stolen Cards

You can stop thieves from using your ATM, debit, or credit card by reporting the loss immediately to the proper company. Call these 24-hour U.S. numbers collect: Visa (tel. 410/581-9994), MasterCard (tel. 636/722-7111), and American Express (tel. 336/393-1111).

Providing the following information will help expedite the process: the name of the financial institution that issued you the card, full card number, the cardholder's name as printed on the card, billing address, home phone number, circumstances of the loss or theft, and identification verification including a Social Security number or birth date and your mother's maiden name. (Packing along a photocopy of the front and back of your cards helps you answer the harder questions.) If you are the secondary cardholder, you'll also need to provide the primary cardholder's identification verification details. You can generally receive a temporary card within two or three business days in Europe.

If you promptly report your card lost or stolen, you typically won't be responsible for any unauthorized transactions on your account, although many banks charge a liability fee of $50.

reservations and confirmations. Those who expect to travel smart, do.

Maximize rootedness by minimizing one-night stands. Plan ahead for banking, laundry, post-office chores, and picnics. Mix intense and relaxed periods. Every trip (and every traveler) needs at least a few slack days. Pace yourself. Assume you will return.

As you read through this book, plan your itinerary. Note the days when sights are closed. Sundays have pros and cons, as they do for traveling in the United States (special events and weekly markets, limited hours, shops and banks closed, limited public transportation, no rush hours). Saturdays are virtually weekdays.

Holiday Weekends: Popular places are even busier on weekends and inundated on three-day weekends. Holiday weekends can make towns, trains, roads, and hotels more crowded than summer. The French are experts at the long weekend, and you're no match for them when it comes to driving and finding hotels during these peak periods.

Major Holidays: In 2005, be ready for unusually big crowds during these holiday periods—Easter week (March 21–29), Labor Day weekend (April 29–May 1), Ascension weekend (May 5–8), Bastille Day (July 14), Assumption (Aug 15), All Saints' Day weekend (Oct 29–Nov 1), Armistice Day weekend (Nov 11–13), and the winter holidays (Dec 17–Jan 3). Many sights close on the actual holiday (confirm closures at local TIs).

Best Two-Week Trip of Provence & the French Riviera (By Train and Bus)

Note that fewer buses and trains run on Sunday.

Day **Plan**

1 Fly into Nice. Settle in at your hotel, then stroll the promenade des Anglais. Sleep in or near Nice.

2 Take our self-guided Old Nice Walk (page 222) in the morning, allowing time to smell the *fougasse* and sample a café. Spend your afternoon at one or more of Nice's fine museums (see Chagall Museum Tour on page 229). Have dinner on the beach. Sleep in or near Nice.

3 Take the train to Antibes and try our self-guided tours of its old city and the Picasso Museum. Consider a hike along Cap d'Antibes. Return to Nice, rest up, and then head into Monaco for dinner and gambling. Sleep in or near Nice.

4 Take a bus north to Vence and St-Paul-de-Vence. (Stop for a stroll and consider a visit to Fondation Maeght and/or Matisse's Chapel of the Rosary.) Sleep in Vence or back in Nice.

5 Take a train from Nice to Isle-sur-la-Sorgue (best to arrive on Saturday or Wednesday and awake to tomorrow's market day). Wander and explore the town. Consider a canoe ride down the crystal-clear Sorgue River. Sleep in Isle-sur-la-Sorgue.

6 Enjoy market day this morning, then take a train to Avignon. Take our self-guided Avignon walking tour this afternoon and enjoy dinner on one of Avignon's many atmospheric squares. Sleep in Avignon.

7 Relax in Avignon this morning, and divide the rest of your day between Nîmes and the Pont du Gard (bus from Avignon to Pont du Gard, bus from Pont du Gard to Nîmes, train from

Tourist Information

The tourist information office (abbreviated as **TI** in this book) is your best first stop in most places. Throughout Provence and the Riviera, you'll find TIs are usually well-organized with English-speaking staff. If you're arriving in town after the office closes, try calling ahead or picking up a map in a neighboring town. Most TIs will help you find a room by calling hotels (for a small fee) or by giving you a complete listing of available bed-and-breakfasts. Towns with a lot of tourism generally have English-speaking guides available for private hire (about $100 for a 2-hr guided town walk).

The French call TIs by different names. *Office de Tourisme* and *Bureau de Tourisme* are used in cities, while *Syndicat d'Initiative* or *Information Touristique* are used in small towns. Also look for *Accueil* signs in airports and at popular sights. These are information booths

Nîmes back to Avignon). If the weather's good, bring your swimsuit and float on your back below the 2,000-year-old Pont du Gard. Sleep in Avignon.

8 Take a bus or train to Orange, visit its Roman theater, then take a bus to Vaison la Romaine (market day is Tuesday, so a Monday arrival is ideal). Set up in Vaison la Romaine for two nights. This requires careful planning as few buses run to Vaison la Romaine.

9 Explore Vaison la Romaine's upper medieval village and lower Roman city, then bike to Séguret and Gigondas, or hike to Le Crestet for lunch (taxi back). Check out Vaison la Romaine's wine cooperative. Sleep in Vaison la Romaine.

10 Take a bus to Orange, and then a train to Arles (big market day on Saturday). Check into Arles for the next two days. Sleep in Arles.

11 Take a taxi to Les Baux and have breakfast with a view. Spend your afternoon back in Arles. Sleep in Arles.

12 Take a train to Cassis. Take a boat trip to the *calanques,* watch the *pétanque* balls roll, and end your day with a taxi ride up Cap Canaille. Sleep in Cassis.

13 Take a train to Aix-en-Provence. Have lunch and take our self-guided walking tour of the city, then return home to Cassis and watch the sunset from the old port, while you savor a bouillabaisse dinner. Sleep in Cassis.

14 Take the short train ride into Marseille (check your bag at the station), explore the city, then take a train back to Nice. Sleep in Nice.

15 Trip over.

staffed with seasonal helpers who provide tourists with limited, though generally sufficient, information. TIs are often closed from noon to 14:00.

TRANSPORTATION

By Car or Train?

Cars are best for three or more traveling together (especially families with small kids), those packing heavy, and those scouring the countryside in search of the perfect hill town—a tempting plan for this region. Trains and buses are best for solo travelers, blitz tourists, and city-to-city travelers. If you intend to focus on Arles, Avignon, Aix-en-Provence, and seaside destinations along the Riviera, go by train. Stations are centrally located in each city, which makes hotel-hunting and sightseeing easy. Buses and taxis pick up where trains leave off. While bus service can be sparse, taxis are generally available and reasonable. If relying on public transportation, seriously evaluate the value of train or bus detours and focus on fewer destinations.

Trains

France's rail system (SNCF) sets the pace in Europe. Its super TGV (*train à grande vitesse;* tay zhay vay) system has inspired bullet trains throughout the world. The TGV runs at 170–220 mph. Its rails are fused into one long, continuous track for a faster and smoother ride. The TGV has changed commuting patterns in much of France and put most of the country within day-trip distance of Paris. The fastest TGV Mediterranean line opened in 2001, with trains screaming from Paris' city center and Charles de Gaulle airport to Avignon in 2.5 hours and to Marseille in three hours. TGV trains serve these cities in Provence and the Riviera: Avignon, Arles, Nîmes, Marseilles, Orange, Aix-en-Provence, Antibes, Cannes, and Nice. Avignon and Aix-en-Provence have separate TGV stations on the edge of town (with handy bus connections into the center)—note carefully which station your train serves (either "Centre-Ville" or "TGV"; if it's not specified, then it's the central station).

Schedules change by season, weekday, and weekend. Verify train schedules shown in this book (to study ahead on the Web, check http://bahn.hafas.de/bin/query.exe/en). The nationwide information line for train schedules and reservations is tel. 3635. Dial this four-digit number, then press "3" (for reservations or to purchase a ticket) when you get the message. This incredibly helpful, time-saving service costs €0.34 per minute from anywhere in France. Ask for an English-speaking agent and hope for the best (allow 5 min per call). The time and energy you save easily justifies the telephone torture, particularly when making seat reservations. Phoned-in reservations must be picked up at the station at least 30 minutes prior to departure.

Bigger stations have helpful information agents (often in red vests) roaming the station and/or at *Accueil* offices or booths. They're capable of answering rail questions more quickly than the information or ticket windows.

Long-distance travelers can save big money with a France Railpass, sold only outside France (through travel agents or Europe Through the Back Door; see Railpass sidebar on page 20). For roughly the cost of a Paris–Avignon–Paris ticket, the France Railpass offers four days of travel (within a month) anywhere in France. You can add up to six additional days for the cost of a two-hour ride each. Save money by getting the second-class instead of the first-class version and/or travel with a companion (the Flexi Saverpass gives two people traveling together a 20 percent discount).

Each day of use allows you to take as many trips as you want in a 24-hour period (you could go from Paris to Chartres, see the cathedral, then continue to Avignon, stay a few hours, and end in Nice— though we don't recommend it). Buy second-class tickets in France for shorter trips and spend your valuable railpass days wisely.

If traveling *sans* railpass, inquire about the many point-to-point discount fares possible (for youths, those over 60, married couples, families, travel during off-peak hours, and more). Remember that second-class tickets provide the same transportation for up to 33 percent less (and many regional trains to less-trafficked places often have only second-class cars).

Reservations, while generally unnecessary for non-TGV trains, are advisable during busy times (e.g., Friday and Sunday afternoons, weekday rush hours, and particularly holiday weekends; see "When to Go," page 6). Reservations are required for any TGV train (usually about €3, more during peak periods) and for *couchettes* (berths, €15) on night trains. Even railpass-holders need reservations for the TGV trains, and only a limited number of reservations are available for passholders. To avoid the more expensive fares, avoid traveling at peak times; ask at the station. Validate (*composter;* kohm-poh-stay) all train tickets and reservations in the orange machines located before the platforms. (Do not *composter* your railpass, but do validate it at a ticket window before the first time you use it.) Watch others and imitate.

For mixing train and bike travel, ask at stations for information booklets *(Train + Vélo).*

Train Tips

- Check the schedules in advance. Upon arrival at a station, find out your departure possibilities. Large stations have a separate information window or office; at small stations, the regular ticket office gives information.
- Reservations for any TGV train as are required and often sell out. You can reserve any train at any station, through SNCF Boutiques (small offices in city centers), or by phone (tel. 36 35). You must pick up phone reservations at the station at least 30 minutes before departure.
- Arrive at the station with plenty of time before your departure in order to find the right platform, confirm connections, and so on. In small towns, your train may depart before the station opens; go directly to the tracks and find your train listed on the overhead signs. *Remember that Avignon and Aix-en-Provence have separate TGV stations that are outside of the center.*
- Write the date on your "flexi" pass each day you travel.
- Validate tickets (not railpasses) and reservations in orange machines before boarding. If you're traveling with a pass and have

French Railpasses

Prices listed are for 2004. My free *Rick Steves' Guide to European Railpasses* has the latest prices and details (and easy online ordering) at www.ricksteves.com/rail. Note that France-only passes are not valid on Paris-Berlin night train.

FRANCE FLEXIPASS

	Adult 1st class	Adult 2nd class	Senior 1st class	Youth 1st class	Youth 2nd class
Any 4 days in 1 month	$252	$218	$228	$189	$164
Extra rail days (max 6)	32	28	29	24	21

Seniors 60+, youth under 26, kids 4-11 half adult fare.

FRANCE FLEXI SAVERPASS

	Adult first class	Adult second class
Any 4 days in 1 month	$215	$186
Extra rail days (max 6)	28	24

Prices are per person for two or more traveling together. OK to mix kids and adults (kids 4–11 half adult fare).

FRANCE RAIL & DRIVE PASS

Any 2 days of rail and 2 days of Avis rental car in 1 month.

France: The map shows approximate point-to-point one-way 2nd class rail fares in $US. 1st class costs 50% more. Add up fares for your itinerary to see if a railpass will save you money.

Car category	1st class	Extra car day
Economy	$205	$39
Compact	219	49
Intermediate	235	55
Full-size car	255	79
Minivan	299	129

Rail and Drive prices are approximate per person, two traveling together. Solo travelers pay about $100 extra, third and fourth members of a group need only buy the equivalent flexi railpass. Extra rail days (6 max) cost $29 per day for first or second class. To order a France Rail & Drive pass, call your travel agent or Rail Europe at 800/438-7245.

a reservation for a certain trip, you must validate the reservation.

- Before getting on a train, confirm that it's going where you think it is. For example, ask the conductor or any local passenger, *"A Antibes?"* (ah ahn-teeb; meaning, "To Antibes?").
- Some trains split cars en route. Make sure your train car is continuing to your destination by asking, *"Cette voiture va à Avignon?"* (seht vwah-tewr vah ah ah-veen-yohn; meaning, "This car goes to Avignon?").
- If a seat is reserved, it will be labeled *réservé,* with the cities to and from which it is reserved.
- Verify with the conductor all transfers you must make:

Key Travel Phrases

Bonjour, monsieur/madame, parlez-vous anglais?
    Pron: bohn-zhoor, muhs-yur/mah-dahm,
        par-lay-voo ahn-glay?
    Meaning: Hello, sir/madam, do you speak English?

Je voudrais un départ pour ___ (destination), *pour le* ___ (date),
vers ___ (general time of day), *la plus direct possible.*
    Pron: zhuh voo-dray uh day-par poor ___ (destination),
        poor luh ___ (date), vehr ___ (time), lah ploo dee-rehk
        poh-see-bluh.
    Meaning/Example: I would like a departure for Avignon,
        on 23 May, about 9:00, the most direct way possible.

"Correspondance à?" (kor-rehs-pohn-dahns ah; meaning, "Transfer to where?").

- To guard against theft, keep your bags right overhead; don't store them on the racks at the end of the car.
- Note your arrival time so you'll be ready to get off.
- Use the train's free WCs before you get off (but not while the train is stopped).

Buses

Regional bus service is relatively good in Provence and the Riviera. Buses take over where the trains stop. You can get nearly anywhere in Provence and the Riviera by rail and bus...if you're well-organized, patient, and allow enough time. Review our bus schedule information and always verify times at the local tourist office or bus station; call ahead when possible. A few bus lines are run by SNCF (France's rail system) and are included with your railpass (show railpass at station to get free bus ticket), but most bus lines are independent of the rail system and are not covered by railpasses. Train stations often have bus information where train-to-bus connections are important—and vice versa for bus companies. On Sunday, regional bus service virtually disappears.

Bus Tips

- Read the train tips above and use those that apply.
- Use TIs often to help plan your trip; they have regional bus schedules and are happy to assist you.
- Keep in mind that service is sparse on Sunday. Wednesday bus schedules are often different during the school year.
- Be at bus stops at least five minutes early.
- On schedules, *en semaine* means Monday through Saturday.

Rental Cars and Rail 'n' Drive Passes

Car rental is cheapest if arranged in advance from home. Call various companies, look online, or arrange a rental through your hometown travel agent, who can also help you out if anything goes wrong during your trip. The best rates are weekly, with unlimited mileage or leasing (see leasing info below). You can pick up and drop off in medium-size or larger cities anytime. Big companies have offices in more cities and towns. Small rental companies can be cheaper, but aren't as flexible.

You can rent a car on the spot just about anywhere. In many cases, this is a worthwhile splurge. All you need is your American driver's license and money (about €60/day, including 100 kilometers, or 60 miles, per day). If you want a car for only a day (e.g., for the Côtes du Rhône wine route or Luberon villages), you'll find it cheaper to rent it in France—most U.S.-arranged rentals have a three-day minimum (which is still cheaper than two days of a car rental arranged in Europe).

When you drive a rental car, you are liable for its replacement value. CDW (Collision-Damage Waiver) insurance gives you the peace of mind that comes with low-deductible coverage for about $15 a day; a few "gold" credit cards provide this coverage for free if you use their card for the rental. Quiz your credit-card company on the worst-case scenario or consider the $7-a-day policy offered by Travel Guard (U.S. tel. 800/826-1300, www.travelguard .com).

For a trip of three weeks or more, leasing is a bargain. By technically buying and then selling back the car, you save lots of money on tax and insurance (CDW is included). Leasing, which you should arrange from the United States, usually requires a 22-day minimum contract, but Europe by Car leases cars in France for as few as 17 days for $700 (U.S. tel. 800/223-1516, www.europebycar.com). Auto France has good deals on leasing Peugeot cars (U.S. tel. 800/572-9655, fax 201/934-7501, www.autofrance.net).

Rail 'n' drive passes allow you to mix car and train travel economically (available only outside of France, from your travel agent). Generally, big-city connections are best done by train, and rural regions are best done by car. With a rail 'n' drive pass, you get an economic "flexi" railpass with "flexi" car days. This allows you to combine rail and drive into one pass. For a very reasonable package price, you can take advantage of the high speed and comfort of the TGV trains for longer trips, and rent a car for as little as one day at a time for the day trips that can't be done without one. As with normal rental cars, you can pick up a car in one city and drop it off in another city without problems. While you're only required to reserve the first car day, it's safer to reserve all days, as cars are not always available on short notice.

STOP AND LEARN THESE ROAD SIGNS

Speed Limit (km/hr)

Yield

No Passing

End of No Passing Zone

One Way

Intersection

Main Road

Freeway

Danger

No Entry

No Entry for cars

All Vehicles Prohibited

Parking

No Parking

Customs

Peace

Driving

An international driver's license is not necessary in France. Seat belts are mandatory, and children under age 10 must be in the back seat. Gas *(essence)* is expensive—about $5 per gallon. Diesel *(gazole)* is less—about $3.80 per gallon—so rent a diesel car if you can. Gas is most expensive on autoroutes and cheapest at big supermarkets (closed at night and on Sunday). Many gas stations close on Sunday.

Go metric. A liter is about a quart (four quarts to a gallon). A kilometer is six-tenths of a mile. We figure kilometers to miles by cutting them in half and adding back 10 percent of the original (120 km: 60 + 12 = 72 miles, 300 km: 150 + 30 = 180 miles).

Quick-and-Dirty Road Sign Translation

Cédez le Passage	Yield
Centre Commercial	Grouping of large, suburban stores (not city center)
Centre-Ville	City center
Doublage Interdit	No passing
Feu	Traffic signal
Horadateur	Remote parking meter, usually at the end of the block
Parc de Stationnement	Parking lot
Parking Interdit/ Stationnement Interdit	No parking
Priorité à Droite	Right-of-way
Rue Piétonne	Pedestrian-only street
Sauf Riverains	Local access only

Signs Unique to Autoroutes:

Bouchon	Traffic jam ahead
Fluide	No slowing ahead, fluid conditions
Péage	Toll
Telepéage	Toll booths—for locals with automatic toll payment only
Toutes Directions	All directions (leaving city)
Autres Directions	Other directions (leaving city)

Four hours of autoroute tolls cost about €20, but the alternative to these super "feeways" is often being marooned in rural traffic—especially near the Riviera. Autoroutes usually save enough time, gas, and nausea to justify the splurge. Mix high-speed "autorouting" with scenic country-road rambling (be careful of sluggish tractors on country roads). You'll usually take a ticket when entering an autoroute and pay when you leave. Shorter autoroute sections (including along the Riviera) have periodic unmanned toll booths, where you can pay by dropping coins into a basket (change given, but keep a good supply of coins handy to avoid waiting) or by inserting a credit card. Autoroute gas stations usually come with well-stocked mini-marts, clean rest rooms, sandwiches, maps, local products, and cheap vending-machine coffee (€1). Many have small cafés or more elaborate cafeterias with reasonable prices.

Roads are classified into departmental (D), national (N), and autoroutes (A). D routes (usually yellow lines on maps) are slow and often the most scenic. N routes (usually red lines) are the fastest after autoroutes (orange lines). Speed limits, not often marked, are 90 kph for N and D roads, and 130 kph on toll autoroutes (10–20 kph less if it's raining). Green road signs are for national routes; blue are for

Driving in Provence and the French Riviera

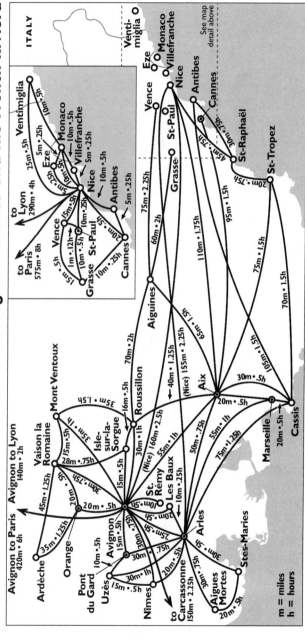

Best Two-Week Trip of Provence & the French Riviera (By Car)

Day Plan

1 Fly into Nice. Settle in at your hotel, then stroll the prome-nade des Anglais. Sleep in or near Nice.

2 Take our self-guided walking tour of Old Nice in the morning (leaving time to smell the *fougasse* and sample a café). Spend your afternoon at one or more of Nice's fine museums (see Chagall Museum Tour on page 229). Have dinner on the beach. Sleep in or near Nice.

3 Take the train to Antibes, then follow our self-guided tours of its old city and the Picasso Museum. Consider a hike along the Cap d'Antibes. Return to Nice, rest up, and head into Monaco for dinner and gambling. Sleep in or near Nice.

4 First thing in the morning, pick up your rental car in Nice. Drive north to Grasse, sample the perfumes, then continue on to the Gorges du Verdon and sleep in tiny Aiguines.

5 Continue west into the Luberon and follow our self-guided *La Provence Profonde* driving tour (page 166). Stay in or near Roussillon.

6 Spend your time comparing hill towns on our self-guided *Le Luberon Classique* driving tour (page 161). Sample a village market, then drive over the hills to the valley of the Côtes du Rhône. Sleep in or near Vaison la Romaine (Monday arrival is ideal since market day is Tuesday).

7 Explore Vaison la Romaine's upper medieval village and lower Roman city. Set sail along the Côtes du Rhône wine road (fol-lowing our self-guided driving tour). Have lunch in sky-high Le Crestet, and consider visiting a winery or wine cooperative.

autoroutes. There are plenty of good facilities, gas stations, and rest stops along most French roads.

Here are a few French road tips: In city centers, traffic merging from the right normally has the right-of-way *(priorité à droite)*, though cars entering the many suburban roundabouts must yield *(cédez le passage)*. It's an art to navigate roundabouts. The key is to know your direction and stay in the outer lane of the circle. When navigating through cities, approach intersections cautiously, stow the map, and follow the signs to *Centre-Ville* (downtown). From there, head to the tourist information office *(Office de Tourisme)*. When leaving or just passing through, follow the signs for *Toutes Directions* or *Autres Directions* (meaning anywhere else) until you see a sign for your specific destination. While locals are eating (12:00–14:00), many sights (and gas stations) are closed, so you can make great time driving. The French drive fast and live to tailgate. U-turns are illegal

Take a walk above Gigondas. If you're here from mid-June to late July when the lavender blooms, the drive to Sault and up Mont Ventoux is a must. Sleep in or near Vaison la Romaine.

8   Start your day touring the Roman theater in Orange and consider a quick stop in Châteauneuf-du-Pape. Continue south and set up in Avignon. In the afternoon, take our self-guided Avignon walking tour and enjoy dinner on one of the town's many atmospheric squares. Sleep in Avignon.

9   Relax in Avignon this morning, then divide the rest of your day between Nîmes and the Pont du Gard. If the weather's good, bring your swimsuit and float on your back below the 2,000-year-old Pont du Gard. Sleep in Avignon.

10   Drive through the Camargue, consider lunch in Stes-Maries-de-la-Mer, and wind up in Arles (big market day on Saturday). Sleep in Arles.

11   Spend your day in Arles. Drive to Les Baux for dinner. Sleep in Arles.

12   Drive to Cassis and stop for lunch and a mid-day visit to Aix-en-Provence or Marseille. Set up in Cassis and watch the sun set from the old port while you savor a bouillabaisse dinner. Sleep in Cassis.

13   Spend all day in Cassis enjoying *la vie douce*. Take a boat trip to the *calanques,* watch the *pétanque* balls roll, and end your day with a drive up Cap Canaille. Sleep in Cassis.

14   Drive to St-Tropez and spend your morning carousing along its old port (searching for Brigitte Bardot). In the afternoon, drive back to Nice, taking the scenic detour from Fréjus to Cannes. Sleep in Nice.

15   Trip over.

throughout France. Be very careful when driving on smaller roads—most are narrow with little ditches on either side that are easy to slide into. We've met several readers who "ditched" their cars (and were successfully pulled out by local farmers).

Parking is a headache in the larger cities, and theft is a problem throughout Provence and the Riviera. Ask your hotelier for ideas, and pay to park at well-patrolled lots (blue *P* signs direct you to parking lots in the cities). Parking structures often require that you take a ticket with you and pay at a machine (called *Caisse,* credit cards usually accepted) on your way back to the car. Curbside metered parking also works (usually free 12:00–14:00, 19:00–9:00, and in August). Look for a small machine selling time (called *horadateur,* usually one per block), plug in a few coins (about €1 gets an hour), push the green button, get a receipt showing the amount of time you have, and display it inside your windshield. Keep a pile of

Best Two-Week Trip (By Car)

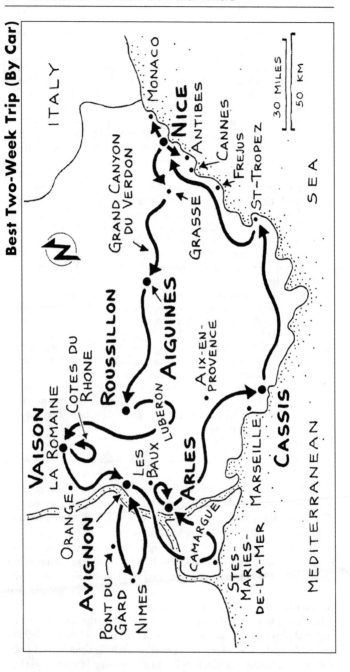

coins in your ashtray for parking meters, public rest rooms, launderettes, and short stints on autoroutes.

Biking

You'll find areas in Provence and the Riviera where public transportation is limited and bicycle touring might be a good idea. For
many, biking is a romantic notion whose novelty wears off after the
first hill or wind gust—realistically evaluate your physical condition
and understand the limitations bikes present. Start with an easy
pedal to a nearby village or through the vineyards, then decide how
ambitious you want to be. Most find that two hours on a narrow,
hard seat is enough. We've listed bike-rental shops where appropriate and suggested a few of our favorite rides. TIs always have
addresses for bike-rental places. For a good touring bike, figure
about €10 for a half day and €16 for a full day. You'll pay more for
better equipment; generally the best is available through bike shops,
not at train stations or other outlets. French bikers usually do not
wear helmets, though most rental outfits have them.

COMMUNICATING

The Language Barrier and that French Attitude

You've no doubt heard that the French are "mean and cold and
refuse to speak English." This is an out-of-date preconception left
over from the days of Charles de Gaulle—and it's especially incorrect
in this region. In these southern lands kissed by the sun and sea,
you'll find your hosts more jovial and easygoing (like their Italian
neighbors just over the border) than in the comparatively serious
north. Still, be reasonable in your expectations: Waiters are paid to
be efficient, not chatty. And Provençal postal clerks are every bit as
speedy, cheery, and multilingual as ours are back home.

The biggest mistake most Americans make when traveling to
France is trying to do too much with limited time. This approach is
a mistake in the bustling north, and a virtual sin in the relaxed south.
Hurried, impatient travelers who miss the subtle pleasures of people-
watching from a sun-dappled café often misinterpret French atti-
tudes. By slowing your pace and making an effort to understand
French culture by living it, you're much more likely to have a richer
experience. With the five weeks of paid vacation and 35-hour work
week that French workers get as non-negotiable rights, your hosts
can't comprehend why anyone would rush through their vacation.

The French take great pride in their customs, clinging to their
belief in cultural superiority despite the fact that they're no longer a
world superpower. Let's face it: It's tough to keep on smiling when
you've been crushed by a Big Mac, Mickey Moused by Disney, and
drowned in instant coffee. Your hosts are cold only if you decide to

see them that way. Polite and formal, the French respect the fine points of culture and tradition. Here, strolling down the street with a big grin on your face and saying hello to strangers is a sign of senility, not friendliness (seriously). They think that Americans, while friendly, are hesitant to pursue more serious friendships. Recognize sincerity and look for kindness. Give them the benefit of the doubt.

French communication difficulties are exaggerated. To hurdle the language barrier, bring a small English/French dictionary, a phrase book (look for ours, which contains a dictionary and menu decoder), a menu reader (if you're a gourmet eater), and a good supply of patience. In transactions, a small notepad and pen minimize misunderstandings about prices; have vendors write the price down. If you learn only five phrases, learn and use these: *bonjour* (good day), *pardon* (pardon me), *s'il vous plaît* (please), *merci* (thank you), and *au revoir* (goodbye). The French place great importance on politeness. Begin every encounter with *"Bonjour, madame/monsieur"* and end every encounter with *"Au revoir, madame/monsieur."*

The French are language perfectionists—they take their language (and other languages) seriously. Often they speak more English than they let on. This isn't a tourist-baiting tactic, but timidity on their part about speaking another language less than fluently. Start any conversation with, *"Bonjour, madame/monsieur. Parlez-vous anglais?"* and hope they speak more English than you speak French.

Telephones

You'll want a locally purchased phone card for making hotel/restaurant reservations, verifying hours at sights, phoning home and checking e-mail (at some places, see below).

Phone Cards: Instead of putting coins in pay phones, you can buy cards with pre-paid time. Look for them at any post office and from most newsstands and tobacco shops *(tabacs)*, including at train stations and airports. There are two kinds of cards available.

1. A *télécarte* (tay-lay-kart) can be used only in a public phone booth. The *télécarte* represents the efficient card-operated system that has replaced coin-operated public phones throughout Europe. Insert the card in the phone and dial away. There are two denominations: *une petite* costs about €7; *une grande* about €15. To use the *télécarte*, simply take the phone off the hook, insert the card, and wait for a dial tone; the price of the call (local or international) is automatically deducted.

2. A *carte à code* (cart ah code) comes with a dial-up code that can be used from any phone, including the one in your hotel room (if it's set on pulse, switch it to tone). Cards are marked as national (France only), international, or for both, but all work for calls inside and outside the country. (You get a better rate if your card corresponds to the type of call you're making.) If you're not sure what

kind of calls you'll make, buy one that does both. *Le Ticket de Téléphone, 365-Universel,* and *Kosmos* seem like the most common calling-card brands, with denominations in €7, €10 (sometimes), and €15 amounts. They're all are good values—my €15 international card lasted for four weeks of regular calls home.

These cards all work the same way and are simple to use, once you learn the rules (English instructions provided). Scratch to get your code. After you dial the access code, the message tells you to enter your code and then press (*touche;* toosh) the pound key (#, *dièse;* dee-ehz) or the star key (*, *étoile;* eh-twahl); once the next message arrives, dial your number, again followed by pound or star (you don't have to listen through the entire sales pitch). While per-minute rates are much cheaper with a *carte à code* than with a *télécarte,* it's slower to use (more numbers to dial)—so local calls are quicker with a *télécarte* from a phone booth.

When spelling out your name on the phone, you'll find that some letters are pronounced differently in French: *a* is pronounced "ah," *e* is pronounced "eh," and *i* is pronounced "ee." To avoid confusion, say "*a,* Anne," "*e,* euro," and "*i,* Isabelle," etc.

U.S. Calling Card Services: Since direct-dialing rates have dropped, calling cards (offered by AT&T, MCI, and Sprint) are no longer the good value they used to be. In fact, they are a rip-off. You're likely to pay a $4 connection fee and $3 for the first minute; if you get an answering machine, it'll cost you $7 to say, "Sorry I missed you." Now it's much cheaper to make your international calls with a phone card purchased in Europe.

Dialing Direct: France has a direct-dial 10-digit telephone system. There are no area codes. To call to or from anywhere in France, you dial the 10 numbers directly. (All Paris numbers start with 01.)

To call France from another country, start with the international access code (00 if you're calling from a European country; 011 from the United States and Canada), dial France's country code (33), and then drop the initial 0 of the 10-digit local number and dial the remaining nine digits. For example, the phone number of a good hotel in Paris is 01 47 05 49 15. To call it from home, dial 011 33 1 47 05 49 15.

To dial out of France, start your call with its international code (00), then dial the country code of the country you're calling, then the number you're calling. For example, to call our office in the United States, dial 00 (France's international access code), 1 (U.S. country code), then 425/771-8303 (our area code plus local number).

For a list of international access codes and country codes, see the appendix. European time is six/nine hours ahead of the East/West Coasts of the United States.

Mobile Phones: You can buy relatively cheap mobile phones in Europe to make both local and international calls (parents with independent-minded traveling teens find these phones invaluable). Typical American mobile phones don't work in Europe, and those that do have horrendous per-minute costs.

For about $120, you can get a phone with $20 worth of calls that will work in the country where you purchased it. (You can buy more time at newsstands or mobile phone shops.) Pricier phones (about $150–200) work in most countries once you pick up the necessary chip per country (about $25). If you're interested, stop by any European shop that sells mobile phones; you'll see prominent store window displays. Depending on your trip, ask for a phone that works only in that country or one that can be used throughout Europe. If you're on a budget, skip mobile phones and buy phone cards instead.

E-mail and Mail

E-mail: E-mail has caught on among hoteliers; today very few lack an e-mail address. Many hotels have computers in their lobby—usually with slow Internet connections—for guests to use. The terminals can be free, or operated with coins or a telephone card.

For high-speed Web access, ask at your hotel if there is a nearby Internet (an-ter-net) café. Post offices that offer Internet access *(cyberposte)* charge less than the cafés; buy a chip-card (for about same prices as phone cards) and you're in business.

The current rage is wireless access, called *Wi-Fi* (wee fee), available to laptop users for a minimal fee at Internet cafés and some post offices and hotels.

Mail: French post offices are called PTT for *Poste, Télégraphe, et Téléphone*—look for signs for *La Poste*. Hours vary, though most are open weekdays 8:00–19:00 and Saturday morning 8:00–12:00. Stamps and phone cards are also sold at *tabac* (tobacco) shops. It costs about €0.90 to mail a postcard to the United States.

To arrange for mail delivery, reserve a few hotels along your route in advance and give their addresses to friends. If you have an American Express card, most AmEx offices will hold your mail for you for free. Allow 10 days for a letter to arrive. Federal Express makes pricey two-day deliveries. E-mailing and phoning are so easy that we've dispensed with mail stops altogether.

SLEEPING

Accommodations in Provence and the Riviera are a good value and generally easy to find. Choose from one- to three-star hotels (two stars is our mainstay), bed-and-breakfasts *(chambres d'hôte)*, hostels, campgrounds, and homes rented on a weekly basis *(gîtes)*. We like places that are clean, small, central, traditional, inexpensive, friendly, and not listed in other guidebooks. Most places we list have at least five of these seven virtues.

Hotels

In this book, the price for a double room will range from €30 (very simple, toilet and shower down the hall) to €200 (maximum plumbing and more), with most clustering around €70.

The French have a simple hotel rating system based on amenities (0–4 stars, indicated in this book by * through ****). One star is simple, two has most of the comforts, and three is generally a two-star with minibars and a fancier lobby. Four stars offer more luxury than you usually have time to appreciate. One- and two-star hotels are the best budget values, though some three-star hotels (and even a few four-star hotels) can justify the extra cost. Lately, the star system has become less reliable. Unclassified hotels (no stars) can be bargains or depressing dumps. Look before you leap, and lay before you pay (upon departure).

Most hotels have lots of doubles and a few singles, triples, and quads. Traveling alone can be expensive, as single rooms (except for the rare closet-type rooms that fit only one twin bed) are simply doubles used by one person—so they cost about the same as a double. Room prices vary within each hotel depending on size, whether the room has a bath or shower, and whether there are twin beds or a double bed (tubs and twins cost more than showers and double beds). A triple is often a double room with a small double bed plus a sliver-sized single, and quad rooms usually have two double beds. Hotels cannot legally allow more in the room than what's shown on their price list. Modern hotels generally have a few family-friendly rooms that open to each other *(chambres qui communiquent)*.

Receptionists often don't mention the cheaper rooms—they assume you want a private bathroom or a bigger room. Study the price list on the Web site or posted at the desk. These are the types of rooms and beds:

Une chambre sans douche or **sans WC:** Room without a private shower or toilet (uncommon these days).

Une chambre avec cabinet de toilette: Room with a toilet but no shower (some hotels charge for down-the-hall showers).

Une chambre avec bain et WC: Room with private bathtub and toilet.

Une chambre avec douche et WC: Room with private shower and toilet.

Chambres qui communiquantes: Connecting rooms (ideal for families).

Un grand lit: Double bed (55 inches wide).

Un lit de cent-soixante: Queen-size bed (literally 160 centimeters, or 63 inches wide).

Deux petits lits: Twin beds (30–36 inches wide).

Deux lits séparés: Two beds separated.

Un lit dépliant: Folding bed.

Un bérceau: Baby crib.

Un lit d'enfant: Children's bed.

You can save as much as €20–25 by finding the rare room without a private shower or toilet. A room with a bathtub costs €5–10 more than a room with a shower (and is generally larger). Hotels often have more rooms with tubs than showers and are inclined to give you a room with a tub (which the French prefer).

A double bed is usually €5–10 cheaper than twins, though rooms with twin beds tend to be larger, and French double beds are smaller than American double beds. Hotels occasionally offer queen-size beds, which are 160 centimeters wide (more than 5 feet wide); most doubles are 140 centimeters (about 4.5 feet). To see if a hotel has queen-size beds, ask, *"Avez-vous un lit de cent-soixante?"* (ah-vay-voo uh lee duh sahn-swah-sahnt). Some hotels push two twins together under king-size sheets and blankets.

If you prefer a double bed (instead of twins) and a shower (instead of a tub), you need to ask for it—and you can save up to €20. If you're willing to take either twins or a double, ask generically for *une chambre pour deux* (room for two) to avoid being needlessly turned away.

Hotels in France must charge a daily tax *(taxe du séjour)* that is normally added to the bill. It varies from €0.55 to €1 per day, per person, depending on the hotel's number of stars. While some hotels include it in the price list, most add it to your bill.

You'll almost always have the option of breakfast at your hotel, which is pleasant and convenient, but it's more than the price of breakfast at the corner café, and with less ambience (though you get more coffee at your hotel). Some hotels offer only the classic continental breakfast for about €6–8, but others offer buffet breakfasts for about €8–15 (cereal, yogurt, fruit, cheese, croissants, juice, and hard-boiled eggs)—which we usually spring for. While hotels hope you'll buy their breakfast, it's optional unless otherwise noted.

Some hotels strongly encourage their peak-season guests to take "half pension"—that is, breakfast and either lunch or dinner. By law, they can't require you to take half pension unless you are staying three or more nights, but, in effect, many do during summer. While the food is usually good, it limits your ability to shop around. We've indicated where we think *demi-pension* is a good value.

Hotel rooms are safe. Still, keep cameras and money out of sight. Towels aren't routinely replaced every day; drip-dry and conserve. If that Lincoln Log–like pillow isn't your idea of comfort, American-style pillows (and extra blankets) may be in the closet or available on request. For a pillow, ask for *"Un oreiller, s'il vous plaît"* (uhn ohr-ray-yay, see voo play).

Some hoteliers will ask you to sign their *Livre d'Or* (literally "Golden Book," for client comments). They take this seriously and enjoy reading your remarks.

France is littered with sterile, ultramodern hotels, usually located on cheap land just outside of town, providing drivers with low-stress accommodations. The antiseptically clean and cheap Formule 1 and ETAP chains (about €30–40/room for up to 3 people), the more attractive Ibis hotels (€50–70 for a double), and the cushier Mercure and Novotels hotels (€70–110 for a double) are all run by the same company, Accor (www.accorhotels.com). While far from quaint, these can be a good value. A smaller, up-and-coming chain, Kyriad, has its act together, offering good prices and quality (toll-free in France tel. 08 25 00 30 03, from overseas tel. 01 64 62 46 46, www.kyriad.com; these telephone numbers also work for 8 affiliated chains, including Clarine, Climat de France, and Campanile). For a long listing of various hotels throughout France, see www.france.com.

Making Reservations

It's possible to travel at any time of year without reservations, but given the high stakes and the quality of the gems we've found for this book, we'd recommend making reservations. You can call long in advance from home, or better, book rooms a few days to a week in advance as you travel. (If you have difficulty, ask the fluent receptionist at your current hotel to call for you.) If you like more spontaneity (or if you're traveling off-season), you might make a habit of calling between 9:00 and 10:00 on the day you plan to arrive, when the hotel clerk knows who'll be checking out and just which rooms will be available. We've taken great pains to list telephone numbers with long-distance instructions (see "Telephones," page 30; also see the appendix). Use a public phone, the convenient pre-paid telephone cards, or your mobile phone. Most hotels listed here are accustomed to English-only speakers. A hotel receptionist will trust you and hold a room until 16:00 without a deposit, though some will ask for a credit-card number.

If you know where you want to stay each day (and you don't need or want flexibility), reserve your rooms a month or two in advance from home. This is particularly smart for the Riviera—and anywhere during holidays (see "When to Go," page 6). To reserve from home, e-mail, fax, or call the hotel. Most hotels listed are accustomed to English-only speakers. E-mail is preferred. Phone and fax costs are reasonable. To fax, use the form in the appendix (online at www.ricksteves.com/reservation). If you don't get an answer to your fax request, consider that a "no." (Many little places get 20 faxes a day after they're full, and they can't afford to respond.)

A two-night stay in August would be "2 nights, 16/8/05 to 18/8/05" (Europeans write the date in this order—day/month/year—and hotel jargon uses your day of departure).

If you receive a response from the hotel stating its rates and room availability, it's not a confirmation. You must confirm that you indeed want a room at the given rate. One night's deposit is generally required. A credit-card number is often accepted as a deposit (though you may need to send a signed traveler's check or, rarely, a bank draft in the local currency). To make things easier on yourself and the hotel, be sure you really intend to stay at the hotel on the dates you requested. These small, family-run businesses lose money if they turn away customers while holding a room for someone who doesn't show up. Understandably, most hotels bill no-shows for one night. *If you must cancel, give at least two days' notice.* Long-distance calls are cheap and easy from public phone booths. Don't let these people down—I promised you'd call and cancel if for some reason you won't show up.

Reconfirm your reservations a few days in advance for safety. Don't needlessly confirm rooms through the tourist office; they'll take a commission.

Bed-and-Breakfasts *(Chambres d'Hôte)*

B&Bs offer double the cultural intimacy for a good deal less than most hotel rooms. This book and local tourist offices list B&Bs. *Chambres d'hôte* (abbreviated CH in this book) are found mainly in the smaller towns and the countryside. They are listed by the owner's family name. While some post small *Chambres* or *Chambres d'hôte* signs in their front windows, many are found only through the local tourist office. We list reliable CHs that offer a good value and/or unique experience (such as CHs in renovated mills, châteaux, and wine *domaines*). Almost all have private bathrooms in all rooms, but no reception area or lounges to stretch out in. Doubles with breakfast generally cost between €35 and €50, and fancier ones run €60–70 (breakfast may or may not be included—ask). While your French hosts may not speak English, they will almost always be enthusiastic and pleasant. You'll also find many English-run CHs in these sunny regions (we've listed several). The owners are a great resource of tourist information (since they moved here because they love the region), and of course, communication is easy.

Hostels *(Auberge de Jeunesse)*

Hostels charge about €14 per bed. Get a hostel card before you go (contact Hostelling International, 202/783-6161, www.hiayh.org). Travelers of any age are welcome if they don't mind dorm-style accommodations or meeting other travelers. Travelers without a hostel card can generally spend the night for a small extra "one-night membership" fee. Cheap meals are sometimes available, and kitchen facilities are usually provided for do-it-yourselfers. Expect youth groups in spring, crowds in the summer, snoring, and incredible variability in quality from one hostel to the next. Family rooms are sometimes available on request, but it's basically boys' dorms and

Sleep Code

To help you sort easily through these listings, I've divided the rooms into three categories based on the price for a standard double room with bath:

$$$ **Higher Priced**
$$ **Moderately Priced**
$ **Lower Priced**

To give maximum information in a minimum of space, I use the following code to describe the accommodations. Prices listed are per room, not per person. Unless otherwise noted, breakfast is included (but usually optional). English is generally spoken.

S = Single room (or price for 1 person in a double).

D = Double or Twin. Double beds are usually big enough for non-romantic couples.

T = Triple (often a double bed with a single bed moved in).

Q = Quad (an extra child's bed is usually cheaper).

b = Private bathroom with toilet and shower or tub.

s = Private shower or tub only (the toilet is down the hall).

no CC = Does not accept credit cards; pay in local cash.

SE = Speaks English.

NSE = Does not speak English. Used only when it's unlikely you'll encounter English-speaking staff.

* = French hotel rating system, ranging from zero to four stars.

According to this code, a couple staying at a "Db-€70, no CC, SE" hotel would pay a total of 70 euros (about $84) for a double room with a private bathroom. The hotel accepts cash only (no credit cards), and the staff speaks English.

girls' dorms. You usually can't check in before 17:00 and must be out by 10:00. There is often a 23:00 curfew. Official hostels are marked with a triangular sign that shows a house and a tree.

Camping

In Europe, camping is more of a social than an environmental experience. It's a great way for American travelers to make European friends. Camping costs about €14 per campsite per night, and almost every destination recommended in this book has a campground within a reasonable walk or bus ride from the town center and train station. A tent and sleeping bag are all you need. Many

Tipping

Tipping *(donner un pourboire)* in France isn't as automatic and generous as it is in the United States, but for special service, tips are appreciated, if not expected. As in the United States, the proper amount depends on your resources, tipping philosophy, and the circumstance—but some general guidelines apply.

Restaurants: Almost all restaurants include tax and a 15 percent service charge *(service compris)* in their prices, but it's polite to round up for a drink or meal well-served. This bonus tip is usually about 5 percent of the bill (for example, if your bill is €19, leave €20). For exceptional service, tip up to 10 percent. In the rare case where service is not included (the menu would state *service non compris* or *s.n.c.*), a 15 percent tip is appropriate. When you hand your payment plus a tip to your waiter, you can say, *"C'est bon"* (say bohn), meaning, "It's good." It's best to tip in cash even if you pay with your credit card. Otherwise, the tip may never reach your server. If you order your food at a counter, don't tip.

Taxis: To tip a cabbie, round up. For a typical ride, round up to the next euro on the fare (to pay a €13 fare, give €14); for a long ride,

---

campgrounds have small grocery stores and washing machines, and some even come with discos and miniature golf. Hot showers are better at campgrounds than at many hotels. Local TIs have camping information. You'll find more detailed information in the annually updated *Michelin Camping/Caravanning Guide,* available in the United States and at most French bookstores.

Gîtes and Apartments

Throughout France, you can find reasonably priced rental homes, and nowhere are there more options than in Provence and the Riviera. Because this region is small, and all the sights are within an easy drive, it makes a lot of sense to spend your vacation at one home base.

Gîtes (zheet) are country homes (usually urbanites' second homes) that the government rents out to visitors who want a week in the countryside. The original objective of the *gîte* program was to save characteristic rural homes from abandonment and to make it easy and affordable for families to reacquaint themselves with the French countryside. The government offers subsidies to renovate such homes, then coordinates rentals to make it financially feasible for the owner. Today France has more than 8,000 *gîtes.* One of your authors restored a farmhouse a few hours north of Provence, and even though he and his wife are 100 percent American, they received the same assistance French owners do.

Gîtes are best for drivers (usually rural, with little public-transport access) and ideal for families and small groups (since they can sleep round up to the nearest €5 (for a €51 fare, give €55). If the cabbie hauls your bags and zips you to the airport to help you catch your flight, you might want to toss in a little more—but not more than €5. If you feel like you're being driven in circles or otherwise ripped off, skip the tip.

Special Services: Tour guides at public sites often hold out their hands for tips after they give their spiel; if we've already paid for the tour, we don't tip extra, though some tourists do give a euro or two, particularly for a job well done. If the tour was free, then we tip the guide €1–2 per person in our group or family. We don't tip at hotels, but if you do, give the porter a euro for carrying bags and leave a couple of euros in your room at the end of your stay for the maid if the room was kept clean. In general, if someone in the service industry does a super job for you, a tip of a couple of euros is appropriate...but not required.

When in doubt, ask. If you're not sure whether (or how much) to tip for a service, ask your hotelier or the TI. They'll fill you in on how it's done on their turf.

many for the same price). Homes range in comfort from simple cottages and farmhouses to restored châteaux. Most have at least two bedrooms, a kitchen, a living room, a bathroom or two, and no sheets or linens (though you can usually rent them for extra). Like hotels, all *gîtes* are rated for comfort from one to four (using ears of corn—*épis*—rather than stars). Two or three *épis* are generally sufficient quality, but I'd lean towards three for more comfort. Prices generally range from €300–1200 per week, depending on house size and amenities such as pools. For more information on *gîtes,* visit www.gites-de-france.fr/eng or www.gite.com. Our readers also report finding long lists of non-*gîte* homes for rent through TIs and on the Internet, though these are usually more expensive than staying in a *gîte.*

While less common than *gîtes,* **apartments** can be rented in cities and towns along the Riviera (one-week minimum). Tourist offices have lists. Avignon, Aix-en-Provence, Nice, and other Riviera towns have the biggest selection.

EATING

The French eat long and well—nowhere more so than in the South. Relaxed tree-shaded lunches with a chilled rosé, three-hour dinners, and endless afternoons at outdoor cafés are the norm. The French have a legislated 35-hour workweek...and a self-imposed 36-hour eat-week. Local cafés, cuisine, and wines should become a highlight of any French adventure. It's sightseeing for your palate. Even if the rest of you is sleeping in cheap hotels, let your taste buds travel first class in France. (They can go coach in England.) You can eat well without going broke—but choose carefully: You're just as likely to blow a small fortune on a mediocre meal as you are to dine wonderfully for €20. For specific suggestions on what to order where, see our cuisine suggestions in our introductions of Provence (page 49) and the Riviera (page 197).

Breakfast

Petit déjeuner (puh-tee day-zhuh-nay) is typically café au lait, hot chocolate, or tea; a roll with butter and marmalade; and a croissant. While breakfasts are available at your hotel (from €8–15), they're cheaper at corner cafés (but don't come with coffee refills). It's fine to buy a croissant or roll at a bakery and eat it with your cup of coffee at a café. Better still, some bakeries offer worthwhile breakfast deals with juice, a croissant, and coffee or tea for about €4 (look for the bakery chain La Brioche Dorée). If you crave eggs for breakfast, drop into a café and order *une omelette* or *œufs sur le plat* (fried eggs). You could also buy (or bring from home) plastic bowls and spoons, buy a box of cereal and a small box of milk, and eat in your room before heading out for coffee.

Picnics

For most lunches—*déjeuner* (day-zhuh-nay)—we picnic or munch a take-away sandwich from a *boulangerie* (bakery) or a crêpe from a *crêperie*.

Picnics can be first-class affairs and adventures in high cuisine. Be daring. Try the smelly cheeses, ugly pâtés, sissy quiches, and baby yogurts. Local shopkeepers are accustomed to selling small quantities of produce. Try the tasty salads-to-go and ask for a plastic fork (*une fourchette en plastique;* ewn foor-sheht en plah-steek). A small container is *une barquette* (ewn bar-keht).

Gather supplies early; you'll want to visit several small stores to assemble a complete meal, and many close at noon (see also "Market Day" on page 294). Look for a *boulangerie*, a *crémerie* or *fromagerie* (cheeses), a *charcuterie* (deli items, meats, and pâtés), a *pâtisserie* (delicious pastries), and an *épicerie* or *magasin d'alimentation* (small grocery with veggies, drinks, and so on).

Open-air markets *(marchés)* are fun and photogenic and close at about 13:00 (many are listed in this book; local TIs have complete lists). Local *supermarchés* offer less color and cost, more efficiency, and adequate quality. Department stores often have supermarkets in the basement. On the outskirts of cities, you'll find the monster *hypermarchés*. Drop in for a glimpse of hyper-France in action.

Sandwiches, Quiche, and Pizza

Everywhere in Provence and the Riviera, you'll find bakeries and small stands selling baguette sandwiches, quiche, and pizza-like items to go for €3–5. Usually filling and tasty, they also streamline the picnic process. (If you don't want your sandwich drenched in mayonnaise, ask for it *sans mayonnaise;* sahn my-oh-nehz). Here are some sandwiches you'll see:

Jambon beurre (zhahn-bohn bur): Ham and butter (boring).

Fromage beurre (froh-mahzh bur): Cheese and butter (also boring).

Poulet crudités (poo-lay krew-dee-tay): Chicken with tomatoes, lettuce, carrots, and cucumbers.

Thon crudités (tohn krew-dee-tay): Tuna with tomatoes, lettuce, carrots, and cucumbers.

Jambon crudités (zhahn-bohn krew-dee-tay): Ham with tomatoes, lettuce, carrots, and cucumbers.

Jambon or *Poulet à la provençal* (zhahn-bohn/poo-lay ah lah proh-vehn-sahl): Ham or chicken, usually with marinated peppers, tomatoes, and eggplant.

Look also for grilled *panini* sandwiches *à la italienne.*

Café Culture

French cafés (or brasseries) provide reasonable light meals and a refuge from museum and church overload. Feel free to order only a bowl of soup or a salad at a café.

Cafés generally open by 7:00, but closing varies wildly. Food is served throughout the day, so if you want a late lunch or an early dinner—find a café instead of a restaurant (which opens only for lunch and dinner).

It's easier for the novice to sit and feel comfortable when you know the system. Check the price list first. Prices, which must be posted prominently, can vary a great deal between cafés. Cafés charge different prices for the same drink depending on where you want to be seated. Prices are posted: *comptoir* (counter/bar) or the more expensive *salle* (seated).

Your waiter probably won't overwhelm you with friendliness. Notice how hard they work. They almost never stop. Cozying up to clients (French or foreign) is probably the last thing on their minds.

The **standard menu items** (generally served day and night) are the *croque monsieur* (grilled ham-and-cheese sandwich) and *croque madame* (*croque monsieur* with a fried egg on top). The *salade composée* (kohm-poh-zay) is a hearty chef's salad. Sandwiches are least expensive but plain unless you buy them at the *boulangerie* (bakery). To get more than a piece of ham *(jambon)* on a baguette, order a sandwich *jambon crudité*, which means garnished with lettuce, tomatoes, cucumbers, and so on. Omelettes come lonely on a plate with a basket of bread. The **daily special**—*plat du jour* (plah dew zhoor)—is your fast, hearty hot plate for €10–14. At most cafés, feel free to order only appetizers—which many find lighter, more fun, and more interesting than a main course. Regardless of what you order, bread is free; to get more, just hold up your breadbasket and ask, *"Encore, s'il vous plaît."*

For tips on beverages, see page 43.

Restaurants

Choose restaurants filled with locals, not places with signs boasting, "We Speak English." Consider our suggestions and your hotelier's opinion, but trust your instinct. If the menu *(la carte)* isn't posted outside, move along. Refer to our restaurant recommendations to get a sense of what a reasonable meal should cost.

Restaurants in the south open for dinner at 19:00 and are typically most crowded about 20:30 (the early bird gets the table). Last seating is usually about 21:00 (22:00 in cities, possibly earlier in small villages during the off-season). When lunch is served at restaurants, it generally begins at 11:30 and goes until 14:00, with last orders taken around 13:30.

La carte is the menu; if you ask for *le menu,* you'll get a fixed-price meal. This fixed-price *menu* (which can also be called *formule*) gives you a choice of soup, appetizer, or salad *(entrée);* a choice of three or four main courses *(plat principal)* with vegetables; plus a cheese course and/or a choice of desserts. (The same *menu* can cost €6 more at dinner.) Most restaurants offer a reasonable *menu-enfant* (kids' menu). Service is included, but wine or drinks are generally extra. Wines are often listed in a separate *carte des vins.*

To order à la carte, ask the waiter for help in deciphering *la carte.* Go with the waiter's recommendations and anything *de la maison* (of the house), unless it's an organ meat *(tripes, rognons, andouillette).* Galloping gourmets should bring a menu translator (the *Marling Menu Master* is excellent). The *entrée* is the first course, and *le plat principal* is the main course. The *plat du jour* (plate of the day), mentioned in "Café Culture," above, is served all day at bistros and cafés, but only at lunch (when available) at restaurants. Because small dinner salads are usually not offered on *la carte,* two travelers can split a big salad (of which several are usually available), then each get a *plat principal.* If all you want for dinner is a salad, find a café instead of a restaurant (restaurants expect you to order a main course).

By American standards, the French undercook meats: rare or *saignant* (seh-nyahn) is close to raw; medium or *à point* (ah pwahn) is rare; and well-done or *bien cuit* (bee-yehn kwee) is medium.

To get a waiter's attention, simply say, *"S'il vous plaît"* (see voo play)—"please."

Beverages at Cafés and Restaurants

House **wine** at the bar is cheap and good in this region (about €3 per glass). At a restaurant, a bottle or carafe of house wine—invariably good enough for Rick Steves, if not always Steve Smith—costs €6–11. To get inexpensive wine, order regional table wine (*un vin du pays;* uhn van duh pay) in a pitcher (*un pichet;* uhn pee-shay), rather than a bottle (though finer restaurants usually offer only bottles of wine). If all you want is a glass of wine, ask for *un verre de vin rouge* for red wine or *blanc* for white wine (uhn vehr duh van roozh/blahn). A half carafe of wine is *un demi-pichet* (uhn duh-mee pee-shay); a quarter carafe (ideal for one) is *un quart* (uh kar).

The local **beer,** which costs about €3 at a restaurant, is cheaper on tap (*une pression;* oon pres-yohn) than in the bottle (*bouteille;* boo-teh-ee). France's best beer is Alsatian; try Kronenbourg or the heavier Pelfort. *Une panaché* (oon pah-nah-shay) is a refreshing French shandy (beer and 7-Up).

Try some regional specialty **drinks.** For a refreshing before-dinner drink, order a *kir* (keer): a thumb's level of *crème de cassis* (black currant liqueur) topped with white wine. If you like brandy, try a *marc* (regional brandy, e.g., *marc de Bourgogne*) or an Armagnac, cognac's cheaper twin brother. *Pastis,* the standard southern France aperitif, is a sweet anise (licorice) drink that comes on the rocks with a glass of water. Cut it to taste with lots of water.

The French are willing to pay for **bottled water** with their meal (*eau minérale;* oh mee-nay-rahl) because they prefer the taste over tap water. If you prefer a free pitcher of tap water, ask for *une carafe d'eau* (oon kah-rahf doh). Otherwise, you may unwittingly buy bottled water.

Soft drinks cost about €3 in restaurants. Kids love the local lemonade (*citron pressé;* see-trohn preh-say) and the flavored syrups mixed with bottled water (*sirops à l'eau;* see-roh ah loh), try *un diablo menthe* (7-Up with mint syrup; uh dee-ah-bloh mahnt). The ice cubes melted after the last Yankee tour group left.

If you order coffee or tea, here's the lingo:

Coffee

Un express (uh nex-prehs): A shot of espresso.

Une noisette (oon nwah-zeht): An espresso with a shot of milk.

Un café au lait (uh kah-fay oh lay): Coffee with lots of milk, also called *un grand crème* (large size; uh grahn krehm) or *un petit crème* (average size; uh puh-tee krehm) in big cities.

Un grand café noir (uh grahn kah-fay nwahr): A cup of black coffee, closest to American style.

Un décaffiné (uh day-kah-fee-nay): A decaf coffee; can modify any of the above drinks.

By law, the waiter must give you a glass of tap water with your coffee if you request it; ask for *"un verre d'eau, s'il vous plaît"* (uh vehr doh, see voo play).

Tea

Un thé nature (uh tay nah-toor): A cup of plain tea.
Un thé au lait (uh tay oh lay): Tea with milk.
Un thé citron (uh tay see-trohn): Tea with lemon.
Un infusion (uh an-few-see-yohn): Herbal tea. Provence is known for its herbal and fruit teas. Look for *tilleul* (linden), *verveine* (verbena), or interesting blends such as *poire-vanille* (pear-vanilla).

TRAVELING AS A TEMPORARY LOCAL

We travel all the way to Europe to enjoy differences—to become temporary locals. You'll experience frustrations. Certain truths that we find "God-given" or "self-evident," like friendly waiters, ice in drinks, bottomless cups of coffee, hot showers, and bigger being better, are suddenly not so true. One of the benefits of travel is the eye-opening realization that there are logical, civil, and even better alternatives.

Paris is an understandably proud city. To enjoy its people, you need to celebrate the differences. A willingness to go local ensures that you'll enjoy a full dose of Parisian hospitality.

While updating our guidebooks, we hear over and over again that our readers are considerate and fun to have as guests. Thank you for traveling as temporary locals who are sensitive to the culture. It's fun to follow you in our travels.

Send Us a Postcard, Drop Us a Line

If you enjoy a successful trip with the help of this book and would like to share your discoveries, please fill out the survey at www .ricksteves.com/feedback or e-mail us at rick@ricksteves.com. We personally read and value all feedback.

Judging from all the happy postcards we receive from travelers who have used this book, it's safe to assume you'll enjoy a great, affordable vacation—with the finesse of an independent, experienced traveler.

From this point, "we" (your co-authors) will drop our respective egos and become "I."

Thanks, and *bon voyage!*

BACK DOOR TRAVEL PHILOSOPHY
From *Rick Steves' Europe Through the Back Door*

Travel is intensified living—maximum thrills per minute and one of the last great sources of legal adventure. Travel is freedom. It's recess, and we need it.

Experiencing the real Europe requires catching it by surprise, going casual..."through the Back Door."

Affording travel is a matter of priorities. (Make do with the old car.) You can travel—simply, safely, and comfortably—anywhere in Europe for $100 a day (even less in Provence and the Riviera) plus transportation costs. In many ways, spending more money only builds a thicker wall between you and what you came to see. Europe is a cultural carnival, and, time after time, you'll find that its best acts are free and the best seats are the cheap ones.

A tight budget forces you to travel close to the ground, meeting and communicating with the people, not relying on service with a purchased smile. Never sacrifice sleep, nutrition, safety, or cleanliness in the name of budget. Simply enjoy the local-style alternatives to expensive hotels and restaurants.

Extroverts have more fun. If your trip is low on magic moments, kick yourself and make things happen. If you don't enjoy a place, maybe you don't know enough about it. Seek the truth. Recognize tourist traps. Give a culture the benefit of your open mind. See things as different but not better or worse. Any culture has much to share.

Of course, travel, like the world, is a series of hills and valleys. Be fanatically positive and militantly optimistic. If something's not to your liking, change your liking. Travel is addictive. It can make you a happier American, as well as a citizen of the world. Our Earth is home to six billion equally important people. It's humbling to travel and find that people don't envy Americans. They like us, but, with all due respect, they wouldn't trade passports.

Globe-trotting destroys ethnocentricity. It helps you understand and appreciate different cultures. Travel changes people. It broadens perspectives and teaches new ways to measure quality of life. Many travelers toss aside their hometown blinders. Their prized souvenirs are the strands of different cultures they decide to knit into their own character. The world is a cultural yarn shop. And Back Door travelers are weaving the ultimate tapestry.

Come on, join in!

PROVENCE

"There are treasures to carry away in this land, which has not found a spokesman worthy of the riches it offers."
—Paul Cézanne

This magnificent region is shaped like a giant wedge of quiche. From its sunburned crust, fanning out along the Mediterranean coast from the Camargue to Marseille, it stretches north along the Rhône Valley to Orange. The Romans were here in force and left many ruins—some of the best anywhere. Seven popes, great artists such as Vincent van Gogh and Paul Cézanne, and author Peter Mayle all enjoyed their years in Provence. The region offers a splendid recipe of arid climate, oceans of vineyards, dramatic scenery, captivating cities, and adorable hill towns by the dozen.

Explore the ghost town that is ancient Les Baux and see France's greatest Roman ruins, the Pont du Gard and the theater in Orange. Admire the skill of ball-tossing *boules* players in small squares in every Provençal village and city. Spend a few starry, starry nights where van Gogh did, in Arles. Youthful but classy Avignon bustles in the shadow of its brooding pope's palace. Stylish and self-confident Aix-en-Provence lies 30 minutes from the sea and feels more Mediterranean. It's a short hop from Arles or Avignon into the splendid scenery and villages of the Côtes du Rhône and Luberon regions that make Provence so popular today. Should you need an urban fix—and want to understand southern France—Marseille is a must. If you prefer a Provençal beach fix, find Cassis, barely east of Marseille.

Planning Your Time

With limited time, make Arles or Avignon your sightseeing base—particularly if you have no car (with a car, head for the hill towns).

Arles has a blue-collar quality; the entire city feels like van Gogh's bedroom. It also has this region's best-value hotels and is handy to Les Baux, St. Rémy, and the Camargue. Avignon—three times larger than Arles—feels sophisticated, offers more nightlife and shopping, and makes a good base for exploring Nîmes, the Pont du Gard, and Orange. Italophiles prefer smaller Arles, while poodles pick urban Avignon. Many enjoy nights in both cities.

The bare minimum in Provence: one full day for sightseeing in Arles (best on Wed or Sat, when the morning market rages), a day for Nîmes and the Pont du Gard, and a full day for Avignon. You'll need at least two days for the Provençal villages. Allow two days in Cassis, using one of the days for a day trip to Marseille or Aix-en-Provence (or both). Ideally, see the cities—Arles, Nîmes, Avignon, Aix-en-Provence, and Marseille—by train, then rent a car for the countryside.

To measure the pulse of rural Provence, spend at least a few nights in the smaller towns. (They come to life on market days, but can be pretty dead on Mondays, when the shops are generally closed.) I've described many towns in the Côtes du Rhône and Luberon. The Côtes du Rhône is ideal for wine connoisseurs and easy to include for those heading to or from the north. The Luberon is for hill-town lovers and works well for itineraries heading east, toward Aix-en-Provence or the Riviera. Don't day-trip to these very different areas; nights spent in Provençal villages are what books are written about. Two nights in each area make a terrific start.

The small port town of Cassis is a worthwhile Mediterranean meander between Provence and the Riviera (and more appealing than Riviera resorts). It has easy day-trip connections to Marseille and Aix-en-Provence.

Depending on the length of your trip, here are my recommended priorities for Provence:

3 days:	Arles, Les Baux, Pont du Gard, Avignon
5 days, add:	Nîmes, Orange, Côtes du Rhône villages
7 days, add:	Cassis, Marseille, Aix-en-Provence
9 days, add:	Luberon hill towns, Camargue

Getting Around Provence

By Bus or Train: Public transit is good between cities and decent to some towns, but marginal at best to the villages. Frequent trains link Avignon, Arles, and Nîmes (about 30 min between each). Avignon has good train connections with Orange. Marseille is well connected to all cities in Provence and has particularly frequent service to Cassis and Aix-en-Provence (about 30 min to each).

Buses connect many smaller towns. From Arles, you can catch a bus to Stes-Maries-de-la-Mer (Camargue) or St. Rémy. From Avignon, you can bus to Pont du Gard, St. Rémy, Isle-sur-la-Sorgue (also by train), and less easily to Vaison la Romaine and some Côtes du Rhône villages.

Overall, St. Rémy and Isle-sur-la-Sorgue are the most accessible small towns. While a tour of the villages of Luberon is possible only by car or bus excursion from Avignon, nearby Isle-sur-la-Sorgue is an easy hop by train or bus from Avignon.

The TIs in Arles and Avignon have information on bus excursions to regional sights that are hard to reach *sans* car; see "Tours of Provence," below.

By Car: The region is made-to-order for a car. The yellow Michelin Local maps #332 and #340 are a godsend. Be wary of thieves: Park only in well-monitored spaces and leave nothing in your car.

I've described key sights and three full-day excursions deep into the countryside (see Côtes du Rhône and Luberon chapters)—all better done as overnights.

Avignon (pop. 100,000) is a headache for drivers; Arles (pop. 35,000) is easier. Les Baux and St. Rémy work well from Arles or Avignon (or vice versa). Nîmes and the Pont du Gard are a short hop west of Avignon and on the way to or from Languedoc for drivers. The town of Orange ties in tidily with a trip to the Côtes du Rhône villages and with destinations farther north. If you're heading north from Provence, consider a three-hour detour through the spectacular Ardèche Gorges (see Côtes du Rhône chapter).

Tours

It's possible to take half-day or full-day excursions to most of the sights described in this book from Arles or (better) Avignon. Local TIs have brochures on all of these excursions and can help you make a reservation. Here are two options:

Visit Provence—The tour company, based in Avignon, offers a great variety of half-day or full-day guided tours in eight-seat mini-vans (€50/half-day, €100/day). For example, a half-day tour to both the Châteauneuf-du-Pape vineyards, with wine-tasting, and to Orange (includes Triumphal Arch, Roman Theater, and audioguide for Theater) costs €50. Other day trips include: Les Baux and Arles; St. Rémy, Les Baux, and Pont du Gard; and Aix-en-Provence, Cassis, and Marseille (last tour of the day for this one allows a drop-off at the TGV station in Marseille, saving money and time if you're headed to the Côte d'Azur next). Not all tours include entry fees for sights, but reservations are required for all. Ask about their cheaper large-coach excursions (tel. 04 90 14 70 00, www.provence-reservation.com).

Lieutaud—The company operates cheap, unguided, big-bus excursions from Arles and Avignon to many hard-to-reach places at a fraction of the price you'd pay for a taxi. Different half-day and full-day

Top 10 Roman Sights in Provence

1. Pont du Gard aqueduct and its museum
2. Roman Theater in Orange
3. Ancient History Museum in Arles
4. Maison Carrée in Nîmes
5. Arena in Nîmes
6. Arena in Arles
7. Ruined aqueduct near Fontvieille
8. Roman city of Glanum
9. Roman city of Vaison la Romaine
10. Roman bridge St. Julien (near Roussillon)

Top 10 Provençal Towns and Villages

1. Roussillon
2. Uzès (officially in Languedoc)
3. Joucas
4. Isle-sur-la-Sorgue
5. Nyons
6. Lourmarin
7. Le Crestet
8. Gigondas
9. Vaison la Romaine
10. Séguret

trips are available every day, but no admission fees are included. Here are a few examples: Pont du Gard (€15/half-day, runs twice weekly, usually Tue and Thu); Vaison la Romaine and Orange (€19/half-day, 1 weekly, usually Mon); St. Rémy Wednesday morning market (€15/half-day); and Nîmes, Arles, and the Camargue (€28/day, usually Fri). They also offer weekly excursions to Les Baux or the Luberon, including Musée de la Lavande, Gordes, and Roussillon (tel. 04 90 86 36 75, www.cars-lieutaud.fr).

Provence's Cuisine Scene

Provence has been called France's "garden market," stressing farm-fresh food (vegetables, fruit, and meats) prepared in a simple way, meant to be savored with family and friends. Grilled foods are typical, as are dishes derived from lengthy simmering—in part a reflection of long days spent in the fields. Colorful and lively, Provençal cuisine assaults the senses with an extravagant use (by French standards) of garlic, olive oil, and herbs. Order anything *à la provençale,* and you'll be rewarded with aromatic food heightened by rich and pungent sauces. Thanks to the Riviera, many seafood dishes show up on Provençal menus (see "The Riviera's Cuisine Scene," page 197).

Unlike other French regions, the food of Provence is inviting for nibblers. Appetizers (hors d'oeuvres) often consist of bowls of olives (look for the plump and full-flavored black *tanche* or the green,

buttery *picholine*), as well as plates of fresh vegetables served with lusty sauces ready for dipping. These same sauces adorn dishes of hard-boiled eggs, fish, or meat. Look for tapenade, a paste of pureed olives, capers, anchovies, herbs, and sometimes tuna. True anchovy-lovers seek out *anchoiade* (a spread of garlic, anchovy, and parsley) or *bagna caouda* (warm sauce of anchovies and melted butter or olive oil). Aioli—a rich, garlicky mayonnaise spread over vegetables—is another Provençal favorite. In the summertime, entire village festivals celebrate this sauce. Look for signs announcing *aioli monstre* (literally "monster aioli"), and for a few euros, immerse yourself in a very local eating experience (pass the breath mints, please).

Despite the heat, soup is a favorite in Provence. Look for *soupe au pistou*, a flavorful vegetable soup with a sauce (called *pistou*) of basil, garlic, and cheese—pesto minus the pine nuts. Or try *soupe à l'ail* (garlic soup). For seafood soups, see "The Riviera's Cuisine Scene," page 197.

Provençal main courses venerate fresh vegetables and meats (eat seafood on the Riviera and meat in Provence). Ratatouille is a mixture of Provençal vegetables (typically eggplant, zucchini, onions, and peppers) in a thick, herb-flavored tomato sauce. It's readily found in charcuteries and often served at room temperature, making it the perfect picnic food. Ratatouille veggies also show up on their own, stuffed and served in spicy sauces. Look for *aubergines* (eggplants), *tomates* (tomatoes), *poivrons* (sweet peppers), and *courgettes* (zucchini—especially *fleurs de courgettes*, stuffed and batter-fried zucchini flowers). *Tians* are gratin-like vegetable dishes named for the deep terra-cotta dish in which they are cooked and served. *Artichauts à la barigoule* are stuffed artichokes flavored with garlic, ham, and herbs (*barigoule* is from the Provençal word for thyme, *farigoule*). Also look for *riz de Camargue*—the reddish, chewy, nutty-tasting rice that has taken over the Camargue area, which is otherwise useless for agriculture.

The famous herbs of Provence influence food long before it's cooked. The locally renowned lambs of the *garrigue* (shrub-covered hills), as well as rabbits and other small edible beasts in Provence, dine on wild herbs and spicy shrubs—essentially pre-seasoning their delicate meat. Look for lamb (*agneau,* most often leg of lamb, *gigot d'agneau*), grilled and served no-frills, or the delicious *lapin à la provençale*—rabbit served with garlic, mustard, tomatoes, and herbs in white wine. Locals have a curious passion for quail *(caille)*. These tiny, bony birds are often grilled and served with any variety of sauces, including sauces sweetened with Provençal cherries or honey and lavender. Daube, named for the traditional cooking vessel *daubière*, is generally beef simmered until it is spoon-tender and served with noodles. *Taureau* (bull's meat), usually raised in the marshy Camargue, melts in your mouth.

There are a few dishes to avoid: *Pieds et paquets* is a scary dish of sheep's feet and tripe (no amount of Provençal sauce can hide the flavor here). *Tourtes de blettes* is a confused "pie" made with Swiss chard; both savory and sweet, it can't decide whether it should be a first course or dessert (it shows up as both).

Eat goat cheese *(fromage de chèvre)* in Provence. Look for *banon à la feuille* (dipped in *eau-de-vie* to kill bad mold, then wrapped in a chestnut leaf), spicy *picodon* (the name means "spicy" in the old language), or the fresh, creamy *brousse du Rove* (often served mixed with cream and sugar for dessert). On Provençal cheese platters, you'll often find small rounds of bite-size *chèvres*, each flavored with a different herb or spice—and some even rolled in chopped garlic (more breath mints, please).

Desserts tend to be fairly light and fruit-filled, or traditionally French. Look for fresh tarts made with seasonal fruit, Cavaillon melons (served cut in half with a trickle of the sweet Rhône wine Beaumes-de-Venise), and ice cream or sorbet sweetened with honey and flavored with various herbs such as lavender, thyme, or rosemary.

Wines of Provence

Provence was the first area in France to be planted with grapes, around 600 B.C., by the Greeks. Romans built on what the Greeks started, realizing even back then that Provence had an ideal climate for growing wine: mild winters and long, warm summers (but not too hot—thanks to the cooling winds). This sun-baked, wine-happy region offers Americans a chance to sample wines blended from many different grapes—resulting in flavors unlike anything we get at home (yes, we have good Cabernet Sauvignons, Merlots, and Pinot Noirs, but Rhône wines are new to most of us). Provence's shorts-and-T-shirt climate and abundance of hearty, reasonably-priced wines make for an enjoyable experience, particularly if you have a little wine-tasting background. See "Provençal Wine-Tasting 101," below, to learn the basics.

In France, wine production is strictly controlled by the government to preserve the overall quality. This obligates vintners to use certain grapes that grow best in that region, and to follow certain wine-growing procedures. The *Appellation d'Origine Contrôlée* (AOC) label found on many bottles is the government's seal of approval when a wine meets a series of requirements. The type and percentages of grapes used, vinification methods, and taste are all controlled and verified.

Provençal vintners can blend from 13 different grapes—unique in France. (In Burgundy and Alsace, only one grape variety is used for each wine—so Pinot Noir, Chardonnay, Riesling, Tokay, and Pinot Gris are each 100 percent from that grape.) This blending allows Provençal winemakers great range in personalizing their wine. For reds, most vintners blend half a dozen or so different grapes. The most prevalent grapes are Grenache, Mourvèdre, Syrah, Carignan, and Cinsault. For whites, Grenache-Blanc, Roussanne, Marsanne, Bourboulenc, and Clairette grapes are most common.

There are three primary growing areas in Provence: Côtes du Rhône, Côtes de Provence, and Côteaux d'Aix-en-Provence. A few wines are also grown along the Provençal Mediterranean coast. All regions produce rich, fruity reds and dry, fresh rosés. Only about 5 percent of wine produced here is white (and most Provençal whites are unexceptional).

In Provence, I drink rosé instead of white. Don't confuse these rosés with the insipid blush stuff found in the United States; French rosé is often crisp and fruity, a perfect match to the hot days and Mediterranean cuisine. Rosé wines are made from red grapes whose juice is white, until crushed with red grape skins. The white juice is left in contact with the dark-red skins just long enough to produce the pinkish color (usually a few hours). Rosés from Tavel (20 min northeast of Avignon) are the most respected, but you'll find many good producers at affordable prices in other areas as well. Americans unaccustomed to drinking rosés should give it a try here.

Provençal Wine Tasting 101

The American wine-tasting experience (I'm thinking Napa Valley) is generally informal, chatty, and entrepreneurial (baseball caps and golf shirts with logos). Although Provençal vintners are friendly, welcoming, and more easygoing than in other parts of France, it's a more serious, wine-focused experience—without the distractions of the marketing at U.S. vineyards. Visit several private wineries or stop by a *cave coopérative*—an excellent opportunity to taste wines from a number of local vintners in a single, less intimidating setting.

Provençal vintners are happy to work with you, *if* they can figure out what you want. When you enter a winery, it helps to know what you like (drier or sweeter, lighter or full-bodied, fruity or more tannic, and so on). The people serving you may know those words in English, but you're better off knowing and using the key words in French (see page 53).

For reds, you'll be asked if you want to taste younger wines that still need maturing or older wines, ready to drink now. (Whites and rosés are always ready to drink.) The French like to sample younger

French Wine Lingo

Here are the steps you should follow when entering any wine-tasting:

1. Greetings, Sir/Madam: *Bonjour, Monsieur/Madame.*
2. We would like to taste a few wines: *Nous voudrions déguster quelques vins.* (noo voo-dree-ohn day-goo-stay kehl-kuh van)
3. We want a wine that is ___ and ___: *Nous voudrions un vin ___ et ___.* (noo voo-dree-ohn uhn van ___ ay ___)

Fill in the blanks with your favorites from this list:

English	French	Pronounced
wine	*vin*	van
red	*rouge*	roozh
white	*blanc*	blahn
rosé	*rosé*	roh-zay
light	*léger*	lay-zhay
full-bodied, heavy	*robuste*	roh-boost
fruity	*fruité*	frwee-tay
sweet*	*doux*	doo
tannic	*tannique*	tah-neek
fine	*fin, avec finesse*	fahn, ah-vehk fee-nehs
ready to drink	*prêt à boire*	preh ah bwar (mature)
not ready to drink	*fermé*	fair-may
oak-y	*goût de la chêne*	goo duh lah sheh-nuh
from old vines	*de vieille vignes*	duh vee-yay-ee veen-yah
sparkling	*pétillant*	pay-tee-yahn

*With the exception of the fortified white Beaumes-de-Venise, few Provençal wines would be considered "sweet."

wines and determine how they will taste in a few years, allowing them to buy at cheaper prices and stash the bottles in their cellars. Americans want it now—for today's picnic. While many Americans like a big, full-bodied wine, most French tend to prefer more subtle flavors. They judge a wine by virtue of what food it would go well with—and a big, oak-y wine would overwhelm most French cuisine.

Remember that the vintner is hoping that you'll buy at least a bottle or two. If you don't buy, you may be asked to pay a minimal fee for the tasting. They all know that Americans can't export much wine, and they don't expect to make a big sale—but they do hope you'll look for their wines in the United States.

Côtes du Rhône Wines

The Côtes du Rhône, which follows the Rhône River from just south of Lyon to near Avignon, is the king of Provence wines. Our focus is on the southern, Provençal section, roughly from Vaison la Romaine to Avignon (though wine-lovers should take note of the big, complex reds found in the northern Rhône wines of St. Joseph, Hermitage, and Cornas, as well as the seductive white of Condrieu). The wines of the southern Rhône are consistently good—and sometimes exceptional. The reds are full-bodied, rosés are dry and fruity, and whites are dry and fragrant, often with hints of flowers. Côtes du Rhône whites aren't nearly as good as the reds, though the rosés are refreshing and ideal for lunch on the terrace. For more on this wine region, including a self-guided driving tour of local villages and vintners, see the Côtes du Rhône chapter (page 125).

There are many sub-areas of the southern Côtes du Rhône recognized as producing distinctly good wines, thus awarded their own *appellations* (like Châteauneuf-du-Pape, Gigondas, Beaumes-de-Venise, Côtes de Ventoux, Tavel, and Côtes du Luberon). Wines are often named for the villages that produce them. Wines made from grapes coming from several local vintners are called "Côtes du Rhône Villages" and are less expensive because the grapes can come from a larger area.

Here's a summary of what you might find on a Côtes du Rhône *carte des vins* (wine list):

Châteauneuf-du-Pape: Wines from this famous village are almost all reds (often blends; the most dominant grapes are typically Grenache, Mourvèdre, and Syrah). These wines have a velvety quality and can be spicy, with flavors of licorice and prunes. Châteauneuf-du-Pape wines merit lengthy aging. Considered among the best producers are Château de Beaucastel, Le Vieux Télégraphe, and Château la Nerthe.

Gigondas: These wines have many qualities of Châteauneuf-du-Pape, but remain lesser-known and therefore cheaper. Gigondas red wines are spicy, meaty, and can be pretty tannic. Again, aging is necessary to bring out the full qualities of the wine. Look for Domaine du Terme, Château de Montmirail, or Domaine de Coyeux for good quality.

Beaumes-de-Venise: While reds from this village are rich and flavorful, Beaumes-de-Venise is most famous for its Muscat—a sweet, fragrant wine often served as an apéritif or with dessert. It often has flavors of apricots and peaches, and it should be consumed

On the Label

appellation	area in which a wine's grapes are grown
bouchonné	"corked" (spoiled from a bad cork)
bouquet	bouquet (smell when first opened)
cave	cellar
cépage	grape variety (syrah, chardonnay, etc.)
côte, côteau	hillside or slope
domaine	wine estate
étiquette	label
fût, tonneau	wine barrel
grand vin	excellent wine
millésimé	wine from a given year
mis en bouteille au Château/à la Domaine	estate-bottled (bottled where it was made)
vin de table	table wine (can be a blend of several wines)
vin du pays	wine from a given area (a step up from vin du table)

within two years of bottling. Try Domaine de Coyeux, Domaine de Durban, and Château Redortier.

Rasteau: This village sits across the valley from Gigondas and shares many of its qualities at lesser prices. Rasteau makes fine rosés, robust (at times "rough") and fruity reds, and a naturally sweet wine (Vin Doux Naturel). Their Côtes du Rhône Villages can be excellent. The cooperative in Rasteau is good, though you should not miss a visit to Domaine de Girasols (see page 137).

Sablet: This village lies down in the valley below Gigondas and makes decent, fruity, and inexpensive reds and rosés.

Tavel: The queen of French rosés is 15 minutes northwest of Avignon, close to the Pont du Gard. Tavel produces a rosé that is distinctly dry, crisp, higher in alcohol, and more full-bodied than other rosés from the region. Look for any rosé from Tavel.

Côtes de Provence Wines

The lesser-known vineyards of the Côtes de Provence run east from Aix-en-Provence almost to St-Tropez. Many wines from this area are sold in an unusual curvy bottle. Typical grapes are Cinsault, Mourvèdre, Grenache, Carignan, and a little Cabernet Sauvignon and Syrah. The wines are commonly full-bodied and fruity, and are meant to be drunk when they're young. It's not unusual to chill a red from this area. This region is most famous for its "big" rosés that can be served with meat and garlic dishes (rosé accounts for 60 percent of production). The reds can be delicious. They cost less than Côtes du Rhônes, with similar characteristics.

For one-stop shopping, make a point to find the superb **La Maison des Vins Côtes de Provence** on the RN-7 in Les Arcs-sur-Argens (a few minutes north of the A-8 autoroute, about halfway between Aix-en-Provence and Nice). This English-speaking wine shop and tasting center represents hundreds of producers and sells their wines at vineyard prices, offering free tastings of up to 16 wines (tel. 04 94 99 50 20, www.caveaucp.fr).

Côteaux d'Aix-en-Provence Wines

This large wine region, between Les Baux and Aix-en-Provence, produces some interesting reds, whites, and rosés. Commonly used grapes are the same as in Côtes de Provence, though several producers (mainly around Les Baux) use a higher concentration of Cabernet Sauvignon that helps distinguish their wines.

Provençal Mediterranean Wines

Barely east of Marseille, Cassis and Bandol sit side-by-side, overlooking the Mediterranean. Though very close together, they are technically designated as separate wine-growing areas, given the distinctive nature of their wines. Cassis is one of France's smallest wine regions and is known for its strong, fresh, and very dry whites, arguably the best in Provence. Bandol is known for its luscious, velvety reds, made primarily from the Mourvèdre grape.

ARLES

By helping Julius Caesar defeat Marseille, Arles (pronounced arl) earned the imperial nod and was made an important port city. With the first bridge over the Rhône River, Arles was a key stop on the Roman road from Italy to Spain, the Via Domitia. After reigning as the seat of an important archbishop and a trading center for centuries, the city became a sleepy place of little importance in the 1700s. Vincent van Gogh settled here a hundred years ago, but left only a chunk of his ear (now gone). American bombers destroyed much of Arles in World War II as the townsfolk hid out in its underground Roman galleries. Today Arles thrives again, with its evocative Roman ruins, an eclectic assortment of museums, made-for-ice-cream pedestrian zones, and squares that play hide-and-seek with visitors. It's an understandably popular home base from which to explore France's trendy Provence region.

ORIENTATION

Arles faces the Mediterranean and turns its back on Paris. While the town is built along the Rhône, it completely ignores the river (the part of Arles most damaged by Allied bombers in World War II, and therefore the least charming today).

Landmarks hide in Arles' medieval tangle of narrow, winding streets. Virtually everything is close—but first-time visitors can walk forever to get there. Hotels have good, free city maps, and Arles provides helpful street-corner signs that point you toward sights and hotels. Racing cars enjoy Arles' medieval lanes, turning sidewalks into tightropes and pedestrians into leaping targets.

Tourist Information

The main TI is on the ring road, esplanade Charles de Gaulle

(April–Sept daily 9:00–18:45, Oct–March Mon–Sat 9:00–17:45, Sun 10:30–14:30, tel. 04 90 18 41 20). There's also a TI at the train station (open year-round, Mon–Sat 9:00–13:00, closed Sun). Both charge €1 to reserve hotel rooms. Pick up the good city map, note the bus schedules, and get English information on nearby destinations such as the Camargue wildlife area. Ask about bullfights and bus excursions to regional sights (see "Helpful Hints," below). Ask if buses to Les Baux have been reinstated.

Excursions from Arles: The TI can book bus excursions to many destinations that require a car to reach. These are the best half-day excursions I saw: Pont du Gard and Les Baux for €50, Luberon villages for €50, and Camargue for €36. (Read about these sights in Near Arles chapter.) An all-day trip to the lavender fields is offered in summer for €100 (go only in late June–July when fields are blooming). See also "Tours" in the Provence chapter, page 48.

Arrival in Arles

By Train and Bus: The train and bus stations are next to each other on the river, a 10-minute walk from the town center (baggage storage not available). Get what you need at the train station TI before leaving (see above). To reach the old town, turn left out of either station and walk 10 blocks, or take bus #3 from the shelter right across from the train station (2/hr, €0.80, buy ticket from driver). Taxis generally do not wait at either station, but you can summon one by asking the TI or calling 04 90 96 90 03 (rates are fixed, allow €8–10 to any hotel I list).

By Car: Follow signs to *Centre-ville,* then follow signs toward *Gare SNCF* (train station). You'll come to a huge roundabout (place Lamartine) with a Monoprix department store to the right. Park along the city wall or in nearby lots; pay attention to No Parking signs on Wednesday and Saturday until 13:00 (violators will be towed to make way for Arles' huge outdoor produce markets). Some hotels have limited parking. Theft is a big problem; leave nothing in your car. From place Lamartine, walk into the city between the two stumpy towers.

Helpful Hints

Launderettes: One is at 12 rue Portagnel; another is nearby at 6 rue de la Cavalerie, near place Voltaire (both daily 7:00–21:00, you can stay later to finish if you're already inside, English instructions).

Internet Access: Cyber City is central (daily 10:00–22:00, 41 rue du Quatre Septembre, tel. 04 90 96 87 76).

Bike Rental: Try the Peugeot store (15 rue du Pont, tel. 04 90 96 03 77). While Vaison la Romaine and Isle-sur-la-Sorgue make better biking bases, rides to Les Baux (20 miles round-trip, very steep climb) or into the Camargue (40 miles round-trip, forget it in the wind) are possible from Arles—provided you're in great shape.

Car Rental: Avis is at the train station (tel. 04 90 96 82 42), Europcar and Hertz are downtown (2 bis avenue Victor Hugo, Europcar tel. 04 90 93 23 24, Hertz tel. 04 90 96 75 23), and National is just off place Lamartine toward the station (4 avenue Paulin Talabot, tel. 04 90 93 02 17).

Local Guide: Jacqueline Neujean, an excellent guide, knows Arles like the back of her hand (2 hrs/€90, tel. 04 90 98 47 51).

Cooking Courses: Friendly American Madeleine organizes a fun variety of wine appreciation and cooking courses from her B&B in the city center. See Maison d'Hotes en Provence, below, under "Sleeping in Arles."

Serious Coffee or Tea: Recharge at Café de la Major (closed Sun, near Forum Square at 7 bis rue Réattu, tel. 04 90 96 14 15).

Public Pools: Arles has three public pools (indoor and outdoor). Ask at the TI or your hotel.

Getting Around Arles

Everything's within walking distance. Only the Ancient History Museum requires a long walk (you can take the bus instead, €0.80, details in sight listing, below). The elevated riverside walk provides Rhône views and a direct (if odorous) route to the Ancient History Museum, with an easy return to the train station. Keep your head up for *Starry Night* memories, but eyes down for decorations by dogs with poorly-trained owners.

Arles' **taxis** charge a set fee of about €8, but only the Ancient History Museum is worth a taxi ride (figure €30 each way to Les Baux, tel. 04 90 96 90 03).

SIGHTS

The worthwhile **Monument Pass** *(le pass monuments)* covers Arles' many sights and is valid for one week (adults-€13.50, under 18-€12, sold at each sight). Otherwise, it's €3–4 per sight and €5.50 for the Ancient History Museum. While any sight is worth a few minutes, many aren't worth the individual admission. Start at the Ancient History Museum for a helpful overview, then dive into the sights (ideally in the order described below). Remember, many begin closing rooms 30 minutes early.

▲▲▲**Ancient History Museum (Musée de l'Arles Antique)**— Begin your town visit here—it's Roman Arles 101. Models and original sculptures (with meager help from the English brochure) re-create the Roman city, making workaday life and culture easier to imagine.

Arles

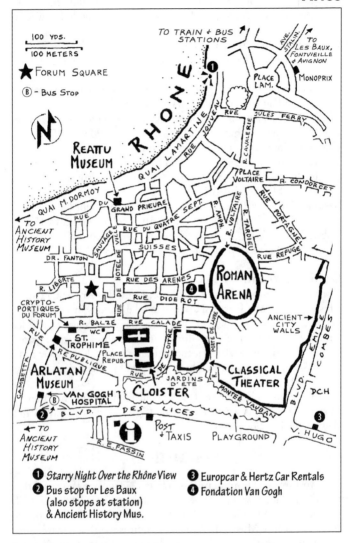

1 Starry Night Over the Rhône View
2 Bus stop for Les Baux
(also stops at station)
& Ancient History Mus.
3 Europcar & Hertz Car Rentals
4 Fondation Van Gogh

You're greeted by an impressive row of pagan and early-Christian sarcophagi (2nd through 5th centuries). These would have lined the Via Aurelia outside the town wall. Pagan sarcophagi show simple slice-of-Roman-life scenes, while the Christian ones feature Bible stories. In the early days of the Church, Jesus was often portrayed beardless and as the good shepherd, with a lamb over his shoulder.

Next, you'll find models of every Roman structure in Arles you can visit today. These are the highlight for me, as they breathe a little life into buildings as they looked 2,000 years ago. Find the Forum model and commit it to memory for when you visit the real thing later. Check out the pontoon bridge (over the widest, and therefore slowest, part of the river), find the arena (with its moveable stadium cover, which sheltered spectators from sun or rain), and locate Arles' chariot racecourse (where you are now). While virtu-

ally nothing is left of the racecourse (a.k.a. circus), the model shows that it must have rivaled Rome's Circus Maximus. Looking at the model, you can see that an emphasis on sports—with huge stadiums at the edge of town—is not unique to modern America. The model of the entire city puts it all together, illustrating how little Arles seems to have changed over two millennia—warehouses still on the opposite side of the river and houses clustered around the city center.

All of the statues are original, except for the greatest—the *Venus of Arles*—which Louis XIV took a liking to and had moved to Versailles. It's now in the Louvre (and, as locals say, "When it's in Paris...bye-bye"). Jewelry, fine metal and glass artifacts, and well-crafted mosaic floors make it clear that Roman Arles was a city of art and culture.

Built at the site of the chariot racecourse (the arc of which is built into the parking lot), this air-conditioned, all-on-one-floor museum is a 25-minute walk from Arles along the river or a bus ride with a short walk (€5.50, daily March–Oct 9:00–19:00, Nov–Feb 10:00–17:00, tel. 04 90 18 88 88, www.arles-antique.org—in French only).

Bus #1 gets you within a five-minute walk. Catch the bus in downtown Arles on boulevard des Lices (€0.80, pay driver, runs every 20 min, daily except Sun); to find the museum turn left exiting the bus and then keep right, passing Hôtel Mercure. To return by bus, cross the bridge in front of museum and keep right, passing Hôtel Mercure; the bus stop (look for glass shelter) will be on your left across from the next roundabout; you want direction *Trebon*.

To reach the museum by foot from the city center, turn left at the river and take the riverside path to the big modern building just past the new bridge. The museum can call a taxi for your return (allow €8–10).

▲▲**Forum Square (Place du Forum)**—Named for the Roman forum that once stood here, this square was the political and religious center of Roman Arles. Still lively, this café-crammed square is popular for a *pastis* (see "Eating," page 72). The bistros on the square, while no place for a fine dinner, can put together a good

Arles at a Glance

▲▲▲**Ancient History Museum** Filled with models and sculptures, this is Roman Arles 101. **Hours:** Daily March–Oct 9:00–19:00, Nov–Feb 10:00–17:00.

▲▲▲**Roman Arena** Big amphitheater once used by gladiators, today for occasional bullfights. **Hours:** Daily May–Sept 9:00–18:00, March–April and Oct 9:00–17:30, Nov–Feb 10:00–16:30.

▲▲**Forum Square** Lively, café-crammed square, once the Roman forum. **Hours:** Always open.

▲▲**St. Trophime Church and Cloisters** Church with excellent Romanesque entrance. **Hours:** Daily May–Sept 9:00–18:30, March–April and Oct 9:00–17:30, Nov–Feb 10:00–16:30.

▲▲**Fondation Van Gogh** Small gallery with works by major contemporary artists paying homage to van Gogh (but no Vincent originals). **Hours:** April–mid-Oct daily 10:30–20:00, mid-Oct–March Tue–Sun 11:00–17:00, closed Mon.

▲**Arlatan Museum** Shares the treasures and pleasures of Provençal life from the 18th and 19th centuries, including costumes, furniture, bullfighting memorabilia, baby paraphernalia, manger scenes, and Christmas feasts. **Hours:** Daily April–Sept 9:30–12:30 & 14:00–18:00, Oct–March until 17:00.

Classical Theater Ruined Roman theater, recently restored and still used for events. **Hours:** Daily May–Sept 9:00–11:30 & 14:00–18:30, April and Oct 9:00–11:30 & 14:00–17:30, Nov–March 10:00–11:30 & 14:00–16:30.

enough salad or *plat du jour*—and when you sprinkle on the ambience, that's €10 well spent.

At the corner of Grand Hôtel Nord-Pinus, a plaque shows how the Romans built a foundation of galleries to make the main square level. The two columns are all that survive of a temple. Steps leading to the entrance are buried (the Roman street level was about 20 feet below you).

The statue on the square is of Frédéric Mistral. This popular poet, who wrote in the local dialect rather than French, was a champion of Provençal culture. After receiving the Nobel Prize in Literature in 1904, Mistral used his prize money to preserve and display the folk identity of Provence. He founded the regional folk museum (see Arlatan Museum, below) at a time when France was rapidly centralizing. (The famous local mistral wind—literally "master"—has nothing to do with his name.)

The bright-yellow café is famous as the subject of one of Vincent van Gogh's first works in Arles. While his painting showed the café in a brilliant yellow from the glow of gas lamps, the facade was bare limestone, just like the other cafés on this square. The café's current owners have painted it to match van Gogh's version...and to cash in on the Vincent-crazed hordes who pay too much to eat or drink here.

Cryptoportiques du Forum—The only Baroque church in Arles (admire the wooden ceiling) provides a dramatic entry to this underground system of arches and vaults that supported the southern end of the Roman Forum (and hid French resistance fighters during World War II). The galleries of arches demonstrate the extent to which Roman engineers would go to follow standard city plans: If the land doesn't suit the blueprint, change the land. While remarkable, there's not much to it beyond the initial "Oh, wow!" (€3.50, daily May–Sept 9:00–12:00 & 14:00–18:00, April and Oct 9:00–11:30 & 14:00–17:30, Nov–March 10:00–11:30 & 14:00–16:30, leave Forum Square with Grand Hôtel Nord-Pinus on your right and turn right on rue Balze).

▲▲St. Trophime Church, Cloisters, and Republic Square (Place de la République)—This church, named after a 3rd-century bishop of Arles and located on a fun square, sports the finest Romanesque main entrance (west portal) I've seen anywhere. Get a good view of it from...

République Square: This square used to be called "place Royale"...until the French Revolution. The obelisk was the centerpiece of Arles' Roman Circus. The lions at its base are the symbol of the city, whose slogan is "far from the anger of the lion." This is a popular gathering place for young Arlesians at night. Find a seat and watch the peasants—pilgrims, locals, and street musicians. There's nothing new about this scene.

Tympanum (on church facade): Like a Roman triumphal arch, the church trumpets the promise of Judgment Day. The tympanum (the semicircular area above the door) is filled with Christian symbolism. Christ sits in majesty, surrounded by symbols of the four

evangelists: Matthew, the winged man; Mark, the winged lion; Luke, the ox; and John, the eagle. The 12 apostles are lined up below Jesus. It's Judgment Day...some are saved and others aren't. Notice the condemned (on the right)—a chain gang doing a sad bunny-hop over the fires of hell. For them, the tune trumpeted by the three angels at the very top is not a happy one. Below the chain gang, St. Stephen is being stoned to death, with his soul leaving through his mouth and instantly being welcomed by angels. Ride the exquisite detail back to a simpler age. In an illiterate medieval world, long before the vivid images of our Technicolor time, this was a neon billboard over the town square. (A chart just inside the church on the right helps explain the carvings.)

Inside St. Trophime: The tall, 12th-century Romanesque nave is decorated by a set of tapestries showing scenes from the life of Mary (17th-century, from French town of Aubusson). Immediately to the left of entry, a chapel is built on an early-Christian sarcophagus from Roman Arles (from around A.D. 300). On its right side, the three Magi give gifts to baby Jesus, and a frieze below shows the flight to Egypt. Under the left transept, another Roman sarcophagus shows Jews hopping over the Red Sea as they leave Egypt. Amble around the Gothic apse and check out the relic chapel. This church is a stop on the ancient pilgrimage route to Santiago de Compostela in northwest Spain. For 800 years, pilgrims on their way to Santiago have paused here. Even today, modern-day pilgrimages are advertised near the church's entry (free, daily May–Sept 9:00–18:30, March–April and Oct 9:00–17:30, Nov–Feb 10:00–16:30).

The adjacent **cloisters** are the best in Provence (enter from square, through courtyard to right of church). Enjoy the sculpted capitals of the rounded 12th-century Romanesque columns and the pointed 14th-century Gothic columns. The second floor offers only a view of the cloisters from above (€3.50, same hours as church).

To get to the next sight, the Classical Theater, face the church, walk left, then take the first right on rue de la Calade.

Classical Theater (Théâtre Antique)—Precious little survives from this Roman theater, which served as a handy town quarry throughout the Middle Ages. Walk to a center aisle and pull up a stone seat. Built in the 1st century B.C., this theater seated 10,000. To appreciate its original size, look to the upper left side of the tower and find the protrusion that supported the highest of three seating levels. Today, 3,000 can attend events in this restored facility. Two lonely Corinthian columns look out from the stage over the audience. The orchestra section is defined by a semicircular pattern in the stone. Stepping up onto the left side of the stage, look down to the narrow channel that allowed the curtain to disappear below, like magic. Go backstage and browse through broken bits of Rome, and loop back to the entry behind the grass (€3, you can see much of the theater by peeking through the fence for free, daily May–Sept 9:00–11:30 & 14:00–18:30, April and Oct 9:00–11:30 & 14:00–17:30, Nov–March 10:00–11:30 & 14:00–16:30; for more on Roman theaters, read about Orange in the Near Avignon chapter, page 121). A block uphill is the...

▲▲▲Roman Arena (Amphithéâtre)—Nearly 2,000 years ago, gladiators fought wild animals here to the delight of 20,000 screaming fans. Today, local daredevils fight wild bulls. In Roman times, games were free (sponsored by city bigwigs) and fans were seated by social class. The many exits allowed for rapid dispersal after the games—fights would break out among frenzied fans if they couldn't leave

quickly. Through medieval times and until the early 1800s, the arches were bricked up and the stadium became a fortified town—with 200 humble homes crammed within its circular defenses. Three of the medieval towers survive (the one above the ticket booth is open and rewards those who climb it with a good view). To see two still-sealed arches, complete with cute medieval window frames, turn right as you leave, walk to the Andaluz restaurant, and look back (€4, daily May–Sept 9:00–18:00, March–April and Oct 9:00–17:30, and Nov–Feb 10:00–16:30; for more on Roman amphitheaters, see page 112 in Nîmes section). Bullfight posters around the Arena advertise upcoming spectacles.

Turn left out of the Arena and find...

▲▲Fondation Van Gogh—Refreshing to any art lover, and especially interesting to van Gogh fans, this small gallery features works by major contemporary artists and pays homage to Vincent through thought-provoking interpretations of his art. Many pieces are explained in English by the artists. The black-and-white photographs (both art and shots of places Vincent painted) complement the paintings (€7, not covered by Monument Pass, great collection of van Gogh prints and postcards for sale in free entry area, April–mid-Oct daily 10:30–20:00, mid-Oct–March Tue–Sun 11:00–17:00, closed Mon, facing Roman Arena at 24 bis rond-point des Arènes, tel. 04 90 49 94 04, www.fondationvangogh-arles.org).

▲Arlatan Museum (Musée Arlatan)—Built on the remains of the Roman Forum (see the courtyard), this museum houses the treasures of daily Provençal life. It was given to Arles by Nobel Prize winner Frédéric Mistral (see Forum Square, above). Mistral's vision was to give locals an appreciation of their cultural roots, presented in tableaux that unschooled villagers could understand—"a veritable poem for the ordinary people who cannot read." Even though there are no English descriptions, the museum offers a unique and intimate look at local folk culture from the 18th and 19th centuries.

A one-way route takes you through 30 rooms. The first few rooms display folk costumes chronologically until about 1900, when the traditional dress was replaced by the modern nondescript norm. You'll then see fine freestanding wedding armoires (given to brides by parents and filled with essentials to begin a new home). Finely

Van Gogh in Arles

"The whole future of art is to be found in the south of France."
—Vincent van Gogh, 1888

Vincent was 35 years old when he arrived in Arles in 1888, and it was here that he discovered the light that would forever change him. Coming from the gray skies and flatlands of the Netherlands and Paris, he was bowled over by everything Provençal—jagged peaks, gnarled olive trees, brilliant sunflowers, and the furious wind. Van Gogh painted in a flurry in Arles, producing more paintings than at any other period of his too-brief career—more than 200 in just a few months. (The fact that locals pronounced his name "vahn-saw van gog" had nothing to do with his psychological struggles here.) Sadly, none of van Gogh's paintings remain in Arles—but you can still visit the places that inspired him. Around downtown Arles, you'll find 17 steel-and-concrete van Gogh **"easels"** that mark places Vincent painted, including the *Café at*

crafted wooden cages—called *panetières*—hung from walls and kept bread away from mice. *Santons* were popular figurines giving nativity scenes a Provençal look. The second floor shows local history and a large room covers lifestyles of residents of the Camargue. A fascinating case shows antique *Coursa Provanciale* bullfighting memorabilia, including a stuffed champion bull named Lion, who died of old age.

The last two rooms are the collection's pride and joy. In one, a rich mom is shown with her newborn. Her friends visit with gifts representing four physical and moral qualities hoped for in a new baby—good as bread, full as an egg, wise as salt, and straight as a match. The cradle is fully stocked with everything needed to raise an infant in 1888.

The next room shows "the great supper"—a traditional feast served on Christmas Eve before midnight Mass. It's 1860, and everything on the table is locally produced. Traditionally 13 sweets—for Jesus and the 12 apostles—were served. Grandma and grandpa warm themselves in front of the fireplace; grandpa pours wine on a log for good luck in the coming year (€4, pick up excellent English brochure, daily April–Sept 9:30–12:30 & 14:00–18:00, Oct–March until 17:00, 29 rue de la République, tel. 04 90 96 08 23).

Réattu Museum (Musée Réattu)—Housed in a beautiful 15th-century mansion, this mildly interesting, mostly-modern art collection includes 57 Picasso drawings (some two-sided and all done in a flurry

Night on Forum Square. Each comes with a photo of the actual painting (see photo at left) and provides fans with a fun opportunity to compare the scene then and now. The TI has a €1 brochure that locates all the easels.

The **hospital** where Vincent was sent to treat his self-inflicted ear wound is today a cultural center (called *Espace Van Gogh* and *Mediathèque*). It surrounds a garden that the artist loved (and the only flower garden I've seen in Arles). Only the courtyard is open to the public; find the "easel" to see what Vincent painted here (free, near the Arlatan Museum on rue Président Wilson). Vincent was sent from here to the mental institution in nearby St. Rémy (see page 82) before Dr. Paul Gachet invited him to Auvers-sur-Oise, near Paris.

From place Lamartine, walk to the river, then look toward the town to find where Vincent set his easel for this *Starry Night Over the Rhône* painting, where stars boil above the skyline of Arles. Riverfront cafés that once stood here were destroyed by bridge-seeking bombs in World War II, as was the bridge whose remains you see on your right.

of creativity—I liked the bullfights best), a room of Henri Rousseau's Camargue watercolors, and an unfinished painting by the neoclassical artist Jacques Réattu, none with English explanations (€4, extra for special exhibits, daily May–Sept 9:00–12:00 & 14:00–18:30; March–April and Oct until 17:00; Nov–Feb 13:00–17:00; 10 rue du Grand Prieuré, tel. 04 90 96 37 68).

EVENTS

▲▲**Wednesday and Saturday Markets**—Twice a week in the morning, Arles' ring road erupts into an open-air market of fish, flowers, produce, and you-name-it. The Wednesday market runs along boulevard Emile Combes, between place Lamartine and Avenue Victor Hugo; the segment nearer place Lamartine is all about food, the upper half is about clothing, tablecloths, purses, etc... The Saturday market is along boulevard des Lices near the TI. Join in, buy flowers, try the olives, sample some wine, and swat a pick-pocket; both markets open until 12:00. On the first Wednesday of the month, it's a grand flea market.

Much of the market has a North African feel, thanks to the Algerians and Moroccans who live in Arles (see page 10). They came to do the lowly city jobs that locals didn't want, and now mostly do the region's labor-intensive agricultural jobs (picking olives, harvesting fruit, and working in local greenhouses).

▲▲**Bullfights (Courses Camarguaises)**—Occupy the same seats fans have used for nearly 2,000 years, and take in Arles' most mem-

orable experience—a bullfight *à la provençale* in the ancient Arena. These are more sporting than bloody Spanish bullfights. The bulls of Arles (who, locals stress, "die of old age") are billed even more boldly than their human foes in the posters. A bull has a ribbon *(cocarde)* above its forehead laced between its horns. The bullfighter, with a special hook, has 15 minutes to snare the ribbon. Local businessmen encourage a fighter by hollering out how much money they'll pay for the *cocarde*. If the bull pulls a good stunt, the band plays the famous *Toreador Song* from *Carmen*. The following day, newspapers have reports on the fight, including how many *Carmens* the bull earned.

Three classes of bullfights—determined by the experience of the fighters—are advertised in posters: The *course de protection* is for rookie bullfighters. The *trophée de l'Avenir* comes with better fighters. And the *trophée des As* features top professionals. During Easter and the fall rice harvest festival (Féria du Riz), the Arena hosts actual Spanish bullfights (look for *corrida*) with outfits, swords, spikes, and the whole gory she-bang (tickets €5–10, Easter–Oct on Sat, Sun, and holidays). Don't pass on a chance to see *Toro Piscine*, a silly spectacle for warm summer evenings where the bull ends up in a swimming pool (uh huh, get more details at TI). Nearby villages stage bullfights in small wooden bull-rings nearly every weekend; the TI has the latest schedule.

SLEEPING

In Arles
Hotels are a great value here; many are air-conditioned, though few have elevators.

$$$ **Hôtel d'Arlatan***, built over the site of a Roman basil-ica, is classy in every sense of the word. It has sumptuous public spaces, a tranquil terrace, a designer pool, a turtle pond, and antique-filled rooms, most with high, wood-beamed ceilings and stone walls. In the lobby of this 15th-century building, a glass floor looks down into Roman ruins (standard Db-€88, bigger Db-€105–125, still bigger-Db-€145, Db/Qb suites-€180–250, excellent buffet break-fast-€11, air-con, elevator, parking-€11, 26 rue Sauvage, 1 block below Forum Square, tel. 04 90 93 56 66, fax 04 90 49 68 45, www.hotel-arlatan.fr, hotel-arlatan@wanadoo.fr, SE).

Sleep Code

(€1 = about $1.20, country code: 33)
S = Single, **D** = Double/Twin, **T** = Triple, **Q** = Quad,
b = bathroom, **s** = shower only, no **CC** = Credit Cards not
accepted, **SE** = Speaks English, **NSE** = No English, * = French
hotel rating system (0–4 stars). Unless otherwise noted, credit
cards are accepted.

To help you sort easily through these listings, I've divided
the rooms into three categories based on the price for a standard
double room with bath:

$$$ **Higher Priced**—Most rooms €85 or more.
$$ **Moderately Priced**—Most rooms between €55–85.
$ **Lower Priced**—Most rooms €55 or less.

The next three hotels are worthy of three stars; each is an
exceptional deal:

$$ Hôtel de l'Amphithéâtre**, a carefully decorated boutique
hotel, is just steps from the Roman Arena. Public spaces are very sharp
with a museum quality, and the owners pay attention to every detail of
your stay. The Belvedere room for €140 has the best view over Arles
I've seen (Db-€52–72, superior Db-€82, Tb-€92, Qb-€120, air-con,
elevator, parking-€5, 5 rue Diderot, one block from Arena, tel. 04 90
96 10 30, fax 04 90 93 98 69, www.hotelamphitheatre.fr, contact
@hotelamphitheatre.fr, helpful Fabrice and Denis SE).

$$ Hôtel du Musée** is a quiet, delightful manor-home hide-
away with 20 comfortable, air-conditioned rooms, a flowery two-
tiered courtyard, and a snazzy art-gallery lounge. The rooms in the
new section are worth the few extra euros and steps. Claude and
English-speaking Laurence are gracious owners. The price ranges
listed are for rooms in the old (lower rates) or new building (Sb-
€43–50, Db-€55–65, Tb-€65–80, Qb-€80, buffet breakfast-€7, elevator, parking-€7, 11 rue du Grand Prieuré, follow signs to Réattu
Museum, tel. 04 90 93 88 88, fax 04 90 49 98 15, www.hoteldumusee
.com.fr, contact@hoteldumusee.com.fr).

$$ Hôtel Calendal**, located between the Roman Arena and
Classical Theater, is Provençal chic and does everything right, with
smartly appointed rooms—some with views overlooking the Arena—
surrounding a large, palm-shaded courtyard. They even have my
Provence video on DVD in the lobby. Enjoy the great buffet
breakfast (€8), the salad-and-pasta-bar lunch buffet (€14), and the
seductive ambience. Price ranges reflect room size (Db facing street-
€45–70, Db facing garden-€72–85, Db with balcony-€90–100,
air-con, Internet access, reserve ahead for parking-€10,

Arles Hotels and Restaurants

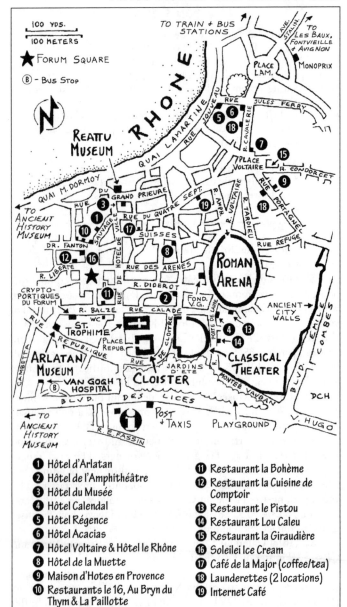

① Hôtel d'Arlatan
② Hôtel de l'Amphithéâtre
③ Hôtel du Musée
④ Hôtel Calendal
⑤ Hôtel Régence
⑥ Hôtel Acacias
⑦ Hôtel Voltaire & Hôtel le Rhône
⑧ Hôtel de la Muette
⑨ Maison d'Hotes en Provence
⑩ Restaurants le 16, Au Bryn du Thym & La Paillotte

⑪ Restaurant la Bohème
⑫ Restaurant la Cuisine de Comptoir
⑬ Restaurant le Pistou
⑭ Restaurant Lou Caleu
⑮ Restaurant la Giraudière
⑯ Soleilei Ice Cream
⑰ Café de la Major (coffee/tea)
⑱ Launderettes (2 locations)
⑲ Internet Café

5 rue Porte de Laure, just above Arena, tel. 04 90 96 11 89, fax 04 90 96 05 84, www.lecalendal.com, contact@lecalendal.com, SE).

$$ Hôtel de la Muette, with eager-to-please owners (NSE), is a good choice when the places listed above are full. Located in a quiet corner of Arles, the place is well kept with stone walls, wood beams, and air conditioning (Db-€55–60, Tb-€60–70, Qb-€80, no elevator, 15 rue de Suisses, tel. 04 90 96 15 30, fax 04 90 49 73 16, http//perso.wanadoo.fr/hotel-muette, hotel.muette@wanadoo.fr).

$$ Maison d'Hôtes en Provence, run by engaging American Madeleine and her soft-spoken French husband Erique, combines an interesting B&B experience—four spacious and funky but comfortable rooms—with optional Provençal cooking workshops. Foodies should check out their Web site for its appealing and affordable range of gourmet classes (Db-€65, extra person-€15, good family room, across from launderette at 11 rue Portagnel, tel. & fax 04 90 49 69 20, www.cuisineprovencale.com, actvedel@wanadoo.fr).

$ Hôtel Régence, one of the best deals in Arles, has a riverfront location, immaculate and comfortable rooms, good beds, safe parking, and easy access to the train station (Db-€35–48, Tb-€40–57, Qb-€60–67, choose river view or quieter courtyard rooms, most with shower, air-con, no elevator but only two floors, excellent buffet breakfast-€5, Internet access, 5 rue Marius Jouveau, from place Lamartine turn right immediately after passing between towers, tel. 04 90 96 39 85, fax 04 90 96 67 64, www.hotel-regence.com, contact @hotel-regence.com, the gentle Nouvions speak some English).

$ Hôtel Acacias, just off place Lamartine and inside the old city walls, is a modern, pastel paradise, with smallish, reasonably-priced rooms with all the comforts, including cable TV and hairdryers (Db-€46–55, Tb-€61–79, Qb-€78–87, buffet breakfast-€6, air-con, elevator, 1 rue Marius Jouveau, tel. 04 90 96 37 88, fax 04 90 96 32 51, www.hotel-acacias.com, contact@hotel-acacias.com, Christophe and Sylvie SE).

$ Hôtel Voltaire rents 12 small and spartan rooms with ceiling fans and nifty balconies overlooking a caffeine-stained square. It's perfect for starving artists, a block below the Arena. Smiling owner Mr. Ferran (fur-ran) loves the States (his dream is to travel there), and hopes you'll add to his postcard collection. He also serves daily lunch and dinner; see "Eating," below (D-€28, Ds-€30, Db-€36, 1 place Voltaire, tel. 04 90 96 49 18, fax 04 90 96 45 49, levoltaire @aol.com).

$ Hôtel le Rhône greets you with neon-yellow outside and hardworking owners inside—Benedicte and Hervé, refugees from northern France. Their 11 cute, spotless little rooms are decorated with cheery colors (D-€26, Ds-€31, Db-€38–40, some rooms have balconies over the square, 11 place Voltaire, tel. 04 90 96 43 70, fax 04 90 93 87 03, hotellerhone@wanadoo.fr).

Near Arles, in Fontvieille

Many drivers, particularly those with families, prefer staying in the peaceful countryside with easy access to the area's sights. Just 10 minutes from Arles and Les Baux, and 20 minutes from Avignon, little Fontvieille slumbers in the shadows of its big-city cousins (though it has its share of restaurants and boutiques). See also "Sleeping," page 80.

$$$ **Le Peiriero***** is a pooped parent's dream come true, with a grassy garden, massive pool, table tennis, badminton, massage parlor, and (believe it or not) a miniature golf course. The spacious family loft rooms, capable of sleeping up to five, have full bathrooms on both levels. This complete retreat also comes with a terrace café and restaurant (Db-street side-€84, Db-garden side-€105, Db with terrace-€120, Tb-€96–135, Tb loft-€160, breakfast buffet-€12, dinner *menu*-€24, air-con, free parking, 34 avenue des Baux, just east of Fontvieille on road to Les Baux, tel. 04 90 54 76 10, fax 04 90 54 62 60, www.hotel-peiriero.com, info@hotel-peiriero.com, SE).

EATING

You can dine well in Arles on a modest budget—in fact, it's hard to blow a lot on dinner here (all my listings have *menus* for €22 or less). The bad news is that restaurants here change regularly, so double-check my suggestions. All restaurants listed have outdoor seating except La Bohème. Before dinner, go local on the Forum Square and enjoy a *pastis*. This anise-based apéritif is served straight in a glass with ice, plus a carafe of water—dilute to taste.

For **picnics,** a big, handy Monoprix supermarket/department store is on place Lamartine (Mon–Sat 8:30–19:25, closed Sun).

On or near Forum Square

Great atmosphere and mediocre food at fair prices await on Forum Square. A half-block below the Forum on rue du Dr. Fanton lies a lineup of these three tempting places:

Le 16, with warm ambience inside and out, is ideal for a fresh salad or one-course dinner. It offers a daily *plat du jour* and seasonal *menu* (closed Sat–Sun, just below Forum Square on 16 rue du Dr. Fanton, tel. 04 90 93 77 36).

La Paillotte, a few doors down, has rosy tablecloths under wood-beamed comfort inside, a nice terrace outside, and fine regional cuisine at affordable prices (€15–21 *menus*, closed Wed, 28 rue du Dr. Fanton, tel. 04 90 96 33 15).

Au Bryn du Thym, almost next door, is reliable and specializes in traditional Provençal cuisine. Arrive early for an outdoor table (€19 *menu*, closed Tue, 22 rue du Dr. Fanton, tel. 04 90 49 95 96).

La Bohème seems lost a block above Forum Square. Here you dine under a long, vaulted ceiling with good budget options (€14 vegetarian *menu*, €18 Provençal *menu*, closed Sun–Mon, 6 rue Balze, tel. 04 90 18 58 92).

La Cuisine de Comptoir (signed CDC) is the place urbanites go to lose that Provençal decor and pretend they're in Paris. It's a cool little bistro serving light *tartine* dinners (dishes served over toasted bread) at inexpensive prices (closed Sun, just off Forum Square's lower end at 10 rue de la Liberté, tel. 04 90 96 86 28).

Near the Roman Arena

For about the same price as on Forum Square, you can enjoy regional cuisine with a point-blank view of the Arena. Of the two restaurants sitting side by side, I prefer **Le Pistou.** Arrive early to get an outdoor table with a view (*menus* from €18, closed Tue, at top of Arena, 30 rond-point des Arènes, tel. 04 90 18 20 92).

On the same block as the recommended Hôtel Calendal lies a mini-restaurant row, with several reasonable options. **Lou Caleu** is the best (though not cheapest), with very Provençal cuisine and *menus* at €18 and €26 (closed Mon, 27 rue Porte de Laure, tel. 04 90 49 71 77).

La Giraudière, a few blocks below the Arena on place Voltaire, is mauve-pretty and offers reliable regional cuisine under a heavy-beamed ceiling. Come here to dine inside, and show this book to get a free *kir* (€22–35 *menus*, closed Tue, air-con, tel. 04 90 93 27 52).

The recommended **Hôtel Calendal** hosts an all-you-can-eat salad-and-pasta bar (daily 12:00–16:00 for €14); the selection is as good as the quality. Retreat from the city and enjoy a healthy lunch in the hotel's palm-shaded garden.

The recommended **Hôtel Voltaire** serves daily a nothing-fancy three-course dinner (or lunch) for €11 and hearty salads for €8–10 (try *salade fermière*) on place Voltaire.

Dessert

For the best ice cream in Arles, find **Soleilei,** with all-natural ingredients and unusual flavors such as *fadoli*—olive oil–flavored ice cream (daily, across from recommended La Vitamine restaurant at 9 rue du Dr. Fanton).

TRANSPORTATION CONNECTIONS

From Arles by bus to: Nîmes (5/day, 1 hr), **St. Rémy** (6/day, 45 min), **Camargue/Stes-Maries-de-la-Mer** (5/day Mon–Sat, 4/day Sun, 1 hr). There are two bus stops in Arles: the *Centre-ville* stop is at 16 boulevard Clemenceau (2 blocks below main TI, next to Café le Wilson); the other is at the train station. Bus info: tel. 04 90 49 38 01 (NSE). Ask about buses to **Les Baux** (it's possible they will be reinstated by the time you read this).

From Arles by train to: Paris (17/day, two direct TGVs in 4 hrs, 15 with transfer in Avignon in 5 hrs), **Avignon Centre-Ville** (11/day, 20 min, afternoon gaps), **Avignon TGV** (2/hr, 20 min, take SNCF bus), **Nîmes** (9/day, 25 min), **Orange** (4/day direct, 35 min, more with transfer in Avignon), **Aix-en-Provence Centre-Ville** (10/day, 2 hrs, requires at least one transfer, in Marseille), **Marseille** (20/day, 1 hr), **Carcassonne** (6/day, 3 hrs, 3 with transfer in Narbonne), **Beaune** (10/day, 4.5 hrs, 9 with transfer in Nîmes or Avignon and Lyon), **Nice** (11/day, 4 hrs, 10 with transfer in Marseille), **Barcelona** (2/day, 6 hrs, transfer in Montpellier), **Italy** (3/day, transfer in Marseille and Nice; from Arles, it's 4.5 hrs to Ventimiglia on the border, 8 hrs to Milan, 9.5 hrs to Cinque Terre, 11 hrs to Florence, and 13 hrs to Venice or Rome).

NEAR ARLES

*Les Baux, St. Rémy,
and the Camargue*

The diverse terrain around Arles harbors several worthwhile and easy day trips. The medieval ghost town of Les Baux still haunts the eerie Alpilles mountains, while busy little St. Rémy awaits over the Alpilles with Roman ruins and memories of Vincent van Gogh. For a completely different experience, the flat Camargue knocks on Arles' southern door with saltwater lakes, flamingos, wild horses, and wild black bulls.

Les Baux

Crowning the rugged Alpilles (ahl-pee) Mountains, this rock-capping castle town is a memorable place to visit. Even with the tourist crowds, the place evokes a strong community that lived a rugged life—thankful more for their top-notch fortifications than their dramatic views. While mobbed with tourists through most of the day, those arriving by 9:00 or after 17:00 enjoy a more peaceful scene. Sunsets are dramatic, and nights in Les Baux are pin-drop peaceful. After dark, the castle is closed—but beautifully illuminated.

ORIENTATION

Les Baux is actually two visits in one: castle ruins on an almost lunar landscape and, below, a medieval town packed with shops, cafés, and tourist knickknacks. See the castle, then savor or blitz the lower town on your way out. There's no free parking; get as close to the top as you can and pay €4 (good for 3 days, take ticket and walk toward town, pay at machine next to telephone and bakery, 30 steps below town entry).

One cobbled street leads into town, where you're greeted first by

Sights Near Arles

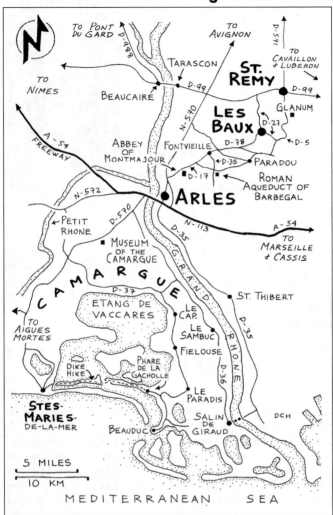

the TI (daily April–Sept 9:00–19:00, Oct–March 9:00–12:00 & 13:00–18:00, in Hôtel de Ville, tel. 04 90 54 34 39). The main drag leads directly to the castle (15-min uphill walk).

Getting to Les Baux

By Car: Les Baux is a 20-minute drive from Arles. From Arles, follow signs to Avignon, then Les Baux. Drivers can combine Les Baux with St. Rémy (15 min away) and the ruined Roman aqueduct of Barbegal (both described below).

By Foot: Les Baux is a beautiful three-hour hike from St. Rémy; see "Hike to Les Baux" on page 84.

By Bus: Longtime bus service with Arles was canceled in 2004 for "local political reasons." It might be reinstated—someday; ask. Consider taking a bus to St. Rémy (about €4 from Arles or Avignon) and then a taxi from there (figure €15 one-way). This allows you to combine two worthwhile stops while saving euros.

By Taxi: Figure €30 for a taxi one-way from Arles (tel. 06 80 27 60 92).

SIGHTS

The Castle Ruins

Many of the ancient walls of Les Baux's striking castle still stand in testament to the proud past of this village. The climbing is fun, the views are sensational, and the mistral wind just might blow your socks off. Buy your ticket in the old olive-mill room and study the museum exhibits (models of the town in the 13th and 16th centuries, interesting photos showing the town before tourism and today). Pick up the informative and included audioguide.

A 12th-century regional powerhouse, Les Baux was razed in 1632 by a paranoid Louis XIII, who was afraid of these troublemaking upstarts. The sun-bleached "dead city" ruins are carved into, out of, and on top of a rock 650 feet above the valley floor. As you wander out on the wind-blown field past kid-thrilling medieval siege weaponry,

try to imagine 6,000 people living behind stone walls on this cliff. Notice the water-catchment system (a slanted field that caught rain water and drained it into a cistern—necessary during a siege). In the little chapel across from the museum, the slideshow ("Van Gogh, Gauguin, and Cézanne: Painting in the Land of the Olive Trees") provides a relaxing 10-minute interlude. Early July through late August, medieval events take place in the open area (visitors' crossbow shooting range might be continued in 2005, check at TI as you enter; castle entry-€7, daily Easter–Oct 9:00–19:00, July–Aug until 20:00, Nov–Easter 9:30–17:00).

Lower Town

You can shop and eat your way back to your car or the bus station through the new town. Or you can take your first left, go downhill, and check out these minor but fun sights as you descend from the castle:

Yves Brayer Museum (Musée Yves Brayer)—This is an appealing exhibit of paintings (van Gogh-like Expressionism, without the

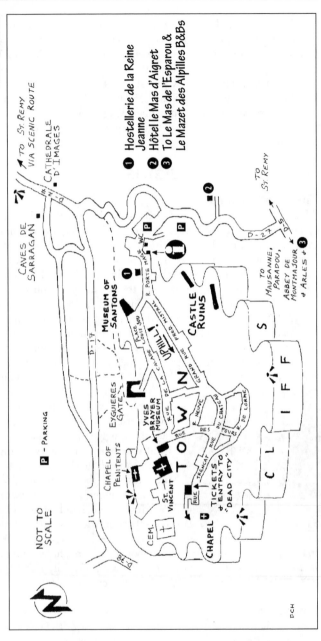

Les Baux

1 Hostellerie de la Reine Jeanne
2 Hôtelle Mas d'Aigret
3 To Le Mas de l'Esparou & Le Mazet des Alpilles B&Bs

NOT TO SCALE

P - PARKING

tumult) by Yves Brayer, who spent his final years in the 1970s here in Les Baux (€4, daily 10:00–12:30 & 14:00–18:30).

Downhill, around the corner, is...

St. Vincent Church—This 12th-century Romanesque church was built short and wide to fit the terrain. The center chapel on the right houses the town's traditional Provençal processional chariot. Each Christmas Eve a ram pulled this cart—holding a lamb, symbolizing Jesus, and surrounded by candles—to this church.

In front of the church is the old-town laundry—with a pig-snout faucet and 14th-century stone washing surface with drains designed for short women.

Around the corner, toward a great view, is the...

Chapel of Penitents—Notice the nativity scene painted by Yves Brayer, which shows the local legend that Jesus was born in Les Baux.

Staying left as you round the old laundry and heading down-hill, you'll pass plenty of cafés with wonderful views. You'll see the town's fortified wall and one of its two gates. Farther below you'll come to the...

Museum of Santons—The museum displays a collection of *santons*, popular folk figurines, which decorate local Christmas mangers (free entry). Notice how the nativity scene proves once again that Jesus was born in Les Baux. These painted clay dolls show off local dress and traditions. Find the old couple leaning into the mistral wind.

Near Les Baux

A half-mile beyond Les Baux, D-27 leads to dramatic views of the hill town with pull-outs and walking trails at the pass, and two sights that fill cool, cavernous caves in former limestone quarries that date back to the Middle Ages. (The limestone is easy to cut, but gets hard and nicely polished when exposed to the weather.)

Caves de Sarragan, with the best Les Baux views from its park-ing lot, is occupied by the Sarragan Winery, which invites you in for a taste. While this place looks like it's designed for groups, the friendly, English-speaking staff welcomes individuals (free, daily April–Sept 10:00–12:00 & 14:00–19:00, Oct–March until 18:00, tel. 04 90 54 33 58).

Cathédrale d'Images, in a similar cave nearby, offers a mes-merizing sound-and-slide show. Its 48 projectors flash countless images set to music on the quarry walls as visitors wander around, immersed in the year's theme (€7, daily 10:00–18:00). The D-27 continues to St. Rémy and makes a good loop if you return via D-5 from St. Rémy.

Speaking of quarries, in 1821 the rocks and soil of the area were discovered to contain an important mineral for the making of alu-minum. It was named after the town—bauxite.

Sleep Code

(€1 = about $1.20, country code: 33)
S = Single, **D** = Double/Twin, **T** = Triple, **Q** = Quad,
b = bathroom, **s** = shower only, **no CC** = Credit Cards not
accepted, **SE** = Speaks English, **NSE** = No English, * = French
hotel rating system (0–4 stars). Unless otherwise noted, credit
cards are accepted.

To help you easily sort through these listings, I've divided
the rooms into three categories, based on the price for a standard
double room with bath:

$$$ **Higher Priced**—Most rooms €85 or more.
$$ **Moderately Priced**—Most rooms between €55–85.
$ **Lower Priced**—Most rooms €55 or less.

For more accommodations, see also "Sleeping near Arles," page
72, and "Sleeping in St. Rémy," page 85.

SLEEPING

In or near Les Baux

$$$ **Le Mas d'Aigret*** crouches barely past Les Baux on the road to
St. Rémy. Lie on your back and stare up at the castle walls rising
beyond your swimming pool in this mini-oasis. Most of the average
size, artfully designed rooms have private terraces and views over the
valley, and the restaurant is troglodyte-chic (no view Db-€100, larger
Db with balcony-€135, Tb-€175, prices include breakfast, air-con,
some daytime road noise with view rooms, €30 *menu* at restaurant, tel.
04 90 54 20 00, fax 04 90 54 44 00, www.masdaigret.com, contact
@masdaigret.com, SE).

$$ **Le Mas de l'Esparou** *chambre d'hôte*, a few minutes below Les
Baux, is welcoming and kid-friendly, with three spacious rooms,
squishy mattresses, a swimming pool, table tennis, and distant views of
Les Baux. Jacqueline loves her job, and her lack of English only makes
her more animated. Monsieur Roux painted the artwork in your room
and has a gallery in Les Baux (Db-€62, extra person-about €16, no
CC, between Les Baux and Maussane les Alpilles on D-5, look for
white sign with green lettering, tel. & fax 04 90 54 41 32, NSE).

$ **Hostellerie de la Reine Jeanne**, an exceptional value, offers
comfy rooms 150 feet to your right after the main entry to the live city
where you can watch the sun set and rise from Les Baux (standard
Ds-€47, standard Db-€51, Db with view deck-€63, cavernous family
suite-€92, air-con in some rooms, ask for *chambre avec terrasse*, good
menus from €20, tel. 04 90 54 32 06, fax 04 90 54 32 33, www
.la-reinejeanne.com, reine.jeanne@wanadoo.fr, affable Alain SE).

$ **Le Mazet des Alpilles** is a small home with three tidy air-conditioned rooms just outside the unspoiled village of Paradou, five minutes below Les Baux. It may have space when others don't (Db-€53, ask for largest room, child's bed available, no CC, follow brown signs from D-17, in Paradou look for route de Brunelly, tel. 04 90 54 45 89, fax 04 90 54 44 66, lemazet@wanadoo.fr, charming Annick speaks just enough English).

Between Les Baux and Arles

These sights make easy stops for drivers.

Abbey of Montmajour—This brooding hulk of a ruin, just a few minutes' drive from Arles toward Les Baux, was once a thriving abbey and a convenient papal retreat (c. 950). Today the vacant abbey church is a massive example of Romanesque architecture. The surrounding fields were a favorite of van Gogh's, who walked here from Arles to paint his famous wheat fields. These are now rice fields, which wouldn't have looked nearly as good on canvas (abbey entry-€6, daily April–Sept 9:00–19:00, Oct–March 10:00–13:00 & 14:00–17:00, tel. 04 90 54 64 17). For more on abbeys, see "Medieval Monasteries" on page 162.

▲**Roman Aqueduct of Barbegal**—To be all alone with evocative Roman ruins, drivers can take a quick detour to the crumbled arches of ancient Arles' principal aqueduct. Coming from Arles, take D-17 toward Fontvieille, then, 1.5 miles before Fontvieille, follow signs for *L'Aqueduc Romain* on D-82 (it's signed coming from Fontvieille to Arles as well, on the left). In less than two miles, park at the pull-out (no sign, just after *Los Pozos Blancos* sign, where the ruins of the aqueduct cross the road). Leave no valuables in your car; the gravel twinkles with the remains of wing windows.

Follow the dirt path to the right through the olive grove and along the aqueduct ruins for 200 yards. Approaching the bluff with the grand view, you'll see that the water canal split into two troughs: One takes a 90-degree right turn and heads for Arles; the other goes straight to the bluff and over, where it once sent water cascading down to power eight grinding mills. Romans grew wheat on the vast fields you see from here, then brought it down to the mega-water-mill of Barbegal. Historians figure this mill produced enough flour each day to feed 12,000 hungry Romans. (If you saw the model of this eight-tiered mill in Arles' Ancient History Museum, the milling is easy to visualize and quite an exciting experience.) Returning to your car, find the broken bit of aqueduct—positioned like a children's slide—and study the waterproofing mortar that lined all Roman aqueducts.

St. Rémy-de-Provence

Sophisticated and sassy, St. Rémy gave birth to Nostradamus and cared for a distraught artist. A few min-
utes from the town center, you can visit the once-thriving Roman city called Glanum, the mental ward where Vincent van Gogh was sent after lopping off his lobe, and an art center dedicated to his memory. Best of all, elbow your way through its raucous Wednesday market (until 12:30). A racecourse-like ring road
hems in a pedestrian-friendly center that's well-stocked with fine foods and the latest Provençal fashions.

ORIENTATION

The **TI** is on place Jean Juarés, two blocks toward Les Baux from the ring road (Mon–Sat 9:30–12:30 & 14:00–19:00, Sun 10:00–12:00 & 15:00–17:00, tel. 04 90 92 05 22). Parking in St. Rémy is tricky and always comes with a fee; it's easiest at the TI lot. From St. Rémy's TI, it's a 15-minute walk to Glanum and Clinique St. Paul (van Gogh's mental hospital).

Getting to St. Rémy

By Car: A spectacular 15-minute drive along D-27, over the hills and through the woods, separates St. Rémy and Les Baux. Coming from Les Baux, find D-27 by passing Cathedrale d'Images. If you're driving from St. Rémy to Les Baux, follow signs for Tarascon, and you'll see the D-27 turnoff to Les Baux in a few miles.

By Bus: Buses run from Arles and Avignon to St. Rémy (6/day, 45 min). If arriving at St. Rémy by bus, get off on the ring road, just before the turnoff to Les Baux and the TI.

By Taxi: From Les Baux, figure on €15; from Avignon, allow €40. Tel. 06 80 27 60 92.

SIGHTS

▲**Glanum**—These crumbling stones are the foundations of a Roman market town, located at the crossroads of two ancient trade routes between Italy and Spain. This important town had grand villas and temples, a basilica, a forum, a wooden dam, aqueducts, and more. A massive Roman arch and tower stand proud and lonely near the ruins' parking lot. The arch marked the entry into Glanum, and the tower is a memorial to the grandsons of Emperor Caesar Augustus. The

St. Rémy Area

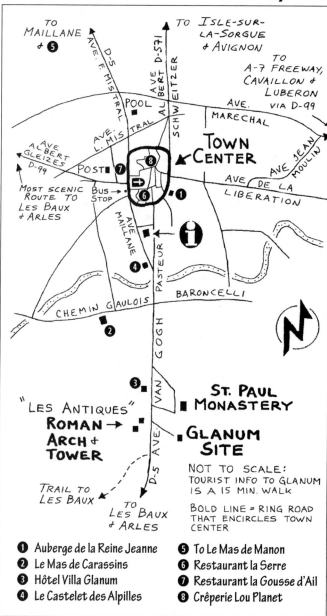

TO MAILLANE ⌀ ❺

AVE. F. MISTRAL   D-5

TO ISLE-SUR-LA-SORGUE & AVIGNON

AVE ALBERT D-571

SCHWEITZER

TO A-7 FREEWAY, CAVAILLON & LUBERON   VIA D-99

AVE. MARECHAL

POOL

AVE. L. MISTRAL

ALBERT GLEIZES AVE   D-99

POST ■ ❼   ❽   TOWN CENTER   AVE JEAN MOULIN

MOST SCENIC ROUTE TO LES BAUX & ARLES

BUS STOP   ⟶   ❻   ■❶

AVE DE LA LIBERATION

AVE MAILLANE

■   ⟵   ❶

PASTEUR

❹

CHEMIN GAULOIS   BARONCELLI

❷

VAN GOGH

❸ ■

ST. PAUL ■ MONASTERY

"LES ANTIQUES" ROMAN ⟶ TOWER ARCH & ■   ■ GLANUM SITE

AVE D-5

TRAIL TO LES BAUX

TO LES BAUX & ARLES

NOT TO SCALE: TOURIST INFO TO GLANUM IS A 15 MIN. WALK

BOLD LINE = RING ROAD THAT ENCIRCLES TOWN CENTER

❶ Auberge de la Reine Jeanne
❷ Le Mas de Carassins
❸ Hôtel Villa Glanum
❹ Le Castelet des Alpilles
❺ To Le Mas de Manon
❻ Restaurant la Serre
❼ Restaurant la Gousse d'Ail
❽ Crêperie Lou Planet

setting is stunning, though shadeless, and the small museum at the entry sets the stage well. While the ruins are, well, ruined, they remind us of the range and prosperity of the Roman Empire. Along with other Roman monuments in Provence, they allow us to paint a more complete picture of Roman life (the city is estimated to have been 7 times as large as the ruins you see). The English handout is helpful, but consider buying one of the two English booklets (one has better photos, the other provides much better background). Inside the ruins, signs give basic English explanations at key locations, and the view from the belvedere justifies the effort (€6, daily May–Aug 9:00–19:00, Sept–April 10:30–17:00).

St. Paul Monastery (Le Monastère St. Paul de Mausole)—Just below Glanum is the still-functioning mental hospital (called Valetudo, formerly Clinique St. Paul) that treated Vincent van Gogh from 1889 to 1890. Pay €3.50 and enter Vincent's temporarily peaceful world: a small chapel, intimate cloisters, and a re-creation of his room. You'll find limited information in English about Vincent's life. Amazingly, he painted 150 works in his 53 weeks here—none of which remain anywhere nearby today. The contrast between the utter simplicity of his room (and his life) and the multimillion-dollar value of his paintings today is jarring. The site is managed by Valetudo, a center specializing in art therapy (daily April–Oct 9:30–19:00, Nov–March 10:15–16:45). Outside the complex, dirt trails lead to Vincent's favorite footpaths with (sometimes vandalized) copies of his paintings located where he painted them.

Food Lovers' Guide to St. Rémy—Wednesday is market day in St. Rémy, but you don't have to fast until then. Foodies will appreciate the three shops that gather on the ring road in St. Rémy, near the turn-off to Les Baux.

Start at Olive-Huiles du Monde, where you can saddle up to a wine-bar-like setting and sample the best olive oil this area; also check out the fine display of other products made from olive oil (daily 10:00–13:00 & 15:00–19:00, 16 boulevard Victor Hugo).

Le Petit Duc, across the road, offers a remarkable introduction to antique cookies. Let friendly owner Anne, who speaks English, take you on a tour (daily 10:00–13:00 & 15:00–19:00, 7 boulevard Victor Hugo).

Just one whiff of Joel Durand's chocolate will lure chocoholics inside. Ask for a sample and learn the letter-coded system (daily 10:00–19:00, 3 boulevard Victor Hugo, next door to Le Petit Duc).

Centre d'Art Présence Vincent van Gogh—Here you'll find a permanent tribute to the painter (including some reproductions), as well as rotating exhibits reflecting the enormous influence of his work on contemporary artists (€3.50, Tue–Sun 10:30–12:30 & 14:30–18:30, closed Mon, inside the ring road on rue Estrine, tel. 04 90 92 34 72).

Hike to Les Baux—These directions will help you find your way on the lovely three-hour hike from St. Rémy to Les Baux (for more details, ask at TI). Start from the signposted slope opposite the Glanum entry. Follow the goat path up into the mountain and arrive at the chimney. Go down the iron ladder, and you'll come to a lake. Walk around the lake on the left-hand side, turning left along the *Mas de Gros* cart track. A mile later, turn right on *Sentier des Crêtes*, and follow the yellow markings to Les Baux. You'll end on the paved road in Val d'Enfer.

SLEEPING

(€1 = about $1.20, country code: 33)

$$$ Le Mas de Carassins***, a 15-minute walk from the center, is impeccably run by friendly Paris refugees, Michel and Pierre. Luxury is affordable here. They pay attention to every aspect of the hotel, from the generously sized pool and gardens to the muted room decor to the optional €26 weekday-only dinner (standard Db-€98, bigger Db-€115, deluxe Db-€120, suite-€165, extra bed-€15, air-con, table tennis, look for signs 200 yards toward Les Baux from TI, 1 Chemin Gaulois, tel. 04 90 92 15 48, fax 04 90 92 63 47, www.hoteldescarassins.com, info@hoteldescarassins.com).

$$ Le Castelet des Alpilles*** is a slightly tired and Old World place, but the location is good (a few blocks toward Les Baux from the TI), the price is fair, and the rooms are plenty comfortable. Rooms are generally big and airy, and the balcony rooms have views of the Alpilles (Db-€65, Db with air-con and view balcony-€87, 6 place Mireille, tel. 04 90 92 07 31, fax 04 90 92 52 03, www.castelet -alpilles.com, hotel.castel.alpilles@wanadoo.fr).

$$ Hôtel Villa Glanum**, right across from the Glanum ruins and with some traffic noise, is a 15-minute walk from the town center. Rooms are small and unimaginative, yet adequate. The best rooms, which come with higher rates, are in bungalows around the pretty pool (Db-€62–82, Tb-€85–100, Qb-€105–120, cheaper off-season, 46 avenue van Gogh, tel. 04 90 92 03 59, fax 04 90 92 00 08, www.villaglanum.com, villa.glanum@wanadoo.fr).

$$ Auberge de la Reine Jeanne** is more central, if less personal. The 11 traditionally decorated, spotless, and spacious rooms (with big beds) take a backseat to the popular restaurant. Some rooms overlook a courtyard filled with tables and umbrellas (Db-€59–68, Tb/Qb-€76, €25 *menu* in fine restaurant, on right side of ring road a few blocks after you enter from Les Baux, 12 boulevard Mirabeau, tel. 04 90 92 15 33, fax 04 90 92 49 65, aubergereinejeanne@wanadoo.fr).

$$ Le Mas de Manon *chambre d'hôte* has rooms two miles from St. Rémy, off a bamboo-lined lane in a lush locale. Salty owners Marie-Odile (SE) and Claude (forget it) run this restored farmhouse with modern rooms at fair prices. A stay here includes all the comforts and a pretty little garden (Db-€60, includes breakfast, no

CC, leave St. Rémy toward Maillane on D-5 and look for signs after 2 miles, Chemin des Lones, tel. & fax 04 32 60 09 86, mobile 06 09 44 92 22, masdemanon@libertysurf.fr).

EATING

The town is packed with fine restaurants, each trying to outdo the other. Join the evening strollers and compare. To dine well in an interior courtyard packed with plants, try **La Serre,** where everything from bread to pâté is homemade (€22 *menu,* closed Mon, a block from where the road to Les Baux meets the ring road in the old center, 8 rue de la Commune, tel. 04 90 92 37 21).

La Gousse d'Ail is no secret, but even so it's a reliable and warm place for a mini-splurge (*menus* from €30, on the ring road just after the turnoff to Maillane at 6 boulevard Marceau, closed Thu, tel. 04 90 92 16 87).

Crêperie Lou Planet, on pleasant place Favier, is cheap and peaceful (daily until 20:00, behind Hôtel de Ville).

The Camargue

The Camargue is a vast wetlands delta, created by the two Rhône rivers (big and little) as they break ranks and rush into the Mediterranean. Over the millennia, a steady flow of sediment has been deposited at the mouth of the rivers—thoroughly land-locking villages that once faced the sea.

Since World War II, large northern tracts of the Camargue have been converted to rice production, and today the delta is a major producer of France's rice and salt. Because the salt-marshy land was long considered useless, it has been relatively untouched, leaving a popular nature destination for the French today.

The Camargue is a protected and "wild" natural-park area, where pink flamingos, wild bulls, mean boar, meaner mosquitoes, and its famous white horses wander freely through lagoons and tall grass. The free-to-roam animals and the migrating birds are the biggest attraction. The bulls are raised for bullfights (by local cowboys called "guardians") and eventually end up on plates in Arles' restaurants. The guardians, who have patrolled the Camargue for centuries on horseback, add a cowboy aura to the region's charm. The Camargue's workhorses—born brown, later turning light gray—remain the most practical way for guardians to patrol the marshy land. In this natural preserve, the graceful pink flamingos flourish. Once an endangered species here, several thousand migrate each fall to warmer climates and return in March to pink up the Camargue.

ORIENTATION

The Camargue's subtle wetlands beauty makes it a worthwhile joyride, but not a must-see sight. The wetlands scenery is unique in France, particularly along the Etang de Vaccares (it's a birder's paradise), and the experience is downright fun if you see a clumsy flamingo in flight. The occasional bulls and wild horses add to the interest, but for me, this is basically a big swamp—interesting to drive through with a few roadside walkabouts, and worthwhile only if you're a birder or in Arles for awhile. The Camargue appeals mostly to Europeans, for whom such expansive areas of wilderness are rare.

Getting to the Camargue

There are several ways to experience the Camargue: horseback, mountain bikes, and jeep safaris. All three options are available in Stes-Maries-de-la-Mer (see below) and jeep safaris are also offered from Arles (ask at TI). Hiking is not popular in the Camargue, as there are few good trails. The best biking is across the Digue (dike) to Phare de la Gacholle (see below).

There are two main driving routes from Arles through the Camargue: to Stes-Maries-de-la-Mer (see below), and toward Salin de Giraud (which I prefer). Here's my favorite route: Leave Arles on D-570 toward Stes-Maries-de-la-Mer, passing the Museum of the Camargue (listed below). Then follow D-37 toward Salin de Giraud and Le Sambuc as it skirts the Etang de Vaccarès lagoon. The lagoon itself is off-limits, but this area has some of the finest views. Turn right off D-37 onto the tiny road at Villeneuve, following La Capelière and La Fiélouse.

This stretch is the best I found, with several pull-outs with viewing stands to help you get above the brush. A small exhibit and walking trail are provided at La Capelière (€3), with some English information on the Camargue. Pick up their brochure, *Ballade Naturalistes,* with a good Camargue map showing walking routes. Birders can look at the register and see what birds have been spotted recently (observations in English are in red). The drive past La Capelière is pretty for another few miles. If you're into this, you can continue all the way to the Phare de La Gacholle lighthouse, where a seven-mile biking/hiking trail leads to Stes-Maries-de-la-Mer, crossing a dike located along the Mediterranean, between sand dunes and wetlands.

Buses serve the Camargue (stopping at Museum of the Camargue and Stes-Maries-de-la-Mer, below) from Arles' bus station (6/day Mon–Sat, 4/day Sun, 1 hr, tel. 04 90 96 36 25). In Stes-Maries-de-la-Mer, walk from the stop to the church (10 min) to get oriented. There are several parking lots and lots of on-street parking for drivers.

The Camargue

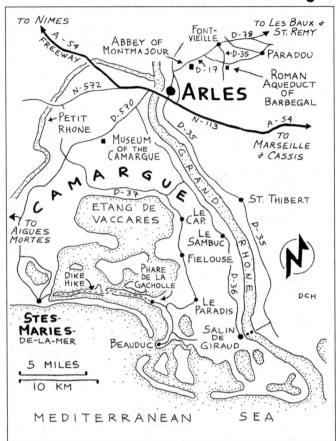

SIGHTS

Museum of the Camargue (Musée Camarguais)—In a traditional Camargue barn on the road to Stes-Maries-de-la-Mer, the folk museum does a good job describing the natural features and traditions of the Camargue. The costumes, tools, and helpful exhibits are all well-described in English. The two-mile nature trail has French-only information (€5, May–Sept daily 9:15–17:45; Oct–April Wed–Mon 10:15–16:45, closed Tue; 8 miles from Arles on D-570 toward Stes-Maries-de-la-Mer at Mas du Pont de Rousty farmhouse, tel. 04 90 97 10 82).

Stes-Maries-de-la-Mer—At the western end of the Camargue lies this whitewashed, Spanish-feeling seafront town with flamingos, bulls, and miles of horses at its doorstep. The place is so popular that it's best avoided on weekends and during holidays. It's a French Coney Island—a trinket-selling, perennially windy place, famous as a mecca for Gypsies. Every May, Gypsies from all over Europe pile in their caravans and migrate to Stes-Maries-de-la-Mer to venerate the statue of St. Sarah (a Gypsy leader who, according to Gypsy tradition, welcomed Mary Magdalene here after Jesus' death). The impressive spectacle is like a sprawling flea market spilling out from the town. Avoid the Gypsy women with flowers, who often cluster near the church—they want your money, not your friendship.

The town of Stes-Maries-de-la-Mer has little to offer except its beachfront promenade, bullring, and towering, five-belled, fortified church. The church interior is worth a look for its unusual decorations and artifacts, including the statue of St. Sarah (church entry free, €2 to climb to church's roof for Camargue and sea views).

Most tourists come to take a horse, jeep, or bike into the Camargue—and there's no lack of outfits ready to take you for a ride. The TI has a long list (daily April–Sept 9:00–19:00, until 20:00 in summer, Oct–March 9:00–17:00, 5 avenue Van Gogh, tel. 04 90 97 82 55, www.saintesmaries.com). For horses, contact the Association Camarguaise de Tourisme Equestre, which represents many places (€13–16/1 hr, €40/half-day, €60–80/day, just outside Stes-Maries-de-la-Mer on the road from Arles, Route d'Arles, tel. 04 90 97 58 45, elevage.parc@wanadoo.fr). You can rent bikes and get advice on the best route at Le Vélo (19 rue de la République in Stes-Maries-de-la-Mer, tel. 04 90 97 74 56). Jeep excursions run €25 for 2.5 hours; Camargue Safaris Gallon has offices in Stes-Maries-de-la-Mer and in Arles, with departures from either office (in Stes-Maries-de-la-Mer at 22 avenue Van Gogh, tel. 04 90 97 86 93; in Arles at 38 avenue Edouard Herriot, tel. 04 90 93 60 31, fax 04 90 96 31 55).

Aigues-Mortes—This strange walled city, on the western edge of the Camargue (20 miles from Nîmes), was built by Louis IX as a jumping-off point for his crusades to the Holy Land. Once a strategically situated port city, today its tall towers and thick fortifications seem oddly out of place, surrounded by nothing but swamps and flamingos. The name "Aigues-Mortes" means "dead waters," which says it all. Skip it unless you need more souvenirs and crowded streets. Drivers can detour to Aigues-Mortes, between Nîmes and Arles, for a quick-and-easy taste of the Camargue. Buses and trains serve Aigues-Mortes from Nîmes (4/day, 50 min).

AVIGNON

Famous for its nursery rhyme, medieval bridge, and brooding Palace of the Popes, contemporary Avignon (ah-veen-yohn) bustles and prospers behind its mighty walls. During the 68 years (1309–1377) that Avignon starred as the *Franco Vaticano*, it grew from a quiet village into the thriving city it remains today. With its large student population and fashionable shops, today's Avignon is an intriguing blend of youthful spirit and urban sophistication. Street performers entertain the international crowds who fill Avignon's ubiquitous cafés and trendy boutiques. If you're here in July, be prepared for the rollicking theater festival (reserve your hotel months in advance). Clean, sharp, and popular with tourists, Avignon is more impressive for its outdoor ambience than for its museums and monuments. See the Palace of the Popes, and then explore the city's thriving streets and beautiful vistas from the parc des Rochers des Doms.

ORIENTATION

The cours Jean Jaurés, which turns into rue de la République, runs straight from the train station to place de l'Horloge and the Palace of the Popes, splitting Avignon in two. The larger eastern half is where the action is. Climb to the parc des Rochers des Doms for a fine view, enjoy the people scene on place de l'Horloge, meander the backstreets (see "Discovering Avignon's Backstreets," below), and lose yourself in a quiet square. Avignon's shopping district fills the traffic-free streets where rue de la République meets place de l'Horloge.

Tourist Information

The main TI is between the train station and the old town, at 41 cours Jean Jaurés (April–Oct Mon–Sat 9:00–18:00, Sun 9:00–17:00;

Nov–March Mon–Fri 9:00–18:00, Sat 9:00–17:00, Sun 10:00–12:00; longer hours during July festival, tel. 04 32 74 32 74, www.avignon-tourisme.com). Other branch offices may be open at either in the Palace of the Popes or at the St. Bénézet Bridge (rue Ferruce, but slow with just one person working).

At any TI, get the good tear-off map and pick up the free and handy *Guide Pratique* (info on car and bike rental, hotels, and museums) as well as their Avignon "passion" map and guide, which includes several good (but tricky-to-follow) walking tours. It comes with the free **Avignon Passion Pass** (valid 15 days). Get the pass stamped when you pay full price at your first sight, and then receive reductions at the others; for example, €2 less at Palace of the Popes and €3 less at Petit Palais.

The TI offers informative English-language **walking tours** of Avignon (€10, €7 with Avignon Passion Pass; April–Oct Tue, Thu, and Sat at 10:00; Nov–March on Sat only, depart from the main TI, 2 hrs). They also have information on bus excursions to popular regional sights, including the wine route, Luberon, and Camargue.

The TI can book **excursions** to many destinations that require a car. See "Tours" in the Provence introduction on page 48.

Arrival in Avignon

By Train: Avignon has two stations, the TGV and Centre-Ville (connected by frequent €1.10 shuttle bus). Avignon's new space-age TGV train station—located away from the center—is big news. While it makes Paris a zippy three-hour ride away, locals say it benefits rich Parisians the most. As Provence is now within easy weekend striking distance of the French capital, rural homes are being gobbled up by urbanites at inflated prices that locals can't afford.

Arrival at TGV Station (Gare TGV): There is no baggage check here, though you can check your bags at the Centre-Ville station (see below). For the shuttle bus *(navette)* to the center of town, go out the north exit *(sortie nord),* down the stairs, and to the left. Look for the shuttle bus or the stop marked *Avignon Centre* (€1.10, 3/hr, buy tickets at info booth or from the driver). It drops you close to the other station (Centre-Ville). To reach the city center from the bus stop, walk down onto cours Jean Jaurés (TI is three blocks down at #41).

A taxi ride between from the station and downtown Avignon costs €12.

If you want to rent a car at the TGV station, take the south exit *(sortie sud)* to find the *location de voitures.*

From downtown Avignon to the TGV Station: The bus stop for the shuttle bus to the station is just in front of the main post office (*poste principal,* across from the main station on cours Président Kennedy). When a market fills that street, the bus waits on the east side of cours Jean Jaurés.

Avignon at a Glance

▲▲**Park, Ramparts, and St. Bénézet Bridge** The park at the hilltop where Avignon was first settled, offering great views of the Rhône River Valley and the famous bridge. **Hours:** Always open.

▲▲**St. Bénézet Bridge** The "pont d'Avignon" of nursery-rhyme fame, once connecting Vatican territory to France. **Hours:** Daily April–Oct 9:00–19:00, July until 21:00, Aug–Sept until 20:00, Nov–March 9:30–17:45.

▲**Palace of the Popes** Fourteenth-century Gothic palace built by the popes that made Avignon their home. **Hours:** Daily April–Oct 9:00–19:00, July until 21:00, Aug–Sept until 20:00, Nov–March 9:30–17:45.

▲**Tower of Philip the Fair** Massive tower across St. Bénézet Bridge, featuring the best view over Avignon and the Rhône basin. **Hours:** Daily April–Sept 10:00–12:30 & 14:00–18:30; Oct–Nov and March Tue–Sun 10:00–12:00 & 14:00–17:00, closed Mon and Dec–Feb.

Place de l'Horloge Avignon's café square with fun ambience; it was once the Roman forum. **Hours:** Always open.

Arrival at Centre-Ville Station (Gare Avignon Centre-Ville): All non-TGV trains serve the central station. You can check bags here (exit the station to the left, look for *consignes* sign, May–Sept 6:00–22:00, Oct–April 7:00–19:00). The bus station *(gare routière)* is 100 yards to the right of the Centre-Ville station as you leave it (beyond and below Ibis Hôtel). From Centre-Ville station, walk through the city walls onto cours Jean Jaurés. The TI is three blocks down at #41.

By Car: Drivers entering Avignon should follow *Centre-Ville* and *Gare SNCF* (train station) signs. Park either near the walls for free (on boulevard Saint-Roch near porte de la République), or more securely in a parking garage or a lot (€4/half-day, €7/day). The Palace of the Popes is just inside the walls, where the "ruined" St. Bénezet Bridge meets the city, and there's a TI in season. Leave nothing in your car. Hotels have advice for smart overnight parking.

Helpful Hints

Book Ahead for July: During the July theater festival, rooms are rare—reserve very early or stay in Arles (page 68) or St. Rémy (page 85).

Palace Square Grand square surrounded by the Palace of the Popes, Petit Palace, and cathedral. **Hours:** Always open.

Petit Palais Museum "Little palace" displaying the Church's collection of medieval Italian painting and sculpture. **Hours:** Oct–May Wed–Mon 9:30–13:00 & 14:00–17:30, June–Sept Wed–Mon 10:00–13:00 & 14:00–18:00, closed Tue.

Fondation Angladon-Dubrujeaud Museum with a small but enjoyable Post-Impressionist collection, including art by Cézanne, van Gogh, Daumier, Degas, and Picasso. **Hours:** Tue–Sun 13:00–18:00, closed Mon year-round and Tue in winter.

Calvet Museum Fine-arts museum with a good collection and no English descriptions. **Hours:** Wed–Mon 10:00–13:00 & 14:00–18:00, closed Tue.

Synagogue Thirteenth-century synagogue rebuilt in a neoclassical Greek-temple style. **Hours:** Mon–Thu 10:00–12:00 & 15:00–17:00, Fri 10:00–12:00, closed Sat–Sun.

Launderette: Handy to most hotels is the launderette at 66 place des Corps-Saints, where rue Agricol Perdiguier ends (daily 7:00–20:00).

Internet Access: Consider Webzone (daily 14:00–24:00, 25 rue Carnot) or ask your hotelier for the nearest Internet café.

English Bookstore: Try Shakespeare Bookshop (Tue–Sat 9:30–12:30 & 14:00–18:30, closed Mon, 155 rue Carreterie, in Avignon's northeast corner, tel. 04 90 27 38 50).

Bike Rental: Consider Provence Bike at the bus station *(gare routière)* for bikes and scooters (52 boulevard St. Roch, tel. 04 90 27 92 61, www.provence-bike.com).

Car Rental: The TGV station has the most car rental agencies (open long hours daily); the Centre-Ville station has fewer companies and shorter hours.

Tourist Trains: Two little trains, designed for tired tourists, leave regularly from the Palace of the Popes (mid-March–mid-Oct daily 10:00–19:00). One does a town tour (€7, 2/hr, 45 min, English commentary) and the other choo-choos you sweat-free to the top of the park, high above the river (€2, schedule depends on demand, no commentary).

Festival d'Avignon

The last thing Avignon needs is an excuse to party. Still, every July since 1947, a theater festival envelops the whole of Avignon, creating a Mardi-Gras-like atmosphere. Contemporary theater groups come from throughout the continent, and each year the festival showcases a different European theater director or artist. Programs come out in May, and most tickets are booked immediately—hotels are 80 percent full by March. The festival is indoors, but venues overflow into the streets. The organizers need 20 different locations for the performances, from actual theater spaces to small chapels to the inner courtyard of the Palace of the Popes, which seats 2,000. There's also a "fringe festival" that adds another 100 venues and countless amateur performances. In July, the entire city is a stage, with mimes, fire breathers, singers, and musicians filling the streets. Most of the performances are in French, some are occasionally in English, and many dance performances don't require language at all (www.festival-avignon.com).

Commanding City Views: Walk or drive across the Daladier Bridge (pont Daladier) for a great view of Avignon and the Rhône River. You can see other great views from the top of park des Rochers des Doms and from the end of the famous broken bridge, St. Bénézet (pont St. Bénézet).

SIGHTS

I've listed sights in the best order to visit, and have added a short walking tour of Avignon's backstreets to get you beyond the surface. Entries are listed at full price and also with the discount card (Avignon Passion Pass). Start your tour where the Romans did, on place de l'Horloge, and find a seat on a stone bench in front of City Hall (Hôtel de Ville).

Place de l'Horloge—The square, which was the town forum during Roman times and the market square through the Middle Ages, is Avignon's café square. (Restaurants here come with a fun ambience, but they also have high prices and low-quality meals.) Named for a medieval clock tower that the City Hall now hides, this square's present popularity arrived with the trains in 1854. Walk a few steps to the center, and look down the main drag, rue de la République. When trains arrived in Avignon, proud city fathers wanted a direct, impressive way to link the new station to the heart of the city (just like in Paris)—so they plowed over homes to create the rue de la République and widened place de l'Horloge.

Walk past the merry-go-round (public WCs behind), veer right and walk into Palace Square, then walk uphill past the Palace of the Popes, and enter...

Avignon

1 Best View of Bridge & Stairs to Ramparts
2 More Views & Orientation Table
3 TGV Shuttle Stop
4 TGV Shuttle Stop on Market Days
5 Launderette
6 To Shakespeare Bookshop

Palace Square (Place du Palais)—This grand square surrounds the forbidding Palace of the Popes, the Petit Palais, and the cathedral.

In the 1300s, the Vatican moved the entire headquarters of the Catholic Church to Avignon. The Church bought Avignon and gave it a complete facelift. Along with clearing out vast spaces like this square and building this three-acre palace, the Church erected more than three miles of protective wall, with 39 towers, "appropriate" housing for cardinals (read: mansions), and residences for the entire Vatican bureaucracy. The city was Europe's largest construction zone. Avignon's population grew from 6,000 to 25,000 in short order. (Today, 13,000 people live within the walls.) The limits of pre-pope Avignon are outlined on the TI map. Rue Joseph Vernet, rue Henri Fabre, rue des Lices, and rue Philonarde all follow the route of the city's earlier defensive wall.

The Petit Palais (Little Palace) seals the uphill end of the square and was built for a cardinal; today, it houses medieval paintings (museum described below). The church to the left of the Palace of the Popes is Avignon's cathedral. It predates the Church's purchase of Avignon by 200 years. Its small size reflects Avignon's modest, pre-pope population. The gilded Mary was added in 1859.

Notice the stumps in front of the Conservatoire National de Musique. Nicknamed *"bites,"* slang for the male anatomy, they effectively keep cars from double-parking in areas designed for people. Many of the metal ones slide up and down by remote control to let privileged cars come and go.

Petit Palace Museum (Musée du Petit Palais)—This palace displays the Church's collection of medieval Italian painting and sculpture. All 350 paintings deal with Christian themes. A visit here before going to the Palace of the Popes helps furnish and people that otherwise barren building (€6, €3 with Avignon Passion Pass, Oct–May Wed–Mon 9:30–13:00 & 14:00–17:30; June–Sept Wed–Mon 10:00–13:00 & 14:00–18:00, closed Tue year-round; at north end of the Palace Square, tel. 04 90 86 44 58).

▲▲Park (Parc des Rochers des Doms), Ramparts, and St. Bénézet Bridge (Pont St. Bénézet)—With a short loop, you can enjoy a park, hike to a commanding river view, walk a bit of the wall, and visit Avignon's beloved broken bridge.

Park: Hike (or catch the tourist train, see "Helpful Hints," above) from the Palace of the Popes to the rocky top where Avignon was first settled. While the park itself is a delight, with many lookout points, don't miss the climax—a grand view of the Rhône River Valley and the broken bridge. On the largest terrace in the north side of the park, an orientation table explains the view; all around the terrace, several tableaus provide a little history in English.

On a clear day, the tallest peak you see is Mont Ventoux ("windy mountain"). St. André Fortress (across the river) was built by the French in 1360, shortly after the Pope moved to Avignon, to counter the papal incursion into this part of Europe. The fortress was in the kingdom of France. Avignon's famous bridge was a key border crossing, with towers on either end—one French and one Vatican.

To find the highest view and where all the teenage lovers hang out, climb the rocky stairs behind the fountain on the north side of the park (watch your step). In the center of the park, you'll also find a small café and public WCs.

Ramparts: From the viewpoint closest to the bridge, find the stairs leading down onto the only bit of the rampart you can walk on. When the pope came in the 1360s, small Avignon had no town wall...so he built one (restored in the 19th century).

St. Bénézet Bridge (Pont St. Bénézet): This bridge, whose construction and location were inspired by a shepherd's religious vision, is the "pont d'Avignon" of nursery-rhyme fame. The ditty (which you've probably been humming all day) dates back to the 15th century: *Sur le pont d'Avignon, on y danse, on y danse, sur le pont d'Avignon, on y danse tout en rond* ("On the bridge of Avignon, we will dance, we will dance, on the bridge of Avignon, we will dance all in a circle").

But the bridge is a big deal even outside of its kiddie-tune fame. This was the only bridge crossing the mighty Rhône in the Middle

Ages, until it was knocked down by a flood. While only four arches survive today, the bridge was huge: Imagine a 22-arch, 3,000-foot-long bridge extending from Vatican territory to the lonely Tower of Philip the Fair, which marked the beginning of France. A Romanesque **chapel** on the bridge is dedicated to St. Bénézet. While there's not much to actually see on the bridge, the audioguide included in the €4 combo-ticket (available with the Palace of the Popes admission) tells a good story. It's also just fun to be in the breezy middle of the river with a fine city view (daily April–Oct 9:00–19:00, July until 21:00, Aug–Sept until 20:00, Nov–March 9:30–17:45, last ticket sold 30 min before closing, tel. 04 90 27 51 16).

As you exit down the stairs, dip into the tiny and free museum, **Musée du Pont,** for some bridge history (daily 9:00–22:00, €0.50 WCs in same courtyard).

To get to the Palace of the Popes from here, exit the courtyard to the right and follow rue Ferruce straight ahead (don't take a right on rue Ferruce towards the river). After a block, look for the brown signs leading you left under the passageway, and up the stairs to the Palace Square.

▲Palace of the Popes (Palais des Papes)—In 1309, a French pope was elected (Pope Clement V). At the urging of the French king, His Holiness decided he'd had enough of unholy Italy. So he loaded up his carts and moved to Avignon for a steady rule under a supportive king. The Catholic Church literally bought Avignon (then a two-bit town), and popes resided here until 1403. From 1378 on, there were twin popes, one in Rome and one in Avignon, causing a schism in the Catholic Church that wasn't fully resolved until 1417.

The papal palace is tourable. The included audioguide leads you through the one-way route and does a decent job of overcoming the lack of furnishings, teaching the basic history while allowing you to tour this largely empty palace at your own pace. As you wander, remember that this palace—the biggest surviving Gothic palace in Europe—was built to accommodate 500 people as the administrative center of the Vatican and home of the pope (you'll walk through his personal  quarters frescoed with happy hunting scenes). In the Napoleonic age, the palace was a barracks, housing 1,800 soldiers. You can see cuts in the wall where high ceilings gave way to floor beams.

The film auditorium shows a continuous 20-minute video in French that features images of the papal court, both in the Vatican and in Avignon. Nearby, a staircase leads to the tower for a view and windswept café.

A room at the end of the tour is dedicated to the region's wines, of which the pope was a fan. Sniff Le Nez du Vin (54 tiny bottles designed to develop your "nose"). Châteauneuf-du-Pape is a nearby village where the pope summered in the 1320s. Its famous wine is a direct descendant of his wine. You're welcome to taste some here (free or split the €6 tasters deal, which comes with a souvenir tasting cup).

You'll exit to the rear of the palace, where my backstreets walking tour begins (below). To return to the Palace Square, make two rights after exiting (€10, €8 with Avignon Passion Pass, combo-ticket available with St. Bénézet Bridge, daily April–Oct 9:00–19:00, July until 21:00, Aug–Sept until 20:00, Nov–March 9:30–17:45, last entry one hour before closing, tel. 04 90 27 50 74, www.palais -des-papes.com).

▲▲Discovering Avignon's Backstreets—Use the map in this book or the TI map to navigate this easy, level, 30-minute walk. This self-guided tour begins in the small square behind the Palace of the Popes, where visitors exit. (If you skipped the interior of the Palace of the Popes, walk down the Palace Square with the palace to your left and take the first left down the narrow, cobbled rue Peyrolerie; notice how it was cut through the rock. You'll pop out into a small square behind the Palace of the Popes. Veer left and you're ready to go.)

Hôtel la Mirande: Located on the square, Avignon's finest hotel welcomes visitors. Find the atrium lounge and consider a coffee break amid the understated luxury (afternoon tea with a pastry, €15, is served 15:00–18:00). Inspect the royal lounge and dining room (recommended on page 106); cooking courses are offered in the basement below. Rooms start at €300.

Turn left out of the hotel and left again on rue Peyrolerie ("street of coppersmiths"), then take your first right on rue des Ciseaux d'Or and on the small square ahead you'll find the...

Church of St. Pierre: The original chestnut doors were carved in 1551, when tales of New World discoveries raced across Europe (notice the Indian headdress). The fine Annunciation (lower left) shows Gabriel giving Mary the exciting news in impressive Renaissance 3-D.

Follow the alley to the left, which turned into a tunnel when it was covered with housing as the town's population grew. It leads into what was the cloister of St. Pierre (place des Châtaignes), named for chestnut trees, but now replaced by plane trees. For recommended restaurants near the Church of St. Pierre, see page 105. Continue around the church.

With the church on your right, cross busy place Carnot to the Banque Chaix. The building opposite, with its beams showing, is a rare vestige from the Middle Ages. Notice how the building widens the higher it gets. A medieval loophole based taxes on ground-floor area—everything above was tax-free. Walking left down the pedestrian street, rue des Fourbisseurs ("street of animal furriers"), notice how the top floors almost meet. Fire was a constant danger in the Middle Ages, as flames leapt easily from one home to the next. In fact, the lookout guard's primary responsibility was watching for fires, not the enemy. Virtually all of Avignon's medieval homes have been replaced by safer structures.

Turn left on the traffic-free rue du Vieux Sextier ("street of the balance," for weighing items); another left under the first arch leads to...

Avignon's Synagogue: Jews first came to Avignon with the Diaspora of the 1st century. Avignon's Jews were nicknamed "the Pope's Jews" because of the protection that the Pope offered to Jews expelled from France. While this synagogue dates from 1220s, in Revolutionary times it was completely rebuilt in a neoclassical Greek-temple style by a non-Jewish architect. This is the only synagogue under a rotunda that you'll see anywhere. The arc holding the Torah is in the east, next to a list of Jews deported from here to

Auschwitz in 1942, after Vichy France was gobbled up by the Nazis. To visit the synagogue, press the buzzer and friendly Rabbi Moshe Aman will be your guide (Mon–Thu 10:00–12:00 & 15:00–17:00, Fri 10:00–12:00, closed Sat–Sun).

From here, retrace your steps to rue du Vieux Sextier. Cross it, then go through the arch and down the yellow alley. Turn left on rue de la Bonneterie ("street of hosiery"), which leads to the big, boxy...

Market (Les Halles): In 1970, the open-air market was replaced by this modern one, which may be ugly, but it provides plenty of parking upstairs. Step inside for a sensual experience of organic breads, olives, and festival-of-mold cheeses. The rue des Temptations cuts down the center. The cafés and cheese shops are on the left—as far as possible from the stinky fish stall on the right (Tue–Sun until 13:00, closed Mon).

Continue on 5 minutes from Les Halles, on rue de la Bonneterie, which eventually becomes...

Rue des Teinturiers: This "street of the dyers" is Avignon's headquarters for all that's hip. You'll pass the Gray Penitents chapel. The facade shows the GPs, who dressed up in robes and pointy hoods to do their anonymous good deeds back in the 13th century (long before the KKK dressed this way).

You'll see the work of amateur sculptors, who have carved whimsical car barriers out of limestone. Earthy cafés, galleries, and a small stream (a branch of the Sorgue River) with waterwheels line this tie-dyed street. This was the cloth industry's dyeing and textile center in the 1800s. Those stylish Provençal fabrics and patterns you see for sale everywhere started here, after a pattern imported from China.

Waterwheel: At the waterwheel, imagine the Sorgue River, which hits the mighty Rhône here in Avignon, being broken into several canals in order to turn 23 such wheels. Around 1800, this powered the town's industries. The little cogwheel above the big one could be shoved into place, kicking another machine into gear behind the wall.

Across from the wheel at #41, **La Cave Breysse** would love to serve you a fragrant glass of regional wine (€2.50 per glass). Choose from the blackboard by the bar that lists all the bottles open today. You're welcome to take it out and sit by the canal (wine with salads and lunch plates, flexible hours, normally Tue–Sat 11:00–15:00, wine only Tue–Sat 18:00–22:30, closed Sun–Mon, Christine Savory and Tim Sweet SE).

To get back to the real world, double-back on rue des Teinturiers, turning left on rue des Lices, which traces the first medieval wall—*lices* is the no-man's-land along a wall. You'll pass a four-story arcaded building that was a home for the poor in the 1600s, an army barracks in the 1800s, a fine arts school in the 1900s, and a deluxe condominium today (much of this neighborhood is going high-class residential). Eventually you'll return to rue de la République, Avignon's main drag.

More Sights

Fondation Angladon-Dubrujeaud—This museum mixes a small but enjoyable collection of art from Post-Impressionists (including Paul Cézanne, Vincent van Gogh, Honoré Daumier, Edgar Degas, and Pablo Picasso) with re-created art studios and furnishings from many periods. It's a quiet place with a few superb paintings (€6, €4 with Avignon Passion Pass, Tue–Sun 13:00–18:00, closed Mon year-round and Tue in winter, 5 rue Laboureur, tel. 04 90 82 29 03, www.angladon.com).

Calvet Museum (Musée Calvet)—This museum impressively displays its wide-ranging collection covering prehistory to 20th-century art with no English information. You'll find everything from neolithic artifacts to medieval tapestries to porcelain plates to Impressionist paintings (€6, €3 with Avignon Passion Pass, Wed–Mon 10:00–13:00 & 14:00–18:00, closed Tue, on quieter west half of town at 65 rue Joseph Vernet; its antiquities collection is a few blocks away at 27 rue de la République—same hours and ticket; tel. 04 90 86 33 84).

Near Avignon, in Villeneuve-lès-Avignon

▲**Tower of Philip the Fair (Tour Philippe-le-Bel)**—Built to protect access to St. Bénézet Bridge in 1307, this massive tower offers the best view over Avignon and the Rhône basin. It's best late in the day (€1.60, €0.90 with Avignon Passion Pass, April–Sept daily 10:00–12:30 & 14:00–18:30; Oct–Nov and March Tue–Sun 10:00–12:00 & 14:00–17:00, closed Mon and Dec–Feb; tel. 04 32 70 08 57). To reach the tower from Avignon, you can drive (5 min, cross Daladier Bridge, follow signs to Villeneuve-lès-Avignon); take a boat (Bateau-Bus departs from Mireio Embarcadère near Daladier Bridge); or take bus #11 (2/hr, catch bus across from Centre-Ville train station, in front of post office, on cours Président Kennedy).

Sleep Code

(€1 = about $1.20, country code: 33)
S = Single, **D** = Double/Twin, **T** = Triple, **Q** = Quad, **b** = bathroom, **s** = shower only, **no CC** = Credit Cards not accepted, **SE** = Speaks English, **NSE** = No English, * = French hotel rating system (0–4 stars). Unless otherwise noted, credit cards are accepted.

To help you easily sort through these listings, I've divided the rooms into three categories, based on the price for a standard double room with bath:

$$$ **Higher Priced**—Most rooms €85 or more.
$$ **Moderately Priced**—Most rooms between €55–85.
$ **Lower Priced**—Most rooms €55 or less.

SLEEPING

Hotel values are distinctly better in Arles, though these are all solid values. Avignon is particularly popular during its July festival when you must book ahead and can expect inflated prices. (Note that only a few hotels have elevators, specifically the first three listed near place de l'Horloge.)

Near Avignon's Centre-Ville Station

The next three listings are a 10-minute walk from the main train station; turn right off cours Jean Jaurès on rue Agricol Perdiguier.

$$ Hôtel Colbert**** is a fine midrange bet. Parisian escapees Patrice and Annie, who both speak English, are your hosts. They care for this restored manor house, and it shows, from the peaceful patio to the warm room decor throughout (Sb-€43–53, Db-€60–70, Tb-€70–90, air-con, 7 rue Agricol Perdiguier, tel. 04 90 86 20 20, fax 04 90 85 97 00, www.lecolbert-hotel.com, colbert.hotel@wanadoo.fr).

At **$$ Hôtel le Splendid***, ever-smiling Madame Prel-Lemoine rents 17 cheery rooms with good beds, ceiling fans, and small bathrooms (Sb-€42–45, Db-€54–64, 17 rue Agricol Perdiguier, tel. 04 90 86 14 46, fax 04 90 85 38 55, www.avignon-splendid-hotel.com, contact@avignon-splendid-hotel.com).

$ Hôtel du Parc*, across the street at #18, is a little less sharp, but cheaper than Hôtel le Splendid, with entertaining Avignon native Madame Rous thrown in for free. Rooms have pretty stone walls; the best overlook the park. Madame bakes all her own bread and pastry for breakfast (S-€28, Ss-€35, D-€35, Ds-€44, Db-€48, Tb-€65, no TVs or phones, tel. 04 90 82 71 55, fax 04 90 85 64 86, hotel.du.parc.84@wanadoo.fr).

Avignon Hotels and Restaurants

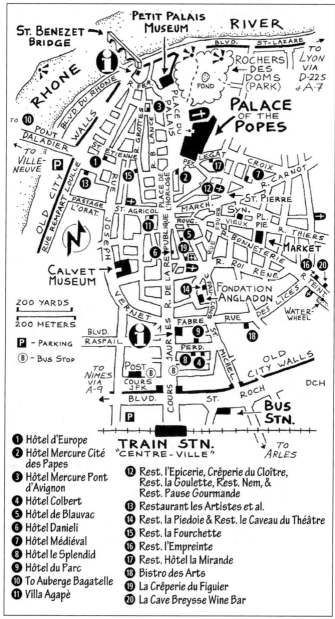

① Hôtel d'Europe
② Hôtel Mercure Cité des Papes
③ Hôtel Mercure Pont d'Avignon
④ Hôtel Colbert
⑤ Hôtel de Blauvac
⑥ Hôtel Danieli
⑦ Hôtel Médiéval
⑧ Hôtel le Splendid
⑨ Hôtel du Parc
⑩ To Auberge Bagatelle
⑪ Villa Agapè

⑫ Rest. l'Epicerie, Crêperie du Cloître, Rest. la Goulette, Rest. Nem, & Rest. Pause Gourmande
⑬ Restaurant les Artistes et al.
⑭ Rest. la Piedoie & Rest. le Caveau du Théâtre
⑮ Rest. la Fourchette
⑯ Rest. l'Empreinte
⑰ Rest. Hôtel la Mirande
⑱ Bistro des Arts
⑲ La Crêperie du Figuier
⑳ La Cave Breysse Wine Bar

In the Center, near Place de l'Horloge

At $$$ **Hôtel d'Europe******, you can be a vagabond in the palace at Avignon's most prestigious address—if you get one of the 15 surprisingly reasonable "standard rooms." Enter into a fountain-filled courtyard, linger in the lounges, and enjoy every comfort. The hotel is located on the handsome place Crillon near the river (standard Db-€134, spacious Db standard-€164, first-class Db-€224, deluxe Db-€312, superior Db-€420, breakfast-€25, elevator, Internet access, garage-€16, 12 place Crillon, near Daladier Bridge, tel. 04 90 14 76 76, fax 04 90 14 76 71, www.heurope.com, reservations@heurope.com, SE).

$$$ **Hôtel Mercure Cité des Papes***** is a modern hotel chain within spitting distance of the Palace of the Popes. It has 73 smartly designed, smallish rooms, musty halls, air-conditioning, elevators, and all the comforts (Db-€113–130, extra bed-€14, many rooms have views over place de l'Horloge, 1 rue Jean Vilar, tel. 04 90 80 93 00, fax 04 90 80 93 01, h1952@accor-hotels.com, SE). **Hôtel Pont d'Avignon***** is nearby, just inside the walls, near St. Bénézet Bridge (87 rooms, same chain, same price, rue Ferruce, tel. 04 90 80 93 93, fax 04 90 80 93 94, h0549@accor-hotels.com, SE).

$$ **Hôtel de Blauvac**** and friendly owner Veronica offer 16 mostly spacious, high-ceilinged rooms (many with an additional upstairs loft) and a sky-high atrium. It's a grand old manor home near the pedestrian zone (Sb-€60–70, Db-€65–75, Tb- €80–90, Qb-€95, €10 less off-season, 11 rue de la Bancasse, 1 block off rue de la République, tel. 04 90 86 34 11, fax 04 90 86 27 41, www .hotel-blauvac.com, blauvac@aol.com).

$$ **Hôtel Danieli**** is a *Hello, Dolly!* fluffball of a place that rents 29 colorful and comfortable rooms on the main drag. It has air-conditioning and lots of tour groups (Sb-€61–73, Db-€72–85, Tb-€83–100, Qb-€100–120, elevator, 17 rue de la République, tel. 04 90 86 46 82, fax 04 90 27 09 24, www.hotel-danieli-avignon .com, contact@hotel-danieli-avignon.com, kind owner Madame Shogol SE).

$$ **Hôtel Médiéval**** is burrowed deep a few blocks from the St. Pierre church in a massive stone mansion with a small flower-filled garden. The 34 unimaginative yet adequate rooms have firm beds (Db-€56–70, Tb-€79, kitchenettes available but require 3-day minimum stay, 15 rue Petite Saunerie, 5 blocks east of place de l'Horloge, behind Church of St. Pierre, tel. 04 90 86 11 06, fax 04 90 82 08 64, hotel.medieval@wanadoo.fr).

Chambre d'Hôte

$$$ **Villa Agapè**, just off busy place de l'Horloge right in the center of town, is an oasis of calm and good taste. Run by helpful Madame de La Pommeraye, the villa has three handsomely decorated rooms, a

peaceful courtyard, and a soaking pool to boot (Db-€100–140, extra person-€30, includes breakfast, 2-night minimum in high season; from place de l'Horloge walk one block toward the TI and train station and turn right on rue St. Agricol, it's on the left above the pharmacy, ring buzzer, 13 rue St. Agricol; tel. 04 90 85 21 22, fax 06 07 98 71 30, www.villa-agape.com, michele@villa-agape.com). For a weeklong stay, ask about renting her entire house, where you get Madame's room, study, kitchen, and everything.

Sleeping Cheaply near Avignon

$ **Auberge Bagatelle's hostel/campground** offers dirt-cheap beds, a lively atmosphere, a busy pool, a café, a grocery store, a launderette, great views of Avignon, and campers for neighbors (D-€25, dorm bed-€12, across Daladier Bridge on the island l'Ile de la Barthelasse, bus #10 from main post office, tel. 04 90 86 30 39, fax 04 90 27 16 23, camping.bagatelle@wanadoo.fr).

EATING

Skip the overpriced places on place de l'Horloge (Les Domaines and La Civette near the carousel are the least of evils here) and find a more intimate location for your dinner. Avignon has many delightful squares filled with tables ready to seat you.

Near the Church of St. Pierre

This church has enclosed squares on both sides, offering outdoor yet intimate ambience.

L'Epicerie is charmingly located and popular, with the highest-quality cuisine around St. Pierre church, including a good selection of à la carte items (€20 main dishes, closed Sun, cozy interior good in bad weather, 10 place St. Pierre, tel. 04 90 82 74 22).

Pass under the arch by L'Epicerie restaurant and enter enchanting place des Châtaignes, filled with the tables of four restaurants: **Crêperie du Cloître** (big salad and main-course crêpe for about €13, closed Sun–Mon); **Restaurant la Goulette** (Tunisian specialties, *tagine* or couscous-€17, closed Mon); **Restaurant Nem** tucked in the corner of the square (Vietnamese, family-run, *menus* from €10, closed Tue–Wed); and **Pause Gourmande** (lunch only, *plats du jour*-€7, always a veggie choice, closed Sun).

Crillon Square (Place Crillon)

This large, open square just off the river provides more atmosphere than quality. Several cafés offer inexpensive bistro fare with *menus* from €14, *plats* from €12, and many tables to choose from. **Restaurant les Artistes** is one of several (daily, 21 place Crillon, tel. 04 90 82 23 54).

Elsewhere in Avignon

Bistro des Arts, with a colorful interior and pleasant service, is a good choice for Provençal dishes (daily, 24 rue des Lices, tel. 04 90 85 67 21).

La Crêperie du Figuier has good crêpes and salads that won't break the bank (dinner crêpe or salad for €11, closed Sun, 3 rue du Figuier, tel. 04 90 82 60 67).

At **La Piedoie,** a few blocks northeast of the TI, eager-to-please owner-chef Thierry Piedoie serves fine traditional and Provençal dishes in an intimate, elegant setting (interior seating only, €36 *menu,* closed Wed, 26 rue des Trois Faucons, tel. 04 90 86 51 53).

Le Caveau du Théâtre is the antithesis of its neighbor, La Piedoie, with wild posters decorating a carefree interior. Wine and good-value dishes are the specialties (€13 *plats,* €18 *menus,* fun ambience for free, closed Sun, 16 rue des Trois Faucons, tel. 04 90 82 60 91).

La Fourchette is cozy, indoor-only, traditional, and well-respected. It's a block from place de l'Horloge toward the river (*menus* from €29, closed Sat–Sun, 17 rue Racine, tel. 04 90 85 20 93).

L'Empreinte is good for North African cuisine in a trendy location (copious couscous for €11–16, take-out and veggie options available, daily, 33 rue des Teinturiers, tel. 04 32 76 31 84).

Hôtel la Mirande is the ultimate Avignon splurge. Reserve ahead here for understated elegance and Avignon's top cuisine (€28 lunch *menu,* €50 dinner *menu,* €85 tasting *menu,* closed Tue–Wed, behind Palace of the Popes, 4 place de la Mirande, tel. 04 90 86 93 93, fax 04 90 86 26 85, www.la-mirande.fr).

TRANSPORTATION CONNECTIONS

Trains

Remember, there are two train stations in Avignon: the new suburban TGV station and the Centre-Ville station in the city center (€1.10 shuttle buses connect to both stations, 3/hr, 10 min). Only the Centre-Ville station has baggage check (see "Arrival in Avignon," above). Car rental is available at both stations (better at TGV). Some cities are served both by slower local trains from the Centre-Ville station and by faster TGV trains from the TGV station; I've listed the most convenient stations for each trip.

From Avignon's Centre-Ville station to: Arles (12/day, 20 min), **Orange** (10/day, 15 min), **Nîmes** (14/day, 30 min), **Isle-sur-la-Sorgue** (6/day, 30 min), **Lyon** (10/day, 2 hrs, also from TGV station—see below), **Carcassonne** (8/day, 7 with transfer in Narbonne, 3 hrs), **Barcelona** (2/day, 6 hrs, transfer in Montpellier).

From Avignon's TGV station to: Arles (2/hr, by SNCF bus, 30 min), **Nice** (10/day, 4 hrs, a few direct, most require transfer in

Marseille), **Marseille** (10/day, 70 min), **Aix-en-Provence TGV** (10/day, 75 min), **Lyon** (12/day, 1.5 hrs, also from Centre-Ville station—see above), **Paris'** Gare de Lyon (14/day, 3 with transfer in Lyon, 2.5 hrs), **Paris'** Charles de Gaulle airport (7/day, 3 hrs).

Buses

The bus station (*gare routière,* tel. 04 90 82 07 35) is just past and below the Ibis Hôtel to the right as you exit the train station (information desk open Mon–Fri 10:15–13:00 & 14:00–18:00, Sat 8:00–12:00, closed Sun). Nearly all buses leave from this station. The biggest exception is the SNCF bus service that runs from the Avignon TGV station to Arles (10/day, 30 min). The Avignon TI has schedules. Service is reduced or nonexistent on Sunday and holidays.

From Avignon by bus to: Pont du Gard (5/day in summer, 3/day off-season, 40 min, see details under "Pont du Gard," page 117). Consider visiting Pont du Gard, continuing on to Nîmes or Uzès (see next chapter), and returning to Avignon from there. (To catch the bus from Pont du Gard to Nîmes and Uzès, stand at the same Pont du Gard bus stop you arrived at.) Try these plans: Take the 12:05 bus from Avignon, arriving at Pont du Gard at 12:50. Then take either the 14:45 bus from there to Nîmes (trains run hrly back to Avignon), or a 16:00 bus (Mon–Fri only) on to Uzès, arriving at 16:30, with a return bus to Avignon at 18:30.

By bus to other regional destinations: St. Rémy (6/day, 45 min, handy way to visit its Wed market); **Isle-sur-la-Sorgue** (5/day, 45 min); **Vaison la Romaine, Sablet,** and **Séguret** (2–3/day during school year, called *période scolaire,* 1/day otherwise and 1/day from TGV station, 90 min); **Gordes** (via Cavaillon, 1/day, not on Wed or Sun, 2 hrs, spend the night or taxi back to Cavaillon); **Nyons** (1/day, 2 hrs).

NEAR AVIGNON

Nîmes, Pont du Gard, Uzès, and Orange

While Avignon lacks Roman monuments of its own, some of Europe's most impressive Roman sights are an easy, breezy day trip away. The Pont du Gard aqueduct is a magnificent structure to experience, as is the city it served 2,000 years ago, Nîmes, which wraps a variety of intriguing Roman monuments together in a bustling bigger-city package. The pedestrian-friendly town of Uzès, which lies between Nîmes and the Pont du Gard, offers a refreshing break from power monuments and busy cities. Twenty minutes north of Avignon, the ancient town of Orange may have vineyards at its doorstep, but it's the best-preserved Roman theater in existence that gets (and deserves) all the attention. Train travelers should see "Tours" (page 48) in the Provence chapter for organized tour options.

Nîmes

Nîmes joins Arles and Avignon on the list of Provence's "big three." While Arles and Avignon have more touristic appeal, Nîmes—which feels richer and more sure of itself—is completely lacking in overnight tourists. This thriving town of classy shops and serious businesses is studded with world-class Roman monuments. (And if you've visited the magnificent Pont du Gard, you must be curious where all that water went.) Nîmes' streets are far cleaner than Arles', yet it's a long way from the polished sophistication you find in Aix-en-Provence or Avignon. It's just a nice town—even the train station area is pleasant.

Since the Middle Ages, Nîmes has exported a famous fabric—the word *denim* actually comes from here (*denim* from *de Nîmes,* meaning "from Nîmes"). Denim caught on in the United States in the 1800s, when a Bavarian immigrant, Levi Strauss, exploited its use in the American West.

Near Avignon

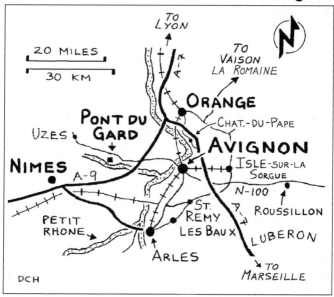

Today Nîmes is officially considered part of the Languedoc region (for administrative purposes only), yet historically the town has been a key player in the evolution of Provence. Only 30 minutes by train from Arles or Avignon (€7 one-way to either), and three hours from Paris on the TGV, Nîmes is worth a visit if you want a taste of today's urban Provence. The city keeps its peaceful, pedestrian-friendly old center a secret for its well-heeled residents. While most understandably prefer sleeping in Arles or Avignon, a night here provides a good escape from tourist crowds and a truer taste of a Provençal city.

ORIENTATION

Nîmes has no river or natural landmark to navigate by, so it's easy to become disoriented. For a quick visit, limit yourself to the manageable triangle formed by the ring of roads formed by boulevard Victor Hugo, boulevard Amiral Courbet, and boulevard Gambetta.

The town's landmarks can be connected by 10-minute walks: It's 10 minutes from the train station to the Arena, 10 minutes from the Arena to Maison Carrée, and 10 minutes from Maison Carrée to either the Castellum or the Fountain Garden.

Tourist Information: The TI is across the street and a few steps out the front door of Maison Carrée (Mon–Fri 8:00–19:00, Sat 9:00–19:00, Sun 10:00–18:00, 6 rue Auguste, tel. 04 66 67 29 11, www.ot-nimes.fr). Pick up the excellent "Travel Guide" map that describes the city's museums and a worthwhile old-town walk.

Arrival in Nîmes

By Car: Follow signs for *Centre-Ville,* then *Arènes,* and pay to park underneath the Arena. (There's a good lot under *Gare SNCF,* the SNCF train station, as well.)

By Train and Bus: Trains and buses use the same station, which is handy for travelers who want to combine the Pont du Gard with Nîmes. (The bus information office is in the rear of the train station.) There is no baggage check at either station.

The Arena is a 10-minute walk straight out of the station. Head up the left side of avenue Feuchères, veer left at the end of the street, then curve right and you'll see the Arena. The Maison Carrée and TI are a pleasant 10-minute stroll from the Arena through Nîmes' traffic-free old town. Check return schedules before leaving the station, as service can be sparse.

Helpful Hints

Internet Access: An Internet café is behind la Maison Carrée on 25 place du Maison Carrée (daily 10:00–24:00).

Local Guide: Sylvie Pagnard does fine walks (3 hrs-€130, 8 hrs-€350, tel. 04 66 20 33 14, mobile 06 03 21 37 33, sylviepagnard @aol.com).

SNCF Boutique: This small office, centrally located in the old city, gives you an easy place to buy train tickets without having to go to the station (Tue–Sat 8:30–18:30, closed Sun–Mon, 11 rue de l'Aspic).

Taxi and Tours: Call 04 66 29 40 11 for a cab or for an English-language tour of Nîmes by taxi (figure €30 per hour for up to 6 persons). It's a €35 taxi ride to Pont du Gard.

Car Rental: Avis is at the train station.

View and WCs: For a great view over the ancient monument and a quiet break above the world, ride the elevator to the top-floor café of the glass building (Museum of Contemporary Art) that faces Maison Carrée (lunch available, Tue–Sun 10:00–18:00, closed Mon). The basement has the best public WCs in Nîmes (same hours as café).

SIGHTS

Except for the Arena, all sights I recommend in Nîmes are free. I've described my favorite sights below in a logical order for a good day-long visit, starting from the Arena (near the train station, which offers the best parking in town).

▲▲**Arena (Amphithéâtre)**—Nîmes' Arena (dating from about A.D. 100, more than 425 feet in diameter and 65 feet tall) is considered

Nîmes

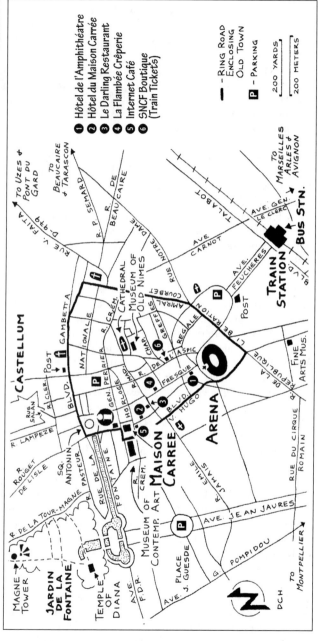

1 Hôtel de l'Amphithéâtre
2 Hôtel du Maison Carrée
3 Le Darling Restaurant
4 La Flambée Crêperie
5 Internet Café
6 SNCF Boutique (Train Tickets)

— = Ring Road Enclosing Old Town

P = Parking

200 YARDS
200 METERS

the best-preserved of the Roman world. It's a fine example of Roman engineering...and propaganda. In the spirit of "give them bread and circuses," it was free. No gates, just 60 welcoming arches, numbered to allow entertainment-seekers to come and go freely. The agenda was to create a populace that was thoroughly Roman—enjoying the same activities and entertainment, all thinking as one (not unlike Americans' nationwide obsession with the same reality-TV shows). The

24,000 seats could be filled and emptied in minutes (through passageways called *vomitoires*).

Climb to the very top—it's a rare opportunity to enjoy the view from the nosebleed seats of a Roman arena. An amphitheater is literally a double theater—two theaters facing each other, designed so that double the people could view a *Dirty Harry*–type spectacle (without the fine acoustics provided by the back wall of a theater stage). You may think of this as a "colosseum," but that's not a generic term. Rome's Colosseum was a one-of-a-kind arena—named for a colossal statue of Nero that stood nearby.

The floor where the action took place was the *arena* (literally "sand"—which absorbed the blood, as in bullfights today). The Arena's floor, which covered passages and storage areas underneath, came with the famous elevator for surprise appearances of wild animals. (While Rome could afford exotic beasts from the tropics, places like Nîmes made do with snarling local beasts...bulls, wild boars, lots of bears, and so on.) The standard fight was as real as professional wrestling is today—mostly just crowd-pleasing. Thumbs down and kill the guy? Maybe in Rome, but only rarely (if ever) here.

After Rome fell, and stability was replaced by Dark Age chaos, a huge structure like this was put to good use—bricked up and made a fortress. In the 13th century, after this region was incorporated into France, the Arena became a gated community housing about 700 people—with streets, plumbing, even gardens on the top level. Only in 1809 did Napoleon decide to scrape away the people and make this a historic monument, thus letting the ancient grandeur of Roman France shine.

Since 1850, Nîmes' Arena has been a venue for spectacles, even Spanish-style bullfights. Since 1988, an inflatable dome has provided a roof over the lower seats (from the glass half-walls down), which gives the city a winter venue of 7,000 seats for concerts, ice-skating, opera, and concerts. Elton John played here in July of 2003 (€5, daily mid-March–mid-Oct 9:00–19:00, winter 10:00–17:00).

Roman Nîmes

Born a Celtic city (around 500 B.C.), Nîmes joined the Roman Empire in the first century B.C. Because it had a privileged status within the Roman Empire, Nîmes was never really considered part of the conquered barbarian world. It rated highly enough to merit one of the longest protective walls in the Roman world and to have a 30-mile-long aqueduct (Pont du Gard) built to serve its growing population.

Today, the physical remains of Roman Nîmes testify to its former importance. The city's emblem—a crocodile tied to a palm tree—is a reminder that Nîmes was a favorite retirement home for Roman officers who conquered Egypt (the crocodile is Egypt, and the palm tree symbolizes victory). All over town, little bronze croc-palm medallions shine on the sidewalks. In the City Hall, 400-year-old statues of crocodiles actually swing from the top of a monumental staircase.

▲**Old City**—Those coming to Nîmes only for its famous Roman sights are pleasantly surprised by its old center. Connect the Arena and Maison Carrée with a stroll through Nîmes' "conservation zone." As you wander, study how elements in the building from the medieval and Renaissance times artfully survive: Shops' interiors incorporate medieval brick with stone arches, windows expose Gothic finery, and Renaissance staircases grace peaceful courtyards. The TI map outlines a handy old-town walk, but even aimless wandering will reward you with good memories of Nîmes.

From opposite the Arena's ticket office, follow rue des Arènes into place du Marché. Place du Marché has an inviting café ambience, including a wispy palm tree and crocodile fountain. (Le Caladon Café/Pâtisserie is the class act of the square—check out its old-time interior.) Leave the square, heading to the right, then turn left on rue de l'Aspic, the town's primary shopping spine. Rue de l'Aspic leads to place de l'Horloge, the center of the old town. From here, pedestrian-friendly streets take off in all directions.

To get to Nîmes' thriving, colorful, and modern market hall (Centre Commerciale), go straight. Most will take a left on rue de l'Horloge (leading to Maison Carrée), but historians will want to detour a few blocks to the right, towards picturesque place aux Herbes and the **Museum of Old Nîmes.** The museum fills a 17th-century bishop's palace with exhibits on life in the city, starting with the Middle Ages. It offers you the best chance to bring the intriguing architectural remnants of historic Nîmes to life (free, April–Sept 10:00–18:00, Oct–March 11:00–18:00, closed Mon).

▲▲**Maison Carrée**—This temple rivals Rome's Pantheon as the most complete and beautiful building that survives from the Roman

Empire. The temple survived in part because it's been in constant use for the last thousand years—church, city hall, private stable, archives during the Revolution, people's art gallery after the Revolution (like Paris' Louvre), and finally as the monument you visit today. It's a textbook example of a "pseudo-peripteral temple" (surrounded by columns, half of which support the roof over a porch, and half of which merely decorate the rest of the building) and a "six-column temple" (6 columns wide, 11 columns along each side).

The lettering across the front is long gone, but the tiny surviving "nail holes" presented archeologists with a fun challenge: Assuming each letter would leave a particular series of nail holes as evidence, derive the words. Archaeologists agree that this temple was built to honor Caius and Lucius, the grandsons (and adopted sons) of Emperor Augustus. And from this information, they date the temple from the year A.D. 4. With further analysis of the even tinier holes below those, I derive that, even in ancient times, the temple was free and open daily (mid-March–mid-Oct 9:00–19:00, winter 10:00–17:00).

Maison Carrée (literally "square house"—named before they had a word for "rectangle") was the centerpiece of a fancy plaza surrounded by a U-shaped commercial, political, and religious forum. This marked the core of Roman Nîmes. As was the case in all Roman temples, only the priest went inside. Worshippers gathered for religious rituals at the foot of the steps. Climb the steps as a priest would—starting and ending with your right foot...*dexter* (from the Latin for "right") rather than *sinister* ("left"). Put your right foot forward for good karma.

Inside, a drawing shows the temple in action 2,000 years ago. The interior has thoughtful English descriptions, mosaics discovered during 1991 excavations, some statues from pre-Roman Celtic Nîmes, and a chart describing the nail-holes puzzle (if you want to play the game at home).

The modern building that faces the temple is Nîmes' **Museum of Contemporary Art,** designed by Norman Foster (Tue–Sun 10:00–18:00, closed Mon, good view café and WCs, see "Helpful Hints," above).

To reach the Fountain Garden (next sight described), walk down rue Corneille with the Museum of Contemporary Art on your right, merge onto rue Gretry, and take your second right.

▲**Fountain Garden (Jardin de la Fontaine) and the Spring of Nemo**—Centuries before the Romans arrived in Nîmes, Nemo's Spring was here (named, like the town itself, for a Celtic god).

When the Romans built a shrine to Emperor Augustus around the spring, rather than bulldoze the Nemo temple, they built alongside it—welcoming Nemo into their own pantheon (as was their more-gods-the-merrier tradition). Today the spring remains, though the temple is gone.

Walk into the center of the park and look into the canal. In the early 1700s, Nîmes needed a reliable source of water for its textile industry—to power its mills and provide water for the indigo dyes for the fabric *serge de Nîmes* (denim). Around 1735, the city began a project to route a canal through the city, and discovered this Roman temple. The city eventually agreed to fund a grander project that ultimately resulted in what you see today: a lavish Versailles-type park, complete with an ornate system of canals and boulevards. The industrial canals built then still wind throughout the city. This was just 50 years after the construction of Versailles and, to the French, this place has a special significance. These were the first grand public gardens not meant for a king, but for the public.

Hiding behind trees in the left rear corner of Fountain Garden, find the...

Temple of Diana—This 1st-century "temple," which modern archaeologists now believe was more likely a Roman library, has long been considered one of the best examples of ancient stoneworking. Its roof—a round Roman barrel vault laced together with still-visible metal pegs—survived until a blast during the Catholic-Protestant Wars of Religion in the 1500s.

At first glance, all the graffiti is obnoxious. But it's actually part of the temple's story. For centuries, France had a highly esteemed guild of stone, metal, and wood workers called the Compagnon, which began as Gothic-church builders in the Middle Ages. As part of their almost mystic training, these craftsmen would visit many buildings, including the great structures of antiquity, like this, for inspiration. Walk through the side aisle for a close look at the razor-accurate stonework and the 17th-, 18th-, and 19th-century signatures of the Compagnon craftsmen this building inspired. Notice how their signatures match their era—no-nonsense "enlightened" chiseling of the 18th century gives way to ornate script in the Romantic 19th century.

The park and temple are free and open daily (April–Oct 7:30–22:00, Nov–March 7:30–18:30). Consider a well-deserved coffee break at the park's café.

To reach the next sight described (about a 20-min walk), turn left out of the park onto quai de la Fontaine, merge onto busy boulevard Gambetta, and then turn left on rue du Fort.

Castellum—A couple of blocks off boulevard Gambetta to the north, on rue de la Lampèze, is an exposed excavation site showing a modest-looking water distribution tank that was the grand finale of the 30-mile-long Pont du Gard aqueduct. Discovered in the 1850s, this is one of only two known Roman distribution tanks (the other is in Pompeii). The water needs of Roman Nîmes grew beyond the capacity of its local springs. Imagine the jubilation on the day (in A.D. 50) that this system was finally operational. Suddenly the town had an abundance of

water—for basic needs as well as fun extras like public fountains. Notice the big hole marking the end of the aqueduct, a pool, and two layers of water distribution holes. The lower holes were for top-priority needs, by providing water via stone and lead pipes to the public wells that graced neighborhood squares. The higher holes—which got water only when the supply was plentiful—routed water to the homes of the wealthy, to public baths, and to non-essential fountains. The excavation site is free (daily April–Oct 7:30–22:00, Nov–March 7:30–18:00; for more on this impressive example of Roman engineering, see "Pont du Gard" on page 117).

SLEEPING AND EATING

(€1 = about $1.20, country code: 33)
Few tourists sleep here, so hotels are a bargain, yet few have elevators, e-mail addresses, or air-conditioning.

$$ **Hôtel de l'Amphitheatre**** is ideally located a spear's toss from the Arena. It's quiet, with well-kept rooms run by helpful Hervé (Db-€51–57, no elevator, 4 rue des Arènes, tel. 04 66 67 28 51, fax 04 66 67 07 79, http://perso.wanadoo.fr/hotel-amphitheatre).

$ **Hôtel du Maison Carrée**** is a shy little place near Maison Carrée (Sb-€35, Db-€45, 14 rue de la Maison Carrée, tel. 04 66 67 32 89).

Eating: Nîmes' many fine squares host lunch-perfect cafés. Prices are the same at most places; find the square that fits you best (I like place aux Herbes).

For dinner, Nîmes' old town is quiet after hours, cafés close, and the options are fewer. **La Flambée Crêperie** is a safe dinner choice near Maison Carrée (2-course crêpe dinner-€10, 3 courses-€14, closed Sun, 3 rue Fresque). **Le Darling** is darling and traditional, yet reasonable (€18–25 *menus*, closed Sun–Mon, a long block behind Maison Carrée, 40 rue de la Madeleine, tel. 04 66 67 04 99).

Sleep Code

(€1 = about $1.20, country code: 33)
S = Single, **D** = Double/Twin, **T** = Triple, **Q** = Quad,
b = bathroom, **s** = shower only, **no CC** = Credit Cards not
accepted, **SE** = Speaks English, **NSE** = No English, * = French
hotel rating system (0–4 stars). Unless otherwise noted, credit
cards are accepted.

To help you easily sort through these listings, I've divided
the rooms into three categories, based on the price for a standard
double room with bath:

$$$ **Higher Priced**—Most rooms €85 or more.
  $$ **Moderately Priced**—Most rooms between €55–85.
   $ **Lower Priced**—Most rooms €55 or less.

TRANSPORTATION CONNECTIONS

Trains and buses depart from the same station in Nîmes.

From Nîmes by train to: Arles (9/day, 20 min), **Avignon** (14/day, 30 min), **Carcassonne** (8/day, 2.5 hrs, transfer in Narbonne), **Paris** (10/day, 3 hrs).

By bus to: Uzès (8/day, 1 hr), **Pont du Gard** (5/day, 30 min), **Aigues-Mortes** (4/day, 50 min), **Arles** (5/day, 1 hr).

Pont du Gard

Throughout the ancient world, aqueducts were like flags of stone that heralded the greatness of Rome. A visit to this sight still works to proclaim the wonders of that age. This perfectly preserved Roman aqueduct was built as *the* critical link of a 30-mile canal that, by dropping one inch for every 350 feet, supplied nine million gallons of water per day (about 100 gallons per second) to Nîmes—one of ancient Europe's largest cities. Though most of the aqueduct is on or below the ground, at the Pont du Gard it spans a canyon on a massive bridge—one of the most remarkable surviving Roman ruins anywhere.

Getting to the Pont du Gard

By Car: Pont du Gard is an easy 25-minute drive due west of Avignon (follow signs to Nîmes) and 45 minutes northwest of Arles (via Tarascon). The *Rive Gauche* parking is off D-981, which leads from Remoulins to Uzès. (Parking is also available on the *Rive Droite* side, but it's farther away from the museum.)

By Bus: Buses run to Pont du Gard *(Rive Gauche)* from Nîmes, Uzès, and Avignon. Combining Nîmes and Pont du Gard makes a good day-trip excursion from Avignon (5/day summer, 3/day off-season, 40 min; see Avignon's "Transportation Connections" on page 106; from Nîmes: 5/day in summer, 3/day off-season, 30 min).

Bus stops are at the traffic roundabout 300 yards from the Pont du Gard. The stop from Avignon and to Nîmes is on the opposite side of the roundabout from the Pont du Gard; the stop from Nîmes and to Avignon is on the same side as the Pont du Gard, just to the left as you enter the traffic circle. Make sure you're waiting for the bus on the correct side of the traffic circle.

ORIENTATION

There are two riversides to the Pont du Gard: the left and right banks (*rive gauche* and *rive droite*). Park on the *rive gauche*, where you'll find the museums, ticket booth, cafeteria, WC, and shops—all built into a modern plaza. You'll see the aqueduct in two parts: first, a fine new museum complex, then the actual river gorge spanned by the ancient bridge.

Cost: While it's free to see the aqueduct itself, the various optional activities each have a cost: parking (€5), museum (€6), informative 25-minute film (€3, see below), and a kids' space called *Ludo* (€4.50, scratch-and-sniff experience in English of various aspects of Roman life and the importance of water). The new extensive outdoor *garrigue* natural area, featuring historic crops and landscapes of the Mediterranean, is free (though €4 gets you a helpful English booklet). All are designed to give the sight more meaning—and they do—but for most visitors, only the museum is worth paying for. The €10 combo-ticket—which covers all sights and parking—is best for drivers. If you get the combo-ticket, check the movie schedule; the 25-minute film is silly but offers good information in a flirtatious French style...and a cool, entertaining, and cushy break. During summer months, a free nighttime sound-and-light show plays against the Pont du Gard.

Hours: The museum is open daily (Easter–Nov 9:30–19:00, mid-June–Aug until 21:30, Dec–Easter until 18:00, closed most of Jan, tel. 08 20 09 33 30). The aqueduct itself is free and open until 22:00 (same hours as the parking lot).

Canoe Rental: Consider seeing the Pont du Gard by canoe. Collias Canoes will pick you up at the Pont du Gard (or elsewhere, if prearranged) and shuttle you to the town of Collias. You'll float down the river to the nearby town of Remoulins, where they'll pick you up and take you back to the Pont du Gard (two-person canoe-€27, usually 2 hrs, though you can take as long as you like, tel. 04 66 22 85 54, SE).

SIGHTS

▲**Museum**—The state-of-the-art museum's multimedia approach (well-described in English) shows how water was an essential part of the Roman "art of living." You'll see examples of lead pipes, faucets, and siphons; walk through a rock quarry; and learn how they moved those huge rocks into place and how those massive arches were made. While actual artifacts from the aqueduct on display are few, the exhibit shows the immensity of the undertaking as well as the payoff. Imagine the excitement as this extravagant supply of water finally tumbled into Nîmes. A relaxing highlight is the scenic video helicopter ride along the entire 30-mile course of the structure, from its start at Uzès all the way to the Castellum in Nîmes.

▲▲▲**Viewing the Aqueduct**—A park-like path leads to the aqueduct. Until a few years ago, this was an actual road—adjacent to the aqueduct—that has spanned the river since 1743. Before you cross the bridge, pass under it and hike 350 feet along the riverbank for a grand viewpoint from which to study the second-highest standing Roman structure (Rome's Colosseum is 2 yards taller).

This was the biggest bridge in the whole 30-mile-long aqueduct. It seems exceptional because it is: The arches are twice the width of standard aqueducts, and the main arch is the largest the Romans ever

built—80 feet (so it wouldn't get its feet wet). The bridge is about 160 feet high, and was originally about 1,100 feet long. Today, 12 arches are missing, reducing the length to 790 feet.

While the distance from the source (in Uzès) to Nîmes was only 12 miles as the eagle flew, engineers chose the most economical route, winding and zigzagging 30 miles. The water made the trip in 24 hours with a drop of only 40 feet. Ninety percent of the aqueduct is on or under the ground, but a few river canyons like this required bridges. A stone lid hides a four-foot-wide, six-foot-tall chamber lined with waterproof mortar that carried a stream for more than 400 years. For 150 years, this system provided Nîmes with good drinking water. Expert as the Romans were, they miscalculated the backup caused by a downstream corner, and had to add the thin extra layer you can see just under the lid to make the channel deeper.

The bridge and the river below provide great fun for holidaygoers. While parents suntan on inviting rocks, kids splash into the gorge from under the aqueduct. Some daredevils actually jump from the aqueduct itself—not knowing that crazy winds scrambled by the structure cause painful belly flops and sometimes even accidental deaths. For the most refreshing view, float flat on your back under the structure (bring a swimsuit and sandals for the rocks).

The appearance of the entire gorge changed in 2002, when a huge flood flushed lots of greenery downstream. Those floodwaters put Roman provisions to the test. Notice the triangular-shaped buttresses at the lower level—designed to split and divert the force of any flood *around* the feet of the arches rather than *into* them. The 2002 floodwaters reached the top of those buttresses. Anxious park rangers winced at the sounds of trees crashing onto the ancient stones...but the arches stood strong.

The stones that jut out—giving the aqueduct a rough, unfinished appearance—supported the original scaffolding. The protuberances were left, rather than cut off, in anticipation of future repair needs. The lips under the arches supported the wooden templates that allowed the stones of the round arches to rest on something until the all-important keystone was dropped into place. Each stone weighs four to six tons. The structure stands with no mortar—taking full advantage of the innovative Roman arch, made strong by gravity.

Hike over the bridge for a closer look. Across the river, a high trail (marked *Panorama*) leads upstream and offers commanding views. On the exhibit side of the structure, a trail marked *Accès l'Aqueduc* leads up to surviving stretches of the aqueduct. For a peaceful walk alongside the top of the aqueduct (where it's on land and no longer a bridge), follow the red-and-yellow markings. Remains of this part are scant because of medieval cannibalization—frugal builders couldn't resist the pre-cut stones as they constructed local churches. The ancient quarry (about a third of a mile downstream on the exhibit side) may open in 2005.

Uzès

Like Nîmes and the Pont du Gard, this intriguing, less-trampled town is officially in Languedoc, not Provence. Uzès (oo-zehs) feels like it must have been important—and it was, as a bishopric from the 5th century until 1789. It's best seen slowly on foot, with a long coffee break in its arcaded and mellow main square, the place aux Herbes (not so mellow during the colorful Wed morning and even bigger all-day Sat markets).

At the **TI,** pick up the brief English-language self-guided walking-tour brochure (May–Sept Mon–Fri 9:00–18:00, Sat–Sun

10:00–13:00 & 14:00–17:00; Oct–April Mon–Fri 9:00–12:00 & 13:30–18:00, Sat 10:00–13:00, closed Sun; on ring road on place Albert 1er, tel. 04 66 22 68 88).

The city itself—traffic-free and tastefully restored—is the sight. In spite of all those bishops, there are no important museums. Skip the dull, overpriced palace of the Duché de Uzès (€9, French-only tour). The unusual and circular Tour Fenestrelle is all that remains of a 12th-century cathedral. Plant enthusiasts might enjoy the Medieval Garden, a "living herbarium" (€2, daily 14:00–18:00, sometimes open longer hours, includes a little shot of lemongrass tea).

Uzès is a short hop west of Pont du Gard and is well-served by bus from Nîmes (8/day, 60 min) and Avignon (3/day, 60 min).

Orange

Orange is notable for its Roman arch and grand theater. Orange, while otherwise insignificant, has more than its share of Roman monuments, because it was an important city in ancient times— strategically situated on the Via Agrippa connecting Lyon and Arles. It was actually founded as a nice place for Roman army officers to enjoy their retirement. Even in Roman times, career military men retired after only 20 years. Does the emperor want thousands of well-trained, relatively young guys hanging around Rome? No way. What to do? "How about a nice place in the south of France...?"

ORIENTATION

Tourist Information: The TI is opposite the Roman Theater's stage wall (daily 10:00–13:00 & 14:15–18:00, place des Frères Mounet, tel. 04 90 34 70 88).

Arrival in Orange
By Train: Orange's **train station** (no baggage check, though if you ask nicely at *Accueil* they might keep your bags up to 2 hours) is a 15-minute walk from the Roman Theater (or a €7 taxi ride, tel. 06 09 32 57 71): Walk straight out of the station down avenue Frédéric Mistral, merge left onto Orange's main shopping street (rue de la République), turn left on rue Caristie and you'll hit the stage wall.

By Bus: Buses from Avignon, Vaison la Romaine, and other wine villages arrive at the big square, place Pourtoules. To reach the Roman Theater, walk toward the hill and turn right at the end of place Pourtoules.

By Car: Drivers follow signs to *Centre-Ville*, then *Théâtre Antique*. Park as close to the Roman Theater's huge wall as possible. (*Parking Théâtre Antique* is large and close to theater, with another TI nearby).

SIGHTS

▲**Roman "Arc de Triomphe"**—Technically the only real Roman arches of triumph are in Rome's Forum, built to commemorate various emperors' victories. The great Roman arch of Orange is actually a municipal arch erected (about A.D. 19) to commemorate a general, named Germanicus, who protected the town. The 60-foot-tall arch is on a noisy traffic circle (north of city center on avenue Arc de Triomphe).

▲▲**Roman Theater (Théâtre Antique)**—Orange's ancient theater is the best-preserved in existence, and the only one in Europe with its acoustic wall still standing (two others in Asia Minor also survive).

After you enter (to the right of the actual theater), you'll see a huge dig—the site of the Temple to the Cult of the Emperor.

Climb the steep stairs to the top of the theater to appreciate the acoustics (eavesdrop on people by the stage) and contemplate the idea that, 2,000 years ago, Orange residents enjoyed grand spectacles with high-tech sound and lighting effects—such as simulated thunder, lightning, and rain.

This is the standard Roman theater design: a semi-circular orchestra, a half-circle of theater seats, and a small stage with a high back wall—originally covered with a marble veneer and colorfully painted. A huge awning could be unfurled from the 130-foot-tall stage wall to provide shade.

A grandiose Caesar overlooks everything. If it seems like you've seen this statue before, you probably have. Countless sculptures identical to this one were mass-produced in Rome and shipped throughout the empire to grace buildings like this theater for propaganda purposes. To save money on shipping and handling, only the heads of these statues were changed with each new ruler. The permanent body wears a breastplate emblazoned with the imperial griffin (body of a lion, head and wings of an eagle) that only the emperor could wear. When a new emperor came to power, new heads were made in Rome and shipped off throughout the empire to replace the pop-off heads on all these statues. (Imagine John Kerry's head on George W. Bush's body. Now pop off Kerry's head and pop on anybody else's.)

Archaeologists believe that a puny, vanquished Celt was included at the knee of the emperor and touching his ruler's robe respectfully—a show of humble subservience to the emperor. It's interesting to consider how an effective propaganda machine can con the masses into being impressed by their leader.

The horn has blown. It's time to grab your seat: row two, number 30. Sitting down, you're comforted by the "EQ GIII" carved into the seat (Equitas Gradus #3...three rows for the Equestrian order.) You're not comforted by the hard limestone bench (thinking it'll probably last 2,000 years). The theater is filled with 10,000 people. Thankfully, you mix only with your class (the nouveau riche—merchants, tradesmen, and city big shots). The people above you are the working-class, and way up in the "chicken roost" section is the scum of the earth—slaves, beggars, prostitutes, and youth hostelers. Scanning the orchestra section (where the super-rich sit on real chairs), you notice the town dignitaries hosting some visiting VIPs.

Okay, time to worship. They're parading a bust of the emperor from its sacred home in the adjacent temple around the stage. Next is the ritual animal sacrifice called *la pompa* (so fancy that future generations will use that word for anything full of such...pomp). Finally, you settle in for an all-day series of spectacles and dramatic entertainment. All eyes are on the big stage door in the middle—where the Julia Robertses and Jack Nicholsons of the day will appear. (Lesser actors come out of the side doors.)

The play is good, but many come for the half-time shows—jugglers, acrobats, and strip-tease dancers. In Roman times, the theater was a festival of immorality. An ancient writer commented, "The vanquished take their revenge on us by giving us their vices through the theater."

With an audience of 10,000 and no amplification, acoustics were very important. At the top of the side walls, a slanted line of stones marks the position of a long-gone roof—not to protect from the weather, but to project the voices of the actors into the crowd. For further help, actors wore masks with leather caricature mouths that functioned as megaphones.

The Roman Theater was all part of the "give them bread and circuses" approach to winning the support of the masses (not unlike today's philosophy of "give them tax cuts and the Fox News Channel"). The spectacle grew from 65 days of games per year when the theater was first built (and when Rome was at its height) to about 180 days each year by the time Rome finally fell.

Cost and Hours: Your ticket includes a worthwhile audioguide and entrance to the small museum across the street. Pop in to see a few theater details and a rare grid used as the official property-ownership registry; each square represented a 120-acre plot of land (theater entry–€7.50, daily April–Sept 9:00–19:00, until 20:00 in summer, closes at 18:00 or 17:00 off-season, tel. 04 90 51 17 60). Vagabonds wanting to see the theater for free can hike up nearby stairs (*escalier est* off of rue Pourtoules is closest) to view it from the bluff high above.

TRANSPORTATION CONNECTIONS

From Orange by train to: Avignon (10/day, 15 min), **Arles** (4/day direct, 35 min, more with transfer in Avignon), **Lyon** (16/day, 2 hrs).

By bus to: Vaison la Romaine (2–3/day, 45 min), **Avignon** (hrly, 55 min). Buses to Vaison la Romaine and other wine villages depart from the big square, place Pourtoules (turn right out of the Roman Theater and right again on rue Pourtoules).

COTES DU RHONE

The sunny Côtes du Rhône wine road—one of France's best—starts at Avignon's doorstep and winds north through an appealingly rugged, mountainous landscape carpeted with vines, peppered with warm stone villages, and presided over by the Vesuvius-like Mont Ventoux. The wines of the Côtes du Rhône (grown on the *côtes,* or hillsides, of the Rhône Valley) are easy on the palate and on your budget. But this hospitable place offers more than famous wine—its hill-capping villages inspire travel posters, and its vistas are fantastic. Yes, there are good opportunities for enjoyable wine-tasting, but there is also a soul to this area...if you take the time to look.

Planning Your Time

Vaison la Romaine is the small hub of this region, offering limited bus connections with Avignon and Orange, bike rental, and a mini-Pompeii in the town center. Nearby, you can visit the world's best-preserved Roman Theater in Orange (see previous chapter), drive to the top of Mont Ventoux, follow my self-guided driving tour of Côtes du Rhône villages and wineries, and pedal to nearby villages for a breath of fresh air. The Dentelles de Montmirail mountains are laced with a variety of exciting trails, ideal for hikers.

Two nights make a good start for exploring this area. Drivers should head for the hills (read the "Côtes du Rhône Villages: Self-Guided Driving Tour" before deciding where to stay). Those without wheels find that Vaison la Romaine makes an easier home base.

ORIENTATION

Getting Around the Côtes du Rhône

By Bus: Buses run to the Côtes du Rhône from Avignon and Orange (2–3/day, 45 min from Orange, 90 min from Avignon) and connect

The Côtes du Rhône Area

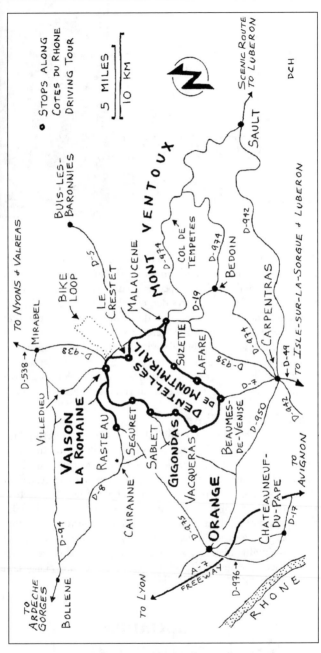

several wine villages (including Gigondas, Sablet, and Beaumes-de-Venise) with Vaison la Romaine and Nyons to the north.

By Train: Trains get you as far as Orange (from Avignon: 10/day, 15 min), where buses make the 45-minute trip to Vaison la Romaine (2–3/day).

By Car: Pick up the Michelin Local map #332 to navigate (landmarks like Dentelles de Montmirail and Mont Ventoux make it easier to get your bearings). If connecting the Côtes du Rhône with the Luberon, consider doing it scenically via Mont Ventoux (follow signs to Malaucène, then to Mont Ventoux, allowing 2 hrs to Roussillon). This route is one of the most spectacular in Provence.

By Tour: Lieutard offers big-bus excursions to Vaison la Romaine and Orange (see page 48).

Côtes du Rhône Market Days

Monday: Bedoin (good market, between Vaison la Romaine and Mont Ventoux)

Tuesday: Vaison la Romaine (great market with produce and antiques/flea market)

Wednesday: Malaucène (good market, near Vaison la Romaine with produce and antiques/flea market)

Thursday: Nyons (great market with produce and antiques/flea market) and Vacqueyras

Friday: Châteauneuf-du-Pape (small market)

Saturday: Valréas (small market north of Vaison la Romaine)

Vaison la Romaine

With quick access to vineyards, villages, and Mont Ventoux, this lively little town of 6,000 makes a great base for exploring the Côtes du Rhône region by car or bike. You get two villages for the price of one: Vaison la Romaine's "modern" lower city is like a mini-Arles, with worthwhile Roman ruins, a lone pedestrian street, and too many cars. The car-free medieval hill town looms above, with meandering cobbled lanes, a dash of art galleries and cafés, and a ruined castle (good view from its base).

ORIENTATION

The city is split in two by the Ouvèze River. The Roman bridge connects the newer city (Ville-Basse) with the hill-capping medieval city (Ville-Haute).

Tourist Information

The superb TI is in the newer city, between the two Roman ruin sites, at place du Chanoine Sautel (May–Sept Mon–Sat 9:00–12:00 & 14:00–18:45, Sun 9:00–12:00; Oct–April Mon–Sat 9:00–12:30 & 14:00–17:45, closed Sun; tel. 04 90 36 02 11, www.vaison-la -romaine.com). Say *bonjour* to *charmante* and ever-so-patient Valerie, ask about festivals and evening programs, get bus schedules, and pick up information on walks and bike rides from Vaison la Romaine. Also ask about *Nocturiales,* nighttime sound-and-light visits of the Roman ruins (summers only).

Arrival in Vaison la Romaine

By Bus: The unmarked bus stop to Orange and Avignon is in front of the Cave la Romaine winery. Buses from Orange or Avignon drop you across the street (2–3/day, 45 min from Orange, 90 min from Avignon). Tell the driver you want the stop for the Office de Tourisme. When you get off the bus, walk 5 minutes down avenue Général de Gaulle to reach the TI and hotels.

By Car: Follow signs to *Centre-Ville,* then *Office de Tourisme;* park free across from the TI.

Helpful Hints

Market Day: Sleep in Vaison la Romaine on Monday night, and you'll wake to an amazing Tuesday market. But be warned: Mondays are quiet, and the town's two best restaurants are closed. If you do spend a Monday night, avoid parking at market sites.

Launderette: The self-service Laverie la Lavandière is on cours Taulignan near avenue Victor Hugo (daily 8:00–20:00). The friendly owners (who work next door at the dry cleaners) will do your laundry while you sightsee—when you pick it up, thank them with a small tip.

Internet Café: Le Cyber Café de Net & Cie is on the outskirts of town (Mon–Fri 9:00–19:00, Sat 9:00–12:00 & 14:00–18:00, closed Sun, 30 ZA de l'Ouvèze, across from cemetery and Renault shop, tel. 04 90 28 97 41).

Bike Rental: Try Mag 2 Roues, near the TI on cours Taulignan (tel. 04 90 28 80 46).

Car Rental: Try Vaison Pneus (avenue Marcel Pagnol, tel. 04 90 28 89 81).

Taxi: To call a taxi, dial 04 90 46 81 36 or 06 82 93 68 42.

Local Guide: Let sincere Anna-Marie Melard bring those Roman ruins to life for you (€35 for a tour of the ruins, tel. 04 90 36 50 48).

SIGHTS AND ACTIVITIES

In Vaison la Romaine

Roman Ruins—Ancient Vaison la Romaine had a treaty that gave it the preferred "federated" relationship with Rome (rather than simply

Vaison la Romaine

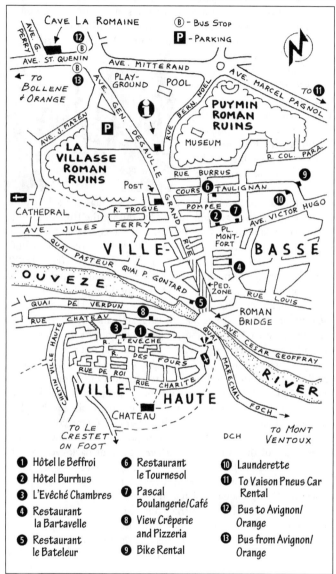

1 Hôtel le Beffroi

2 Hôtel Burrhus

3 L'Evêché Chambres

4 Restaurant la Bartavelle

5 Restaurant le Bateleur

6 Restaurant le Tournesol

7 Pascal Boulangerie/Café

8 View Crêperie and Pizzeria

9 Bike Rental

10 Launderette

11 To Vaison Pneus Car Rental

12 Bus to Avignon/ Orange

13 Bus from Avignon/ Orange

being a colony). This, along with a healthy farm economy (olives and vineyards), made it a most prosperous place—as a close look at its sprawling ruins indicates. Two thousand years ago, about 6,000 people called Vaison la Romaine home. When the barbarians

arrived, the Romans were forced out, and the Vaison townspeople fled into the hills (see sidebar on page 138). The town has only recently reached the same population as during its Roman era— that's mind-boggling.

Vaison la Romaine's Roman ruins are split by a modern road into two sites: Puymin and La Villasse. Each is well-presented, offering a good picture of life during the Roman Empire (€7, price includes both sets of ruins, plus the cloister at the Notre-Dame de Nazareth cathedral; daily June–Sept 9:30–18:00, Oct–March 10:00–12:30 & 14:00–18:00, Nov–Feb 10:00–16:00, English-language tours about once a week in summer, check with TI). Visit **Puymin** first. The brief but helpful English flier explains the site (pick it up when you pay). Inside the site, climb the hill to the museum (exhibits explained in English loaner booklet). Behind the museum is a 6,000-seat theater (just enough seats for the number of residents). Nearest the entry are the scant but impressive remains of a sprawling mansion. Back across the modern road in **La Villasse,** you'll explore a "street of shops" and the foundations of more houses.

Lower Town (Ville-Basse)—Vaison la Romaine's nondescript modern town stretches out from its car-littered main square, place Montfort. The cafés grab the north side of the square, conveniently sheltered from the prevailing *mistral* wind, and they enjoy the generous shade of the ubiquitous *platane* trees (cut back each year to form a leafy canopy). A few blocks away, the stout Notre-Dame de Nazareth cathedral, with an evocative cloister, is a good example of Provençal Romanesque (cloister entry covered by €7 Roman ruins ticket—see above). The pedestrian-only Grand Rue is a lively shopping street leading to the river gorge and the Roman bridge.

Roman Bridge—Two thousand years ago, the Romans cut this sturdy, no-nonsense vault into the canyon rock, and it has survived ever since. Until the 20th century, this was the only way to cross the Ouvèze River. The metal plaque on the wall *(Crue du 22-09-92)* shows the high-water mark of the record flood that killed 30 people and washed away the valley's other bridges. The flood swept away the modern top of this bridge...but couldn't budge the 55-foot Roman arch.

Upper Town (Ville-Haute)—While there's nothing of particular importance to see in the fortified medieval old town atop the hill, the cobbled lanes and charming fountains make you want to break out a sketchpad. Vaison la Romaine had a prince/bishop since the 4th century. He came under attack by the Count of Toulouse in the 12th century. Anticipating a struggle, the bishop abandoned the lower town and built a château on this rocky outcrop (around 1195). Over time, the rest of the townspeople followed, vacating the lower town and building their homes at the base of the château behind the upper town's fortified wall.

To reach the upper town, hike up from the Roman Bridge (passing memorials for both World Wars) through the medieval gate, under the lone tower crowned by an 18th-century wrought-iron bell cage. The château is closed, but a trail to it rewards you with a fine view.

▲**Market Day**—In the 16th century, the pope gave Vaison la Romaine market-town status. Each Tuesday since then, the town has hosted a farmers' market. Today, merchants gather with gusto, turning the entire place into a festival of produce. This amazing Tuesday-morning market is worth noting as you plan your itinerary (see "Helpful Hints," above, and "Market Day" information on page 127).

Hiking—The TI has good information on relatively easy hikes into the hills above Vaison la Romaine. It's about 90 minutes to the tiny hill town of Le Crestet, though great views begin immediately. To find this trail, drive or walk up past the upper town with the castle on your left, find the chemin des Fontaines, and stay the course as far as you like. Cars are not allowed on the road after about a mile.

Biking—This area is not particularly flat, and it's often hot and windy, making bike-riding a dicey option. But if it's calm out and you lack a car, the five-mile ride to cute little Villedieu is doable (small roads, lovely views). With a little more energy, you can pedal beyond Villedieu on the beautiful road to Mirabel (ask in Villedieu for directions). You can also connect the following villages for a good 11-mile loop ride: Vaison la Romaine, St. Romain-en-Viennois, Puyméras, Faucon, and St. Marcellin-lès-Vaison (TI has details).

Wine Tasting—Cave la Romaine, a five-minute walk up avenue Général de Gaulle from the TI, offers a variety of great-value wines from nearby villages in a pleasant, well-organized tasting room (daily 8:30-13:00 & 14:00-19:00, avenue St. Quenin, tel. 04 90 36 55 90).

Near Vaison la Romaine

▲**Mont Ventoux and Lavender**—The drive to Mont Ventoux is worth ▲▲▲ if skies are crystal-clear, or in any weather from late June to early August when the lavender blooms. It also provides a scenic connection between the Côtes du Rhône villages and the Luberon. Allow an hour to drive to the top of this 6,000-foot mountain, where you'll be greeted by cool temperatures, plenty of people, and more white stones than you can imagine.

Lavender

Whether or not you travel to Provence during the late-June and July lavender blossom, you'll see examples of this particularly local product everywhere—in shops, on tables in restaurants, and in your hotel room. And if you do come during lavender season, you'll experience one of Europe's great color events—where brilliant fields of purple lavender meet equally brilliant yellow fields of sunflowers. While lavender season is hot, you'll find the best fields in the cooler hills, since the flowers need an elevation of at least 2,500 feet to grow best. The flowers are harvested in full bloom (beginning in mid-July), then distilled to extract the oils for making soaps and perfume.

While lavender seems like an indigenous part of the Provence scene, it wasn't cultivated here until about 1920, when it was imported by the local perfume makers. Since lavender is not native to Provence, growing it successfully requires great care. Three kinds of lavender are grown in Provence: true lavender (traditionally used by perfume makers), spike lavender, and lavandin (a cloned hybrid of the first two). Today, a majority of Provence lavender fields are lavandin—which is also mass-produced at factories, a trend that is threatening to put the true lavender grower out of business.

Mont Ventoux is Provence's rooftop, with astonishing Pyrénées-to-Alps views—but only if it's clear (which it often isn't). Even under hazy skies, it's an impressive place. The top has a barren, surreal lunar-landscape quality, but it's packed with souvenirs, bikers, and hikers. Miles of poles stuck in the rock identify the route (the top is usually snowbound Dec–April). **Le Vendran** restaurant (near the old observatory and Air Force control tower) offers snacks and meals with commanding views. An orientation board is available on the opposite side of the mountaintop.

Between Mont Ventoux and the Luberon, you'll pass through several climate zones and astonishingly diverse landscapes. The scene alternates between rocky canyons, lush meadows, and wildflowers. Thirty minutes east of Mont Ventoux, lavender fields forever surround the rock-top village of Sault (pronounced soh), which produces 40 percent of France's lavender essence and has good view cafés.

Getting to Mont Ventoux: To reach Mont Ventoux from Vaison la Romaine, go to Malaucène, then wind up D-974 for 40

Sleep Code

(€1 = about $1.20, country code: 33)

S = Single, D = Double/Twin, T = Triple, Q = Quad, b = bathroom, s = shower only, **no CC** = Credit Cards not accepted, **SE** = Speaks English, **NSE** = No English, * = French hotel rating system (0–4 stars). Unless otherwise noted, credit cards are accepted.

To help you sort easily through these listings, I've divided the rooms into three categories based on the price for a standard double room with bath:

$$$ **Higher Priced**—Most rooms €85 or more.
$$ **Moderately Priced**—Most rooms between €55–85.
$ **Lower Priced**—Most rooms €55 or less.

minutes to the top (or take D-19 to pleasant little Bedoin, with a fun Monday market; from there, D-974 offers a longer, prettier route to the top). If continuing to Sault (worthwhile only when the lavender blooms) or the Luberon (worthwhile anytime—see next chapter), follow signs to Sault, then Gordes. The "Les Routes de la Lavande" brochure suggests driving and walking routes in the area (available online at www.routes-lavande.com or at Sault TI, tel. 04 90 64 01 21).

▲**Ardèche Gorges (Gorges de l'Ardèche)**—These gorges, which wow visitors with abrupt chalky-white cliffs, follow the Ardèche River through immense canyons and thick forests. To reach the gorges from Vaison la Romaine, drive west 45 minutes, passing through Bollène and Pont Saint-Esprit to Vallon Pont d'Arc (which offers all-day canoe-kayak floats through the gorges). If continuing north, connect Privas and Aubenas, then head back via the autoroute. Endearing little Balazuc—a village north of the gorges, with narrow lanes, flowers, views, and a smattering of cafés and shops—makes a fine stop.

SLEEPING

Hotels here are a good value. Those in the medieval upper town (Ville-Haute) are quieter, cozier, cooler, and a 15-minute walk uphill from the parking lot next to the TI. If you have a car, consider staying in one of the charming Côtes du Rhône villages near Vaison la Romaine (see page 143).

$$$ **Hôtel Le Beffroi*****, in the upper town, is red-tile-and-wood-beamed classy, with mostly spacious rooms (some with views), a good restaurant, pleasing public spaces, a garden with view tables,

and a small pool with more views. The rooms are split between two buildings a few doors apart; the main building is more characteristic (standard Db-€85–100, superior Db-€125, *menus* from €27, driving here is a challenge—tiny lanes—and parking is tight, rue de l'Evêché, tel. 04 90 36 04 71, fax 04 90 36 24 78, www.le -beffroi.com, lebeffroi@wanadoo.fr, Nathalie SE).

$$ L'Evêché Chambres, almost next door to Le Beffroi in the upper town, is a cozy, five-room, melt-in-your-chair bed and breakfast. The owners (the Verdiers) have an exquisite sense of interior design and are into art—making this place feel like a wood-beamed, leather-couch art gallery (Sb-€65–70, standard Db-€70–80, Db suite-€95–120, the *solanum* suite is worth every euro, Tb-€105–140, rue de l'Evêché, tel. 04 90 36 13 46, fax 04 90 36 32 43, eveche@aol.com).

$ Hôtel Burrhus**—part art gallery, part hotel—is easily the best value in the lower town. It's central and laid back, with a large, shady terrace over the raucous place Montfort and a floorplan that will confound even the ablest navigator. Ask for one of their new rooms, which are bigger, with cool colors and contemporary decor...worth paying extra for (Db-€45–52, new Db-€54–70, extra bed-€15, air-con in most rooms, for maximum quiet request a back room, 1 place Monfort, tel. 04 90 36 00 11, fax 04 90 36 39 05, www.burrhus.com, info@burrhus.com).

EATING

Vaison la Romaine is a small town with a handful of good, popular places—arrive by 19:30 or reserve a day ahead, particularly on weekends. You can eat very well on a moderate budget in the lower town (where you'll find all of my listings), or go for medieval ambience rather than memorable food in the atmospheric upper town (has a view *crêperie* and an air-conditioned pizzeria, open daily and with fair prices). With a car, it's worth venturing to nearby Côtes du Rhône villages to eat (see page 145).

La Bartavelle is *the* place to savor traditional French cuisine in the lower town. Serious yet helpful owner Richard Cayrot has put together a tourist-friendly mix-and-match menu of local options. You get access to the top-end selections even on the €20 bottom-end *menu*—just fewer courses (closed Mon, 12 place Sus-Auze, air-con, reserve ahead, tel. 04 90 36 02 16).

Le Bateleur, almost on the river, is a shy little place with 10 tables and a cuisine that's more Provençal than traditional. It's colorful, formal, and good enough to be popular with the locals—reserve ahead (€25 and €35 *menus,* closed Mon, near Roman bridge at 1 place Théodore Aubanel, air-con, tel. 04 90 36 28 04).

Le Tournesol offers the best €17 dinner value in town—with mostly Provençal dishes and friendly service (June–Oct daily,

Nov–May closed Tue–Wed, 30 cours Taulignan, tel. 04 90 36 09 18, owner Patrick S a little E).

Pascal Boulangerie/Café is the best value among the many cafés on place Montfort (at the far end, breakfast and lunch only, closed Thu).

TRANSPORTATION CONNECTIONS

The most central bus stop is at Cave Vinicole.

From Vaison la Romaine by bus to: Avignon (2–3/day, 90 min), **Orange** (2–3/day, 45 min). Bus info: tel. 04 90 36 09 90.

Châteauneuf-du-Pape

This most famous of the Côtes du Rhône wine villages is inundated with tourists and shops. (I prefer the less-famous wine villages farther north, described in the driving tour below.) Châteauneuf-du-Pape means "new castle of the pope," named for the pope's summer retreat—now a ruin capping the beautiful-to-see, little-to-do hill town (more interesting during the Friday market). Wine-loving popes planted the first vines here in the 1300s.

Approaching from Avignon, signs announce, "Here start the vineyards of Châteauneuf-du-Pape." Pull over and stroll into a vineyard with a view of the hill town. Notice the rocky soil—perfect for making a good wine grape. Those stones retain the sun's heat (plentiful here) and force the vines to struggle, resulting in a lean grape— lousy for eating, but ideal for producing strong wines (see "Côtes du

Rhône Wines," page 54). Eight different grapes are blended to make the local specialty, which has been strictly controlled for 80 years. Grenache is the most prominent grape in the blend. A white wine is also available (blend of 5 grapes), but the reds are best.

The **Wine Museum** (Musée du Vin) is a good way to begin your Côtes du Rhône exploration (free, daily 9:00–12:00 & 14:00–18:00, on route d'Avignon, at start of the village if coming from Avignon, tel. 04 90 83 70 07). After a brief self-guided tour of the wine-making process (English explanations in the notebooks reward good students), enjoy a tasting. You'll need to tell them what you want; see "French Wine Lingo," page 53. For a clear contrast, taste a "ready-to-drink" wine (*prêt à boire;* pret ah bwar), then a wine from "old vines" (*vieille vignes;* vee-yay-ee veen-yuh).

The town **TI** has a long list of wineries that welcome visitors (place du Portail, tel. 04 90 83 71 08).

Côtes du Rhône Villages:
Self-Guided Driving Tour

This driving tour introduces you to the characteristic best of the Côtes du Rhône wine road. While circling the region's rugged Dentelles de Montmirail mountain peaks, you'll experience all that's unique about this region—its natural beauty, glowing limestone villages, inviting wineries, and rolling hills of vineyards. As you drive, notice how some vineyards grow at angles, planted this way to compensate for the strong effect of the mistral wind.

This trip provides a crash course in Rhône Valley wine, an excuse to meet the locals who make the stuff, and breathtaking scenery—especially late in the day, when the famous Provençal sunlight causes colors to absolutely pop.

ORIENTATION

Officially, the Côtes du Rhône vineyards follow the Rhône River from just south of Lyon to Avignon. Our focus is the southern Provençal section of the Côtes du Rhône, centering on the small area between Châteauneuf-du-Pape (see previous page) and Vaison la Romaine. This eight-stop tour starts just outside wine-happy Rasteau, then returns to Vaison la Romaine and winds clockwise around the Dentelles de Montmirail, visiting the mountaintop village of Le Crestet, adorable little Suzette, and the famous wine villages of Beaumes-de-Venise, Gigondas, and Séguret. I've listed several wineries *(domaines)* along the way. Before you go, study up with "Provençal Wine Tasting 101," page 52. But this easy loop is a shame to miss even if wine isn't your thing.

Without a car, it's tougher, but a representative sampling is doable by bike or bus (2–3 buses/day from Avignon and Orange stop at some Côtes du Rhône villages; consider bus one way and taxi back). While it's possible as a day trip by car from Arles or Avignon (allow an entire day for the 80-mile round-trip from Avignon), you'll have a more relaxing and intimate experience if you sleep in one of the villages (see page 143).

The best one-day plan: Try to get the first two stops done before lunch (most wineries are closed 12:00–14:00), then complete the loop in the afternoon. This route is picnic-friendly, but there are few shops along the way—stock up before you leave. In addition to being closed at lunchtime, most wineries are also closed on Sundays, holidays, and during the harvest (mid-Sept).

Côtes du Rhône Driving Tour

5 MILES
10 KM

TO ARDÈCHE GORGES D-94

MIRABEL

VILLEDIEU

BIKE LOOP

VAISON LA ROMAINE

D-938

D-8 RASTEAU

D-5

LE CRESTET

CAIRANNE   SÉGURET ❽

❶

❷

MALAUCÈNE

D-975   SABLET

DENTELLES DE MONTMIRAIL

D-974

TO ORANGE & AVIGNON   GIGONDAS ❼

❸

❹ SUZETTE

VACQUERAS

❺ LAFARE

❻

D-19

BÉDOIN

D-974

D-938

TO ORANGE & A-7

BEAUMES-DE-VENISE

D-950

D-974

TO MONT VENTOUX

CARPENTRAS →

D-942

← D-49

D-942

TO AVIGNON

TO ISLE-SUR-LA-SORGUE & LUBERON

DCH

❶ Domaine des Girasols Winery   ❺ Domaine de Coyeux Winery
❷ Le Crestet   ❻ Domaine de Durban Winery
❸ La Col de la Chaine   ❼ Gigondas
❹ Suzette   ❽ Séguret

THE TOUR BEGINS

Our tour starts just south of Vaison la Romaine, near Rasteau. From Vaison la Romaine, follow signs to Avignon or Orange, then follow signs to Roaix and stay on D-975. A well-marked turnoff between Roaix and Rasteau leads uphill to...

❶ **Domaine des Girasols:** Friendly Françoise, her American husband John (both SE), or mama (Marie-Elizabeth, SE "a leetle") will take your palate on a tour of some of my favorite wines. This is the ideal place to get oriented, because the helpful owners produce a

The Life of a Hill Town in Provence

Heat-seeking northerners have made Provence's hill towns prosperous and worldly. But before the 1960s, no one wanted to live in these sun-drenched, rock-top settings. Like lost ships in search of safe harbor, people took refuge here only out of necessity.

When the Romans settled Provence (125 B.C.), they brought stability to the warring locals, and hill-towners descended en masse to the Roman cities (such as Arles, Orange, Nîmes, and Vaison la Romaine). There they enjoyed theaters, fresh water from aqueducts, and commercial goods brought via the Roman road that stretched from Spain to Italy (passing along the north edge of the Luberon).

When Rome fell (A.D. 476), barbarians swept in to rape and pillage, forcing locals back up into the hills, where they'd remain for almost a thousand years. These Dark Ages were when many of the villages we see today were established. Most grew up around castles, as peasants depended on their lord for security. The hill-towners gathered stones from nearby fields and built their homes side by side to form a defensive wall, terracing the hillsides to maximize the scarce arable land. They would gather inside heavy stone Romanesque churches to pray for salvation. Medieval life was not easy behind those walls—barbarians, plagues, crop failures, droughts, thieves, wars, and the everyday battle with gravity.

Just when they thought the coast was clear to relocate down below, France's religious wars (1500s) chased the hill-towners back up. As Protestants and Catholics duked it out, hilltop villages prospered, welcoming refugees. Little Séguret (pop. 100 today) had almost 1,000 residents; the village of Merindal (near Avignon) sprouted from nowhere; and Fort de Buoux (near Apt, nothing but ruins today) was an impregnable fortress. The turmoil of the Revolution (1789) continued to make peaceful hill towns desirable.

Over the next century, hill towns slept peacefully as the rest of France modernized. Most of the hill towns you'll visit housed between 200 and 600 people and were self-sufficient, producing just what was needed (farmers, lawyers, and telemarketers were at equilibrium).

wide variety of wines and understand Americans. Papa Joyet bought this winery about 10 years ago, trading a vegetable business in the big city of Lyon for vineyards in little Rasteau. The setting is postcard-perfect, their wines are now available in the U.S., and son-in-law John (a big Oakland Raiders fan) studied winemaking in the Napa Valley. Mama made those beautiful quilts you see in the tasting room (Mon–Sat 9:00–12:00 & 14:00–18:00, Sun by appointment only, tel. 04 90 46 11 70).

Next, return to Vaison la Romaine and follow signs towards Carpentras, taking the uphill detour five minutes to the ridge-top village of...

Many town fountains and communal washrooms date from this time. Animals were everywhere, outnumbering humans four to one.

But 20th-century life down below required fewer stairs—and was closer to the convenience of trains, planes, and automobiles. So after World War I, down the hill-towners moved. To build in the flatlands, they pillaged hill towns' stones, roof tiles, and you-name-it, leaving those villages in ruin. By mid-century, most of these lovely villages became virtual ghost towns (in 1965, Le Crestet had but 15 residents—less than a third of its current population).

In recent years, hill towns have bounced back. Lavender production took off, and the government launched irrigation projects. But most of all, real estate boomed as Parisians, northern Europeans, and (to a lesser extent) Americans discovered the rustic charm of hill-town life. They invested huge sums—far more than most locals could afford—to turn ancient stone structures into modern vacation homes (in most cases, buying several houses and combining them into one). Today's hill towns survive in part thanks to these outsiders' deep pockets.

Today most villages have organizations to preserve their traditions and buildings (like *Les Amis du Séguret,* "Friends of Séguret"). Made up of older residents, these groups raise money, sponsor festivals and dances, and even write collective histories of their villages. Many fear that younger folks won't have the motivation to carry on this tradition.

But hope springs eternal, as there appears to be a movement of locals back to these villages. Some northerners are finding hill-town life less romantic as their knee replacements fail. Meanwhile, the popularity of organic produce makes it financially viable for hill-town farmers with smaller plots to pursue their healthy dream of living off the land. Finally, the Internet has allowed some hill-towners to live in remote villages and telecommute, rather than move into bigger cities. Could the cycle be restarting? Armed with their laptops, will hill-towners once again prosper when the next wave of barbarians comes?

❷ **Le Crestet:** This village—founded after the fall of the Roman Empire, when laws were lost and people gathered in high places like this for protection from marauding barbarians—followed the usual hill-town evolution (see above). The outer walls of the village did double duty as ramparts and house walls. The castle above (from about A.D. 850) provided a final safe haven if attacked. The Bishop of Vaison la Romaine was the first occupant, lending little Crestet a certain prestige. With about 500 residents in 1200, Crestet was a very important town in this region. The village reached its zenith in the mid-1500s, when 660 people called Le Crestet home. Le Crestet began its gradual decline when the bishop moved to

Vaison la Romaine in the 1600s, though the population remained fairly stable until World War II. Today, about 35 people live within the walls year-round (about 55 during the summer).

As you drive up to Le Crestet, stop by Charley Schmitt's house to pick up his well-done self-guided tour in English (on the road up to the village, it's the first house on the right after passing the "No Bus Allowed" sign; look for the small solar panel over his door). Charley has spent the last 40 years of his life studying and sketching this village, and he knows every stone. He's 85, speaks no English (his daughter translated the walking tour), and would be honored to sell you his brochure for €3.

Walking-tour brochure in hand, park at the entry of the village and wander the peaceful lanes. Appreciate the amount of work it took to put these locally found stones in place. Notice the elaborate water channels. Le Crestet was served by 18 cisterns in the Middle Ages, and disputes over water were a common problem. Don't miss the peaceful church (€0.50 turns the lights on) and its beautiful stained-glass window behind the altar. Light a candle. The village's only business, café-restaurant **Le Panoramic,** has an upstairs terrace with a view that justifies the name...even if the food is overpriced (see page 145).

Carry on and re-connect with the road below, following signs to Malaucène. As you enter Malaucène, turn right on D-90 (direction: Suzette) just before the Total station. The scenery gets better fast. You'll pass almond and cherry orchards in less than a mile (to the right and left, respectively) as you climb to the mountain pass...

❸ **La Col de la Chaîne (Chain Pass) and the Dentelles de Montmirail:** Get out of your car at the pass (about 1,000 feet) and enjoy the breezy views. Wander around. The peaks in the distance—thrusting up like the back of a stegosaurus—are the Dentelles de Montmirail, a small range running just nine miles basically north to south and reaching 2,400 feet in elevation. Those rocky tops were blown bare by the viscous mistral wind. Below, pine and oak trees mix with scotch broom, which blooms brilliant yellow from April to June. The village below is Suzette (you'll be there soon). The crops growing in front of you contain the classic Mediterranean mix—olives, vines, citrus fruit, and figs. The yellow-signed hiking trail leads to the castle-topped village of Le Barroux (3.5 miles, mostly downhill).

You'll pass countless yellow trail signs along this drive, as the Dentelles provide fertile ground for walking trails. Barely up the road is a small lavender field that is a sight to behold in July (see sidebar on page 132). To sleep nearby, try **La Ferme Dégoutaud,** just ahead (see page 145).

With the medieval castle of Le Barroux topping the horizon in the distance (off to the left), drive on to little...

❹ **Suzette:** Tiny Suzette floats on its hilltop, with a small 12th-century chapel, one café, a handful of residents, and the gaggle of houses where they live. Park in Suzette's lot, below and to the left as you enter. Find the big orientation board above the lot (Rome is to your right, 620 kilometers away, or 385 miles). Look out to the broad shoulders of Mont Ventoux. At 6,000 feet, it always seems to have some clouds hanging around. The top looks like it's snow-covered; if you drive up there, you'll see it's actually white stone (see page 131, above).

Look to the village. Suzette's homes once huddled in the shadow of an imposing castle, destroyed during the religious wars of the mid-1500s. **Les Coquelicots** café makes a perfect lunch or drink stop (light meals and snacks; see page 146); if it's warm, consider returning for dinner. Back across the road from the orientation table is a tasting room for **Château Redortier** wines (English brochure and well-explained list of wines provided; skip their white, but try the good rosé and two reds). **La Treille's** lovely rooms are on the road just behind you (see page 145).

Continuing in the direction of Beaumes-de-Venise (not Le Barroux), you'll drop down into the lush little village of La Fare. Just after La Fare lies a worthwhile detour and great wine-tasting opportunity...

❺ **Domaine de Coyeux:** The private road winds up and up to this impossibly beautiful setting, with the best views of the Dentelles I found. Olive trees line the final approach, and *Le Caveau* signs lead to a polished tasting room. These wines have an excellent reputation in the area, yet are served in a very relaxed manner. Start with the dry Muscat, then try their delectable Côtes du Rhône Villages red, and finish with their trademark sweet Muscat (wines range from €6.50–10/bottle, Mon–Sat 10:00–12:00 & 14:00–18:00, closed Sun, tel. 04 90 12 42 42, some English spoken). After tasting, take time to wander about the vineyards.

Drive on toward Beaumes-de-Venise. On the way, **Restaurant le Redortier** is worth considering for a bite (see page 146). You'll drop out of the hills as you approach Beaumes-de-Venise. To find my next winery, stay straight at the first *Centre-Ville* sign as the road bends left, then carefully track *Domaine de Durban* signs for three incredibly scenic miles to...

❻ **Domaine de Durban:** In this stunning setting, mellow Natasha Leydier will welcome you to her wines. This *domaine* produces appealing whites, reds, and Muscats. Start with the 100 percent Viognier, then try their Viognier-Chardonnay blend. Next, their two reds are very different from each other: one is fruity, and the other—aged in oak—is tannic (both could use another year before drinking, but seemed fine to me). Finish with their well-respected Muscat de Venise (wines cost €4.50–10/bottle, Mon–Sat 9:00–12:00 & 14:00–18:30, closed Sun, tel. 04 90 62 94 26). Picnics are not allowed, though strolling amid the gorgeous vineyards is.

Returning to Beaumes-de-Venise, follow signs for *Centre-Ville*, then Vacqueyras. You'll pass Beaumes-de-Venise's massive cooperative, which represents many growers in this area (big selection, but too slick for my taste; daily 8:30–12:30 & 14:00–19:00). Continue following signs for Vacqueyras (a famous wine village with another cooperative), and then signs for Gigondas and *Vaison par la route Touristique*. Park in the little square of prosperous...

❼ **Gigondas:** This town produces some of the region's best red wines and is ideally situated for hiking, mountain biking, and driving into the mountains. Take a walk above the town—the church is an easy destination with good views over the heart of the Côtes du Rhône vineyards. Several good tasting opportunities await you on the main square. **Le Caveau de Gigondas** is best, with a vast selection of tiny bottles for sampling filled directly from the barrel, and a donation-if-you-don't-buy system (daily 10:00–12:00 & 14:00–18:30, 2 doors down from TI). Here you can compare wines from a variety of private producers in an intimate, low-key surrounding. A good list of wines is provided, and the staff is generally helpful. Because of a self-imposed gag rule (so they don't favor the production of a single winery in this co-op showcase), you need to know what you want (see "French Wine Lingo," page 53). To dine very well or to sleep nearby, consider **Hôtel les Florets,** a half-mile above town (closed Wed, see page 143).

Gigondas' info-packed **TI** has a list of welcoming wineries, *chambres d'hôte,* and good hikes or drives into the mountains (open daily, closed 12:00–14:00, place du Portail, tel. 04 90 65 85 46). The €2.50 *Chemins et Sentiers du Massif des Dentelles* hiking map is helpful, though not critical, since routes are well-signed. Route #1 is an ideal one-hour walk above Gigondas to superb views from the Belvedere du Rocher du Midi (route #2 extends this hike into a 3-hr loop).

From Gigondas, follow signs to the circular wine village of Sablet—with generally inexpensive yet tasty wines (the TI and wine cooperative share a space in the town center). Next is our finale, the white village of...

❽ **Séguret:** Blending into the hillside with a smattering of shops, two cafés, made-to-stroll lanes, and a natural spring, this place is popular. Follow signs and park in the lot. The bulky entry arch just above the lot came with a massive gate, which kept bad guys out for centuries. Walk to its right to appreciate how the homes' outer walls provided security in the Middle Ages.

Enter the village through the first passageway *(poterne)* you pass in the arch and get lost. Find Séguret's open washbasin, a hotbed of social activity and gossip over the ages. Public washbasins like this were used right up until World War II. Find the community bread oven *(four banal),* used for festivals and celebrations. Consider climbing to the unusual 12th-century church for views. A twisting fig tree

---

Cicadas

In the countryside, listen for *les cigales.* They sing in the heat, and are famous for announcing the arrival of summer (locals say their song also marks the coming of the tourists...and more money). Locals love these ugly, long-winged bugs, an integral part of Provençal life. You'll see souvenir cicadas made out of every material possible. If you look closely—they are well-camouflaged—you can find live specimens on tree trunks and branches. Cicadas live for about two years, all but the last two weeks of which are spent quietly underground as larvae. But when they go public, their non-stop chirping begins with each sunrise and doesn't stop until sunset.

---

growing out of a stone arch greets you en route. The church is usually closed, but worth a look from the outside, as it's built into the rocky hill. High above, on the top of the hill, a castle once protected Séguret. All that's left is a tower that you can only make out from a distance. A four-star hotel/restaurant lies behind the church with more views. At Christmas, this entire village transforms itself into one big crèche scene (a Provençal tradition that has long since died out in other villages). To dine, consider **La Bastide Bleue,** just below Séguret (listed in "Eating," below).

From Séguret, Vaison la Romaine is only minutes away, and your driving tour is finished.

SLEEPING

(€1 = about $1.20, country code: 33)
There are great opportunities near Vaison la Romaine for drivers who want to experience rural France and get better values.

Near Vaison la Romaine
These five accommodations are within a 10-minute drive of Vaison la Romaine.

$$$ At **Château de la Baude****,** young Londoner James Ludlam has taken a low-slung Provençal château and transformed it top to bottom. Goldfish greet guests in the courtyard fountain, and six large rooms pamper guests in tastefully decorated and muted tones (unusual in this colorful region). Enjoy the gym, huge pool, and a tennis court that comes with rackets and a ball machine (Db-€150–200, no CC, accepts checks in U.S. dollars, 500 yards from Villedieu, look for signs, tel. 04 90 28 91 53, www.chateaudelabaude .com, reservations@chateaudelabaude.com, SE).

$$$ **Hôtel les Florets**,** a half-mile above Gigondas, is

Sleep Code

(€1 = about $1.20, country code: 33)
S = Single, **D** = Double/Twin, **T** = Triple, **Q** = Quad,
b = bathroom, **s** = shower only, **no CC** = Credit Cards not
accepted, **SE** = Speaks English, **NSE** = No English, * = French
hotel rating system (0–4 stars). Unless otherwise noted, credit
cards are accepted.

To help you sort easily through these listings, I've divided
the rooms into three categories based on the price for a standard
double room with bath:

  $$$ **Higher Priced**—Most rooms €85 or more.
  $$ **Moderately Priced**—Most rooms between €55–85.
  $ **Lower Priced**—Most rooms €55 or less.

surrounded by pine trees at the foothills of the Dentelles de
Montmirail. It comes with a huge terrace van Gogh would have
loved, thoughtfully designed rooms, and an exceptional restaurant
(Db-€90, Tb-€110, annex rooms are best, restaurant closed Wed,
Gigondas, tel. 04 90 65 85 01, fax 04 90 65 83 80). See page 142.

$$$ Château de Taulignan***, on the outskirts of Vaison la
Romaine, is a romantic country château guarded by vineyards and
pine trees, and offering 12 large rooms (with big beds). It's kid-
friendly and comes with a big pool, table tennis, a lush lawn, and
dreamy strolling. Owners Michel and Helen are lovingly restoring
the castle, stone by stone (Db-€85–100, buffet breakfast-€10, can-
cellation fees apply to any room—no matter how far ahead you
cancel, tel. 04 90 28 71 16, fax 04 90 28 75 04, www.taulignan.com,
reservation@taulignan.com). It's five minutes from Vaison la
Romaine's TI; follow signs to Carpentras and look for *Château de
Taulignan* signs to the left just as you leave Vaison la Romaine.

$$ L'Ermitage *chambre d'hôte*—five minutes outside Vaison la
Romaine, under the hill town of Le Crestet—is well-run by British
ex-pat Nick and native Nicole, who were born for this business.
Their rustic farmhouse comes with three big, simple rooms and a
pool with magnificent views. They also rent apartments on a weekly
basis (Db-€70, Tb-€85, includes breakfast, apartment-€650/week,
no CC, turn right off D-938 at Loupiotte restaurant, from Vaison la
Romaine follow signs to Carpentras, tel. 04 90 28 88 29, fax 04 90
28 72 97, www.lermitage.net, nick.jones@wanadoo.fr, SE).

$$ L'Ecole Buissonnière *chambres* are run by another charming
Anglo-French team, Monique and John, who share their peace and
quiet 10 minutes from Vaison la Romaine in a creatively restored
farmhouse with three cozy, half-timbered rooms and convivial public

spaces. John, who was a guardian in the Camargue, is generous with his in-depth knowledge of the area. The outdoor kitchen allows guests to picnic in high fashion in the well-tended garden (Db-€51–59, Tb-€66–74, Qb-€82–88, includes breakfast, no CC, between Villedieu and Buisson on D-75, tel. 04 90 28 95 19, ecole.buissonniere@wanadoo.fr).

In or near Suzette

These two places are both a 20-minute drive from Vaison la Romaine.

$$ **La Treille** *chambre d'hôte* lie on D-90 between Malaucène and Beaumes-de-Venise in the tiny hamlet of Suzette. Welcoming Madame Garrigou runs this flowery stone home with spacious rooms, some with commanding views and small kitchens. Most rooms are cool, with earth tones, private terraces, and big bathrooms. The pool comes with territorial views, and home-cooked meals may be available—ask (Db-€65–85, Tb/Qb-€89–99, includes breakfast, room size determines price, tel. 04 90 65 03 77, mobile 06 71 73 56 23, fax 04 90 62 93 39).

$$ **La Ferme Dégoutaud** is a splendidly situated and utterly isolated *chambre d'hôte* about halfway between Malaucène and Suzette (well-signed, a mile down a dirt road). Friendly Véronique rents three farm-rustic rooms with many thoughtful touches, a view pool, and table tennis. Ask and she'll cook you dinner—€20 for the homemade works, including drinks (Db-€58–64, includes breakfast, tel. & fax 04 90 62 99 29, www.degoutaud.fr.st, le.degoutaud@wanadoo.fr). If you plan to spend a week, inquire about her apartments.

EATING

Near Vaison la Romaine

Drivers enjoy a wealth of country-Provençal dining opportunities in rustic settings, handy to many of the rural accommodations. I've listed these places by distance from Vaison la Romaine (nearest to farthest).

Le Panoramic, in hill-capping Le Crestet, serves average salads, pizzas, and *plats* for more than you should spend at what must be Provence's greatest view tables (open daily for lunch and dinner, tel. 04 90 28 76 42). Come for a drink and view, but if you're really hungry, eat elsewhere. Drivers should pass on the first parking lot and keep climbing to park at place du Château. The restaurant is to your right as you face the view.

Loupiotte is a simple café-restaurant on the road between Vaison la Romaine and Malaucène, below Le Crestet. They offer pizza (try *le vegeterienne*), pasta, salads, *plats* (consider the grilled lamb with vegetables and fries for €11), and *menus* (from €16). It's nothing fancy, but a good value (closed Mon, tel. 04 90 36 29 50).

Les Coquelicots, a small café surrounded by vines and views in miniscule Suzette, is idyllic. The food is simple, but the setting is memorable (pizza, grilled meats, omelets, May–Sept closed Tue–Wed, Oct–April weekends only, tel. 04 90 62 38 99). At least stop for a drink.

Hôtel les Florets, in nearby Gigondas, is a traditional, family-run place that justifies the drive. Dinners are a sumptuous blend of classic French cuisine and Provençal accents, served with class by English-speaking Thierry (*menus* from €23). See page 142.

La Bastide Bleue sits right on the road just below Séguret. It's blue-shutter Provençal, with outdoor tables in an enclosed courtyard and a warm interior (2-course *menu*-€19, 3-course *menu*-€23, open Thu–Tue for dinner only, closed Wed, just below Séguret, route de Sablet, tel. & fax 04 90 46 83 43).

La Maison Bleue on Villedieu's adorable little square is a pizza-and-salad place with great outdoor ambience; skip it if the weather forces you inside (open for lunch and dinner, closed Wed, tel. 04 90 28 97 02).

Auberge d'Anaïs—at the end of a dirt road 10 minutes from Vaison—is where I go for a true Provençal experience. It has outdoor tables with lights strung overheard, grand views, reliable local cuisine, and Madame Anaïs at the helm. Ask for a table *sur la terrasse* (good *menus* from €15, closed Mon, tel. 04 90 36 20 06). From Vaison la Romaine, follow signs to Carpentras, then St. Marcellin; signs will guide you from there.

Restaurant le Redortier, in tiny La Fare between Suzette and Beaumes-de-Venise, offers reasonably-priced lunch and dinner options on an outdoor terrace flanked by interior seating. The cuisine is a blend of traditional and Provençal. Madame will take good care of you. Her specialties are lamb with eggplant and duck with fresh pasta (*menus* from €17, good lunch salads and *plats,* closed Tue–Wed, tel. 04 90 65 07 16).

HILL TOWNS
OF THE
LUBERON

Not Quite a Year in Provence

The Luberon region, stretching 30 miles along a ridge of rugged hills east of Avignon, hides some of France's most appealing hill towns and landscapes. Those intrigued by Peter Mayle's books love joyriding through the region, connecting I-could-live-here villages, crumbled castles, and meditative abbeys. Mayle's best-selling *A Year in Provence* describes the ruddy local culture from an Englishman's perspective, as he buys a stone farmhouse, fixes it up, and adopts the region as his new home. This book is a great read while you're here.

The Luberon terrain in general (much of which is a French regional natural park) is as appealing as its villages. Gnarled vineyards and wind-sculpted trees separate tidy stone structures from abandoned buildings—little more than rock piles—that seem to challenge city slickers to fix them up. White rock slabs bend along high ridges, while colorful hot-air balloons survey the sun-drenched scene from above.

The wind is an integral part of life here. The infamous mistral, finishing its long ride in from Siberia, hits like a hammer (see page 7).

Planning Your Time

There are no obligatory museums, monuments, or vineyards in the Luberon. Treat this area like a vacation from your vacation. Downshift your engine. Follow my self-guided driving tours and brake for the views. Get out of your car and take a walk.

To enjoy the ambience of the Luberon, you'll want at least two nights and a car (only Isle-sur-la-Sorgue is accessible by train and bus). For the ultimate Luberon experience, travelers with cars should base in or near Roussillon or Joucas.

If you lack wheels or prefer streams to hills, stay in Isle-sur-la-Sorgue, located halfway between Avignon and the Luberon.

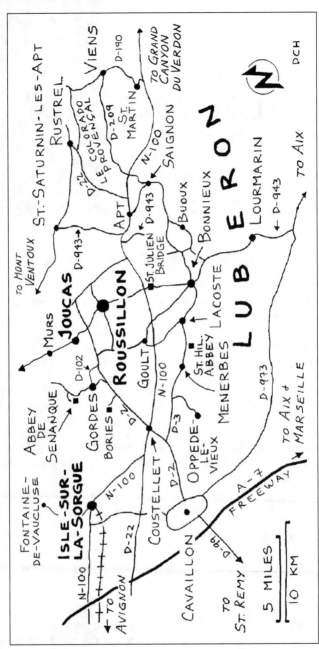

Adequate train service from Avignon and Marseille connects Isle-sur-la-Sorgue with the real world. Flat terrain, tree-lined roads, and nearby villages also make Isle-sur-la-Sorgue good for biking.

Getting Around the Luberon

By Car: Luberon roads are scenic and narrow. With no big landmarks, it's easy to get lost in this area—but getting lost is the point. Pick up the Michelin Local map #332 to navigate. If connecting this region with the Côtes du Rhône, consider doing so via Mont Ventoux—one of Provence's most spectacular routes (see page 127).

By Bus: You have to be determined to reach Luberon hill towns (such as Roussillon) without a car. From Avignon, take a bus to Cavaillon (3/day Mon–Sat, none Sun), where you'll transfer to another bus to Gordes (1–2/day Mon–Sat, none Sun, bus info tel. 04 90 71 03 00). From Gordes, you'll have to taxi to Roussillon (about €15).

By Train: Trains get you as far as Isle-sur-la-Sorgue (station called "L'Isle-Fontaine de Vaucluse") from Avignon (6/day, 30 min) or from Marseille (4/day, 4 hrs). There are no buses from Isle-sur-la-Sorgue to Luberon hill towns; you'll have to rent a bike or take a taxi (tel. 06 08 09 19 49).

Luberon Market Days

Monday: Cavaillon (produce and antiques/flea market).

Tuesday: Gordes and Lacoste (both small).

Thursday: Roussillon (cute) and Isle-sur-la-Sorgue (good, but smaller than its Sun market).

Friday: Lourmarin (very good) and Bonnieux (pretty good).

Saturday: Apt (huge produce and antiques/flea market).

Sunday: Isle-sur-la-Sorgue (granddaddy of them all, produce and antiques/flea market) and Coustellet (very good and less touristy).

Isle-sur-la-Sorgue

This sturdy market town—literally "Island on the Sorgue River"—sits within a split in its crisp, happy little river. (Do not confuse Isle-sur-la-Sorgue with the nearby and plain town of Sorgue.)

Isle-sur-la-Sorgue makes a good base for exploring the Luberon and Avignon (30 min to each by car). After the arid cities and

villages elsewhere in Provence, the presence of water at every turn is a welcome change. Called the "Venice of Provence," the Sorgue's extraordinarily clear and shallow flow divides like cells in Isle-sur-la-Sorgue, producing water, water everywhere. The river is incredibly important to the region's economy. The fresh spring water of the many branches of the Sorgue (that divide in Isle-sur-la-Sorgue) has provided nourishment for crops and power for key industries for centuries.

ORIENTATION

While Isle-sur-la-Sorgue is renowned for its market days, it is otherwise a pleasantly average town with no important sights and a steady trickle of tourism. It's calm at night and downright dead on Mondays.

Tourist Information: The TI has a line on rooms in private homes, all of which are outside the town (Tue–Sat 9:00–12:30 & 14:00–18:00, Sun 9:00–12:30, closed Mon, in town center, next to church, tel. 04 90 38 04 78).

Helpful Hints

Launderette: It's just off the pedestrian street, rue de la République, at 23 impasse de la République (daily 8:00–20:30).

Internet: Try Webanna (daily 9:00–19:00, closed Sun and Mon morning, 10 rue André Autheman, tel. 04 90 38 15 87).

Bike Rental: The TI has addresses for local bike-rental shops. These towns make good biking destinations from Isle-sur-la-Sorgue: Velleron (5 miles north, flat, a tiny version of Isle-sur-la-Sorgue with waterwheels, fountains, and an evening farmer's market Mon–Sat 18:00–20:00); Lagnes (3 miles east, mostly flat, a pretty and well-restored hill town with views from its ruined château); and Fontaine-de-Vaucluse (7 miles northeast, uphill, see "Near Isle-sur-la-Sorgue," below).

Car Rental: Budget France is on rue André Autheman (tel. 04 90 20 64 13).

Taxi: Call tel. 06 09 06 92 06 or 06 08 68 12 33.

Parking: Market days are a challenge. If you don't arrive early, traffic is a mess and parking is a headache. You can circle the ring road and look for parking signs. There's a pay lot behind the post office and several lots just west of the roundabout with roads to Carpentras and Fontaine-de-Vaucluse. There's lots of freestyle parking on roads leaving the city. Don't leave anything visible in your car.

Grocery Store: A big Spar market is on the main ring road, near the Peugeot Car shop and the train station (Mon–Sat 9:00–12:00, Sun 15:00–19:00).

SIGHTS AND ACTIVITIES

In Isle-sur-la-Sorgue

▲**Wander and Explore**—The town has crystal-clear water babbling under pedestrian bridges stuffed with flower boxes, and its old-time carousel is always spinning. Navigate by the town's splintered streams and nine mossy waterwheels, which, while still turning, power only memories of the town's wool and silk industries.

Start your tour at the church next to the TI—where all streets seem to converge—and make forays into the town from there. The 12th-century **church** (Notre-Dame des Anges) has a festive Baroque interior and seems overgrown for today's town. Walk in. The curls and swirls and gilded statues date from an era that was all about Louis XIV, the Sun King. This is propagandist architecture, designed to wow the faithful into compliance. (It was made possible thanks to profits generated from its river-powered industries.) When entering a church like this, the heavens should open up and convince you that whoever built this had unearthly connections.

Wander down rue Danton, in front of the church, to lose the crowds and find three big, forgotten **waterwheels.** These helped put Isle-sur-la-Sorgue on the map in the 1800s. Along with Avignon, this was Provence's cloth-dyeing and textile center. Those stylish Provençal fabrics and patterns you see for sale everywhere were made possible by this river.

Double back to the church, turn left, and find the small stream. Breakaway streams like this run under the town like subways run under Paris. Take a right on the first street after the stream; it leads under a long arch (along rue J. J. Rousseau). Follow this, and keep (mostly) straight all the way to the main river, and then follow it left. You'll come to **Le Bassin** (a pond), where the river enters the town and divides into many branches (across from the recommended Café de Bellevue restaurant). Track as many branches as you can see, then find the round lookout point and take in the pretty scene.

Fishing was Isle-sur-la-Sorgue's first important economic activity—until the waterwheels took over. The sound of the rushing water makes it clear that even small rivers like this are capable of generating power. The river's defensive benefits are also obvious from here. Isle-sur-la-Sorgue was able to prosper in the Middle Ages in spite of its location (situated in a flat valley), thanks to the natural protection this river provided. Walls with big moats ran along the river, but they were destroyed during the French Revolution.

Take a refreshing **riverfront stroll** (or drive) from here. Cross back over the busy roundabout, and head to the left of the orange Delices de Luberon store (or stop to sample its great tapenade selection). You can follow the main river upstream, along the bike lane, as far as you like. The little road meanders about a mile, following the serene course of the clear-as-a-bell river, past waterfront homes, and beneath swaying trees, all the way to Hôtel le Pescador and a riverside café. The wide and shallow Partage des Eaux, where the water divides before entering Isle-sur-la-Sorgue, is perfect for a refreshing swim on a hot day.

▲▲**Market Days**—The town erupts into a market frenzy each Sunday and Thursday, with hardy crafts and local produce. The Sunday market is astounding and famous for its antiques; the Thursday market is more intimate (see market tips on page 149).

Antique Toy and Doll Museum (Musée du Jouet et de la Poupée Ancienne)—The town's lone sight is a fun and funky toy museum (adults-€3.50, kids-€1.50, daily 12:00–17:30, 26 rue Carnot).

Near Isle-sur-la-Sorgue

Fontaine-de-Vaucluse—You'll read and hear a lot about this village, impressively located at the source of the Sorgue River, where the medieval Italian poet Petrarch mourned for his love, Laura. The river seems to magically appear from nowhere (the actual source is a murky, green water hole) and flows through the town past a lineup of cafés, souvenir shops, and enough tourists to make Disney envious. While the setting is beautiful, the trip is worth it only if the spring is flowing—ask your hotelier and arrive by 9:00 or after 19:00 to avoid crowds.

Canoe Trips on the Sorgue—Another reason to travel to Fontaine-de-Vaucluse is to canoe down the river. If  you're really on vacation and committed to going French, consider this five-mile, two-hour trip. A guide escorts small groups in canoes starting in Fontaine-de-Vaucluse and ending in Isle-sur-la-Sorgue; you'll return to Fontaine-de-Vaucluse via shuttle bus (call for departure times: Canoe Evasion, €18, tel. 04 90 38 26 22, and Kayaks Verts, €18, tel. 04 90 20 35 44).

SLEEPING

Pickings are slim for good sleeps in Isle-sur-la-Sorgue, though the few I've listed provide solid values.

$$$ **La Prévoté***** offers the town's most luxurious digs. Its five meticulously decorated rooms—located above their fine restaurant— are each different, but all are done in earth tones. The rooms here

Sleep Code

(€1 = about $1.20, country code: 33)
S = Single, **D** = Double/Twin, **T** = Triple, **Q** = Quad, **b** = bathroom, **s** = shower only, **no CC** = Credit Cards not accepted, **SE** = Speaks English, **NSE** = No English, * = French hotel rating system (0–4 stars). Unless otherwise noted, credit cards are accepted.

To help you sort easily through these listings, I've divided the rooms into three categories based on the price for a standard double room with bath:

$$$ **Higher Priced**—Most rooms €85 or more.
$$ **Moderately Priced**—Most rooms between €55–85.
$ **Lower Priced**—Most rooms €55 or less.

have high ceilings, a few exposed beams, beautiful furnishings, and most overlook a branch of the river (standard Db-€130, larger Db-€150, suite Db-€170, no elevator, one block from the church on 4 bis J. J. Rousseau, tel. & fax 04 90 38 57 29, http://laprevote.site .voila.fr, la.prevote@wanadoo.fr).

$$ Hôtel les Névons**, two blocks from the center (behind the PTT or post office), is concrete motel–modern outside. Inside, however, it does everything right, with comfortable, air-conditioned rooms, a few family suites, puce-colored halls, a small rooftop pool, and eager-to-please owners, Mireille and Jean-Philippe (Db-€55–60, big Db-€69, Tb-€65–70, Qb-€75–85, includes breakfast, has Internet access, easy and secure parking, 205 chemin des Névons, tel. 04 90 20 72 00, fax 04 90 20 56 20, www.hotel-les -nevons.com, info@hotel-les-nevons.com).

$$ Le Pont des Aubes Chambres, run by sweet Martine (SE), has two huggable rooms in an old, green-shuttered farmhouse right on the river. From here you can cross the bridge and walk 15 minutes along the river into Isle-sur-la-Sorgue, or stroll to the recommended Le Mas Blanc restaurant (Db-€65, Tb-€80, no CC, a mile from town at 189 route d'Apt, tel. & fax 04 90 38 13 75, patriceaubert @wanadoo.fr). Martine also rents one-room apartments by the week for €310–350.

$ Hôtel le Cours de l'Eau is a gruff place with bargain beds above a café. It's sufficiently clean and nearly quiet (D-€26, Db-€37, on ring road opposite Café de la Sorgue at place Gambetta, tel. & fax 04 90 38 01 18, NSE).

EATING

Restaurant choices (like hotels) are limited in town. Choose between waterfront ambience and quality cuisine. These places are worthwhile, though having a car opens up a world of opportunity.

Begin your dinner with a glass of wine at the cozy **Le Caveau de la Tour de l'Isle** (part wine bar, part wine shop, open Tue–Sat until about 20:00, closed Sun–Mon, 12 rue de la République).

L'Oustau de l'Isle, which serves the town's most reliable and affordable fine cuisine, is well-suited for special dinners (*menus* from €23, open daily, closed Wed–Thu off-season, has backyard terrace, near post office at 21 avenue des Quatre Otages, tel. 04 90 38 54 83).

La Prévoté is the place to really do it up. Its dining room is covered in wood beams, and the place feels country-classy but not stuffy. It has a branch of the Sorgue running through it, visible through glass windows (*menus* from €42, closed Tue–Wed, 4 rue J. J. Rousseau, on narrow street that runs along left side of church as you face it, tel. 04 90 38 57 29).

Café de Bellevue is my favorite riverfront café, with van Gogh colors, a great setting on Le Bassin (get a waterfront table), and yellow bulbs that create a warm ambience after dark. The owners—friendly American ex-pat Richard from North Carolina and Serge (see if you can find the American)—run this place with panache, celebrating American events like the Fourth of July. Show this book and they'll offer you a free aperitif (€15 *menu*, reasonably-priced *plats* and salads, closed Mon, located at the top of town, tel. 04 90 38 03 63).

The **Fromenterie** bakery next to the PTT (post office) sells really rich quiches.

Experience a decent riverside meal or snack in a dreamy Partage des Eaux setting at café-restaurant **Le Guinguette** (€16 *menu*, salads and *plats*, closed Mon, follow directions for river walk above, tel. 04 90 38 10 61).

The Heart of the Luberon

Fifteen minutes east of Isle-sur-la-Sorgue lies this protected area, where canyons and ridgelines rule. Because the Luberon is a natural reserve (Parc Naturel Régional du Luberon), development is strictly controlled—notice the absence of mega-stores and roadside sprawl. Here, still-proud hill towns stand guard over long-forgotten valleys, while carefully managed vineyards (producing mostly inexpensive wines) play hopscotch with cherry groves, lavender fields, and cypress trees.

While the hill towns can be seen as subtly different variations on the same theme, each has a distinct character. Look for differences:

the color of shutters, the pattern of stones, the way flowers are planted, or the number of tourist boutiques. Every village has something to offer—it's up to you to find and celebrate it.

Stay in Roussillon or Joucas. By village standards, Roussillon is always lively, while Joucas is perennially peaceful. When restaurant-hunting, read descriptions of the villages in this chapter—many good finds are embedded. For aerial views high above this charmed land, consider a hot-air balloon trip (see "Joucas," page 159).

Roussillon

With all the trendy charm of Santa Fe on a hilltop, Roussillon will cost you at least a roll of film (and €2 for parking). Roussillon has been a protected village since 1943 and has benefited from a complete absence of modern development. An enormous deposit of ochre gives the earth and buildings here that distinctive red color, and provides this village with its economic base. This place is popular; it's best to visit early or late in the day.

ORIENTATION

Roussillon sits atop Mont Rouge (Red Mountain) at about 1,000 feet above sea level. The village curls around this hospitable mountain, and the exposed ochre cliffs are a short walk south.

Two parking lots are available: one on the northern edge (by the recommended Hôtel Rêves d'Ocres) and another on its southern flank, closer to the ochre cliffs. If you approach from Gordes or Joucas, you'll end up at the northern lot. If you're coming from the N-100 and the south, you'll park at the southern lot. Thursday is Roussillon's market day, and every day is Christmas for thieves—take everything out of your car.

Tourist Information: The little TI is in the center, between the two lots and across from the David restaurant. It posts a list of hotels, *chambres d'hôte*, and late-night doctors. Walkers should get info on trails from Roussillon to nearby villages (April–Oct Mon–Sat 9:00–12:00 & 13:30–18:30, Sun 14:00–18:30; Nov–March Mon–Sat 13:30–17:30, closed Sun, tel. 04 90 05 60 25).

Boules (Pétanque)

The game of *boules*—also called *pétanque*—is the horseshoes of Provence and the Riviera. It's played in every village, almost exclusively by men, on level dirt areas kept specifically for this purpose. It was invented here in the early 1900s, and today every French boy grows up playing *boules* with Papa and *Ton-Ton* (Uncle) Jean. It's a social-yet-serious sport and endlessly entertaining to watch—even more so if you understand the rules.

Boules is played with heavy metal balls (*boules,* about the size of baseballs) and a small wooden target ball (*le cochonnet,* about the size of a ping-pong ball). Whoever gets their *boule* closest to the *cochonnet* wins. It's most commonly played in teams of two, though individual competition and teams of three are not uncommon. (There are *boules* leagues and professional players who make little money, but are national celebrities.) Most teams have two specialists, a *pointeur* and a *tireur.* The *pointeur* goes first and tries to lob his balls as close to the target as he can. The *tireur*'s job is to blast away opponent's *boules.*

SIGHTS

▲**The Village**—Start at one of Roussillon's two parking lots. For centuries, animals grazed at the lot closer to the ochre cliffs. It then became a school playground, and when there weren't enough kids to support a school, it became a parking lot. Climb a few minutes from either parking lot (follow signs to *Castum,* pass the Hollywood-set square and church) to the summit of the town. During the Middle Ages, the church tower marked the entrance to the fortified town. Duck into the pretty 11th-century church of St. Michel, and notice the well-worn center aisle and the propane heaters—winters can be frigid in this area. The castle stood just above the church on the top of Mont Rouge. Find the orientation plaque and the dramatic viewpoint, often complete with a howling mistral. While nothing remains of the castle today, the strategic advantage of this site is clear: You can see forever. As you head back down to the village, notice the clamped-iron beams that shore up ancient walls. Examine the different hues of yellow and orange. These lime-finished exteriors, called *chaux* (literally "limes"), need to be re-done about every 10 years. Locals choose their exact color...but in this town of ochre, it's never white.

Here's the play-by-play: Each player gets three *boules*. A coin toss determines which team goes first. The starting team scratches a small circle in the dirt, in which players must stand (with both feet on the ground) when launching their *boules*. Next, the starting team tosses the *cochonnet* (about 6–10 yards)—that's the target. The *boule* must be tossed underhand, and can be rolled, thrown sky-high, or rocketed at its target. Most lob it like a slow pitch in softball, with lots of backspin. The starting team's *pointeur* shoots, then the other team's *pointeur* shoots until he gets closer. Once the second team lands a *boule* closer, the first team is back up. If the opposing team's *boule* is very near the *cochonnet*, the *tireur* will likely attempt to knock it away. If the team decides that they can lob one in closer, the *pointeur* shoots.

Once all *boules* have been launched, the tally is taken. This is where it gets tense, as the difference in distance often comes down to millimeters. Faces are drawn, lips are pursed, and eyes are squinted as teams try to sort through the who's-closer process. I've seen all kinds of measuring devices, from shoes to belts to tape measures. The team with the ball closest to the target receives one point, and the teams keep going until someone gets 13 points.

See how local (or artsy) you can look in what must be the most scenic village square in Provence (place du Pignotte) and watch the river of shoppers. Is anyone playing *boules* at the opposite end? You could paint the entire town without ever leaving the red-and-orange corner of your palette. Many do. While Roussillon receives its share of day-trippers, evenings are romantically peaceful.

▲▲**Ochre Cliffs**—Roussillon was Europe's capital for ochre production until World War II. A stroll to the south end of town, beyond the upper parking lot, will show you why. A brilliant orange path leads through the richly-colored ochre canyon (formerly a quarry), explaining the hue of this village (€2, daily 10:00–17:30; beware—light-colored clothing and orange powder don't mix).

The value of Roussillon's ochre cliffs was known in Roman times. Once excavated, the clay ochre was rinsed with water to separate it from sand, and bricks of the stuff were dried and baked for deeper hues. The procedure for extracting the ochre did not change much over 2,000 years. Ochre mining became industrialized in late 1700s. Used primarily for wallpaper, linoleum, and wallpaper, ochre reached its zenith just before World War II (after that, cheaper substitutes took over).

SLEEPING

(€1 = about $1.20, country code: 33)

In Roussillon

The TI posts a list of hotels and *chambres d'hôte.*

$$ Hôtel Rêves d'Ocres**, the only hotel in the town center, is run by helpful Sandrine and laid-back Ouaheb (pronounced Web). They have been trying to sell the hotel—be ready for changes from this description. It's warm and comfortable, with spacious rooms. Eight of these have view terraces, most with views to Gordes (Db without balcony-€72, Db with balcony-€80, Tb-€95, air-con, route de Gordes, tel. 04 90 05 60 50, fax 04 90 05 79 74, www.hotelrevesdocres.com, contact@hotelrevesdocres.com).

$ Madame Cherel rents very simple rooms with firm mattresses and seems just this side of a youth hostel. There's a common view terrace and good reading materials available (D-€32–35, no CC, 3 blocks from upper parking lot, between gas station and school, La Burlière, tel. 04 90 05 68 47). Chatty and sincere Cherel speaks English, is a wealth of regional travel tips, and rents mountain bikes to guests only (€15/day).

Near Roussillon

The next two listings, for drivers only, are most easily found by turning north off N-100 at the Roussillon/Les Huguets sign (second turn-off to Roussillon coming from Avignon).

$$ Hôtel Les Sables d'Ocre** is a modern and kid-friendly spread, with 22 bright, small, but adequate rooms, a big pool, lots of grass, air-conditioning, and a well-tended garden (Db-€64, spring for the Db with garden balcony-€78, Tb loft-€95–115, a half-mile after leaving Roussillon toward Apt at intersection of D-108 and D-104, tel. 04 90 05 55 55, fax 04 90 05 55 50, www.roussillon-hotel.com, sablesdocre@free.fr).

$$ Les Puches *chambre d'hôte* offers three white rooms in a stone home, with terraces overlooking a sleek pool, for a good price (Db-€66, no CC, 1.25 miles below Roussillon toward Apt on D-104, a little past Hôtel Les Sables d'Ocre, tel. 04 90 05 68 39, fax 04 90 05 69 14, www.les-puches.com, contact@les-puches.com).

EATING

Choose ambience over cuisine if dining in Roussillon, and enjoy any of the places on the main square. It's a festive place, where children dance while parents dine, and dogs and cats look longingly for leftovers. Restaurants change with the mistral here—what's good one year disappoints the next. Consider my suggestions and go with what looks best (or look over my suggestions in other Luberon villages).

On the square, **Le Bistrot de Roussillon** (closed Tue, tel. 04 90 05 74 45) and **Minka's Café** (closed Wed, tel. 04 90 05 62 11) go *mano a mano* at dinner, each vying for customers' loyalty. Both are good values, with similar prices, tables on the square, and red-hill-view terraces in the back, though le Bistrot seems more reliable (good *plats* from €14 and *menus* from €20). The little **Crêperie-Saladerie** below serves scrumptious and beefy omelets and good salads. **Le Castrum,** on the square, serves good *tartes* with salad (open lunch only). **Chez David,** across from the TI, has views from interior tables; it's elegant, with a good reputation—for a price (*menus* from €30, closed Wed, tel. 04 90 05 60 13).

Near Roussillon

Many of the restaurants that pepper the countryside around Roussillon are worth a drive. Read my descriptions of the villages below for ideas, and remember that Isle-sur-la-Sorgue is a manageable 30 minutes away. These restaurants merit a visit: **Ferme de la Huppe** (closed Wed–Thu, between Joucas and Gordes, 5 min by car from Roussillon), **Hostellerie des Commandeurs** (closed Wed, in Joucas, 5 min by car from Roussillon), **Le Fournil** (closed Mon, in Bonnieux, 10-min drive from Roussillon), **L'Hôtel St. Hubert** (closed Mon, in St-Saturnin-lès-Apt, 15-min drive from Roussillon), and **L'Auberge de la Loube** (closed Wed–Thu, in Buoux, 20-min drive from Roussillon).

Joucas

This understated, quiet, and largely overlooked village slumbers

below the Gordes buzz. Vertical stone lanes with carefully arranged flowers and well-restored homes play host to occasional artists and a smattering of locals. There's not much to do or see here, except eat, sleep, and relax. Joucas has one tiny grocery, one café, one pharmacy, a good kids' play area, and two solid-value accommodation options. Sleep here for a central location and utter silence. For views, walk past the little fountain in the center and up the steep lanes as high as you want.

Several **hiking** trails leave from Joucas (Gordes and Roussillon are each 3 miles away). Serious hikers should take the three-mile hike to Murs (yellow signs point the way from the top of the village), though you don't have to go far to enjoy the natural beauty on this trail.

Montgolfières are hot-air balloons that ply the thin air above the Luberon every calm morning. The Montgolfières-Luberon outfit has two flight options: the Four-Star Flight (€230, 1.5 hrs, includes picnic and champagne) and the economy-class Tourist Flight (€145, 45 min, includes glass of bubbly). For either flight, meet on main road below Joucas at 7:00 (reserve a few days ahead, maximum 7 passengers, tel. 04 90 05 76 77, fax 04 90 05 74 39).

SLEEPING AND EATING

(€1 = about $1.20, country code: 33)

$$$ **La Ferme de la Huppe***** has a Gordes address, but it's closer physically and spiritually to Joucas. This farmhouse-elegant hacienda is an excellent splurge if you need pampering. The 10 rooms gather on two levels behind the stylish pool, decor is understated and rustic, and the dinners are memorable (small Db-€85, bigger Db-€105–120, really bigger Db-€145–165, dinner *menu* €37, restaurant closed Wed–Thu, air-con promised for 2005, between Joucas and Gordes, on the D-156 road to Goult, just off the D-2, tel. 04 90 72 12 25, fax 04 90 72 01 83, gerald.konings@wanadoo.fr).

$$ **La Maison de Mistral** *chambre d'hôte* offers creatively designed and comfortable rooms, all with valley views and a break-fast terrace for lingering. But the best reason to sleep here is to relax over a chilled rosé with the owners, Pierre and Marie-Lucie Mistral, who want to get to know you. Their lack of English doesn't seem to matter (Db-€60, extra person-€15, includes breakfast, no CC, ask nicely and they might cook you a dinner well worth the cost; dead center in the village by the church, look for the sign on the walking street, rue de l'Eglise; tel. 04 90 05 74 01, mobile 06 23 87 69 02, pmistral@free.fr). Since the Mistrals' daughter runs the town's only hotel, you get access to its pool (see below).

$$ **Hostellerie des Commandeurs****, run by sweet Sophie, lacks the panache of their parent's place, but the modern rooms are comfortable and clean (with wall-to-wall carpeting), the location is great, the pool is big, and their restaurant serves fine-value dinners (*menus* from €17). This place, next to a play field, is good for kids. Ask for a south-facing room for the best views (Db-€55–58, extra bed-€16, above park at village entrance on rue Pietonne, tel. 04 90 05 78 01, fax 04 90 05 74 47, www.lescommandeurs.com, hostellerie @lescommandeurs.com, S enough E).

More Luberon Towns:
Two Self-Guided Driving Tours

Le Luberon is packed with appealing villages and beautiful scenery, but it has only a handful of must-see sights. I've divided the region into two areas that I've labeled *Le Luberon Classique* and *Le Luberon Profonde*. *Le Luberon Classique* has the area's most famous villages and sights (though I've tossed in a few lesser-known stops). *Le Luberon Profonde* is for those wanting to experience a quieter Provence. A day in each area works best. Hotels and restaurants are listed throughout.

Le Luberon Classique

Peter Mayle's *A Year in Provence* nudged tourism in this part of France into overdrive. A visit to Mayle's quintessential Provence includes these very popular villages and sights; I've listed them in logical order for a good day's excursion (see map on page 148).

From either Roussillon or Joucas, follow signs to Gordes and make a hard right when the impressive view of the village first comes in sight. Park at a pullout along this short road, walk to the big stone slab, and admire the view of the hill town.

Gordes: For the last 40 years, Gordes has been the most touristy and trendy town in the Luberon. Recently a virtual ghost town of derelict buildings, it's now completely renovated and filled with people who live in a world without calluses. Parisian big shots love it, many of whom bought homes and restored them, putting property values out of sight for locals. The village has little of interest except its many boutiques and its Tuesday market (which ends at 13:00). The town's 11th-century castle houses a collection of contemporary art. Notice the terrace of the house to your left: Everything is made out of stone here. There are two worthwhile sights near Gordes—the Abbey Notre-Dame de Sénanque and the Village des Bories—both well marked from Gordes and described below.

Abbey Notre-Dame de Sénanque: Arrive before 10:00 or you'll fight crowds and miss the abbey's tranquility. Be the first in to best appreciate this place. This still-functioning Cistercian abbey was built in 1148 as a back-to-basics reaction to the excesses of Benedictine abbeys. These Cistercians worked to recapture the simplicity, solitude, and poverty of the early Church. St. Bernard, the Cistercian's founder, created "a horrible vast solitude" in the forest where his monks could live like the desert fathers of the Old Testament. They strove to be separate from the world. To succeed required industrious self-sufficiency—a skill which these monks had. Their movement spread and colonized Europe with a new form of Christianity.

Medieval Monasteries

France is littered with medieval monasteries, and Provence is no exception. Most have virtually no furnishings (they never had many), which leaves the visitor with little to reconstruct what life must have been like in these cold stone buildings a thousand years ago. A little history can help breathe life into these important yet underappreciated monuments.

After the fall of the Roman Empire, monasteries arose as refuges of peace and order in a chaotic world. While the pope got rich and famous playing power politics, monasteries worked to keep the focus on simplicity and poverty. Throughout the Middle Ages, monasteries were mediators between man and God. In these peacefully remote abbeys, Europe's best minds struggled with the interpretation of God's words. Every sentence needed to be understood and applied. Answers were debated in universities and contemplated in monasteries.

St. Benedict established the Middle Ages' most influential monastic order (Benedictine) in Montecassino, Italy, in A.D. 529. He scheduled a rigorous program of monastic duties that combined manual labor with intellectual tasks. His movement spread north and took firm root in France, where the abbey of Cluny (Burgundy) eventually controlled more than 2,000 dependent abbeys and vied with the pope for control of the Church. Benedictine abbeys grew dot-com rich, and with wealth came excess (such as private bedrooms with baths). Monks lost sight of their purpose and became soft and corrupt. In the late 1100s, a determined and charismatic St. Bernard rallied the Cistercian order by going back to the original rule of St.

In 1200, there were over 500 such monasteries and abbeys in Europe. You can tour Sénanque's purposefully simple church, sublime cloisters, the refectory, and a *chauffoir* (small heated room where monks could copy books year round). A small monastic community still resides here (€4.60, Mon–Sat 10:00–12:00 & 14:00–18:00, Sun 14:00–18:00, good bookshop). For more on monasteries, see the "Medieval Monasteries" sidebar, above.

Village des Bories: This stone-bordered dirt road sets the mood for this open-air museum (turn-off a mile from Gordes toward Coustellet, drive carefully because this narrow road is filled with blind curves). The vertical stones you see on the walls as you approach the site were used for counterweight to keep these walls, built without mortar, intact.

Benedict. Cistercian abbeys thrived as centers of religious thought and exploration from the 13th through the 15th centuries.

Cistercian abbots ran their abbeys like little kingdoms, doling out punishment and food to the monks, and tools to peasant farmers. Abbeys were occupied by two groups: the favored monks from aristocratic families (such as St. Bernard) and a larger group of lay brothers from peasant stock, who were given the heaviest labor and could only join the Sunday services.

Monks' days were broken into three activities: prayer, reading holy texts, and labor. Monks lived in silence and poverty with few amenities—meat was forbidden, as was cable TV. In summer, they got two daily meals; in winter, just one. Monks slept together in a single room on threadbare mats covering solid-rock floors.

With their focus on work and discipline, Cistercian abbeys became leaders of the medieval industrial revolution. Among the few literate people in Europe, monks were keepers of technological knowledge—about clocks, waterwheels, accounting, foundries, grist-mills, textiles, and agricultural techniques. Abbeys became economic engines that helped drive France out of its Middle Aged funk.

As France (and Europe) slowly got its act together in the late Middle Ages, cities reemerged as places to trade and thrive. Abbeys gradually lost their relevance in a brave new humanist world. Kings took over abbot selection, hence further degrading the abbeys' power, and Gutenberg's movable type made monks obsolete. The French Revolution closed the book on abbatial life, with troops occupying and destroying many abbeys. The still-functioning Abbey Notre-Dame de Sénanque, near Gordes, is a rare survivor.

The "village" you tour is composed of dry-laid stone structures, proving that there has always been more stone than wood in this rugged region. Stone villages like this predated the Romans—some say by 2,000 years. This one was inhabited for 200 years (from about 1600 to 1800). You'll also see *bories* (dry-stone huts) in fields, now used to store tools or hay. A look around these hills confirms the relative amounts of building materials: The trees are small and gnarled (not good for construction), but white stone is everywhere just waiting to be used.

The "village" is composed of five "hamlets." You'll duck into several homes, animal pens, a community oven, and more (identified in English). Study the "beehive" stone-laying method and imagine the time it took. They had no scaffolds or support arches, just hammers and patience. They cleared stones from fields, providing building material and cultivating better farmland (€5.50, daily June–Sept 9:00–20:00, Oct–May 9:00–17:30, buy €4 booklet of English translations to learn more).

St. Julien Bridge (Pont St. Julien): This small, three-arched bridge survives as a testimony to Roman engineers—and to the importance of this rural area 2,000 years ago. This is the only surviving bridge on what was once the main road from northern Italy to Provence, the primary route used by Roman armies. This 215-foot-long Roman bridge was built from 27 B.C. to A.D. 14. Mortar had not been invented, so (as with the Pont du Gard) stones were carefully set in place. Amazingly, the bridge survives  today, having outlived Roman marches, a couple hundred floods, and decades of automobile traffic. A new bridge (almost completed) will finally reroute traffic from this beautiful structure.

Notice how thin the layer of stone seems between the arch tops and the road. Those open niches weren't for statues, but instead allowed water to pass through when the river ran high. (At its current trickle, it's hard to fathom.) Walk under an arch and examine the pockmarks in the side—medieval thieves in search of free bronze stole the clamps.

Bonnieux: Spectacular from a distance, this town disappoints up close. It lacks a pedestrian center, though the Friday-morning market briefly creates one. But Bonnieux boasts several excellent restaurants, including **Le Fournil**; reserve ahead for this reliable, rock-sculpted place. They serve creative Provençal specialties in a warm setting (expect €35 per person, closed Mon, best tables outside by the fountain, next to TI at 5 place Carnot, tel. 04 90 75 83 62).

Lacoste: Little Lacoste slumbers across the valley from Bonnieux, in the shadow of its ruined castle. Climb through this photogenic village of arches and stone paths, passing American art students (from the Savannah College of Art and Design) showing their work. Support an American artist, learn about their art, then keep climbing and climbing to the ruined castle base. From the base of Lacoste's ruined castle (serious renovation was underway in 2004), the view of Bonnieux is as good is it gets.

The Marquis de Sade (1740–1814) lived in this castle for more than 30 years. Author of pornographic novels, he was notorious for hosting orgies behind these walls, and for kidnapping peasants for scandalous purposes. He was eventually arrested and imprisoned, and thanks to him, we have a word to describe his favorite hobby—sadism.

If you need inexpensive digs and you find Lacoste appealing, **Café de Sade** is spotless, with six rooms above a little restaurant (D-€36, Db-€50, family room-€65, dorm beds-€15, no CC, sheets €4 extra in dorm only, tel. 04 90 75 82 29, fax 04 90 75 95 68). A good bakery with pizza slices and drinks is nearby. If you need a café with views, walk to the other end of Lacoste and find the **Bar/Restaurant de France**'s outdoor tables overlooking Bonnieux.

Abbey St. Hilaire: A dirt road between Lacoste and Ménerbes leads down to this long-forgotten and pint-size abbey. There's a pure church and a cute little cloister, but it's not really much to see— instead, there's more to experience. The tranquility and isolation sought by monks 800 years ago is still palpable, and it might be just what you need after experiencing the crowds in some of these vil- lages. Once a Cistercian outpost for the bigger abbey at Sénanque, Abbey St. Hilaire is now owned by Carmelite Friars. Pick up the English handout, contribute to the abbey's well-being (free entry, donation requested), and wander around the place. The lone stone bench in front is picnic-ready, and a rugged WC is cut into the rock (across the courtyard).

Ménerbes: Ménerbes is (in)famous as the village that drew Peter Mayle's attention to this region, but offers little of interest for most. To experience Provence pre-tourism, wander into the Café du Progrès time-warp. Specifically the original café, not the outdoor extension that spills into the parking area. Ponder a region that in the last 30 years has experienced such a dramatic change. In 1970, the Luberon was unknown to most travelers. Locals led simple lives and had few ambitions (as depicted in the film *Manon of the Spring* and *Jean de Florette* movies). They blame the theater festival in Avignon for bringing directors here every year, who then recreated perfect Provençal villages on film (Gordes was first). Parisians, Swiss, Brits, and eventually Americans followed, willing to pay any price for their place in the Provençal sun. Property taxes increased—as did the cost of *une bière* at the corner café—and all too soon, villagers found themselves with few affordable options...just several cafés like this.

To explore Ménerbes, follow signs to *Eglise* and walk 10 min- utes to the squat Romanesque church (closed) and graveyard (more great views in all directions and a stone bench for picnics). You're face-to-face with the Grand Luberon ridge. Notice the quarry carved into its side, where the stone for this village came from. Between Ménerbes and Oppède you'll pass the **Corkscrew Museum** (Musée du Tire-Bouchon), worth a stop only if you're a corkscrew enthusiast (1,200 of them on display in glass cases) or want to taste their wines (Domaine de la Citadelle, €4 for the "museum," includes tasting, daily 10:00–12:00 & 14:00–19:00).

Oppède-le-Vieux: This windy barnacle of a town clings to its hillside like a baby to its mother. There's one boutique, a café, and a dusty main square at the base of a short, ankle-twisting climb to a pretty little church and a ruined castle. This off-the-beaten-path fixer-upper of a village has retained its rustic character and shows little inclination for boutiques and smart hotels. It's ideal for those looking to perish in Provence.

Consider a light lunch at one of the town's two cafés (see below) and plan your ascent to the castle. It's 20 minutes straight up, but the Luberon views justify the effort. Walk under the central arch of the building across from the café and climb. At the fork, either way works (right is a bit easier). Find the little church terrace. From here, tiled rooftops paint a delightful picture with the grand panorama; the flat plain of the Rhône delta is visible to the left. The colorful **Notre-Dame d'Alidon church** (1588) is generally open, except at lunch (depends on village volunteers). Pick up the English text and imagine having to climb this distance every Sunday—your entire life. Go behind the church and notice the flowers growing from the stone. From here, mountain goats can climb on what remains of the castle (but be careful—there are no rails).

To find Oppède-le-Vieux, follow signs to Oppède-le-Village, then head to Oppède-le-Vieux and drive towards *le Grand Luberon massif.* You'll be forced to park a few hundred yards from the village, for which you'll get to pay €2.

In Oppède-le-Vieux, **Le Petit Café** serves cheap lunches and offers several surprisingly comfortable rooms scattered around the village. But they seem almost hesitant to rent them, or maybe just indifferent to your visit (Db-€55–70, Tb-€78, bed in small dorm-€25, no CC, most rooms over the café, tel. 04 90 76 74 01, tel. & fax 04 90 76 84 15, daughter Kathy—pronounced kah-tee—SE). If you sleep here, you have parking privileges at the little top lot, but ask.

Goult: Bigger than its sister hill towns, this surprisingly quiet town seems content to be away from the tourist path. (It's the only town listed in this section *not* on one of the driving tours—though it can be easily tagged on to the *Classique* tour). Wander up the hill to the panorama and windmill, and later review its many good restaurants—where you won't have to compete with tourists for a table.

La Provence Profonde

Provence is busy with tourists, but there are still plenty of characteristic and undiscovered spots to explore. The area east of Roussillon feels peaceful and less touristed—come here to get a sense of how most villages were before they became "destinations." Here are the key sights in the order you would pass them coming from Roussillon (see map on page 148).

St-Saturnin-lès-Apt: Most tourists pass by this pleasant place (with a lively Sun market) on their way to more famous destinations. I couldn't find a souvenir shop. Ditch your car below the main entry to the town (just below the old city) and walk up the main drag, following signs to *Le Château.* You'll soon come to a striking church (usually closed) which is a fine example of Provençal Romanesque, with a tall, rounded spire. From here, look for *Le Château* signs pointing up the steps. The ruined "château" grows right out of the rock, making it difficult to tell the man-made from the natural. Climb as high as the sun allows with no shade—the green arrows guide you up. It's a scamperer's paradise, with views to drool over. These are the best village-top views I found in Provence. The small chapel at the very top is closed, so there's no reason to climb all the way to the top. To get back down, find your way through the small opening to the little dam.

Hôtel le St. Hubert is centrally located in the village, with a cozy café wallpapered with wine labels on one side (salads and *plats*) and a classier view restaurant on the other (*menus* from €17, café and restaurant closed Mon). The hotel has eight rooms above (Db-€55, tel. 04 90 75 42 02, fax 04 90 75 49 90).

Le Colorado Provençal: The park has ochre cliffs similar to Roussillon's (listed above), but they're spread over a larger area, with well-signed trails. So if you'd like to hike in orange sand through Bryce Canyon–like rocks, follow signs to the town of Rustrel, the gateway to Le Colorado Provençal.

Rustrel has two parking lots; choose the one at the trailhead. Do *not* park at the big lot right on the main road with the big signs (you'll pay €5.50 and be 15 minutes from the trails). The lower-profile, cheaper, and more convenient *Parking Municipal* at the trailhead is 300 yards toward Apt from the "bad" parking (€3.50, small *café-buvette* available).

Cross the little footbridge and follow either Cheminée de Fée or Sahara trails for the best walks (trails are color-coded and easy to follow, allow about 30–40 min for each with modest elevation gain; Cheminée de Fée is more impressive, but steeper). Light-colored clothing is a bad choice. Signs remind you to please remain on the trails and not to climb the cliffs.

Viens: About 15 minutes above and to the east of Le Colorado Provençal (turn right when leaving Colorado to reach Viens), this

village is where locals from Roussillon go to get away. With a setting like this, it's surprising that modest Viens is not more touristy. The panoramas are higher and more vast than around Roussillon (some lavender fields), and the vegetation is more rugged. Walk the streets of the old town (bigger than it first appears) and visit the few shops scattered about. This is how Gordes must have looked before it became chic.

Le Petit Jardin Café, just below the town's only phone booth, makes a good lunch or dinner stop, with cozy interior tables, a garden terrace, and reasonable prices (*menu du jour*-€11, closed Wed, tel. 04 90 75 20 05). There's a small grocery store and a good bakery a few blocks past the café, toward St. Martin de Castillon. To reach the next village (Saignon), follow signs to St. Martin de Castillon, then turn right on the N-100 toward Apt.

Saignon: Sitting high atop a rock spur, you'll look down upon Apt, a city of only 11,500, which from here looks like a megalopolis after all these villages. If you need a break, climb Le Rocher Belvedere (the Belvedere rock) for grand views over lavender fields. Park as high as you feel comfortable driving, and follow *Le Rocher* signs up to this "ship's prow" (about 3 stories of stairs to the top). You'll find several cafés, a cushy hotel, and a grocery store in the linear village's center.

Saignon is near a brilliant lunch or dinner stop, **Auberge de la Loube,** which is the ultimate in country-coziness and one of Peter Mayle's favorites (great cuisine, allow €20 for lunch and €30 for dinner, closed Wed–Thu, tel. 04 90 74 19 58). Follow Bonnieux signs from Saignon and turn left to Buoux.

Lourmarin: The southernmost Luberon village I include has a fine Friday market, a well-preserved Renaissance château on its fringe (visitable only by French-language tour), and a delightful town center. Existentialist writer Albert Camus *(The Stranger)* lived in Lourmarin in the 1950s, lending it a certain fame that persists today.

MARSEILLE, CASSIS, AND AIX-EN-PROVENCE

In the rush to get between Avignon and the Riviera, most travelers zip through the eastern fringe of Provence. But this area deserves a visit, offering compelling, different-as-night-and-day cities and a strikingly beautiful coastline. Marseille is an unspoiled, untouristy, vibrant port city with 2,600 years of history. The nearby coastal village of Cassis offers the perfect respite from urban sightseeing. And just inland, popular and slick Aix-en-Provence is the yin to Marseille's yang, with beautiful people to match its lovely architecture.

Marseille

Those who think of Marseille as the "Naples of France"—a big, gritty, dangerous port—are about 20 years out of date. Today's Marseille (mar-say) is more like the Barcelona of France: a big, gritty port, sure—but with a distinct culture, a proud spirit, a new prosperity, and a populace excited about cleaning up its act.

France's third-biggest city (and Europe's third-largest port), with a history that goes back to ancient Greek times, challenges you to find its charm. While most tourists won't linger here—it's not their idea of the French Riviera—it'd be a shame to come to the south of France and not check out its leading city. By train or car, it's made-to-order for a quick visit. And with the new TGV line making it just a three-hour trip from Paris, this thriving city seems to be more determined than ever to put on a welcoming face.

ORIENTATION

While Marseille sprawls, keep it simple: a main boulevard (La Canebière) meets the colorful old port with a cluster of small

Marseille, Cassis, and Aix-en-Provence

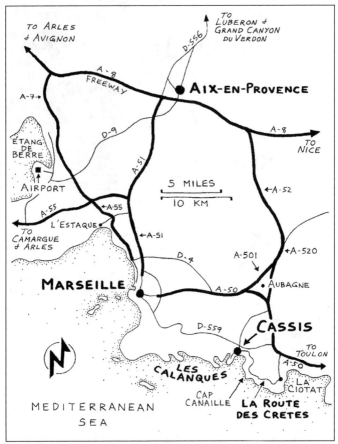

museums and the TI. The characteristic Panier district is the old town, blanketing a hill that tumbles down to the port (Vieux Port). The harborside is a delightful promenade lined with inviting eateries, amusements, and a morning fish market. Everything covered here (except the church on the hill) is within a 15-minute walk of the train station.

Tourist Information: Right at the port, the helpful TI has a good city map, a flier with a self-guided walk through the old town, and fliers on each of the museums (Mon–Sat 9:00–19:00, Sun 10:00–17:00, 4 La Canebière, tel. 04 91 13 89 00).

Arrival in Marseille

By Train: St. Charles Station (Gare St. Charles), newly renovated to celebrate its prestigious status as a TGV station, is modern and user-friendly. Look for free city maps at the kiosk (outside, near exit at track A). Baggage check is at track A. To get from the station to the old port and TI, you can walk, take the Métro, or hop a taxi.

It's a 15-minute downhill **walk** to the port. Leave the station through the exit at track A, veer right, and admire the view from atop the stairs. That's Notre-Dame de la Garde overlooking the city. Walk straight down boulevard d'Athènes, which becomes boulevard Dugommier. Turn right at McDonald's onto the grand boulevard, La Canebière, which leads directly to the port and TI.

By **Métro,** it's an easy two stops from the train station to the port: Go down the escalator opposite track E, buy a €1.50 ticket (from the machines or inside the *Accueil* office), descend the escalator, and take the blue line #1 *(direction La Timone)* to *Vieux Port* (Old Port). Following *Sortie la Canebière* exit signs, you'll pop out at the TI (and smell the fish market).

By **taxi,** allow €6 to the port and €10 to Notre-Dame de la Garde.

By Car: Drivers who are good in big, crazy cities can reasonably navigate Marseille. Leaving the autoroute, signs to *Vieux Port, Centre-Ville,* and *Office du Tourisme* take you right to the port. At the port, turn left and let the blue "P" signs direct you into an underground lot with 625 spaces (locals claim pay lots are patrolled and safe).

By Plane: Marseille's airport (Aéroport Marseille-Provence), 25 minutes from the city center, is small and easy to navigate (tel. 04 42 14 14 14, www.marseille.aeroport.fr). There is a direct shuttle bus service to the St. Charles Station (€9, 3/hr, 25 min, tel. 04 42 14 31 27).

Helpful Hints

Pickpockets: Be on guard. Marseille is one of the few cities in France where you are still likely to run into Gypsy thieves. Looking like beggars, they're usually raggedly-dressed barefoot kids, or a mom with a baby, who hold up newspapers or cardboard to distract you as they pick your pocket. Be firm and rude if you must, but don't let them near you. Big-city thieves thrive in crowds and target tourists.

Le Petit Train: Silly little tourist trains with skimpy recorded information make two handy routes through town. Both leave at least hourly from the port (across from TI, near sprawling Café Samaritaine). One toots you through the Panier district (€5, 60 min). The other saves you the 30-minute climb to the Notre-Dame de la Garde's fantastic view (€5, allow 70 min round-trip, including 30 min to visit the church).

Marseille

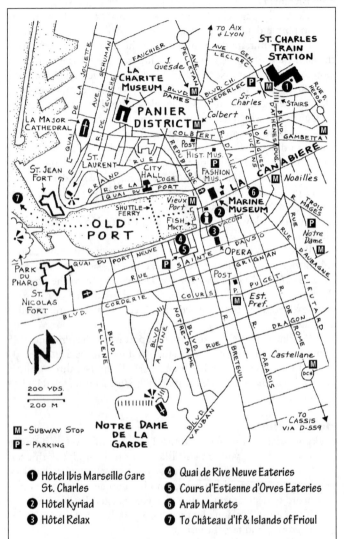

- **M** – Subway Stop
- **P** – Parking

1 Hôtel Ibis Marseille Gare St. Charles

2 Hôtel Kyriad

3 Hôtel Relax

4 Quai de Rive Neuve Eateries

5 Cours d'Estienne d'Orves Eateries

6 Arab Markets

7 To Château d'If & Islands of Frioul

Marseille at a Glance

▲**Old Port** Economic heart of town, featuring lots of boats and a fish market, all protected by two impressive fortresses. **Hours:** Port—always open; fish market—daily until 13:00.

▲**La Charité Museum** Housed in a beautiful building with Celtic, Greek, Roman, and Egyptian artifacts, plus temporary exhibits. **Hours:** June–Sept Tue–Sun 11:00–18:00, Oct–May Tue–Sun 10:00–17:00, always closed Mon.

▲**Marine Museum** Grandiose building with small exhibit on the city's marine history. **Hours:** June–Sept Tue–Sun 10:00–18:00, Oct–May Tue–Sun 10:00–17:00, always closed Mon.

▲**Notre-Dame de la Garde** Marseille's landmark sight: a huge Romanesque-Byzantine basilica, towering above everything, with panoramic views. **Hours:** Daily 7:00–20:00.

Château d'If Island with fortress-turned-prison, featured in Alexandre Dumas' *The Count of Monte Cristo*. **Hours:** Boats depart quai des Belges on the hour 9:00–17:00.

SIGHTS

La Canebière—The boulevard La Canebière (pronounced "can o' bee-air") is the celebrated main drag of Marseille. Strolling this stubby thoroughfare, you feel surrounded by a great city. Two blocks before the harbor, you'll find the museums and stylish shopping district. The boulevard dead-ends at the old port's fish market and TI.

Arab Markets—Marseille's huge Moroccan, Algerian, and Tunisian populations give the city a special spice. For a taste of Africa, leave La Canebière on rue Longue des Capucins (left as you face the port). Suddenly you're immersed in an exotic and fragrant little medina. For a more sprawling Arab market, explore the lanes around boulevard d'Athènes near the train station (such as rue des Convalescents).

▲**Old Port (Vieux Port)**—Marseille's Vieux Port, long the economic heart of town, is carefully protected by two impressive fortresses at its mouth. These citadels were built in the 17th century under Louis XIV, supposedly to protect the city. But locals figured the forts were actually designed to keep an eye on Marseille—a city that was essentially autonomous until 1660, and tough to thoroughly incorporate into the growing kingdom of France.

Today, the serious shipping is away from the center, and the old port is the happy domain of pleasure craft. The fish market along quai des Belges thrives each morning (unless the mistral wind kept the boats home yesterday). The stalls are gone by 13:00, but the smells linger longer. Looking out from here, Le Panier (the old town) rises to your right. The harborfront below Le Panier was destroyed in 1943 by the Nazis, who didn't want a tangled refuge for resistance fighters so close to the harbor. Now it's rebuilt as modern condos and trendy restaurants.

From the Old Port to the New Town: Halfway along the promenade (quai du Port), at the City Hall and moored three-masted restaurant, you'll see the fun little shuttle boat that ferries locals across the harbor to the new town (€0.50, every 10 min, note the funny two-way steering wheel as you sail). Riding this across, you land in the new town—which, because of the 1943 bombings, is actually older than the "old" town along the harborfront.

Directly in front of the ferry landing are a couple of characteristic bars and brasseries, ideal for a salty meal or memorable drink. Nearby are several other handy eating options (see "Eating," below).

Le Panier District (Old Town)—Until the mid-19th century, Marseille was just the hill-capping old town and its fortified port. Today that old town is the best place to wander in search of the town's character. The TI has a self-guided history-trail flier (follow painted red line through old town). Otherwise, simply walk uphill from the City Hall to La Charité Museum (described below); read the thoughtful English information plaques posted at points of historic interest.

The ornate **City Hall** stands across from the old sailboat and the little shuttle ferry. Its bust of Louis XIV overlooks the harbor. Rue de la Prison leads behind the city hall and up the hill. At the crest of the hill—the highest point in the old town—you'll find the peaceful place des Moulins. It's named for the 15 windmills that used to spin and grind from this windy summit. (Today, only the towers of three can be seen.)

The only sight of any importance in Le Panier District is La Charité Museum (see below). From La Charité, you can continue down the other side of the hill, where the towering, striped cathedral stands surrounded by big, noisy streets and an unappealing cruise-ship port. (Plans are in the works to make this port a little more welcoming.) From there, you can follow the ramparts back around to the old port, enjoying a fine view from near Fort Saint Jean. The ugly, boxy building marked "monument" at the base of the fort is a memorial to those lost during the Nazi occupation of the city during World War II.

▲**La Charité Museum (Centre de la Vieille Charité)**—Now a museum, this was once a poorhouse. In 1674, the French king decided that all the poor people on the streets were bad news. He built a huge triple-arcaded home to house a thousand needy sub-

jects. In 1940, the famous architect Le Corbusier declared it a shame that such a fine building was under-appreciated. These days the striking building—wonderfully renovated and beautiful in its arcaded simplicity—is used as a collection of art galleries surrounding a church.

The facade of the church features the figure of Charity taking care of orphans (as the state did with this build-

ing). She's flanked by pelicans (symbolic of charity, for the way they actually pick flesh from their own bosom to feed their hungry chicks). The ground floor houses temporary exhibits. Upstairs, you'll find rooms with interesting collections of Celtic (c. 300 B.C.), Greek, and Roman artifacts from this region. There's also a surprisingly good Egyptian collection, and masks from Africa and the South Pacific (€2–5 depending on exhibits, June–Sept Tue–Sun 11:00–18:00, Oct–May Tue–Sun 10:00–17:00, closed Mon, pleasant restaurant/bar/WC, tel. 04 91 14 58 80).

French Fashion—While handy, cheap, and easy to visit, the **Fashion Museum** (Musée de la Mode) is as skimpy as most of its dresses. Its two rooms are full of creative and colorful dresses from the 1950s to today (€3, June–Sept Tue–Sun 11:00–18:00, Oct–May Tue–Sun 10:00–17:00, closed Mon, 11 La Canebière, in Espace Mode Mediterranée).

For more fashion, cross La Canebière, continue across place du Général de Gaulle, and find the tiny rue de la Tour, Marseille's self-proclaimed "rue de la Mode." It's lined with shops proudly displaying the latest fashions, mostly from local designers. Just beyond that is the impressive 1920s Art Deco facade of Marseille's opera house.

▲**Marine Museum and Chamber of Commerce**—Near the end of La Canebière stands the tall and grandiose Chamber of Commerce building. Step inside and marvel at its flashy 1860s interior (free entry). A relief on the ceiling shows great moments in Marseille's history and a large court with a United Nations of plaques, reminding locals how their commerce comes from trade around the world.

The small ground-floor exhibit on the city's marine history

starts with an impressive portrait of Emperor Napoleon III (who called for the building's construction) and his wife. Sketches show the pomp surrounding its grand opening. The next room allows you to trace the growth of the city through charts of its harbor (€2, June–Sept Tue–Sun 10:00–18:00, Oct–May Tue–Sun 10:00–17:00, closed Mon, tel. 04 91 39 33 33).

For more history (including the remains of an old Roman ship found here), visit the History Museum in the Centre Bourse, a modern shopping center behind the Chamber of Commerce.

▲**Notre-Dame de la Garde**—Crowning Marseille's highest point, 500 feet above the harbor, is the city's landmark sight. This massive Romanesque-Byzantine basilica, built in the 1850s during the reign of Napoleon III, is a harmonious collection of domes, gold, and mosaics. The monumental statue of Mary and the Baby Jesus towers above everything (Jesus' wrist alone is 42 inches around). While the interior is elegant (daily 7:00–20:00), people come here mostly for the commanding city view. This hilltop has served as a lookout, as well as a place of worship, since ancient times.

To get to the church, you can hike 30 minutes from the harbor, catch a taxi (about €10), hop on bus #60 (€1.20, pay driver, runs from south side of port on cours Jean Ballard to church, 3/hr, 10 min, saves you a 30-min uphill hike), or ride the tourist train from the harborfront (see "Helpful Hints," above).

Château d'If—When King François I visited Marseille in the 16th century, he realized the potential strategic importance of a fort on the uninhabited island just outside the harbor. His château was finished in 1531. The impregnable fortress, which never saw battle, became a prison—handy for locking up Protestants during the Counter-Reformation. Among its illustrious inmates was José Faria, a spiritualist priest who was the idol of Paris and whom Alexandre Dumas immortalized in *The Count of Monte Cristo*. Since 1890, it's been open to the public. Tour boats take tourists to this French Alcatraz (round-trip-€8, 30-min trip, daily on the hour 9:00–17:00, departs from quai des Belges, tel. 04 91 59 01 00).

The **Islands of Frioul,** which offer a nature break from the big city with a few hiking paths and cafés, are another 15 minutes away (round-trip with Château d'If-€15, boats run daily on the half-hour 9:30–17:30).

SLEEPING

Stay in Marseille only if you want a gritty, urban experience. Hotel values and ambience are better 20 minutes away, in Cassis (see page 178).

$$ Hôtel Ibis Marseille Gare St. Charles**, with predictable comfort, is right at the train station—on the left as you exit (Db-€80,

Sleep Code

(€1 = about $1.20, country code: 33)
S = Single, **D** = Double/Twin, **T** = Triple, **Q** = Quad, **b** = bathroom, **s** = shower only, **no CC** = Credit Cards not accepted, **SE** = Speaks English, **NSE** = No English, ***** = French hotel rating system (0–4 stars). Unless otherwise noted, credit cards are accepted.

To help you sort easily through these listings, I've divided the rooms into three categories based on the price for a standard double room with bath:

    $$$ **Higher Priced**—Most rooms €85 or more.
    $$ **Moderately Priced**—Most rooms between €55–85.
    $ **Lower Priced**—Most rooms €55 or less.

extra bed-€7, elevator, Square Narvik, tel. 04 91 95 62 09, fax 04 91 50 68 42, www.ibishotel.com).

$$ Hôtel Kyriad**, a block off the port behind the TI, is a shade musty, but offers relative quiet and decent comfort at good rates (Db-€68–74, Tb-€84, elevator, 6 rue Beauvau, Metro Vieux Port, tel. 04 91 33 02 33, fax 04 91 33 21 34, kyriad.vieuxport@wanadoo.fr).

$ Hôtel Relax* is a funky, homey 22-room place with no traffic noise and a lobby any poodle would love. Half of the rooms overlook the square—worth requesting, as the back-side rooms can be gloomy (Db-€45–60 depending on size and plumbing, breakfast-€6, air-con, just 2 blocks off harbor on place de l'Opéra at 4 rue Corneille, tel. 04 91 33 15 87, fax 04 91 55 63 57).

EATING

For the best combination of trendiness, variety, and a fun people scene, consider eating in the new town on or near **quai de Rive Neuve** (about where the shuttle ferry drops people, halfway down the harbor on the left side as you look out to sea). Directly in front of the ferry landing, you'll find some characteristic bars and brasseries. The nearby place aux Huiles leads inland to the **cours d'Estienne d'Orves**—a gentrified Italian-style square lined with thriving outdoor restaurants that offer cuisine ranging from giant salads and fresh seafood to crêpes, Vietnamese dishes, and buffalo wings.

TRANSPORTATION CONNECTIONS

Marseille is well-served by TGV and local trains, and is the hub for many smaller stations in eastern Provence.

From Marseille by train to: Cassis (20/day, 20 min), **Aix-en-Provence Centre-Ville station** (18/day, 35 min), **Nice** (19/day, 2.75 hrs), **Arles** (20/day, 1 hr), **Avignon** (10/day, 70 min), **Paris** (hrly, 3 hrs).

Cassis

Cowering in the shadow of impossibly high cliffs, Cassis (kah-sees) is an unpretentious port town that offers travelers a sunny time-out from their busy vacation. Two hours away from the fray of the Côte d'Azur, Cassis is a poor man's St-Tropez. Outdoor cafés line the small port on three sides, where boaters clean their crafts as they chat up café clients. Cassis is popular with the French and close enough to Marseille to be busy on weekends and all summer. Come to Cassis to dine on true bouillabaisse, swim in the crystal-clear water, and explore its rocky *calanques* and fjord-like inlets.

ORIENTATION

The Massif du Puget mountain hovers over little Cassis, with hills spilling right down to the port. Dramatic and vertical Cap Canaille cliff rises from the southeast. The famous fjord-esque *calanques* hide along the coast, northwest of the port. Hotels, restaurants, and boats line the port on opposite sides.

Tourist Information: The TI sits in the middle of the port among the boats (July–Aug Mon–Fri 9:00–19:00, Sat–Sun 9:30–12:30 & 15:00–18:00; March–June and Sept–Oct Mon–Fri 9:30–12:30 & 14:00–18:00, Sat 10:00–12:00 & 14:00–17:00, Sun 10:00–12:00; Nov–Feb Mon–Sat 9:30–12:30 & 14:00–17:00, closed Sun; quai des Moulins, tel. 04 42 01 71 17, push 5 to talk to an agent). If going to Marseille, pick up a map here.

Arrival in Cassis

By Train: Cassis' hills forced the train station to be built two miles away. Most weekday trains are met by buses that will take you into town (€0.90, 10 min, not available on weekends), and taxis into town cost about €10 with baggage (taxis usually meet arriving trains; if not, call one at tel. 04 42 01 78 96).

By Car: The hills above Cassis make navigating here a challenge. Hotels are all signed, though the signs can be hard to follow. Hotel parking is very limited, and traffic is worse the closer you get to the port. Drivers are better off parking at one of the well-marked pay lots above the port.

Helpful Hints

Tourist Train: The little white *train touristique* is handy to use to connect the upper parking lots with the port and to get you closer to the *calanques*.

Launderette and Internet Access: To reach the combined launderette-Internet café, leave the port walking up rue Victor Hugo, then find 9 rue Autheman (daily 9:00–19:30, self-serve or full-serve, SE). They sell phone cards, too.

Taxi: Call 04 42 01 78 96.

Car Rental: Try Sarl M. H. (4 avenue Jules Ferry, tel. 04 42 01 70 63).

Bike and Scooter Rental: Call Carnoux Bikes at tel. 04 42 73 62 71.

Wine Bar and Shop: Le Chai Cassidain is friendly and well-stocked with area wines (4 blocks from port at 6 rue Séverin Icard, tel. 04 42 01 99 80).

Market Days: The market hops on Wednesdays and Fridays until 12:30 (a few blocks from port, on the streets around place de la Mairie).

SIGHTS

Beaches—Cassis' beaches are pebbly. The big beach behind the TI is sandier than others, though aqua-shoes still help. You can rent a mattress (€10/day) and paddleboats (€10/hr). Underwater springs just off the Cassis shore make the water clean, clear, and a bit cooler than other beaches.

▲La Route des Crêtes—If you have a car, or are willing to spring for a taxi (€35 for a good 45-min trip, 4 people per taxi), consider this enjoyable drive. Go straight up to the top of Cap Canaille and toward the next town, La Ciotat. Acrophobes should skip this narrow, twisty road, which provides numbingly high views over Cassis and the Mediterranean at every turn. From Cassis, follow signs to *La Ciotat/Toulon*, then *La Route des Crêtes*. The towns east of Cassis (La Ciotat, Bandol, etc.) do not merit a detour.

The *Calanques*

Calanques (kah-lahnk) are the narrow inlets created by the prickly extensions of cliffs that border the shore. Until you see the intimate beaches and exotic fjords of translucent blue water, it's hard to understand what all the excitement is about. You can hike or cruise by boat or kayak to many *calanques*, all of which are located along the 13 miles of coast between Cassis and Marseille. The TI has information on hiking and boating to the *calanques*. Bring water, sunscreen, and

Cassis

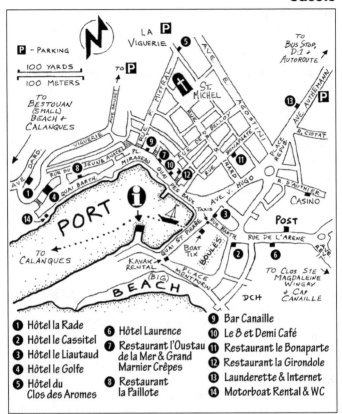

- ❶ Hôtel la Rade
- ❷ Hôtel le Cassitel
- ❸ Hôtel le Liautaud
- ❹ Hôtel le Golfe
- ❺ Hôtel du Clos des Aromes
- ❻ Hôtel Laurence
- ❼ Restaurant l'Oustau de la Mer & Grand Marnier Crêpes
- ❽ Restaurant la Paillote
- ❾ Bar Canaille
- ❿ Le 8 et Demi Café
- ⓫ Restaurant le Bonaparte
- ⓬ Restaurant la Girondole
- ⓭ Launderette & Internet
- ⓮ Motorboat Rental & WC

everything you need for the day, as there are no shops. Don't sleep in too late—the most popular *calanques* are closed by 11:00 in high season and on weekends to limit crowds (ask at TI).

Boats offer trips of various lengths (3 *calanques*-€11, 2/hr, 45 min; 5 *calanques*-€13, 3/day, 65 min; 8–10 *calanques*-€16–20, 1–3/day, 2 hrs; tel. 04 42 01 90 83). The three-*calanques* tour seems most popular. Tickets are sold (and boats depart) from a small booth on the TI side of the port.

Hardy souls can **hike** to three of the *calanques* (Port Miou, Port Pin, and d'En Vau)—though signs are few, shade is nonexistent, and maps lack detail (verify route as you go). For most, the best *calanque* by foot is Calanque Port Pin, about an hour from Cassis (30 min after the linear, boat-lined Calanque Port Miou). It's intimate and well-forested, with a small beach.

If you leave early and like to orienteer, the most spectacular *calanque* to hang out at is **Calanque d'En-Vau.** In high season,

Cassis History

Find a friendly bench in front of Hôtel le Golfe and read this quick town intro: Cassis was born more than 2,500 years ago (on the hill with the castle ruins, across the harbor). Ligurians,

Phoenicians, maybe Greeks, certainly Romans, and plenty of barbarians all found this spot to their liking. The castle tower dates from the eighth century, and the fortress walls from the 13th century—built to defend Cassis against barbarian sea-borne raids. The Michelin family recently sold the fortress, and the buyers plan to turn it into a luxury hotel. Cassis' planning commission might have other ideas.

In the 18th century, things got safer, and people moved their homes back to the waterfront. Since then, Cassis has made its living through fishing, quarrying its famous white stone, and producing its well-respected white wines (which pair well with the local seafood dishes).

Serious tourism arrived in the 1950s, but crowds are sparse by Riviera standards. While foreigners overwhelm nearby resorts, Cassis is popular mostly with the French, and still feels unspoiled. The town's protected status limits the crass development you see elsewhere on the coast. Its harbor is home to plenty of nice boats...but they're chump change compared to the glitzier harbors farther east.

The big cliff towering above the castle hill is Cap Canaille. Europe's highest maritime cliff, it drops 1,200 feet straight down. You can drive or taxi along the top for sensational views (see "La Route des Crêtes," below). You might want to return to this bench at sunset, when the Cap glows a deep red.

Walk to your right, then veer left along the short wall in front of the public WCs. The rocky shore behind you looks cut away just for sunbathers. But Cassis was once an important quarry, and stones were cut right out of this beach for easy transport to ships. The Statue of Liberty's base is made from this rock, and even today Cassis stone remains highly respected throughout the world...but now the quarrymen have been replaced by sunbathers.

access is strictly controlled, and this *calanque* is closed by about 11:00. From Cassis, hiking is the most reliable option. Unless you have rappelling skills, start with the inland route from Cassis, then drop down to the shoreline near the *calanque*, rather than take the challenging shoreline route the entire way (follow the TI map). There is a boat option, but it's not necessarily easier (2/hr, €15, less for one-way tickets). Boats can drop you on a cliff if the sea is calm (short jump), but it's a steep, treacherous hike down to the beach for inexperienced climbers, and an even more difficult hike back up—a bad idea for most. If you *really* want to do this, you can buy a one-way ticket and hike back to Cassis (take the inland route and avoid the more difficult hike up the cliff). Sea currents can make boat drop-off difficult—verify that you can actually get off at Calanque d'En-Vau before buying your ticket.

To cut 45 minutes off the hiking time to Calanque Port Pin and Calanque d'En-Vau, drive or ride the little white **tourist train** (Le Petit Train) to Calanque de Port Miou and walk from there (ask the driver to point you in the right direction).

To explore the *calanques* on your own, you can rent a **kayak** (1-person: €10/1 hr, €15/2 hrs, €25/half day; 2-person: €15/1 hr, €25/2 hrs, €40/half day) or a small **motorboat** (€85/half day, €125/day, €700 cash or credit-card imprint as deposit; rental boats a few steps away from Hôtel le Golfe).

SLEEPING

Cassis hotels are a better value than those on the Côte d'Azur. Many close from November to March, and most come with late-night noise on weekends and in summer. Book early for sea views and bring earplugs. Most hotels have a few invaluable parking spots that you can reserve (do this when booking your room.) The lower rates listed are from mid-September to mid-June.

$$$ Hôtel la Rade*** lies on a busy road above the northwest corner of the port, with great views from poolside chairs. It rents small but adequate rooms with air-conditioning (Db-€105–115, apartments-€170–180, Internet access, route des Calanques, 1 avenue de Dardanelles, tel. 04 42 01 02 97, fax 04 42 01 01 32, www.hotel-cassis.com, larade@hotel-cassis.com, SE).

$$ Hôtel Cassitel** is kinda cute, and located near the TI on the harbor over a sprawling café. The harbor-view rooms come with more night noise (standard Db-€56, large Db-€90, extra bed-€13, garage-€12/day, free Internet access, place Clémenceau, tel. 04 42 01 83 44, fax 04 42 01 96 31, www.hotel-cassis.com, cassitel@hotel-cassis.com, SE).

$$ Hôtel le Liautaud** is on the port near the TI. Noise can be a problem, given its perfectly dead-center location, but its uninspired,

Sleep Code

(€1 = about $1.20, country code: 33)
S = Single, **D** = Double/Twin, **T** = Triple, **Q** = Quad, **b** = bathroom, **s** = shower only, **no CC** = Credit Cards not accepted, **SE** = Speaks English, **NSE** = No English, * = French hotel rating system (0–4 stars). Unless otherwise noted, credit cards are accepted.

To help you sort easily through these listings, I've divided the rooms into three categories based on the price for a standard double room with bath:

$$$ **Higher Priced**—Most rooms €85 or more.
$$ **Moderately Priced**—Most rooms between €55–85.
$ **Lower Priced**—Most rooms €55 or less.

bare-bones-modern rooms are mercifully air-conditioned (Db-€62–72, Tb-€84, 2 rue Victor Hugo, tel. 04 42 01 75 37, fax 04 42 01 12 08, SE).

$$ Hôtel le Golfe**, over a café, has the best views of the port. Half of its cute little blue-and-yellow rooms come with brilliant views and small balconies; the others come with air-conditioning; and all come with friendly English-speaking Michele at the desk (Db with view and noise-€74–89, Db without view and less noise-€64, extra bed-€16, 2 extra beds-€23, 3 parking spaces-€3/day, 3 place Grand Carnot, tel. 04 42 01 00 21, fax 04 42 01 92 08).

$$ Hôtel du Clos des Arômes** is for those who don't need to be right on the port and prefer a quieter, simpler retreat. This place has the most appealing ambience of the hotels I list. *Très provençal,* it comes with a terrific courtyard terrace (Sb-€48, standard Db-€63, bigger Db-€75, Tb or Qb-€85, near Parking Viguerie at 10 rue Abbé Paul Mouton, tel. 04 42 01 71 84, fax 04 42 01 31 76).

$ Hôtel Laurence** offers budget beds, in bland, tight, but clean and air-conditioned rooms. Some come with decks and views (Db-€51, Db with terrace-€79, no CC, 2 blocks off the port beyond Hôtel Cassitel at 8 rue de l'Arène, tel. 04 42 01 88 78, fax 04 42 01 81 04, closed in winter).

EATING

Eat on the port. Shop the lineup of tempting restaurants, consider the recommended places, and then decide for yourself. You can have a simple crêpe or go all-out for bouillabaisse with the same great view. Picnickers can enjoy a "beggars' banquet" at the benches at Hôtel le Golfe or on the beach (small grocery stores open until 19:00).

L'Oustau de la Mer is a good choice, with an ideal location, a loyal following, and fair prices (*menus* from €21, closed Thu, 20 quai des Baux, tel. 04 42 01 78 22).

La Paillote is good if you're in the mood for seafood or bouillabaisse (*menus* from €18, closed Sun–Mon, quai J. J. Barthélémy, tel. 04 42 01 72 14).

Bar Canaille has fabulously fresh seafood platters under bright-yellow awnings (allow €30, closed Wed, 22 quai des Baux, tel. 04 42 01 72 36).

Le Bonaparte is off the harbor and cheaper, with red-and-blue tablecloths and a few outdoor tables (closed Sun–Mon, 14 rue du Général Bonaparte, tel. 04 42 01 80 84).

La Girondole is a good and welcoming place for inexpensive pizza and salads. It's a block off the port and popular with locals (daily in summer, otherwise closed Tue, 1 rue Thérèse Rastit, tel. 04 42 01 13 39).

Le 8 et Demi serves delicious Italian gelato on plastic tables with exceptional portside views (open daily, 8 quai des Baux).

The harborfront **Grand Marnier crêpe stand** serves dessert crêpes, ideal for strollers.

TRANSPORTATION CONNECTIONS

While the train station is two miles from the port, shuttle buses meet most trains, and taxis are reasonable (about €10 into the center). All destinations below require a transfer in Marseille.

From Cassis by train to: Marseille (20/day, 20 min), **Aix-en-Provence** (12/day, 1.5 hrs), **Arles** (7/day, 2 hrs), **Avignon** (7/day, 2 hrs), **Nice** (7/day, 3 hrs, transfer in Toulon or Marseille), **Paris** (7/day, 4 hrs).

Aix-en-Provence

Aix—rhymes with "sex"—is famous for its beautiful women and ability to embrace the good life. It was that way when the French king made the town his administrative capital of Provence, and it's that way today. For a tourist, Aix (pronounced "X") is delightfully free of any obligatory turnstiles. And there's not a single ancient sight to see. It's simply a wealthy town filled with 137,000 people—most of whom, it seems, know how to live well and look good. Aix's 40,000 students give the city a youthful energy.

ORIENTATION

Aix-en-Provence can be seen in an hour's stroll from the TI or station. Cours Mirabeau (the grand central boulevard) divides the stately (boring) Mazarin Quarter from the lively and *très chic* old town. In the old town, several squares (hopping with markets several days a week—see "Helpful Hints," below) are laced together by fine pedestrian shopping lanes that lead to the cathedral.

Tourist Information: The TI anchors the west end of cours Mirabeau at the Rotonde traffic circle. You'll feel like you're taking out a loan here, with individual desks and chairs for each information agent. Get a city map and the walking-tour brochure *In the Footsteps of Cézanne.* Ask about English walking tours (€8, 2–3 times/week), concerts, and special events (TI open daily Mon–Sat 8:30–19:00, Sun 10:00–13:00 & 14:00–18:00, 2 place du Général de Gaulle, tel. 04 42 16 11 61).

Arrival in Aix-en-Provence

By Train: Aix-en-Provence has two train stations—suburban TGV and Centre-Ville. A *navette* bus connects the two (2/hr, 15 min). There is no baggage check anywhere. From the Centre-Ville station, it's a breezy 10-minute stroll to the TI and pedestrian area (walk straight up avenue Victor Hugo, turn left at first intersection—still on Victor Hugo, TI is on the left when you reach traffic circle).

By Car: Follow signs to *Centre-Ville,* then look for Parking Rotonde. If you miss it, follow *Gare Routière* (bus station), and park there.

Helpful Hints

Markets: Aix bubbles over with photogenic open-air morning markets in several of its squares: Richelme (produce daily), Palace of Justice (flea market Tue, Thu, and Sat), and L'Hôtel de Ville (flower market Tue, Thu, and Sat, book market on Sun).

Internet: Try Planet Web (Mon–Sat 9:30–23:00, Sun 13:30–23:00, 20 rue Victor Leydet, tel. 04 42 26 83 01).

Local Guide: Caroline Bernard speaks great English and enjoys teaching visitors about the wonders of her city and region (€50/2 hrs, €80/day, bernardcaro@aol.com, best to contact her through TI).

Launderette: It's at 11 rue des Bernadines (daily 8:00–20:00).

Taxi: Call tel. 04 42 27 71 11 or 06 08 00 13 13.

Car Rental: Hertz and National are on avenue Victor Hugo, across from the Centre-Ville station (Hertz at #43, tel. 04 42 27 91 32; National at #42, tel. 04 42 93 07 85).

English Books: New and used books are available at the helpful Paradox bookshop, on the quiet side of Aix (Mon–Sat

10:00–12:30 & 14:00–18:30, closed Sun, 15 rue du 4 Septembre, tel. 04 42 26 47 99).

Dark Sunglasses: You may want to pick up a pair of especially dark glasses to be more discreet when appreciating the beautiful people of Aix.

SIGHTS

I've listed these streets, squares, and sights in the order of a handy, lazy orientation stroll.

Cours Mirabeau—This Champs-Elysées of Provence divides the old town and the Mazarin Quarter. The grand boulevard is kicked off by La Rotonde fountain (1860, gracing a traffic circle in front of the TI). Designed for the rich and famous to strut their fancy stuff, cours Mirabeau survives much as it was: a single lane for traffic and a very wide pedestrian promenade, shaded by plane trees (see sidebar on page 190) and lined by 17th- and 18th-century mansions (winter homes of the nobility). The higgledy-piggledy old town lined the left side of the boulevard, where it displayed its crustier side of life.

The street follows a plan based on fours: 440 meters long, 44 meters wide, plane trees (originally elms) four meters apart, and decorated by four fountains. The "mossy fountain"—its original little angels covered by 200 years of neglect—trickles with water from the thermal spa.

Cours Mirabeau was designed for showing off. Today, it remains a place for *tendance* (trendiness)—or even *hyper-tendance*. Grab a seat in an upscale café (such as Café le Grillon at #49) and observe.

When you're ready, plunge into the...

Mazarin Quarter (Quartier Mazarin)—Built in a grid plan during the reign of Louis XIV, the Mazarin Quarter remains an elegant residential neighborhood—although each of its mansions now houses several families rather than just one. Study the quarter's Baroque and classical architecture (17th and 18th centuries) as you work your way to the delightful little place des Quatre Dauphins, which marks the center of the Mazarin Quarter.

After a quick nip through the Mazarin Quarter, cross cours Mirabeau and spend the rest of your time in the much livelier...

Old Town—Peaceful pedestrian streets thrive quietly with strolling beauties and romantic street musicians. This is *the* place in Aix for shopping.

Find the recommended **Aux Deux Garçons** (53 cours Mirabeau; see "Eating," below). This café, once frequented by Paul Cézanne, is now popular with the local mafia—don't take photos. Spring for a meal here, or at least a drink, and check out the beautiful interior.

Aix History

Aix was founded in about 120 B.C. as a Roman military camp on the site of a thermal hot spring. The Romans' mission: to defend the Greek merchants of Marseilles against the local Celts. Strategically situated Aix was the first Roman base outside of Italy—the first foreign holding of what would become a vast empire. (The region's name—Provence—comes from its status as the first Roman province.) But Rome eventually fell, and the barbarians destroyed the city in the fourth century. Through the Dark Ages, Aix's Roman buildings were nibbled to nothing by people needing the pre-cut stone. No buildings from Roman Aix survive.

Aix was of no importance through the Middle Ages. Because the area was once owned by Barcelona, Provence has the same colors as Catalunya: gold and red. In 1481, the Count of Provence died. He was hairless (according to my guide). Without a hair, Provence was gobbled up by France. When Aix was made

the district's administrative center, noble French families moved in, kicking off the city's beautiful age (belle époque). They built about 200 *hôtels particuliers* (private mansions)—many of which survive today, giving Aix its classy appearance. As you wander around the town, look up, peek in, and notice the stately architecture.

Aix thrived thanks to its aristocratic population. But when the Revolution made being rich dangerous, Aix's aristocracy and clergy fled. Aix entered the next stage of its history as the "Sleeping Beauty city." Later in the 19th century, the town woke up and resumed its pretentious ways. In Aix, the custom of rich people being bobbed along in sedan chairs survived longer than anywhere else in France. After the Revolution, you couldn't have servants do it—but you could hire pallbearers in their off-hours to give you a lift. If ostentatious were a verb...it happened in Aix.

Aix-en-Provence

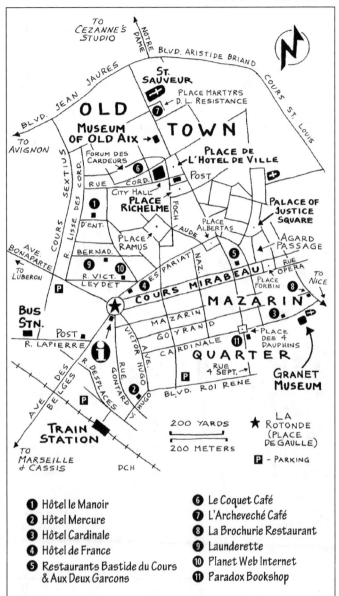

TO CEZANNE'S STUDIO

BLVD. ARISTIDE BRIAND

NOTRE DAME

BLVD. JEAN JAURES

ST. SAUVEUR

PLACE MARTYRS D. L. RESISTANCE

OLD TOWN

COURS ST. LOUIS

TO AVIGNON

MUSEUM OF OLD AIX →

FORUM DES CARDEURS

PLACE DE L'HÔTEL DE VILLE

COURS SEXTIUS

R. LISSE DES CORD.

RUE CORD.

POST

City Hall

PLACE RICHELME

PALACE OF JUSTICE SQUARE

D'ENT.

FOCH

PLACE ALBERTAS

AGARD PASSAGE

AVE. BONAPARTE

BERNAD.

R. VICT. LEYDET

PLACE RAMUS

AUDE

ESPARIAT

NAN

RUE OPERA

TO LUBERON

COURS MIRABEAU

PLACE FORBIN

TO NICE

BUS STN.

MAZARIN

POST

R. LAPIERRE

VICTOR HUGO

AVE.

MAZARIN

GOYRAND

CARDINALE

PLACE DES 4 DAUPHINS

QUARTER

TRAIN STATION

AVE. DES BELGES

R. DESPLACES

RUE GONTARD

HUGO J.

RUE 4 SEPT. →

BLVD. ROI RENE

GRANET MUSEUM

TO MARSEILLE & CASSIS

DCH

200 YARDS

200 METERS

★ LA ROTONDE (PLACE DE GAULLE)

P – PARKING

① Hôtel le Manoir
② Hôtel Mercure
③ Hôtel Cardinale
④ Hôtel de France
⑤ Restaurants Bastide du Cours & Aux Deux Garcons

⑥ Le Coquet Café
⑦ L'Archeveché Café
⑧ La Brochurie Restaurant
⑨ Launderette
⑩ Planet Web Internet
⑪ Paradox Bookshop

Paul Cézanne Sights

Post-Impressionist artist Paul Cézanne (1839–1906) loved Aix. He studied law at the university (opposite the cathedral) and produced most of his paintings in and around Aix—even though this conservative town didn't understand him or his art. Now, as the 100th anniversary of his death approaches (2006), the city is milking anything remotely related to his years here. While you'll find no actual Cézanne artwork in Aix, fans of the artist will want to pick up the *In the Footsteps of Cézanne* self-guided-tour flier at the TI and follow the bronze pavement markers around town.

Cézanne's **last studio** (Atelier Cézanne)—preserved as it was when he died—is open to the public. While there is no art here, his tools and personal belongings make it interesting (€4, daily 10:00–12:00 & 14:30–18:00, until 17:00 in winter, 2 miles from TI at 9 avenue Cézanne, tel. 04 42 21 06 53).

The **Granet Museum (Musée Granet),** Aix's top art gallery, is closed until 2006—when it opens to celebrate the Cézanne centenary.

Leave cours Mirabeau to the left down the tiny passage Agard, 10 steps past Aux Deux Garçons (see map on page 188). You'll reach

the **Palace of Justice Square,** which hosts a bustling flea market (Tue, Thu, and Sat mornings). Leave this square left along the first street you crossed entering it (rue Marius Reinaud), pass the peaceful courtyard square of place d'Albertas, then turn right on rue Aude and make your way to...
Richelme Square (Place Richelme)—This square hosts a lively market (daily 7:00–13:00). It's a quintessential Provençal scene—classic architecture, plane trees, farmers selling local produce, and a guy in the cheese stall who looks just like Paul Cézanne (or Jerry Garcia, if that's more your style).

A few blocks up is the stately...
L'Hôtel de Ville Square (Place de l'Hôtel de Ville)—This square, also known as place de la Mairie, is marked by a Roman column. Stand with your back to the column and face the Hôtel de Ville. The center niche of this 17th-century City Hall once featured a bust of Louis XIV. But since the Revolution, it's filled with Marianne (the Lady of the Republic). To the left, the pediment of the 18th-century Corn Exchange has a fine statue of figures representing the two rivers of Provence: old man Rhône and the Durance. While the Durance River floods frequently (here depicted overflowing its frame), it also brings fertility to the fields (hence the cornucopia). The 16th-century

Plane Trees

Stately old plane trees line roads and provide canopies of shade for town squares all over southern France. These trees are a part of the local scene.

The plane tree is a hybrid between the Asian and American sycamores—created accidentally in a 16th-century Oxford botanical garden. The result was the perfect city tree: fast-growing, resistant to urban pollution, and hearty (it can survive with little water and lousy soil). The plane tree was imported to southern France in the 19th century to replace the traditional elm trees. Napoleon planted them along roads to give his soldiers shade for their long marches. Plane trees were used to leaf up grand boulevards as towns throughout France—including Aix—built their Champs-Elysées wanna-bes.

bell tower to your right is built in part with stones scavenged from ancient Roman buildings. All of this history aside, the square will be a favorite part of your Aix experience for its colorful morning markets: flowers (Tue, Thu, and Sat) and old books (Sun).

Stroll under the bell tower and up rue Gaston de Saporta, to...

Museum of Old Aix (Musée du Vieil Aix)—This museum fills a 17th-century mansion with a scant collection of artifacts. The building interior itself is of most interest. Pop in for a look at the grand staircase and fancy ceilings. The exhibits include lots of *santons*—painted clay figurines popular in old-time manger scenes (€4, Tue–Sun 10:00–12:00 & 14:30–18:00, closed Mon, 17 rue Gaston de Saporta, tel. 04 42 21 43 55).

A bit farther on is the...

Cathedral of the Holy Savior (Saint-Sauveur)—This church was built atop the Roman forum. Its interior is a parade of architectural styles. The small baptistery (immediately on right as you enter) has a Roman font and six ancient columns below a Renaissance cupola. Then you'll see a Romanesque aisle (12th century), a Gothic nave (13–15th centuries), and a Baroque aisle (17th century). To top things off, notice the two organs in the Gothic nave: One works, but the other is a prop, added for looks...an appropriately symmetrical neoclassical touch (18th century).

Sleep Code

(€1 = about $1.20, country code: 33)
S = Single, **D** = Double/Twin, **T** = Triple, **Q** = Quad, **b** = bathroom, **s** = shower only, **no CC** = Credit Cards not accepted, **SE** = Speaks English, **NSE** = No English, * = French hotel rating system (0–4 stars). Unless otherwise noted, credit cards are accepted.

To help you sort easily through these listings, I've divided the rooms into three categories based on the price for a standard double room with bath:

$$$ **Higher Priced**—Most rooms €85 or more.
$$ **Moderately Priced**—Most rooms between €55–85.
$ **Lower Priced**—Most rooms €55 or less.

SLEEPING

Hotel rooms, starting at about €50, are surprisingly reasonable in this stylish city. Reserve ahead for the first two hotels, particularly on weekends. Stars have little meaning in this town.

$$$ Hôtel Mercure Paul Cézanne***, a block up from the Centre-Ville train station, has an Old World lobby and New World rooms with all the comforts (standard Db-€120, deluxe Db-€135, luxury Db-€165, elevator, 40 avenue Victor Hugo, tel. 04 42 91 11 11, fax 04 42 91 11 10, mercure.paulcezanne@free.fr).

$$ Hôtel le Manoir*** is a find—simple, peaceful, and central, built on the heavy arches of a medieval monastery. Most of its 40 smallish rooms hang over a large courtyard, the decor is strictly traditional, and the air is pin-drop quiet (small Db-€55, standard Db-€68–74, big Db-€84, Tb-€74–84, elevator; limited free parking on first-come, first-served basis; 8 rue d'Entrecasteaux, tel. 04 42 26 27 20, fax 04 42 27 17 97, www.hotelmanoir.com, infos @hotelmanoir.com).

$$ Hôtel Cardinale** is a great value on Aix's classy side, across cours Mirabeau from the pedestrian zone. It's a shy, rose-colored place with 29 traditionally furnished and plush rooms over a small, feminine lobby (Sb-€56, Db-€66, Db suite-€80–100, elevator, 24 rue Cardinale, tel. 04 42 38 32 30, fax 04 42 26 39 05, helpful Madame Bernhard SE).

$$ Hôtel de France** couldn't be more central, in the beautiful pedestrian zone near the TI. The place is frumpy, with squishy beds, and could use some upgrading—but that keeps the prices low. Rooms on the noisier street side are bigger than on the courtyard side (Db-€55–64, bigger Db-€64–72, elevator, 63 rue Espariat, tel. 04 42 27 90 15, fax 04 42 26 11 47, hoteldefrance-aix@wanadoo.fr).

EATING

If you're interested in a delicious view more than delicious food, eat with style on cours Mirabeau. If you need to see and be seen, *the* place has always been **Aux Deux Garçons,** a vintage brasserie with waiters in aprons, a magnificent interior, and well-positioned outdoor tables with properly placed silverware on white tablecloths (salads-€11, *plats*-€13, *menus* from €29, open daily, 53 cours Mirabeau, tel. 04 42 26 00 51). Nearby, **Bastide du Cours** offers perhaps the best value and service on le cours Mirabeau (*plats*-€14, 45 cours Mirabeau, tel. 04 42 26 55 41).

Aix's many squares provide good opportunities to dine affordably with ambience. Try the lineup of places just off L'Hôtel de Ville Square on forum des Cardeurs. **Le Coquet** is good for basic café fare and serious people-watching (open daily, 2 forum des Cardeurs, tel. 04 42 23 46 21). My favorite square for dining is place des Martyrs de la Resistance, where two cafés face each other offering similar values; **L'Archeveché** has a wider selection (open Mon–Sat for lunch and dinner, Sun for lunch only, tel. 04 42 21 43 57).

For Provençal cuisine with an Italian and seafood bias, head for the quiet side (Mazarin Quarter) and try the pleasing **La Brochurie.** Options include meats grilled over a wood fire, a good €17 Provençal *menu,* and a €25 seafood *menu* (closed Sun, 5 rue Fernand Dol, tel. 04 42 38 33 21).

TRANSPORTATION CONNECTIONS

Remember, Aix has both a TGV station and a Centre-Ville station (see "Arrival in Aix-en-Provence," above). In some cases, destinations are served from both stations. I've listed the station with the best connection.

By train from Aix's Centre-Ville Station to: Marseille (18/day, 35 min), **Cassis** (12/day, 1.5 hrs, transfer in Marseille), **Arles** (10/day, 2 hrs, transfer at least once—in Marseille).

By train from Aix's TGV Station to: Avignon TGV (10/day, 75 min), **Nice** (10/day, 3.5 hrs, usually change in Marseille), **Paris** (14/day, 3 hrs, may require transfer in Lyon).

THE FRENCH RIVIERA
(La Côte d'Azur)

A hundred years ago, celebrities from London to Moscow flocked to the French Riviera to socialize, gamble, and escape their dreary weather. Belle époque resorts now also cater to budget vacationers at France's most sought-after, fun-in-the-sun destination. This scenic strip is speckled with intriguing museums and countless sun-worshippers. The region got its nickname from turn-of-the-20th-century vacationing Brits, who simply extended the Italian Riviera west to France. But the region—which runs from St-Tropez to the Italian border—is *La Côte d'Azur* to the French. All of my French Riviera destinations are on the sea, except for a few hill towns and the Gorges du Verdon.

This sunny sliver of land has been inhabited for more than 3,000 years. Ligurians were first, then Greeks, then Romans—who, as usual, had the greatest impact. After the fall of Rome, Nice became an important city in the Kingdom of Provence (along with Marseille and Arles). In the 14th century, Nice's leaders voted to throw their beach towel in with the Duke of Savoy's mountainous kingdom (also including several regions of northern Italy), which would later evolve into the Kingdom of Sardinia. It was not until 1860 that Nice (and Savoy) became a part of France—the result of a city-wide vote made possible by Napoleon III and the King of Sardinia.

Nice has world-class museums, a grand beachfront promenade, a seductive old town, and all the drawbacks of a major city (traffic, crime, pollution, and so on). But the day-trip possibilities are easy and exciting: Monte Carlo welcomes everyone with its cash registers open; Antibes has a romantic port and silky sand beaches; and gentle Cannes is the Riviera's self-appointed queen, with an elegant veneer hiding...very little. Yacht-crazy St-Tropez swims alone an hour west (halfway to Cassis and Marseille). The Riviera's overlooked interior offers travelers a world apart, with

The French Riviera

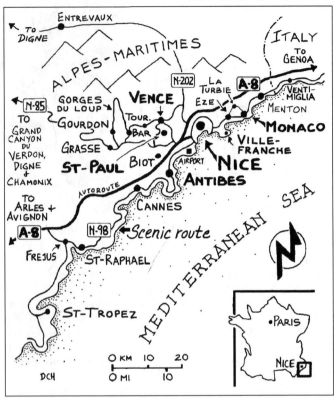

cliff-hanging villages, impossibly steep canyons, and alpine scenery—a refreshing alternative to the beach scene.

Choose a Home Base

My favorite home bases are Nice, Antibes, and Villefranche-sur-Mer.

Nice is the region's capital and France's fifth-largest city. With convenient train and bus connections to most regional sights, this is the most practical base for train travelers. Urban Nice also has a full palette of museums, a beach scene that rocks, the best selection of hotels in all price ranges, and good nightlife options. A car is a headache in Nice, though it's easily stored at one of the many parking garages.

Nearby **Antibes** is smaller, with a bustling center, the best sandy beaches I found, good walking trails, and the Picasso Museum. It has frequent train service to Nice and Monaco, and it's easy for drivers.

Villefranche-sur-Mer is the romantic's choice, with a serene setting and small-town warmth. It has finely-ground pebble beaches, good public transportation to Nice and Monaco, easy parking, and hotels in most price ranges.

Planning Your Time

Ideally, allow two days for Nice itself, a day for Antibes and Cannes, and a day for Monaco and the Corniches. With one more day, visit Italian-esque Villefranche-sur-Mer and lovely Cap Ferrat. Consider using two Riviera bases, and enjoy each for at least two nights— Villefranche-sur-Mer pairs well with Antibes or Nice. And if you must do St-Tropez, visit it when traveling to or from destinations farther west (like Cassis, Aix-en-Provence, and Arles); avoid it on weekend afternoons and all summer.

Monaco has a unique energy at night, and Antibes is best during the day (good beaches and hiking, Picasso Museum). Hill-town and nature lovers should add a night or two inland, to explore the charming hill-capping hamlets near Vence and the Gorges du Verdon. (If you're short on time, you may do better exploring the hill towns of Provence.)

Priorities: Depending on the amount of time you have in the Riviera, spend it this way:

3 days:	Nice, Antibes, and Monaco
5 days, add:	Villefranche-sur-Mer, Cap Ferrat, and hill towns near Vence
7 days, add:	Gorges du Verdon and St-Tropez

Helpful Hints

Museum Pass: The **Riviera Carte Musées pass,** a good value only for serious museum-goers, includes admission to many major Riviera museums such as Nice's Chagall and Matisse museums, Antibes' Picasso Museum and Fort Carré, La Trophée des Alpes, the International Museum of Perfume in Grasse, and the Exotic Gardens in Eze-le-Village. (It does not include Fondation Maeght in St-Paul-de-Vence, the villas between Nice and Monaco, or Monaco sights.) This pass will save you money if you're planning to visit more than two museums in a day, or several museums over a few days (€10/1 day, €17/3 days, €27/7 days, buy at any participating sight).

Events: The Riviera is famous for staging major events. Unless you're actually taking part in the festivities, these events give you only room shortages and traffic jams. Here are the three biggies in 2005: Nice Carnival (Feb 11–27), Grand Prix of Monaco (May 19–22), and Festival de Cannes, better known as the Cannes Film Festival (May 11–22).

Getting Around the Riviera

By Train and Bus: Trains and buses do a good job of connecting places along the coast, though service to inland hill towns varies greatly. The TGV stops in Cannes and Antibes as well as in Nice and Marseille. Nice is well-connected to most sights on the Riviera (see "Getting Around the Riviera" in the Nice chapter). While trains are usually faster, buses can be cheaper and more frequent to destinations near Nice. St-Tropez is remote and requires a bus or boat connection. Details are provided under each destination's "Transportation Connections" section.

By Car: To sample the Riviera's best scenery, drivers should scour the three Corniches between Nice and Monaco; the coastal road between Cannes and St-Tropez; my recommended hill towns; and the Gorges drive linking Vence, the Gorges du Loup, and the Gorges du Verdon. Skip the coastal section between St-Tropez, Hyères, and Marseille. Even if you have a car, trains and buses can be more convenient for waterfront destinations near Nice.

The Riviera's Art Scene

The list of artists who have painted the Riviera reads like a Who's Who of 20th-Century Art. Pierre-Auguste Renoir, Henri Matisse, Marc Chagall, Georges Braque, Raoul Dufy, Fernand Léger, and Pablo Picasso all lived and worked here—and raved about the region's wonderful light. Their simple, semi-abstract, and—most importantly—colorful works reflect the Riviera. You'll experience the same landscapes they painted in this bright, sun-drenched region, punctuated with views of the "azure sea." Try to imagine the Riviera with a fraction of the people and development you see today.

But the artists were mostly drawn to the uncomplicated lifestyle of fishermen and farmers that has reigned here since time began. As the artists grew older, they retired in the sun, turned their backs on modern art's "isms," and painted with the wide-eyed wonder of children, using bright primary colors, basic outlines, and simple subjects.

A terrific concentration of well-organized modern- and contemporary-art museums (many described in this book) litter the Riviera, allowing art lovers to appreciate these artists' works while immersed in the same sun and culture that inspired them. Many of the museums were designed to blend the art with the surrounding views, gardens, and fountains, thus highlighting that modern art is not only stimulating, but sometimes simply beautiful.

Entire books have been written about the modern-art galleries

Top Art Museums and Sights of the Riviera

Chagall Museum (Nice)
Picasso Museum (Antibes)
Matisse Museum (Nice)
Fondation Maeght (St-Paul-de-Vence)
Museum of the Annonciade (St-Tropez)
Chapel of the Rosary (Vence)
Modern and Contemporary Art Museum (Nice)
Fine Arts Museum (Nice)

of the Riviera. If you're a modern-art fan, do some study before your visit to be sure you know about that far-out museum of your dreams. Even those who aren't usually turned on by modern art should take the opportunity to appreciate Picasso in Antibes, and Chagall and Matisse in Nice.

The Riviera's Cuisine Scene

The Riviera adds a Mediterranean flair to the food of Provence. While many of the same dishes served in Provence are available throughout the Riviera (see "Provence's Cuisine Scene," page 49), you should celebrate the differences and look for anything Italian or from the sea. The proximity to the water and historic ties to Italy are clear in this region's dishes.

La salade niçoise (nee-swahz) is where most Riviera meals start. A true specialty from Nice, there are many versions, though most include a base of green salad topped with green beans, boiled potatoes (sometimes rice), tomatoes (sometimes corn), anchovies, olives, hard-boiled eggs, and lots of tuna. Every café and restaurant adds its own twist to this filling dish that goes down well on sultry days.

For lunch on the go, look for a *pan bagnat* (like a *salade niçoise* stuffed into a hollowed-out soft roll). Other tasty bread treats include *pissaladière* (bread dough topped with onions, olives, and anchovies), *fougasse* (a spindly, lace-like bread sometimes flavored with nuts, herbs, olives, or ham), and *socca* (a thin chickpea crêpe, seasoned with pepper and olive oil and often served in a paper cone by street vendors).

Ravioli and potato gnocchi, first made in Nice, are found on menus everywhere (ravioli can be stuffed with a variety of foods, but it's best with seafood). Thin-crust pizza and *pâtes fraîches* (fresh pasta) are generally a good value throughout the Riviera.

Bouillabaisse is the Riviera's most famous dish; look for it in any seafront village or city. It's a spicy fish stew based on recipes handed down from sailors in Marseille. It must contain at least four types of fresh fish, though most have five to 12 kinds. A true bouil-labaisse never has shellfish. The fish is cooked in a tomato-based stock and flavored with saffron (and sometimes anise and orange). The fish is separated from the stock before serving. The flavor of the stock is then heightened by the addition of toasted croutons and a dollop of *rouille* sauce (a thickened reddish mayonnaise heady with garlic and spicy peppers). This dish often requires a minimum order of two to justify its considerable preparation time, so beware of sticker shock, and allow €35–40.

Those on a budget can enjoy other seafood soups and stews. Less pricey but equally good is the local *soupe de poisson* (fish soup). It's flavored like bouillabaisse, with anise and orange, and served with croutons and *rouille* sauce. For a less colorful but still tasty soup, look for *bourride,* a creamy fish soup thickened with an aioli garlic sauce instead of the red *rouille;* or *baudroie,* a fishy soup cooked with vegetables and garlic.

The Riviera specializes in all sorts of fish and shellfish. Look for *"fruits de mer"* or platters of seafood (including tiny shellfish, from which you get the edible part only by sucking really hard), herb-infused mussels, stuffed sardines, squid (slowly simmered with toma-toes and herbs), and tuna *(thon).* The popular *loup flambé au fenouil* is grilled sea bass, flavored with fennel and torched with *pastis* prior to serving.

Cheese and dessert dishes of the Riviera are indistinguishable from those in Provence. Refer to "Provence's Cuisine Scene" (page 49) for suggestions.

Unfortunately, memorable restaurants that showcase the Riviera's cuisine are more difficult to find than in neighboring Provence. Because most visitors come more for the sun than the food, and because the clientele is predominantly international, many restaurants aim for the middle and are hard to tell apart. When dining on the Riviera, I look for views and ambience more than top-quality cuisine.

Wines of the Riviera

Do as everyone else does: Drink wines from Provence. *Bandol* (red) and *cassis* (white) are popular, and from a region nearly on the Riviera. The only wines made in the Riviera are Bellet rosé and white, the latter often found in fish-shaped bottles. For more on Provençal wine, see page 51.

NICE

Nice (sounds like niece), with its spectacular Alps-to-Mediterranean surroundings, eternally entertaining seafront promenade, and fine museums, is an enjoyable big-city highlight of the Riviera. In its traffic-free old city, Italian and French flavors mix to create a spicy Mediterranean dressing. Nice may be nice, but it's hot and jammed in July and August—reserve ahead and get a room with air-conditioning *(une chambre avec climatisation)*. Everything you'll want to see in Nice is walkable or a short bus ride away.

ORIENTATION

Most sights and hotels recommended in this book are near avenue Jean Médecin, between the train station and the beach. It's a 20-minute walk from the train station to the beach (or a €10 taxi ride), and a 20-minute walk along the promenade from the fancy Hôtel Negresco to the heart of Old Nice.

You'll no doubt experience the inconvenience of construction in Nice. Three sleek tramway lines are being built (including one that will run along the promenade des Anglais). It's a huge project, and the first line won't open until 2006 at best. Be ready for traffic re-routes and detours in many places.

Tourist Information

Nice's helpful TI has three locations: at the **airport** (mid-June–mid-Sept daily 8:00–21:00, mid-Sept–mid-June closed Sun); next to the **train station** (mid-June–mid-Sept Mon–Sat 8:00–20:00, Sun 9:00–19:00; mid-Sept–mid-June Mon–Sat 8:00–19:00, Sun 9:00–18:00); and facing the **beach** at 5 promenade des Anglais (mid-Sept–mid-June Mon–Sat 9:00–18:00, closed Sun; mid-June–mid-Sept Mon–Sat 8:00–20:00, Sun 9:00–19:00; tel. 08 92 70 74 07 costs

€0.34/min, www.nicetourisme.com). Pick up the free Nice map (which lists all the sights, with hours and bus lines), the extensive *Practical Guide to Nice*, and information on regional day trips (such as city maps).

Art-lovers should consider buying a **museum pass** for sights in Nice or throughout the Riviera (sold at any participating sight). The Riviera Carte Musées pass covers many regional sights, including four museums in Nice (Chagall, Matisse, Fine Arts, and Modern and Contemporary Art; €10/1 day, €17/3 days, €27/7 days; for more information, see page 195). A Nice-only museum pass, Carte Passe-Musées 7 Jours, is also available (€6/7 days, does not include Chagall Museum).

Arrival in Nice

By Train: All trains stop at Nice's one main station (Nice-Ville, baggage check available but closes at 17:45 and all day Sun and holidays). Avoid the suburban stations, and never leave your bags unattended. The TI is next door (to the left as you exit the station), car rental is to the right, and taxis are in front. To reach most of my recommended hotels, turn left out of the station, then right on avenue Jean Médecin. To get near the beach and the promenade des Anglais from the station, continue on foot for 20 minutes down avenue Jean Médecin, or take bus #15 or #17, each of which run frequently to place Massena (bus #17 continues to the bus station, *gare routière*). Get off at place Massena and walk five minutes through Old Nice to the beach.

By Car: Driving into Nice from the west (such as from Provence), take the first Nice exit (for the airport—called *Côte d'Azur, Central*) and follow signs for *Nice Centre* and *Promenade des Anglais*. Try to avoid arriving at rush hour, when the promenade des Anglais grinds to a halt (Mon–Fri 17:00–19:30). Hoteliers know where to park (allow €10–18/day). The parking garage at the Nice Etoile shopping center on avenue Jean Médecin is handy to many of my hotel listings (ticket booth on 3rd floor, about €18/day, €10 from 20:00–8:00). All on-street parking is metered.

By Plane: For information on Nice's airport, see "Transportation Connections," page 220.

Helpful Hints

Theft Alert: Nice is notorious for pickpockets. Have nothing important on or around your waist, unless it's in a money belt tucked out of sight (thieves target fanny packs); don't leave anything visible in your car; be wary of scooters when standing at intersections; don't leave things unattended on the beach while swimming; and stick to main streets in Old Nice after dark.

Nice

① To Grande Corniche (sky-high route to Monaco)
② To Moyenne Corniche (middle route, best for Monaco & Eze-le-Village)
③ To Basse Corniche (low route to Villefranche-sur-Mer)
④ Start of Old Nice Walk

Museums: Most Nice museums are closed Tuesdays (except the Modern and Contemporary Art Museum), and free the first Sunday of the month. For information on museum passes, see "Tourist Information," above.

Grocery Store: The big Monoprix on avenue Jean Médecin and rue Biscarra has a wide selection and cold drinks (closed Sun).

U.S. Consulate: You'll find it at 7 avenue Gustave V (tel. 04 93 88 89 55, fax 04 93 87 07 38).

Canadian Consulate: It's at 10 rue Lamartine (tel. 04 93 92 93 22).

Medical Help: Riviera Medical Services has a list of English-speaking physicians. They can help you make an appointment or call an ambulance (tel. 04 93 26 12 70).

Rocky Beaches: To make life tolerable on the rocks, swimmers should buy a pair of the cheap plastic beach shoes sold at many shops (flip-flops fall off in the water).

American Express: AmEx faces the beach at 11 promenade des Anglais (where the promenade intersects with Rue du Congrès, tel. 04 93 16 53 53).

English Bookstore: The Cat's Whiskers has a great selection (closed Sun, 26 rue Lamartine, near recommended Hôtel du Petit Louvre, tel. 04 93 80 02 66).

Laundry: The self-service Point Laverie is at the corner of Rue Alberti and Rue Pastorelli, next to Hôtel Vendôme (open daily).

Internet Access: Consider **Web Nice** (daily 9:00–23:00, 25 bis promenade des Anglais, tel. 04 93 88 72 75), **Cyber Café Bio** (cheaper if you buy food or drink, daily 9:00–22:00, near the station at 16 rue Paganini, tel. 04 9 16 89 81), or **Maxi Web** (Mon–Sat 8:00–20:00, closed Sun, 6 bis avenue Durante, tel. 04 93 16 95 56). All three places have familiar American keyboards.

Renting a Bike (and Other Wheels): Roller Station rents bikes (*vélos*, €5/hr, €10/half-day, €15/day), rollerblades (*rollers*, €5/day), and mini-scooters (*trotinettes*, €5/hr, €6/half-day, €9/day). You'll need to leave an ID as deposit (daily 10:00–19:00, across from seaside promenade at 49 quai des Etats-Unis, another location at 10 rue Cassini near place Garibaldi, tel. 04 93 62 99 05). See also City Segway Tours, page 204.

English Radio: Tune into Riviera-Radio at FM 106.5.

Views: For panoramic views, climb Castle Hill (see page 210).

Getting Around Nice

While walking gets you to most places, you'll want to ride the bus to the Chagall and Matisse museums. Bus fare is €1.40, and an all-day pass is €4.

Taxis are expensive but handy for the Chagall and Matisse museums and the Russian Cathedral (figure €10–14 from promenade des Anglais). They normally only pick up at taxi stands *(tête de station)* or if you call (tel. 04 93 13 78 78).

The hokey tourist train is handy for getting to the castle (see "Tours" below).

Getting Around the Riviera

Nice is perfectly located for exploring the Riviera by public transport. Eze-le-Village, Villefranche-sur-Mer, Antibes, St-Paul-de-Vence, and Cannes are all within a 60-minute bus or train ride of each other.

Minivan Excursions: The TI and most hotels have information on minivan excursions from Nice (€50–60/half-day, €80–110/day). **Med-Tour** is one of many (tel. 04 93 82 92 58 or 06 73 82 04 10, www.med-tour.com); **Tour Azur** is a bit pricier (tel. 04 93 44 88 77 or 06 71 90 76 70, www.tourazur.com); and **Revelation Tours** specializes in English tours (tel. 04 93 53 69 85 or 06 60 02 98 42, www.revelation-tours.com). All companies also offer private tours by the day or half day (check with them for their outrageous prices, about €90/hr).

Bus Station: At Nice's efficient bus station on boulevard Jean Jaurès, you'll find a baggage check (called *messagerie*, €2.50/bag, Mon–Sat 8:00–18:00, closed Sun), a snack bar with sandwiches and drinks, clean WCs (€0.50), and several bus companies. Get schedules and prices from the helpful English-speaking clerk at the information desk in the bus station (tel. 04 93 85 61 81). Buy tickets from the driver on the bus.

Schedules: Here's an overview of public transport options to key Riviera destinations with direct service from Nice. Two bus companies, RCA and Cars Broch, provide service on the same route between Nice, Villefranche-sur-Mer, Eze-le-Village, and Monaco (RCA buses run more frequently). For any bus destination between Nice and Monaco (marked here with *), you'll pay the same one-way or round-trip (free return only with same company, remember to keep your ticket). For other destinations, the one-way price is listed. Self-serve ticket machines in train stations make ticket purchase easy and fast.

Destination	Bus from Nice	Train from Nice
Villefranche	4/hr, 20 min, €1.80*	2/hr, 10 min, €1.60
Antibes	3/hr, 60 min, €4.30	2/hr, 25 min, €3.70
Monaco	4/hr, 45 min, €3.90*	2/hr, 20 min, €3.20
Cannes	take the train	2/hr, 30 min, €5.20
St-Paul	every 40 min, 45 min, €4.30	none
Vence	every 40 min, 50 min, €4.80	none
Grasse	every 40 min, 75 min, €6.40	none
Eze-le-Village	every 2 hrs, 25 min, €2.60	none
La Turbie	4/day, 45 min, €3	none

TOURS

Bus Tour—**Le Grand Tour Bus** provides an expensive hop-on, hop-off option on an open-deck bus with headphone commentary. The full route (about 90 min) includes the promenade des Anglais, old port, Cap de Nice, and the Chagall and Matisse museums on Cimiez Hill (€17/1-day pass, €19/2-day pass, cheaper for seniors and students, €10 for last tour of the day at about 18:45, hourly departures, buy tickets on bus, main stop is on promenade des Anglais, across from plage Beau Rivage, look for signs, tel. 04 92 29 17 00).

Tourist Train—For €6, you can spend 40 embarrassing minutes on the tourist train tooting along the promenade, through the old town, and up to the castle with a taped English narration. This is a sweat-free way to get to the castle (every 30 min, meet train opposite Albert I park on promenade des Anglais, tel. 04 93 62 85 48).

Segway Tours—The latest technology to reach the Riviera is now available for three-hour English-language rolls through Nice. These stand-up scooter tours are relaxing, fun, and surprisingly informative (€45, March–Nov daily at 10:30, night tour at 18:30, cash only, reservations required, ages 12 and up, meet at 15 promenade des Anglais in front of Lido Plage, tel. 01 56 58 10 54, www.citysegwaytours.com).

Walking Tour—The TI on the promenade des Anglais organizes guided walking tours of Old Nice from May through October (€12, 1/week, usually Sat mornings, reservations necessary, tel. 08 92 70 74 07).

Local Guide—Pascale Rucker tailors excellent tours to your interests in and around Nice. Book in advance or on short notice (€80/half-day, €140/day, tel. 04 93 87 77 89, mobile 06 16 24 29 52).

SIGHTS

You can get a free pass for bus #15 when traveling between the Chagall and Matisse museums. Ask at either of these museums for this free ticket, which saves you a 15-minute walk (it's uphill from Chagall to Matisse).

▲▲▲**Chagall Museum (Musée National Marc Chagall)**— Inspired by the Old Testament, modern artist Marc Chagall custom-painted works for this building, which he considered a "House of Brotherhood." In typical Chagall style, these paintings are lively, colorful, and simple (some might say simplistic). The museum is an unmissable treat for Chagall fans, and a hit even for people who usually don't like modern art.

Cost, Hours, Location: €5.50, covered by Riviera Carte Musées pass, Oct–June Wed–Mon 10:00–17:00, July–Sept Wed–Mon

Nice at a Glance

▲▲▲**Chagall Museum** The world's largest collection of Chagall's work, popular even with people who don't like modern art. **Hours:** Oct–June Wed–Mon 10:00–17:00, July–Sept Wed–Mon 10:00–18:00, closed Tue.

▲▲**Promenade des Anglais** Nice's four-mile sunstruck seafront promenade. **Hours:** Always open.

▲▲**Matisse Museum** A wonderful collection of Henri Matisse's paintings, providing an easy introduction to the artist. **Hours:** Wed–Mon 10:00–18:00, closed Tue.

▲**Russian Cathedral** Finest Orthodox church outside Russia. **Hours:** Daily 9:00–12:00 & 14:30–18:00, closes 17:00 off-season, chanted services Sat at 17:30 or 18:00, Sun at 10:00, no tourist visits during services.

Modern and Contemporary Art Museum Ultramodern museum with enjoyable collection from the 1960s–1970s, including Warhol and Lichtenstein. **Hours:** Tue–Sun 10:00–18:00, closed Mon.

Molinard Perfume Museum Small museum tracing the history of perfume. **Hours:** Daily 10:00–19:00, sometimes closed Mon off-season.

10:00–18:00, closed Tue, tel. 04 93 53 87 31, www.musee-chagall.fr. ✪ See Chagall Museum Tour on page 229.

▲▲**Matisse Museum (Musée Matisse)**—This museum, worth ▲▲▲ for his fans, contains the world's largest collection of Matisse paintings. It offers a painless introduction to the artist (also see sidebar next page), whose style was shaped by Mediterranean light and by fellow Côte d'Azur artists Pablo Picasso and Pierre-Auguste Renoir.

Henri Matisse, the master of leaving things out, could suggest a woman's body with a single curvy line—leaving it to the viewer's mind to fill in the rest. Ignoring traditional 3-D perspective, he used simple dark outlines saturated with bright blocks of color to create recognizable but simplified scenes composed into a decorative pattern to express nature's serene beauty. You don't look "through" a Matisse canvas, like a window; you look "at" it, like wallpaper.

Matisse understood how colors and shapes affect us emotionally. He could create either shocking, clashing works (Fauvism) or geometrical, balanced, harmonious ones (later works). While other modern artists reveled in purely abstract design, Matisse (almost)

Henri Matisse
(1869–1954)

Here's an outline of Matisse's busy life:

1880s and 1890s—At age 20, Matisse—a budding lawyer—is struck down with appendicitis. Bedridden for a year, he turns to painting as a healing escape from pain and boredom. After recovering, he studies art in Paris and produces dark-colored, realistic still lifes and landscapes. His work is exhibited at the Salon of 1896 and 1897.

1897–1905—Influenced by the Impressionists, he experiments with sunnier scenes and brighter colors. He travels to southern France, including Collioure (on the coast near Spain), and seeks still more light-filled scenes to paint. His experiments are influenced by Vincent van Gogh's bright, surrealistic colors and thick outlines and by Paul Gauguin's primitive visions of a Tahitian paradise. From Paul Cézanne, he learns how to simplify objects into their basic geometric shapes. He also experiments (like Cézanne) with creating the illusion of 3-D not by traditional means, but by using contrasting colors for the foreground and background.

1905—Back in Paris, Matisse and his colleagues (André Derain and Maurice de Vlaminck) shock the art world with an exhibition of their experimental paintings. The thick outlines, simple forms, non-3-D scenes, and—most of all—bright, clashing, unrealistic colors seemed to be the work of "wild animals" *(fauves)*. Fauvism is hot, and Matisse is instantly famous. (Though notorious as a "wild animal," Matisse himself was a gentle, introspective man.)

1906–1910—After just a year, Fauvism is out, and African masks are in. This "primitive" art form inspires Matisse to simplify and distort his figures further, making them less realistic but more expressive.

1910–1917—Matisse creates his masterpiece paintings. Cubism is the rage, pioneered by Matisse's friend and rival for the World's Best Painter award, Pablo Picasso. Matisse dabbles in Cubism, simplifying forms, emphasizing outline, and muting his colors. But

always kept the subject matter at least vaguely recognizable. He used unreal colors and distorted lines not just to portray what an object looks like, but to express the object's inner nature (even inanimate objects). Meditating on his paintings helps you connect with nature—or so Matisse hoped.

As you wander the museum, look for motifs including fruit, flowers, wallpaper, and interiors of sunny rooms—often with a window opening onto a sunny landscape. Another favorite subject is the odalisque (harem concubine)—usually shown sprawled ultimately it proves to be too austere and analytical for his deeply sensory nature. The Cubist style is most evident in his sculpture.

1920s—Burned out from years of intense experimentation, Matisse moves to Nice (spending winters there from 1917, settling permanently in 1921). Luxuriating under the bright sun, he's reborn, and he paints colorful, sensual, highly decorative works. Odalisques (harem concubines) lounging in their sunny, flowery apartments epitomize the lush life.

1930s—A visit to Tahiti inspires more scenes of life as a sunny paradise. Increasingly, Matisse plays around with the lines of the figures he draws to create swirling arabesques and decorative patterns.

1940s—Duodenal cancer (in 1941), requiring two operations, confines Matisse to a wheelchair for the rest of his life. Working at an easel becomes a struggle for him, and he largely stops painting in 1941. But he emerges reborn again. Now in his 70s, he explores a new medium: paper cutouts pasted onto a watercolored surface (*découpages* on gouache-prepared surface). The medium plays to his strengths: The cutouts are essentially blocks of bright color (mostly blue) with a strong outline. Scissors in hand, Matisse says, "I draw straight into the color." (His doctor advises him to wear dark glasses to protect his weak eyes against the bright colors he chooses.) In 1947, Matisse's book *Jazz* is published, featuring the artist's joyful cutouts of simple figures. Like jazz music, the book is a celebration of artistic spontaneity. And like music in general, Matisse's works balance different tones and colors to create a mood.

1947–1951—Matisse's nurse becomes a Dominican nun in Vence. To thank her for her care, he spends his later years designing a chapel there. He oversees every aspect of the Chapel of the Rosary (Chapelle du Rosaire) at Vence, from the stained glass to the altar to the colors of the priest's robe (see page 279). Though Matisse is not a strong Christian, the church exudes his spirit of celebrating life and sums up his work (see page 279).

1954—Matisse dies.

in seductive poses and with a simplified mask-like face.

Notice works from his different periods. Room 9 houses paintings from his formative years as a student. In Room 10, his work evolves through many stages, becoming simpler with time. Upstairs, in and around Room 17, you'll find sketches and models of his famous Chapel of the Rosary in nearby Vence (see page 279) and related religious work. On the same floor, there are rooms dedicated to his paper cutouts and his *Jazz* series. Throughout the building are souvenirs from his travels, which inspired much of his work.

The museum is in a 17th-century Genoese villa, set in an olive grove amid the ruins of the Roman city of Cemenelum. Part of the ancient Roman city of Nice, Cemenelum was a military camp that housed as many as 20,000 people.

Cost and Hours: €4, covered by Riviera Carte Musées pass, Wed–Mon 10:00–18:00, closed Tue, tel. 04 93 81 08 08, www.musee-matisse-nice.org.

Getting to the Matisse Museum: It's a confusing but manageable 45-minute walk from the top of avenue Jean Médecin (and the train station). And it's a 30-minute walk above the Chagall Museum.

Buses #15 and #17 serve the Matisse and Chagall Museums from the eastern side of avenue Jean Médecin (#15 runs more frequently-6/hr, #17-3/hr, €1.40). The bus stop for Matisse (called *Arènes*) is on avenue de Cimiez, two blocks up from Chagall. If connecting the museums by bus, ask for a special free bus pass with your museum ticket (see above).

To **walk** to the Matisse Museum, go to the train-station end of avenue Jean Médecin and turn right onto boulevard Raimbaldi along the overpasses, then turn left under the overpasses onto avenue Raymond Comboul. Once under the overpass, angle to the right up avenue de l'Olivetto to the alley (with the big wall on your right). A pedestrian path soon emerges, and it leads up and up to signs for both Chagall and Matisse.

Modern and Contemporary Art Museum (Musée d'Art Moderne et d'Art Contemporain)—This ultramodern museum features an enjoyable collection of art from the 1960s and 1970s, including works by Andy Warhol and Roy Lichtenstein, and offers frequent special exhibits.

Cost, Hours, Location: €4, covered by Riviera Carte Musées pass, Tue–Sun 10:00–18:00, closed Mon, on promenade des Arts near bus station, tel. 04 93 62 61 62, www.mamac-nice.org.

Molinard Perfume Museum—The Molinard family has been making perfume in Grasse (about an hour's drive from Nice) since 1849. Their Nice store has a small museum in the back illustrating the story of their industry. Back when people believed water spread the plague (Louis XIV supposedly bathed less than once a year), doctors advised people to rub fragrances into their skin and then powder their body. Back then, perfume was a necessity of everyday life.

Room 1 shows photos of the local flowers used in perfume production. Room 2 shows the earliest (18th-century) production method. Petals would be laid on a bed of animal fat. After baking in the sun, the fat would absorb the essence of the flowers. Petals would be replaced daily for two months until the fat was saturated. Models and old photos show the later distillation process (660 pounds of lavender would produce only a quarter-gallon of essence). Perfume is "distilled like cognac and then aged like wine." Room 3 shows the desk of a "nose" (top perfume creator). Of the 150 real "noses" in the world, more than 100 are French. You are welcome to enjoy the testing bottles before heading into the shop.

Cost, Hours, Location: Free, daily 10:00–19:00, sometimes closed Mon off-season, just between beach and place Masséna at 20 rue St. François de Paule, tel. 04 93 62 90 50, www.molinard.com.

Other Nice Museums—These museums are decent rainy-day options. The **Fine Arts Museum** (Musée des Beaux-Arts), with 6,000 works from the 17th to 20th centuries, will satisfy your need for a fine-arts fix (€4, covered by Riviera Carte Musées pass, Tue–Sun 10:00–18:00, closed Mon, 3 avenue des Baumettes, western end of Nice, tel. 04 92 15 28 28). The **Archaeological Museum** (Musée Archeologique) displays Roman ruins and various objects from the Romans' occupation of this region (€4, Wed–Mon 10:00–18:00, closed Tue, near Matisse Museum at 160 avenue des Arènes, tel. 04 93 81 59 57). Nice's city museum, **Museum Masséna** (Musée Masséna), is closed until at least 2006.

▲Russian Cathedral (Cathédrale Russe)—Nice's Russian Orthodox church—claimed to be the finest outside Russia—is worth a visit. Five hundred rich Russian families wintered in Nice in the

late 19th century. Since they couldn't pray in a Catholic church, the community needed a worthy Orthodox house of worship. Czar Nicholas I's widow saw the need and provided the land (which required tearing down her house). Czar Nicholas II gave this church to the Russian community in 1912. (A few years later, Russian comrades—who didn't winter on the Riviera—assassinated him.) Here in the land of olives and anchovies, these proud onion domes seem odd. But, I imagine, so did those old Russians.

Step inside (pick up English info sheet). The one-room interior is filled with icons and candles, and the old Russian music adds to the ambience. The icon wall divides things between the spiritual world and the temporal world of the worshippers. Only the priest can walk between the two worlds, by using the "Royal Door." Take a close look at items lining the front (starting in the left corner). The angel with red boots and wings—the protector of the Romanov family—stands over a symbolic tomb of Christ. The tall, black, hammered-copper cross commemorates the massacre of Nicholas II and his family in 1918. Notice the Jesus icon near the Royal Door. According to a priest here, as the worshipper meditates, staring deep into the eyes of Jesus, he enters a lake where he finds his soul. Surrounded by incense, chanting, and your entire community...it could happen. Farther to the right, the icon of the Virgin and Child is decorated with semi-precious stones from the Ural Mountains. Artists worked a triangle into each iconic face—symbolic of the Trinity.

Cost, Hours, Location: €2.50, daily 9:00–12:00 & 14:30–18:00, closes 17:00 off-season, chanted services Sat at 17:30 or 18:00, Sun at 10:00, no tourist visits during services, no shorts, 10-min walk behind station at 17 boulevard du Tzarewitch, tel. 04 93 96 88 02.

Castle Hill (Colline du Château)—This hill-topping castle, reached by foot or by elevator (runs daily 10:00–18:00, until 20:00 in summer, one-way-€0.70, round-trip-€1, next to beachfront Hôtel Suisse), offers sweeping views over Nice.

ACTIVITIES

▲▲Wandering Old Nice (Vieux Nice)—Offering an intriguing look at Nice's melding of French and Italian cultures, the old town is a fine place to spend some time. Enjoy its belle époque buildings, bustling market squares, tempting shops, and colorful people. ✪ See Old Nice Walk on page 222.

▲▲Strolling the Promenade des Anglais—Sauntering along Nice's four-mile seafront promenade is a must. From the days when wealthy English tourists lined the seaside with grand hotels, to today, as a favorite spot for Europeans to enjoy some fun in the sun—this stretch is *the* place to be in Nice. ✪ See Old Nice Walk on page 222.

▲Wheeling the Promenade—Get a bike and ride along the coast in both directions (about 30 min each way). Roller Station rents bikes, in-line skates, and mini-scooters (see "Helpful Hints," above). Both of the following paths start along the promenade des Anglais.

The path to the west stops just before the airport at perhaps the most scenic *boules* courts in France. Stop and watch the old-timers while away their afternoon tossing those shiny metal balls (see sidebar on page 156).

In the other direction, you'll round the hill—passing a scenic cape and the town's memorial to both World Wars—to the harbor of Nice, with a chance to survey some fancy yachts. Pedal around the harbor and follow the coast past the Corsica ferry terminal (you'll need to carry your bike up a flight of steps). From there, the path leads to a delightful tree-lined residential district.

Relaxing at the Beaches—Nice is where the masses relax on the rocks. After settling into the smooth pebbles, you can play beach volleyball, table tennis, or *boules* (see page 156); rent paddleboats, personal water-craft, or windsurfing equipment; explore ways to use your zoom lens as a telescope; or snooze on comfy beach beds with end tables. You can rent a spot on the beach (mattress and chaise lounge-€12, umbrella-€4, towel-€3). Many hotels have special deals with certain beaches for dis-

counted rental (check with your hotel for details). Consider lunch in your bathing suit (€10 salads and pizzas in bars and restaurants all along the beach). For a peaceful cup of coffee on the beach, stop here first thing in the morning before the crowds hit. *Plage Publique* signs explain the 15 beach no-nos (translated in English).

Near Nice

Narrow-Gauge Train into the Alps (Chemins de Fer de Provence)—

Leave the tourists behind and take your kids on the scenic train-bus-train combination that runs between Nice and Digne through

canyons, along whitewater rivers, between snow-capped peaks, and through many tempting villages (Nice to Digne: 4/day, 3 hrs, €17.50, 25 per-cent discount with railpass, departs Nice from the South Station—Gare du Sud—about 10 blocks behind the city's main station, 4 rue Alfred Binet, tel. 04 97 03 80 80).

Start with a 9:00 departure and go as far as you want. Little **Entrevaux** is a good destination (about 2 scenic hours from Nice, €9) and feels forgotten and still stuck in its medieval shell. Climb high to the citadel for great views. The train ends in **Digne,** where you can catch a main-line train (covered by railpasses) to other des-tinations—or better, take the bus (quick transfer, free with railpass) to **Veynes** (6/day, 90 min), where you can then catch the most scenic two-car train to **Grenoble** (5/day, 2 hrs). From Grenoble, connec-tions are available to many destinations.

To do the entire trip from Nice to Grenoble in one day, you must start with the 9:00 departure from Nice (arrives in Grenoble at about 18:00), but I'd spend the night in one of the tiny villages en route. Clelles has the best hotel: **Hôtel Ferrat****, a simple, family-run moun-tain hacienda at the base of Mont Aiguille (after which Gibraltar was modeled) is a good place to break this train trip. Enjoy your own *boules* court, swimming pool, and good restaurant (Db-€45–58, tel. 04 76 34 42 70, fax 04 76 34 47 47, hotelferrat@wanadoo.fr).

SLEEPING

Don't look for charm in Nice. Go for modern and clean, with a central location and, in summer, air-conditioning. I've divided my sleeping recommendations into three areas: between the train station and Nice Etoile shopping center, near Old Nice and the beaches, and in a more stately area between the station and promenade des Anglais (by boulevard Victor Hugo).

Reserve early for summer visits. The rates listed here are for April through October. Prices generally drop €10–20 from November through March, and can increase dramatically during the Nice Carnival (Feb 11–27 in 2005), Monaco's Grand Prix (May 19–22 in 2005), and the Cannes film festival (May 11–22 in 2005). June is convention month, and Nice is one of Europe's top convention cities—so book ahead.

Near the Train Station

Most hotels near the station are overrun, overpriced, and loud. Here are the pleasant exceptions (most are between Old Nice and the train station, near avenue Jean Médecin and boulevard Victor Hugo). For parking, ask your hotelier, or see "Arrival in Nice: By Car," above.

$$$ Hôtel Vendôme***, a mansion set off the street, gives you a whiff of the belle époque, with pink pastels, high ceilings, and grand staircases. Rooms are modern and come in all sizes. The best have balconies—request *"une chambre avec balcon"* (Sb-€88–95, Db-€105–125, Tb-€120–140, buffet breakfast-€10, air-con, parking-€10/day, 26 rue Pastorelli, tel. 04 93 62 00 77, fax 04 93 13 40 78, www.vendome-hotel-nice.com, contact@vendome-hotel-nice.com).

$$ Hôtel Excelsior***, one block below the station, is a diamond

---

Sleep Code

(€1 = about $1.20, country code: 33)
S = Single, **D** = Double/Twin, **T** = Triple, **Q** = Quad, **b** = bathroom, **s** = shower only, **no CC** = Credit Cards not accepted, * = French hotel rating (0–4 stars). Hotels speak English, have elevators, and accept credit cards unless otherwise noted.

To help you sort easily through these listings, I've divided the rooms into three categories based on the price for a standard double room with bath:

$$$ **Higher Priced**—Most rooms €95 or more.
$$ **Moderately Priced**—Most rooms between €65–95.
$ **Lower Priced**—Most rooms €65 or less.

Nice Hotels

1. Hôtel Excelsior
2. Hôtel Vendome & Launderette
3. Hôtel Clémenceau & Hôtel St. Georges
4. Hôtel du Petit Louvre
5. Hôtel Aria
6. Hôtel Masséna & Hôtel le Guitry
7. Hôtel Suisse
8. Hôtel Lafayette
9. Hôtel Mercure
10. Hôtel le Royal
11. Hôtel Lorrain
12. Hôtel Windsor
13. Hôtel les Cigales
14. Hôtel Splendid & Hôtel Gounod
15. Hôtel l'Oasis
16. To Hôtel Villa Eden
17. Cat's Whiskers Bookstore

in the rough. You'll find turn-of-the-century decor, a small but lush garden courtyard, and pleasant rooms with real wood furnishings. Rooms on the garden are best in the summer; streetside rooms have balconies and get winter sun (standard Db-€90, *prestige* Db-€120, air-con, 19 avenue Durante, tel. 04 93 88 18 05, fax 04 93 88 38 69, www.excelsiornice.com, excelsior.hotel@wanadoo.fr).

$$ Hôtel St. Georges**, a block away, is big and bright, with a backyard garden, reasonably clean and comfortable rooms, and happy Jacques at the reception (Sb-€59, Db-€69, Tb with 3 separate beds-€87, extra bed-€16, air-con, 7 avenue Georges Clémenceau, tel. 04 93 88 79 21, fax 04 93 16 22 85, www.hotelsaintgeorges.fr, nicefrance.hotelstgeorges@wanadoo.fr).

$ Hôtel Clémenceau**, run by the charming La Serres, is an exceptional value with a basic, homey feel. Rooms—some with balconies, some without closets, all air-conditioned—are mostly spacious and traditional (S-€31, Sb-€43, D-€43, Db-€58, Tb-€69, Qb-€84, kitchenette-€8 extra and only for stays of at least 3 nights, no elevator, 3 avenue Georges Clémenceau, 1 block west of avenue Jean Médecin, tel. 04 93 88 61 19, fax 04 93 16 88 96, hotel-clemenceau@wanadoo.fr, Marianne).

$ Hôtel du Petit Louvre* is basic, but a good hostel-like budget bet, with playful owners (the Vilas), art-festooned walls, and adequate rooms (S-€38, Ds-€44, Db-€49, Tb-€57, pay on arrival, 10 rue Emma Tiranty, tel. 04 93 80 15 54, fax 04 93 62 45 08, petilouvr@wanadoo.com).

Near Old Nice

$$$ Hôtel Masséna****, in an elegant building a few blocks from place Masséna, is a consummate business hotel that offers 100 four-star rooms with all the comforts at reasonable rates (small Db-€120, larger Db-€150, still larger Db-€215, extra bed-€30, some non-smoking rooms, Internet access, reserve parking ahead-€18/day, 58 rue Gioffredo, tel. 04 92 47 88 88, fax 04 92 47 88 89, www.hotel-massena-nice.com, info@hotel-massena-nice.com).

$$$ Hôtel Suisse*** has Nice's best ocean views for the money, and is surprisingly quiet given the busy street below. Rooms are comfortable, with air-conditioning and modern conveniences. There's no reason to sleep here if you don't land a view, so I've listed prices only for view rooms—many of which have balconies (Db-€120–155, breakfast-€14, 15 quai Rauba Capeu, tel. 04 92 17 39 00, fax 04 93 85 30 70, hotelsuisse.nice@wanadoo.fr).

$$$ Hôtel Mercure***, wonderfully situated on the water behind cours Saleya, offers tastefully designed rooms (some with beds in a loft) at good rates for the location (Sb-€94, Db-€108–120, buffet breakfast-€12, air-con, 91 quai des Etats-Unis, tel. 04 93 85 74 19, fax 04 93 13 90 94, h0962@accor-hotels.com).

$$ **Hôtel Lafayette*** looks big and average from the outside, but inside it's a cozy, good value that offers 18 sharp, spacious, three-star rooms at two-star rates, all one floor up from the street. Sweet Sandrine will take good care of you (standard Db-€77–93, spacious Db-€87–105, extra bed-€18, central air-con, no elevator, 32 rue de l'Hôtel des Postes, tel. 04 93 85 17 84, fax 04 93 80 47 56, lafayette @nouvel-hotel.com).

$$ **Hôtel le Guitry*** is a small place with 16 rooms. Half are traditional, half are just renovated and *très* plush, and a few have little natural light (Db-€70–90, big family room-€125, central air-con, 6 rue Sacha Guitry, tel. 04 93 80 83 83, fax 04 93 13 02 91, dynamo Geraldine S enough E).

$ **Hôtel Lorrain** is very basic, with kitchenettes in all of its large, linoleum-floored rooms. It's a classic budget place with no frills, conveniently located one block from the bus station and Old Nice (Db-€48, extra bed-€25, 6 rue Gubernatis, push top buzzer to release door, tel. 04 93 85 42 90, fax 04 93 85 55 54, hotellorrain @aol.com).

Uptown, between the Station and Promenade des Anglais

$$$ **Hôtel Windsor*** is a snazzy, well-run garden retreat with contemporary rooms, including some—designed by modern artists—that defy explanation (pass on the *artiste* rooms and ask for a traditional room). It has a swimming pool and gym (both free for guests), and a €10 sauna (Db-€105–155, extra bed-€20, breakfast-€10, rooms over garden worth the higher price, Internet access, 11 rue Dalpozzo, tel. 04 93 88 59 35, fax 04 93 88 94 57, www .hotelwindsornice.com, contact@hotelwindsornice.com).

$$$ **Hôtel Les Cigales*** is a smart little pastel place with tasteful decor, 19 newly renovated rooms, air-conditioning, and a slick upstairs terrace, all well-managed by friendly Mr. Valentino (standard Db-€115, big Db-€160, breakfast-€10, 16 rue Dalpozzo, tel. 04 97 03 10 70, fax 04 97 03 10 71, www.hotel-lescigales.com, infos@hotel-lescigales.com).

$$$ **Hôtel Splendid**** is a worthwhile splurge if you miss your Hilton. The rooftop pool, Jacuzzi, and panoramic breakfast room alone almost justify the cost...but throw in good rooms (some non-smoking), a free gym, Internet access, and air-conditioning, and you're as good as home (Db-€225, deluxe Db with terrace-€250, suites-€335, breakfast-€16, free breakfast with minimum 3-night stay, parking-€19/day, 50 boulevard Victor Hugo, tel. 04 93 16 41 00, fax 04 93 16 42 70, www.splendid-nice.com, info@splendid -nice.com).

$$$ **Hôtel Gounod*** is behind Hôtel Splendid and shares the same owners, who allow its clients free access to Hôtel Splendid's

pool, Jacuzzi, and other amenities. Don't let the lackluster lobby fool you. Its fine rooms are big, air-conditioned, and richly decorated, with high ceilings—though they can be musty (Db-€125–140, palatial 4-person suites-€215, breakfast-€10, parking-€12/day, 3 rue Gounod, tel. 04 93 16 42 00, fax 04 93 88 23 84, www.gounod -nice.com, info@gounod-nice.com).

$$$ **Hôtel Aria***** is a soft-yellow, very sharp big-city refuge with 30 comfortable rooms, half of which overlook a small park. This place is well run and a good value (Db-€95–110, junior suite-€150, extra bed-€20, buffet breakfast-€9, air-con, 15 avenue Auber, tel. 04 93 88 30 69, fax 04 93 88 11 35, www.aria-nice.com, reservation @aria-nice.com).

$$$ **Hôtel le Royal***** stands shoulder-to-shoulder on the promenade des Anglais with the big boys (hôtels Negresco and Westminster). It feels like a retirement home-turned-hotel (don't expect an enthusiastic reception), but offers solid comfort with air-conditioning at €100–200 less than its more famous neighbors. The mini-suites are well worth the extra euros (seaview rooms: Sb-€100, Db-€130, Db mini-suite €150; city-facing rooms: Sb-€80, Db-€100; 23 promenade des Anglais, tel. 04 93 16 43 00, fax 04 93 16 43 02, royal@vacancesbleues.com).

$$$ **Hôtel l'Oasis***** is just that. This orange-pastel hotel sits away from the street, surrounding a large, flowery courtyard. Its 40 non-smoking rooms are also calming, with air-conditioning, earth tones, pleasing fabrics, sharp bathrooms, and reasonable rates. This hotel works with an English travel agency, so many guests are British, and the place is often booked long in advance (Sb-€75, Db-€90–120, Tb-€120, prices include breakfast, 23 rue Gounod, tel. 04 93 88 12 29, fax 04 93 16 14 40).

$$ **Hôtel Villa Eden**** is the one little belle époque time-warp place among the sprawling waterfront hotels lining the promenade des Anglais. This former mansion of a Russian aristocrat new rents 13 rooms with a faded and charming family-run ambience. It's set back enough to lose the street noise and much of the sea view, but if you want to be close to the beach, this is a good budget option (Db-€63–69, extra bed-€15, 10-minute walk beyond Hôtel Negresco, bus #12 or #23 from station, 99 Promenade des Anglais, tel. 04 93 86 53 70, fax 04 93 97 67 97, hotelvillaeden@caramail.com).

EATING

My recommended restaurants are concentrated in the same neighborhoods as my favorite hotels. The promenade des Anglais is ideal for picnic dinners on warm, languid evenings, and the old town is perfect for restaurant-shopping. Gelato-lovers should save room for **Fenocchio** (on place Rossetti in Old Nice, 86 flavors from tomato to

Old Nice Hotels and Restaurants

1. Hôtel Mercure
2. Hôtel Suisse
3. La Cambuse
4. Le Safari
5. Nissa Socca
6. L'Acchiardo
7. Lou Pilha Leva
8. L'Univers
9. Restaurant Castel
10. Fenocchio's Gelato

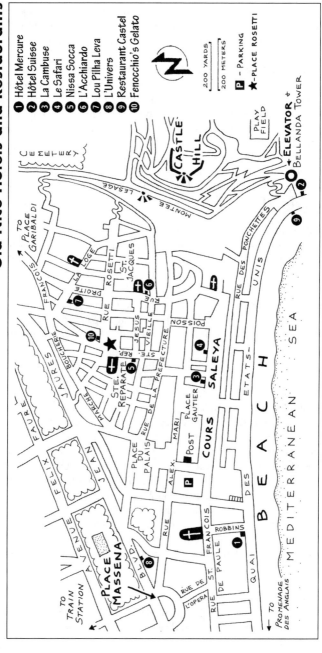

lavender, daily until 23:30). Ice cream cone in hand, you can join the evening parade along the Mediterranean (best view at night is from east end of quai des Etats-Unis, on tip below Castle Hill).

Old Nice, on or near Cours Saleya

Nice's dinner scene converges on cours Saleya (koor sah-lay-yuh)—entertaining enough in itself to make the generally mediocre food of its restaurants a good value. It's a fun, festive place to compare tans and mussels. Even if you're eating elsewhere, wander through here in the evening.

La Cambuse offers a refined setting and fine cuisine for those who want to eat on cours Saleya without sacrificing quality (allow €30–40 per person, open daily, at #5, tel. 04 93 80 82 40).

Le Safari has the best "eating energy" on the cours Saleya and serves all afternoon (open daily, at Castle Hill end at #1, tel. 04 93 80 18 44).

Nissa Socca offers good, cheap Italian cuisine and a lively atmosphere a few blocks from cours Saleya (Mon–Sat from 19:00, closed Sun, arrive early, a block off place Rossetti on rue Ste. Réparate, tel. 04 93 80 18 35).

L'Acchiardo, deeper in the old city, is a budget traveler's friend, with simple, hearty, traditional cuisine at bargain prices in a homey setting (€13 dinner *plats,* closed Sat–Sun, 38 rue Droite, tel. 04 93 85 51 16).

Lou Pilha Leva offers a fun, *très* cheap dinner option with *niçoise* specialties and outdoor-only benches. Order your food from one side and drinks from the other (open daily, located where rue de la Loge and Centrale meet in Old Nice).

L'Univers, a block off place Masséna, has earned a Michelin star while maintaining a warm ambience. This elegant place is as relaxed as a "top" restaurant can be, from its casual decor to the tasteful dinnerware. But when the artfully presented food arrives, you know this is high cuisine (*menus* from €40, closed Sun, 53 boulevard Jean Jaurès, tel. 04 93 62 32 22, plumailunivers@aol.com).

Restaurant Castel is your best beach option. Eating here, you almost expect Don Ho to grab a mic. You're right on the beach below Castle Hill, perfectly positioned to watch evening swimmers get in their last laps as the sky turns pink and city lights flicker on. Lunch views are unforgettable, you can even have lunch at your beach chair if you've rented one. Arrive before sunset and linger long enough to merit the few extra euros the place charges (open daily, salads and pastas–€13–15, main courses–€24, *Panaché de la Mer* is a good sampling of seafood and vegetables, 8 quai des Etats-Unis, tel. 04 93 85 22 66).

Nice Restaurants

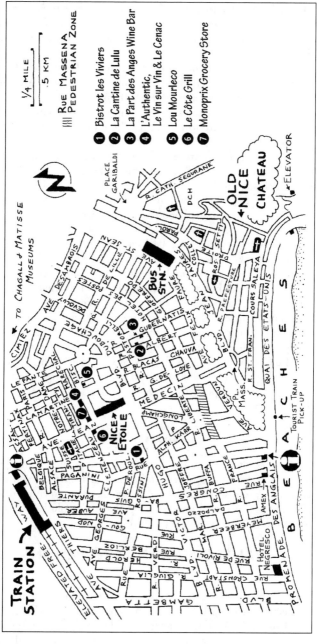

RUE MASSENA
PEDESTRIAN ZONE

1 Bistrot les Viviers
2 La Cantine de Lulu
3 La Part des Anges Wine Bar
4 L'Authentic,
  Le Vin sur Vin & Le Cenac
5 Lou Mourleco
6 Le Côte Grill
7 Monoprix Grocery Store

¼ MILE
.5 KM

Close to Recommended Hotels near the Station

These restaurants lie closer to most of the recommended hotels, within a few blocks of avenue Jean Médecin near the Nice Etoile shopping center.

Reserve ahead at enchanting little **Bistrot Les Viviers** for the most authentic *niçoise* cuisine in this book. Fish is their forte (allow €35 per person for dinner, lunch *menus* from €16, closed Sun, 22 rue Alphonse Karr, 5-min walk west of avenue Jean Médecin, tel. 04 93 16 00 48). Make sure to reserve for the *bistrot*, not their stuffier restaurant next door (prices are same, ambience is different).

Charming **La Cantine de Lulu** is a fine value, wonderfully small, and Czech-owned, with homemade recipes from Nice to Prague (closed Sat–Mon, 26 rue Alberti, tel. 04 93 62 15 33).

La Part des Anges, an atmospheric wine shop with a few tables in the rear, serves a limited, mouthwatering menu with a large selection of wines (open daily for lunch, Fri–Sat only for dinner, reserve ahead, 17 rue Gubernatis, tel. 04 93 62 69 80).

Laid-back cafés line up along the broad sidewalk on rue Biscarra (just east of avenue Jean Médecin behind Nice Etoile, all closed Sun). **L'Authentic, Le Vin sur Vin,** and **Le Cenac** are all reasonable (L'Authentic is best, Le Cenac is cheapest).

Lou Mourleco is *niçoise traditionnel.* Because it serves only what's fresh, the menu changes constantly (*menus* from €20, air-con, closed Sun–Mon, 15 rue Biscarra, tel. 04 93 80 80 11).

Le Côte Grill, a block from Nice Etoile, is bright, cool, and easy, with a salad bar, air-conditioned rooms, and a large selection at reasonable prices (open daily, 1 avenue Georges Clémenceau, tel. 04 93 82 45 53).

NIGHTLIFE

Nice's bars play host to the Riviera's most happening late-night scene, full of jazz and rock 'n' roll. Most activity focuses on Old Nice, near place Rossetti. Plan on a cover charge or expensive drinks. If you're out very late, avoid walking alone. The plush and smoky bar at Hôtel Negresco is fancy-cigar old-English.

TRANSPORTATION CONNECTIONS

For train and bus schedules from Nice to nearby towns, see "Getting Around the Riviera," page 203. Note that most long-distance train connections to other French cities require a change in Marseille.

From Nice by train to: Marseille (19/day, 2.75 hrs), **Cassis** (7/day, 3 hrs, transfer in Toulon or Marseille), **Arles** (11/day, 3.5 hrs, 10 with change in Marseille), **Avignon** (10/day, 4 hrs, a few direct, most require transfer in Marseille), **Paris'** Gare de Lyon

(14/day, 5.5–7 hrs, 6 with change in Marseille), **Aix-en-Provence** TGV station (10/day, 3.5 hrs, transfer in Marseille probable), **Chamonix** (4/day, 11 hrs, 2–3 transfers), **Beaune** (7/day, 7 hrs, transfer in Lyon), **Munich** (2/day, 12 hrs with 2 transfers, one night train with a transfer in Verona), **Interlaken** (1/day, 12 hrs), **Florence** (4/day, 7 hrs, transfers in Pisa and/or Genoa, night train), **Milan** (4/day, 5–6 hrs, 3 with transfers), **Venice** (3/day, 3/night, 11–15 hrs, 5 require transfers), **Barcelona** (3/day, 11 hrs, long transfer in Montpellier, or a direct night train).

Nice's Airport (Aéroport de Nice Côte d'Azur)

Nice's easy-to-navigate airport is on the Mediterranean, about 20 minutes west of the city center. Planes go about hourly to Paris (1-hr flight, about the same price as a train ticket). There are two terminals (1 and 2) used by domestic and international flights. Both terminals have TIs, banks, taxis, and buses to Nice (www.nice.aeroport.fr, tel. 08 20 42 33 33 or 04 89 88 98 28).

Taxis into the center are expensive, charging €30 to Nice hotels and €50 to Villefranche-sur-Mer. Taxis stop outside door *(Porte)* A-1 at Terminal 1 and outside *Porte* A-3 at Terminal 2.

Three **bus** lines run from both terminals into Nice. Bus #99 runs nonstop to the main train station (€3.50, 2/hr, 8:00–21:00, 30 min, drops you within a 10-min walk of many recommended hotels); the yellow "NICE" bus #98 goes to the bus station (*gare routière,* €3.50, 3/hr, 30 min) and will also take you to the train station upon request from 6:00–8:00 and after 21:00 (ask driver for *"la gare SNCF"*). The slower, cheaper local bus #23 serves stops between the airport and train station (€1.40, 4/hr, 50 min, direction: St. Maurice).

Buy tickets in the **bus information office** (Terminal 1 only) or from the driver. To reach the bus information office and bus stops at Terminal 1, turn left after passing customs and exit the doors at the far end (buses #98 and #99 use platform 1, bus #23 uses platform 6). Buses serving Terminal 2 are well-signed to the right as you exit (bus #98 stops at platform 5, bus #99 uses platform 4, and bus #23 uses platform 6).

To get to **Villefranche-sur-Mer** from the airport, take the yellow "NICE" #98 bus to the bus station *(gare routière),* and transfer to the Villefranche-sur-Mer bus (bus #100, €1.70, 4/hr).

Buses also run hourly directly from the airport to **Antibes** (line #200, €8, 20 min) and to **Monaco** (line #110 express on the freeway, €14, 50 min).

OLD NICE WALK

From Promenade des Anglais to Castle Hill

This fun and informative self-guided walking tour gives a helpful introduction to Nice's bicultural heritage and most interesting neighborhoods. It's best done early in the morning (while the outdoor market still thrives). Allow about two hours at a leisurely pace, with a stop for coffee and *socca* (chickpea crêpe).

THE WALK BEGINS

Our tour begins on promenade des Anglais (near the landmark Hôtel Negresco) and ends in the heart of Old Nice.

Promenade des Anglais

Welcome to the Riviera. There's something for everyone along this four-mile-long seafront circus. Watch the Europeans at play, admire the azure Mediterranean, anchor yourself on a blue bench, and prop your feet up on the made-to-order guardrail. Later in the day, come back to join the evening parade of tans along the promenade.

For now, stroll like the belle époque English aristocrats for whom the promenade was built. The broad sidewalks of the promenade des Anglais (literally "walkway of the English") were financed by wealthy English tourists who wanted a safe place to stroll and admire the view. The walk was paved in marble in 1822 for aristocrats who didn't want to dirty their shoes or smell the fishy gravel. This grand promenade leads to the old town and Castle Hill.

• *Start at the pink-domed...*

Hôtel Negresco

Nice's finest hotel (also a historic monument) offers the city's most expensive beds and a free "museum" interior (always open—provided you're dressed decently, absolutely no beach attire). March straight through the lobby (as if you're staying there) into the exquisite Salon Royal. The chandelier hanging from the Eiffel-built dome is made of 16,000 pieces of crystal. It was built in France for the Russian czar's Moscow palace...but because of the Bolshevik Revolution in 1918, he couldn't take delivery. Read the explanation of the dome and saunter around counterclockwise: The bucolic scene, painted in 1913 for the hotel, sets the tone. Nip into the toilets for either a turn-of-the-century powder room or a Battle of Waterloo experience. The chairs nearby were typical of the age (cones of silence for an afternoon nap sitting up).

On your way out, pop into the Salon Louis XIV (right of entry lobby as you leave), where the embarrassingly short Sun King models his red platform boots (English descriptions explain the room).

Walk around the back to see the hotel's original entrance (grander than today's)—in the 19th century, classy people stayed out of the sun, and any posh hotel that cared about its clientele would design its entry on the shady north side.

• *Cross promenade des Anglais, turn left, and—before you begin your seaside promenade—grab a bench at the...*

Bay of Angels (Baie des Anges)

The body of Nice's patron saint, Réparate, was supposedly escorted into this bay by angels in the fourth century. Face the water. To your right is the airport, built on a landfill. On that tip of land way beyond the runway is Cap d'Antibes. Until 1860, Antibes and Nice were in different countries—Antibes was French, but Nice was a protectorate of the Italian kingdom of Savoy-Piedmont, a.k.a. the Kingdom of Sardinia. (During that period, the Var River—just west of Nice—was the geographic border between these two peoples.) In 1850, the people here spoke Italian and ate pasta. As Italy was uniting, the region was given a choice: join the new country of Italy or join France (which was enjoying good times under the rule of Napoleon III). The vast majority voted in 1860 to go French...and *voilà!*

To the far left lies Villefranche-sur-Mer (marked by the tower at land's end—and home to lots of millionaires), then Monaco, then Italy. Behind you are the foothills of the Alps (Alpes Maritimes), which gather threatening clouds that leave alone the Côte d'Azur to enjoy the sunshine more than 300 days each year. While half a million people live here, pollution is carefully treated—the water is routinely tested and very clean.

• *Now head to the left and begin...*

Strolling the Promenade

The block next to Hôtel Negresco has a lush park and the Masséna Museum (city history, closed for renovation). Nearby sit two other belle époque establishments: the West End and Westminster hotels—English names to help those original guests feel at home. These hotels represent Nice's arrival as a tourist mecca a century ago, when the combination of leisure time and a stable economy allowed tourists to find the sun even in winter.

Even a hundred years ago, there was already sufficient tourism in Nice to justify building its first casino (a leisure activity imported from Venice). An elegant casino stood on pilings in the sea until the Germans destroyed it during World War II. While that's gone, you can see the striking 1920s Art Nouveau facade of the Palais de la Mediterranean, a grand casino and theater. Only the facade survives, and today it fronts a luxury condominium. The less charming Casino Ruhl is farther along (just before the park). Anyone can drop in for some one-armed-bandit fun, but for the tables at night you'll need to dress up and bring your passport.

Albert I Park is named for the Belgian king who enjoyed wintering here. While the English came first, the Belgians and Russians were also huge fans of 19th-century Nice. The 1960 statue in the park commemorates Nice's being part of France for 100 years.

• *Walk into the park and continue down the center of the grassy strip between the two boulevards all the way to place Masséna. The modern sculpture you pass—representing the curve of the French Riviera—is an answer to a prayer for local skateboarders. Walk to the fountains and face them. (To save water, they get high pressure only after 17:00.)*

Place Masséna

You're standing on Nice's river, the Paillon (covered since the 1800s). Turn around. You can track the river's route under the green parkway you just walked; it meets the sea at the Casino Ruhl. For centuries, this river was Nice's natural defense. A fortified wall ran along its length to the sea. With the arrival of tourism in the 1800s, Nice expanded over and beyond the river. The  rich red coloring of the buildings around you was the preference of Nice's Italian rulers.

• *Cross the square to the right, towards the Caisse d'Epargne bank and the curved buildings. Follow the steps that lead down past the three palm trees and to rue de l'Opéra (between the curved buildings). Walk down rue de l'Opéra, turning left on...*

Rue St. François de Paule

You've entered Old Nice. Peer into the Alziari olive oil shop at #14 (opposite the city hall). Dating from 1868, the shop produces top-quality, stone-ground olive oil. The proud owner, Gilles Piot, claims that stone wheels create less acidity (since metal grinding builds up

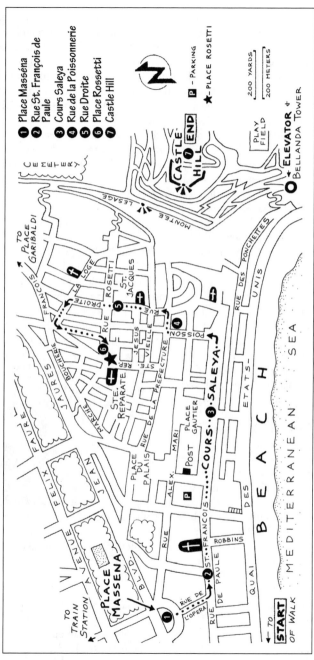

Old Nice Walk

1 Place Masséna
2 Rue St. François de Paule
3 Cours Saleya
4 Rue de la Poissonnerie
5 Rue Droite
6 Place Rossetti
7 Castle Hill

P - PARKING
★ - PLACE ROSETTI

200 YARDS
200 METERS

PLAY FIELD

ELEVATOR +
BELLANDA TOWER

CASTLE HILL 7 END

TO PLACE GARIBALDI

MONTEE LESAGE

RUE DES PONCHETTES

CEMETERY

FRANCOIS DE LA LOGE

ST. JACQUES

RUE ROSETTI

RUE DROITE

6 5

JESUS RUE VIEILLE

4 POISSON

STE. REPARATE

STE. REP.

BOUCHERIE

RUE DE LA PREFECTURE

RUE DE LA PREFECTURE

ETATS-UNIS

MEDITERRANEAN SEA

BEACH

MARCHE

JAURES

FAURE

FELIX

AVENUE JEAN

PLACE DU PALAIS

ALEX MARI

PLACE GAUTIER

POST

P

3 COURS SALEYA

RUE ST. FRANCOIS

QUAI DES ETATS-

DES

ROBBINS

RUE DE PAULE

2 ST. FRANCOIS

RUE

BLVD.

1 PLACE MASSENA

TO TRAIN STATION

AVENUE VERDUN

RUE DE L'OPERA

START OF WALK

TO

heat). Locals fill their own containers from the huge vats (the cheapest one is peanut oil, not olive oil). Consider a gift for the olive-oil lover on your list. A block down on the left (#7), Pâtisserie Auer's grand old storefront has changed little since the pastry shop opened in 1820. The writing on the window says "Since 1820 from father to son." The royal medallions on the back wall remind shoppers that Queen Victoria fed her sweet tooth here. Across the street is Nice's grand opera house, from the same era. Imagine this opulent jewel buried deep in the old town of Nice back in the 19th century. With all the fancy big-city folks wintering here, the rough-edged town needed some high-class entertainment. The four statues on top represent theater, dance, music, and singing.

• *Continue on, sifting your way through tacky souvenirs to the cours Saleya (koor sah-lay-yuh).*

Cours Saleya

Named for its broad exposure to the sun *(soleil)*, this commotion of color, sights, smells, and people has been Nice's main market square since the Middle Ages (produce market held daily until 13:00—except on Monday, when an antique market takes over the square). Amazingly, part of this square was a parking lot until 1980, when the mayor of Nice had an underground parking garage built.

The first section is devoted to freshly cut flowers that seem to grow effortlessly and everywhere in this ideal climate. Carnations, roses, and jasmine are local favorites in what has been the Riviera's biggest flower market since the 19th century. Fresh flowers are perhaps the best value in this otherwise pricey city.

The boisterous produce section trumpets the season with mushrooms, strawberries, white asparagus, zucchini flowers—whatever's fresh gets top billing.

Place Pierre Gautier (also called Plassa dou Gouvernou—bilingual street signs include the old Niçoise language, an Italian dialect) is where the actual farmers set up stalls to sell their produce and herbs directly. For a good overall view, climb the steps closest to the water (stepping over the trash sacks) above the Grand Bleu restaurant.

From your perch, look up to the hill that dominates to the east. The city of Nice was first settled there by Greeks circa 400 B.C. In the Middle Ages, a massive castle stood there, with turrets, high walls, and soldiers at the ready. With the river guarding one side and

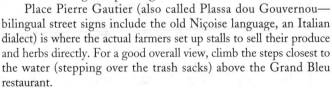

the sea the other, this mountain fortress seemed strong—until Louis XIV leveled it in 1706. Nice's medieval seawall ran along the lineup of two-story buildings where you're standing. Now, look across place Pierre Gautier to the large "palace." This Ducal Palace was where the kings of Sardinia (the city's Italian rulers until about 1860) would reside when in Nice. Today, it's police headquarters.

Resume your stroll down the center of cours Saleya, stopping when you see La Cambuse restaurant on your left. In front, hovering over the black barrel fire with the paella-like pan on top, is the self-proclaimed Queen of the Market, Thérèse (tehr-ehz). When she's not looking for a husband, Thérèse is cooking *socca*, Nice's chickpea crêpe specialty. Spend €2 for a wad of *socca* (careful—it's hot, but good). If she doesn't have a pan out, that means it's on its way (watch for the frequent scooter deliveries). Wait in line...or else it'll be all gone when you return.

• *Continue down cours Saleya. The fine golden building at the end is where Henri Matisse lived for 17 years. Turn left at the Civette du Cours café, and head down...*

Rue de la Poissonnerie

Look up at #4. Adam and Eve are squaring off, each holding a zucchini-like gourd. This scene (post-apple) represents the annual rapprochement in Nice to make up for the sins of a too-much-fun Carnival (Mardi Gras). Nice residents have partied hard during Carnival for more than 700 years. The iron grill above the door allows air to enter the building, but keeps out uninvited guests. You'll see lots of these open grills in Old Nice. They were part of an ingenious system of sucking in cool air from the sea, through the homes, and out through vents in the roof. Across the street, check out the small Baroque church dedicated to St. Rita, the patron saint of desperate causes. She holds a special place in locals' hearts, and this church is the most popular in Nice.

• *Turn right on the next street, then left on "Right" Street (rue Droite), into a world that feels like Naples.*

Rue Droite

In the Middle Ages, this straight, skinny street provided the most direct route from wall to wall, or river to sea. Stop at Esipuno's bakery (at place du Jésus). Thirty years ago, this baker was voted the best in France, and his son now runs the place. Notice the firewood stacked by the oven. Farther along, at #28, Thérèse (whom you met earlier) cooks her *socca* in the wood-fired oven before she carts it to her barrel on cours Saleya. The balconies of the mansion in the next block mark the Palais Lascaris (1647), a rare souvenir from one of Nice's most prestigious families (free, Wed–Mon 10:00–18:00, closed Tue, worth touring for a peek at 1700s Baroque Italy high

life, look up and make faces back at the guys under the balconies).
• *Turn left on the rue de la Loge, then left again on rue Mascoïnat, to reach...*

Place Rossetti

The most Italian of Nice's piazzas, place Rossetti feels more like Rome than Nice. This square comes alive after dark. Fenocchio is popular for its many gelato flavors. Walk to the fountain and stare back at the church. This is the Cathedral of St. Réparate—an unassuming building for a major city's cathedral. The cathedral was relocated here in the 1500s, when Castle Hill was temporarily converted to military-only. The name comes from Nice's patron saint, a teenage virgin named Réparate whose martyred body floated to Nice in the fourth century, accompanied by angels (remember the Bay of Angels?). The interior is overwhelmingly Baroque. Remember that Baroque was a response to the Protestant Reformation. With the Catholic Church's Counter-Reformation, the theatrical energy of churches was cranked up—with reenergized, high-powered saints and eye-popping decor.

• *Back outside the cathedral, the steps leading up rue Rossetti are the most direct path from here to Castle Hill (15 min straight up). If you're pooped, wander back down to quai des Etats-Unis near the beach and ride the elevator (next to Hôtel Suisse, where bayfront road curves right, open daily 10:00–18:00, until 20:00 in summer, one-way-€0.70, round-trip-€1).*

Castle Hill (Colline du Château)

This hill—in an otherwise flat city center—offers good views over Nice, the port (to the east), the foothills of the Alps, and the Mediterranean. The views are best at sunset or whenever the weather's

really clear (park closes at 20:00 in summer, earlier off-season). Until the 1100s, the city of Nice was crammed onto this hilltop, as it was too risky to live in the flatlands below, where marauders were on the rampage. Today, you'll find a waterfall, a playground, two cafés (fair prices), and a cemetery—but no castle—on Castle Hill.

• *To walk back downtown, follow signs from just below the upper café to Vieille Ville (not Le Port), and turn right at the cemetery, then look for the walkway down on your left.*

CHAGALL MUSEUM TOUR
(Musée Chagall)

Even if you're suspicious of modern art, this museum—with the largest collection of Marc Chagall's work in captivity anywhere—is a delight. After World War II, Chagall returned from the United States to settle in nearby Vence. Between 1954 and 1967, he painted a cycle of 17 large murals designed for, and donated to, this museum. These paintings, inspired by the biblical books of Genesis, Exodus, and the Song of Songs, make up the "nave," or core, of what Chagall called the "House of Brotherhood."

ORIENTATION

Cost: €5.50, covered by Riviera Carte Musées pass.

Hours: Oct–June Wed–Mon 10:00–17:00, July–Sept Wed–Mon 10:00–18:00, closed Tue.

Getting There: The museum is at the top of town, a confusing 15-minute walk from the top of avenue Jean Médecin (and the train station). You can get there by bus or on foot. **Buses #15 and #17** serve the museum from the eastern side of avenue Jean Médecin (€1.40, both run 6/hr). The bus stop (Musée Chagall) is on avenue de Cimiez. (If you're also going to the Matisse Museum, ask for a special free bus ticket to connect the two—see page 204.) To **walk** to the Chagall Museum, go to the train-station end of avenue Jean Médecin and turn right onto boulevard Raimbaldi along the overpasses, then turn left under the overpasses onto avenue Raymond Comboul. When you emerge from the

overpass, angle to the right up avenue de l'Olivetto to the alley (with the big wall on your right). A pedestrian path soon emerges, and it leads up and up to signs for the museum.

Information: Tel. 04 93 53 87 31, p.musee-chagall.fr. While Chagall would suggest that you explore his works without help, the €3 museum guidebook is useful in explaining the symbolism.

Length of This Tour: One hour.

THE TOUR BEGINS

The museum consists of two interior rooms with the 17 large murals, a room for special exhibits, an auditorium with stained-glass windows, and a mosaic-lined pond. In the main hall, you'll find the core of the collection (Old Testament Scenes). The adjacent octagonal room houses five paintings—the Song of Songs room.

Old Testament Scenes

Each painting is a lighter-than-air collage of images that draw from Chagall's Russian folk-village youth, his Jewish heritage, biblical themes, and his feeling that he existed somewhere between heaven and earth. He believed that the Bible was a synonym for nature, and that color and biblical themes were key ingredients for understanding God's love for his creation. Chagall's brilliant blues and reds celebrate nature, as do his spiritual and folk themes. Notice the focus on couples. To Chagall, humans loving each other mirrored God's love of creation.

The Creation

God said, "Let us make man in our image, in our likeness..." (Genesis 1:26)

A pure-white angel descends through the blue sky and carries a still-sleeping Adam from radiant, red-yellow heaven to earth. Heaven is a whirling dervish of activity, spinning out all the events of future history, from the tablets of the Ten Commandments to the crucifixion—an overture of many images we'll see in later paintings. (Though not a Christian, Chagall saw the crucifixion as a universal symbol of man's suffering.)

Paradise

God put him in the Garden of Eden... and said, "You must not eat from the tree of the knowledge of good and evil..." (Genesis 2:15–17)

Paradise is a rich, earth-as-seen-from-space pool of blue, green, and white. Amoebic, still-evolving animals float around Adam (celibately practicing yoga) and Eve (with lusty-red hair). On the right, an angel guards the tempting tree, but Eve offers an apple, and Adam reaches around to sample the forbidden fruit.

Chagall's Style

Chagall uses a deceptively simple, almost childlike style to paint a world that's hidden to the eye—the magical, mystical world below the surface. Here are some of his techniques:

- **Deep, radiant colors,** inspired by Fauvism and Expressionism.
- **Personal imagery,** particularly from his childhood in Russia—smiling barnyard animals, fiddlers on the roof, flower bouquets, huts, and blissful sweethearts.
- **A Hasidic Jewish perspective**—the idea that God is everywhere, appearing in everyday things like nature, animals, and humdrum activities.
- **A fragmented Cubist style.** This multi-faceted, multi-dimensional style is perfect to capture the multi-faceted, multi-dimensional, colorful complexity of God's creation.
- **Overlapping images,** like double-exposure photography, with faint images that bleed through—suggesting there's more to life under the surface.
- **Stained-glass-esque**—dark, deep, earthy, "potent" colors, and simplified, iconic, symbolic figures.
- **Gravity-defying compositions**, with lovers, animals, and angels twirling blissfully in mid-air.
- **Happy, not tragic.** Despite the violence and turmoil of World Wars and Revolution, he painted a world of personal joy.
- **Childlike simplicity.** Chagall draws with simple, heavy outlines, filled in with Crayola colors that often spill over the lines. Major characters in a scene are bigger than the lesser characters. The smiling barnyard animals, the bright colors, the magical events presented as literal truth... Was Chagall a lightweight? Or a lighter-than-air-weight?

Driven from Paradise

So God banished him from the Garden of Eden... and placed cherubim and a flaming sword to guard the way... (Genesis 3:23–24)

An angel drives them out with a firehose of blue (there's Adam still cradling his flaming-red *coq*), while a sparkling yellow sword prevents them from ever returning. Deep in the green colors, we get glimpses of the future—Eve giving birth (lower right corner) and the yellow sacrificial goat of atonement (top right).

Marc Chagall
(1887–1985)

1887–1910: Russia
Chagall is born in the small town of Vitebsk, Belarus. He's the oldest of nine children in a traditional Russian, Hasidic Jewish family. He studies realistic art in his hometown. In St. Petersburg, he is first exposed to the modernist work of Paul Cézanne and the Fauves.

1910–1914: Paris
A patron finances a four-year stay in Paris. He hobnobs with the avant-garde, and learns technique from the Cubists, but he never abandons painting recognizable figures or his own personal fantasies. (Some say his relative poverty forced him to paint over used canvases, which gave him the idea of overlapping images that bleed through. Hmm.)

1914–1922: Russia
Returning to his hometown, Chagall marries Bella Rosenfeld (1915), whose love will inspire him for decades. He paints happy scenes despite the turmoil of wars and the Communist Revolution. Moving to Moscow (1920), he paints his first large-scale works, sets for the New Jewish Theatre. These would inspire much of his later large-scale works.

1923–1941: France and Palestine
Chagall returns to France. In 1931, he travels to Palestine, where the

Noah's Ark
Then he sent out a dove to see if the water had receded... (Genesis 8:8)
Adam and Eve's descendants have become so wicked that God destroys the earth with a flood, engulfing the sad crowd on the right. Only righteous Noah (center), his family (lower right), and the animals (including our yellow goat) were spared inside an ark. Here Noah opens the ark's window and sends out a dove to test the waters.

The Rainbow
God said, "I have set my rainbow in the clouds as a sign of the covenant between me and the earth." (Genesis 9:13)
A flaming angel sets the rainbow in the sky, while Noah rests beneath it and his family offers a sacrifice of thanks. The pure-white rainbow's missing colors are found radiating from the features of the survivors.

bright sun and his Jewish roots inspire a series of gouaches (opaque watercolor paintings). These gouaches would later inspire 105 etchings to illustrate the Bible (1931–1952), which would eventually inspire the 17 large canvases of biblical scenes in the Chagall Museum (1954–1967).

1941–1947: United States/World War II
Fearing persecution for his Jewish faith, Chagall emigrates to New York, where he spends the war years. The crucifixion starts to appear in his paintings—not as a Christian symbol, but as a representation of the violence mankind perpetrates on itself. In 1947, his beloved Bella dies, and he stops painting for months.

1947–1985: South of France
After the war, Chagall returns to France, eventually settling in St-Paul-de-Vence. He remarries (Valentina Brodsky, in 1952). His new love, plus the southern sunshine, bring Chagall a revived creativity— he will be extremely prolific for the rest of his life. He experiments with new techniques and media—ceramics, sculpture, book illustrations, tapestry, and mosaic. In 1956, he's commissioned for his first stained-glass project. Eventually he'll do windows for cathedrals in Metz and Reims, and a synagogue of Jerusalem (1960). The Chagall Museum opens in 1973.

Abraham and the Three Angels
In the heat of the day, Abraham looked up and saw three men. He said, "Let a little food and water be brought, so you can be refreshed..." (Genesis 18:1–5)

Abraham refreshes God's angels on this red-hot day, and in return, they promise Abraham a son (in the bubble, at right), thus making him the father of the future Israelite nation.

The Sacrifice of Isaac
Abraham bound his son Isaac and laid him on the altar. Then he took the knife to slay his son. But the angel of the Lord called out to him from heaven, "Abraham!..." (Genesis 22:9–11)

Tested by God, Abraham prepares to kill his only son, but the angel stops him in time. Notice that Isaac is posed exactly as Adam was in *The Creation*. Abraham's sacrifice echoes three sacrifices: the sacrifice all men must make (i.e., Adam, the everyman); the atonement sacrifice (the goat tied to a tree at left); and even God's sacrifice of his own son (Christ carrying the cross, upper right).

Jacob's Ladder

He had a dream in which he saw a ladder resting on the earth with its top reaching to heaven, and the angels of God were ascending and descending on it... (Genesis 28:12)

In the left half, Jacob (Abraham's grandson) slumps asleep and dreams of a ladder between heaven and earth. On the right, a spinning angel with a menorah represents how heaven and earth are bridged by the rituals of the Jewish tradition.

Jacob Wrestles with an Angel

So Jacob wrestled with him till daybreak. Jacob said, "I will not let you go unless you bless me..." (Genesis 32: 24, 26)

Jacob holds on while the angel blesses him with descendants (the Children of Israel) and sends out rays from his hands, creating, among others, Joseph (stripped of his bright red coat and sold into slavery by his brothers).

Moses and the Burning Bush

The angel of the Lord appeared to him in flames of fire from within a bush... (Exodus 3:2)

Horned Moses—Chagall depicts him according to a medieval tradition—kneels awestruck before the burning bush, the event that calls him to God's service. On the left, we see Moses after the call, his face radiant, leading the Israelites out of captivity across the Red Sea, while Pharaoh's men drown (lower half of Moses' robe). The Ten Commandments loom ahead.

Moses Brings Water from the Rock

The Lord said, "Strike the rock, and water will come out of it for the people to drink..." (Exodus 17:5–6)

In the brown desert, Moses nourishes his thirsty people with water miraculously spouting from a rock. From the (red-yellow) divine source, it rains down actual (blue) water, but also a gush of spiritual yellow light.

Moses Receives the Ten Commandments

The Lord gave him the two tablets of the Law, the tablets of stone inscribed by the finger of God... (Exodus 31:18)

An astonished Moses is tractor-beamed toward heaven, where God reaches out from a cloud to hand him the Ten Commandments. While Moses tilts one way, Mount Sinai slants the other, leading our eye up to the left, where a golden calf is being worshipped by the wayward Children of Israel. But down to the right, Aaron and the menorah assure us that Moses will set things right. In this radiant final panel, the Jewish tradition—after a long struggle—is finally established.

Song of Songs

Song of Solomon 7:11
Come, my lover, let us go to the countryside,
let us spend the night in the villages.

Song of Solomon 5:2
I slept but my heart was awake.

Song of Solomon 2:17
Until the day breaks
and the shadows flee,
turn, my lover,
and be like a gazelle
or like a young stag
on the rugged hills.

Song of Solomon 3:4
I held him and would not let him go.

Song of Solomon 7:7
Your stature is like that of the palm,
and your breasts like clusters of fruit.

• *Go into the adjacent octagonal room.*

Song of Songs

Chagall wrote, "I've been fascinated by the Bible ever since my earliest childhood. I have always thought of it as the most extraordinary source of poetic inspiration imaginable. As far as I am concerned, perfection in art and in life has its source in the Bible, and exercises in the mechanics of the merely rational are fruitless. In art as well as in life, anything is possible, provided there is love."

Chagall enjoyed the love of two women in his long life—his first wife Bella, then Valentina, who gave him a second wind as he was painting these late works. Chagall was one of the few "serious" 20th-century artists to portray unabashed love. Where the Bible uses the metaphor of earthly, physical, sexual love to describe God's love for humans, Chagall uses unearthly colors and a mystical ambience to celebrate human love. These red-toned canvases are hard to interpret on a literal level, but they capture the rosy spirit of a man in love with life.

• *To the left of the entry (through the exhibition room with temporary displays) is the auditorium.*

The Auditorium

This room is worth a peaceful sit to enjoy three Chagall stained-glass windows: the creation of light, elements, and planets (a visual big bang that's four "days" wide); the creation of animals, plants, man and woman, and the ordering of the solar system (two "days" wide, complete with fish and birds still figuring out where they belong); and the day of rest, with angels singing to the glory of God (the narrowest—only one "day" wide).

• *As you leave the museum, be sure to pay a visit to...*

The Pond

The great mosaic reflected in the pond evokes the prophet Elijah in his chariot of fire (from the Second Book of Kings)—with Chagall's own addition of the 12 signs of the Zodiac, which he used to symbolize time.

FROM VILLEFRANCHE-SUR-MER TO MONACO

The Riviera's richest stretch of real estate lies between Nice and Monaco. It's packed with worthwhile stops, million-dollar vistas, and sea-splashed walking trails. Ten minutes from Nice, little Villefranche-sur-Mer stares across the bay to elegant Cap Ferrat, while the eagle's-nest village of Eze observes from high above. Between here and Italy—15 minutes away—the dazzlingly minis- cule country of Monaco and Corniche-topping La Turbie also await your visit.

Villefranche-sur-Mer

Villefranche offers travelers an easygoing slice of small-town Mediterranean life just 15 minutes from more high-powered Nice and Monaco. This town feels Italian—with soft orange buildings, steep, narrow streets spilling into the sea, and pasta with pesto. Luxury yachts glisten in the bay, a reminder to those lazing along the harborfront that Monaco is just down the coast. Sand-pebble beaches, a handful of interesting sights, and quick access to Cap Ferrat keep visitors just busy enough.

Originally a Roman port, Villefranche was overtaken by 5th-century barbarians. Villagers fled into the hills, where they stayed and farmed their olives. In 1295, the Duke of Provence—like much of Europe—was threatened by the Saracen Turks. He asked the hill-side olive farmers to move down to the water and establish a front line against the invaders—denying them a base from which to attack Nice. In return for tax-free status, they stopped farming, took up fishing, and established *Ville-* (town) *franche* (without taxes). Since there were many such towns, this one was specifically "Tax-free town on the sea" *(sur Mer)*. Around 1560, the Duke of Savoy built

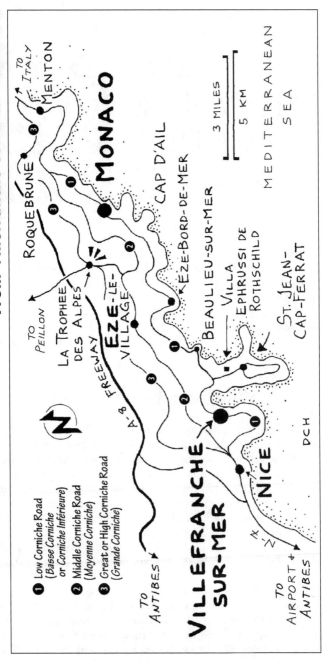

From Villefranche-sur-Mer to Monaco

the town an immense citadel (which you can still tour). Today—because two-thirds of its 8,000 people call this their primary residence—Villefranche feels more like a real community than neighboring Riviera towns.

ORIENTATION

Tourist Information

The TI is in Jardin François Binon, below the main bus stop (July–Aug daily 9:00–19:00, Sept–June Mon–Sat 9:00–12:00 & 14:00–18:30, closed Sun, a 20-min walk or €10 taxi from train station, tel. 04 93 01 73 68, www.villefranche-sur-mer.com). Pick up the brochure detailing a self-guided walking tour of Villefranche and information on boat rides. If you plan to visit Cap Ferrat, ask for the simple brochure-map showing the walks around this peninsula and information on the Villa Ephrussi de Rothschild's gardens (see "The Three Corniches," page 244).

Arrival in Villefranche

By Car: From Nice's port, follow signs for Menton, Monaco, and Basse Corniche. In Villefranche, take the road next to the TI into

the city. For a quick visit to the TI, park at the nearby pay lot. You'll find the free *Parking Fossés* a bit farther down—better for longer visits (well-signed from main road). Some hotels have parking.

By Bus: Buses from Nice and Monaco drop you just above the TI. The old town and most hotels are downhill. The stop for buses going back to Nice is across the street from where you were left (buses run every 10–15 min). Bus #111 to Cap Ferrat uses the same Villefranche stops.

By Train: Villefranche's train station is a level 15-minute walk along the water from the old town (taxi-€10, see below).

Helpful Hints

Launderette: It's just below the main road, opposite 6 avenue Sadi Carnot (daily 8:00–20:00, self-service).

Internet Access: Chez Net, an "Australian International Sports Bar Internet Café," is a fun place to get a late-night drink or check your e-mail (€2.50/15 min, open daily, place du Marché).

Taxi: Beware of taxi drivers who overcharge—the normal weekday, daytime rate to central Nice is about €30; to the airport, figure

Villefranche-sur-Mer

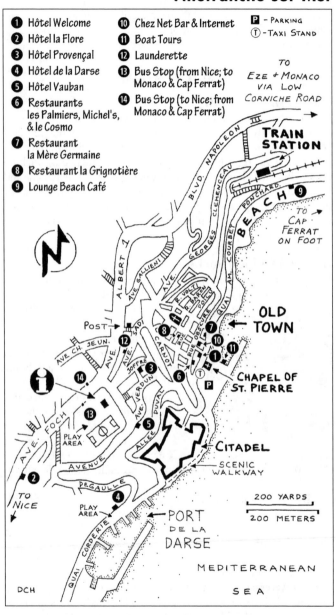

1 Hôtel Welcome
2 Hôtel la Flore
3 Hôtel Provençal
4 Hôtel de la Darse
5 Hôtel Vauban
6 Restaurants les Palmiers, Michel's, & le Cosmo
7 Restaurant la Mère Germaine
8 Restaurant la Grignotière
9 Lounge Beach Café
10 Chez Net Bar & Internet
11 Boat Tours
12 Launderette
13 Bus Stop (from Nice; to Monaco & Cap Ferrat)
14 Bus Stop (to Nice; from Monaco & Cap Ferrat)

P – PARKING
T – TAXI STAND

TO EZE + MONACO VIA LOW CORNICHE ROAD

TRAIN STATION

BEACH

TO CAP FERRAT ON FOOT

OLD TOWN

POST

CHAPEL OF ST. PIERRE

CITADEL

SCENIC WALKWAY

PLAY AREA

TO NICE

PLAY AREA

PORT DE LA DARSE

MEDITERRANEAN SEA

200 YARDS
200 METERS

DCH

about €50; and the trip to the main street level from the waterfront should be around €10 (tel. 04 93 6 70 19).

Market Day: An antiques market enlivens Villefranche on Sundays (on place Amélie Pollonnais by Hôtel le Welcome and in Jardin François Binon by the TI). On Saturday mornings, a small food market sets up by the TI (only in Jardin Binon).

Sports Fans: Lively *boules* action takes place each evening just below the TI and the huge soccer field (see page 156).

SIGHTS

The Harbor—Browse Villefranche's miniscule harbor. Only eight families still fish to make money. Gaze out to sea and marvel at the

huge yachts that call this bay home. (You might see well-coiffed captains being ferried in by dutiful mates to pick up their statuesque call girls.) Local guides keep a list of the world's 100 biggest yachts and talk about some of them like they're part of the neighborhood.

Parallel to the beach and about a block inland, you can walk the mysterious rue Obscura—a covered lane running 400 feet along the medieval rampart.

Chapel of St. Pierre (Chapelle Cocteau)—This chapel, decorated by artist, poet, and filmmaker Jean Cocteau, is the town's cultural highlight. A mean fisherwoman collects a €2 donation for the fishermen's charity, then sets you free to enjoy the chapel's small but delightful interior. In 1955, Jean Cocteau covered the barrel-vaulted chapel with heavy black lines and pastels. Each of the Cocteau scenes—the Gypsies of Stes-Maries-de-la-Mer who dance and sing to honor the Virgin; girls wearing traditional outfits; and three scenes from the life of St. Peter—are explained in English (€2, Tue–Sun 9:30–12:00 & 15:00–19:00, closed Mon, below Hôtel Welcome).

Citadel—The town's immense castle was built by the Duke of Savoy to defend against the French in the 1500s. When the region joined France in 1860, it became just a barracks. In the 20th century, with no military use, the city started using the citadel to house its police station, City Hall, and two art galleries.

Church—The town church features a fine crucifix—carved, they say, from a fig tree by a galley slave in the 1600s.

Boat Rides (Promenades en Mer)—These little cruises, with English handouts, are offered one or two days a week (June–Sept only, €11/1 hr, €16/2 hrs, across from Hôtel Welcome, tel. 04 93 76 65 65).

Beachwalk—A pleasant walk under the citadel, along a nearly beach-level rampart, connects the yacht harbor with the old town and beach. Stroll Villefranche's waterfront beyond the train station away from the town for postcard views back to Villefranche and a quieter beach (ideal picnic benches); consider extending your walk to Cap Ferrat (see page 245). Even if you're sleeping elsewhere, consider an ice-cream-licking village stroll here.

SLEEPING

There's a handful of hotels to choose from in Villefranche. The ones I list have at least half of their rooms with sea views—well worth paying extra for. The rooms at both of my first two listings, while different in cost, are about the same in comfort. Hôtel Welcome sits on the harbor in the center; Hôtel la Flore is a 10-minute walk from the old town, but has a pool and free parking.

$$$ **Hôtel Welcome***** is right on the water in the old town— all 36 balconied rooms overlook the harbor. You'll pay top price for all the comforts in a very smart, professional hotel that seems to do everything right and couldn't be better located ("comfort" Db-€164, bigger "superior" Db-€189, suites-€299–340, extra bed-€35, buffet breakfast-€12, air-con, parking garage-€16/day, 1 quai Amiral Courbet, tel. 04 93 76 27 62, fax 04 93 76 27 66, www.welcomehotel .com, resa@welcomehotel.com.).

$$$ **Hôtel la Flore***** is for you, if your idea of sightseeing is to enjoy the view from your bedroom deck, the dining room, or the pool (Db with no view-€90–125, Db with view and deck-€135, Db mini-suite-€195, extra bed-€34, Qb loft with huge terrace-€220, prices 10–15 percent cheaper Oct–March, air-con, elevator, pool, free parking, fine restaurant, just off main road high above harbor, 5 boulevard Princesse Grace de Monaco, 2 blocks from TI towards Nice, tel. 04 93 76 30 30, fax 04 93 76 99 99, www.hotel-la-flore.fr, hotel-la-flore@wanadoo.fr, SE).

$$$ **Hôtel la Fiancée du Pirate** is best for drivers, as it's above Villefranche on the Middle Corniche. Friendly Nadine (SE) offers 15 clean and comfortable rooms. Choose between larger rooms inside the building with air-conditioning (Db-€95–120), or view rooms on the garden patio (Db-€115–135, no air-con). There's a pool, garden, spacious *salon de thé*, breakfast terrace with partial views of Cap Ferrat and the sea, and even a small children's play area (8 boulevard de la Corne d'Or, Moyenne Corniche N7, tel. 04 93 76 67 40, fax 04 93 76 91 04, www.fianceedupirate.com, info@fianceedupirate.com).

$$ **Hôtel le Provençal**** is a big place crying out for an interior designer. The uninspired yet comfortable-enough rooms are a fair value, with some fine views and balconies (Db-€63–110, most around

---

Sleep Code

(€1 = about $1.20, country code: 33)
S = Single, **D** = Double/Twin, **T** = Triple, **Q** = Quad, **b** = bathroom, **s** = shower only, **no CC** = Credit Cards not accepted, **SE** = Speaks English, **NSE** = No English, * = French hotel rating (0–4 stars). Credit cards are accepted unless otherwise noted.

To help you sort easily through these listings, I've divided the rooms into three categories based on the price for a standard double room with bath:

$$$ **Higher Priced**—Most rooms €95 or more.
$$ **Moderately Priced**—Most rooms between €65–95.
$ **Lower Priced**—Most rooms €65 or less.

€80, Tb-€80–120, extra bed-€10, skip cheaper non-view rooms, 10 percent off with this book and a 2-night stay in 2005, air-con, right below the main road, a block from TI at 4 avenue Maréchal Joffre, tel. 04 93 76 53 53, fax 04 93 76 96 00, www.hotelprovencal.com, provencal@riviera.fr).

$ Hôtel la Darse**, a shy and unassuming little hotel sitting in the shadow of its highbrow brothers, offers a simple low-key alternative right on the water at Villefranche's old port. The dull hallways disguise rooms that are quiet and reasonably comfortable; those facing the sea have million-dollar-view balconies (non-view Db-€52–62, view Db-€64–76, extra bed-€10, from TI walk or drive down avenue Général de Gaulle to the old Port de la Darse, tel. 04 93 01 72 54, fax 04 93 01 84 37, hoteldeladarse@wanadoo.fr, SE). Major renovations are planned in 2005—the hotel might be closed until spring, and prices could increase.

$ Hôtel Vauban*, two blocks down from the TI, is a curious place that makes me feel like I'm in a brothel, with 15 basic rooms and decor as Old World as the owner (non-view Db-€45, view Db-€70, no CC, 11 avenue Général de Gaulle, tel. 04 93 76 62 18, e-what?, NSE).

EATING

Comparison-shopping is half the fun of dining in Villefranche. Make an event out of a pre-dinner stroll through the old city. Check what looks good on the lively place Amélie Pollonnais above the Hôtel Welcome, saunter the string of candlelit places lining the waterfront, and consider the smaller, cheaper eateries embedded in the old city's walking streets.

Les Palmiers is a beachy place buzzing with cheery diners (hearty salads and pizza-€9, open daily, on place Amélie Pollonnais, tel. 04 93 01 71 63).

Michel's, on the other side of the fountain, is more romantic and stylish (allow €35–40 per person, closed Tue, tel. 04 93 76 73 24).

Le Cosmo Restaurant is next door, with great tables overlooking the harbor and the Cocteau chapel's facade (floodlit after some wine, Cocteau pops). It serves nicely-presented gourmet dishes with less fun but better quality than Les Palmiers (fine salads and pastas-€10, great Bandol red wine, open daily, place Amélie Pollonnais, tel. 04 93 01 84 05).

La Mère Germaine, right on the harborfront, is the only place in town classy enough to lure a yachter ashore. It's dressy, with fine service and a harborside setting. The name comes from when the current owner's grandmother fed hungry GIs in World War II. Try the bouillabaisse, served with panache (€57 per person, or a mini-version for €39, €34 *menu,* open daily, reserve harborfront table, tel. 04 93 01 71 39).

Disappear into Villefranche's walking streets and find cute little **La Grignotière,** serving a €29 *gourmet menu* (open daily, 3 rue Poilu, tel. 04 93 76 79 83).

Lounge Beach Café, on the beach below the train station, is worth considering for the best view of Villefranche and decent food at reasonable prices. This place also works well for lunch or a drink with a view (salads, pastas, and à la carte, open daily, tel. 04 93 01 72 57).

Souris Gourmande ("Gourmet Mouse") is handy for a sandwich, to take away or eat there (daily 11:30–19:30, closed Fri in winter, behind Hôtel Welcome, €4 made-to-order sandwiches...be patient and get to know your chef, Albert). Sandwich in hand, there are plenty of great places to enjoy a harborside sit.

TRANSPORTATION CONNECTIONS

The last bus leaves Nice for Villefranche at about 19:45; the last bus from Villefranche to Nice leaves at about 21:00; and one train runs later (24:00).

From Villefranche by train to: Monaco (2/hr, 10 min), **Nice** (2/hr, 10 min), **Antibes** (2/hr, 40 min).

By bus to: Cap Ferrat (6/day, 10 min), **Monaco** (4/hr, 25 min), **Nice** (4/hr, 15 min).

The Three Corniches

Nice, Villefranche-sur-Mer, and Monaco are linked with three coastal routes: the Low, Middle, and High Corniches. The roads are nicknamed for the decorative frieze that runs along the top of a building (cornice). Each Corniche offers sensational views and a different perspective on this exotic slice of real estate.

Low Corniche: The *Basse Corniche* (often called *Corniche Inférieure*) strings ports, beaches, and villages together for a traffic-filled ground-floor view. It was built in the 1860s (along with the new train line) to bring people to the casino in Monte Carlo. When this Low Corniche was finished, many hill-town villagers came down and started the communities that line the sea today. Before 1860, the population of the coast between Villefranche-sur-Mer and Monte Carlo was zero.

Middle Corniche: The *Moyenne Corniche* is higher, quieter, and far more impressive. It runs through Eze (described below) and provides breathtaking views over the Mediterranean, with several scenic pullouts (the one above Villefranche-sur-Mer is particularly stunning).

High Corniche: Napoleon's crowning road-construction achievement, the *Grande Corniche* caps the cliffs with staggering views from almost 1,600 feet above the sea. It is actually the Via Aurelia, used by Romans to conquer the West.

Villas: Driving from Villefranche-sur-Mer to Monaco, you'll come upon impressive villas. A particularly grand entry leads to the sprawling estate built by King Leopold II of Belgium in the 1920s. Those driving up to the Middle Corniche will look down on this yellow mansion that fills an entire hilltop with a lush garden. This estate was later owned by the Agnelli family (of Fiat fame and fortune), and then by the Safra family (American bankers).

The Best Route: For a ▲▲▲ route, **drivers** should take the Middle Corniche from Nice to Eze, follow signs to the High Corniche *(Grande Corniche/La Turbie)* from there, and after La Turbie, drop down into Monaco. **Buses** travel each route; the higher the Corniche, the less frequent the buses (roughly 5/day on Middle and High, 2/hr on Low; get details at Nice's bus station).

The following villages and sights are listed from west to east, as you'll reach them, from Villefranche-sur-Mer to Monaco.

Cap Ferrat

This peninsula, worth ▲, decorates Villefranche-sur-Mer's sea views. An exclusive, largely residential community, it's a peaceful eddy off the busy Nice–Monaco route (Low Corniche). You could spend a day on this peninsula, wandering the port village of St. Jean-Cap-Ferrat, touring the Villa Ephrussi de Rothschild mansion and gardens, and walking on sections of the beautiful trails that follow the coast. If you have a house here, Microsoft mogul Paul Allen is your neighbor. The **TI** is between the port and Villa Ephrussi (at 59 avenue Denis Séméria, tel. 04 93 76 08 90).

Getting to Cap Ferrat from Villefranche: You can go by **car** (Low Corniche) or **taxi** (allow €15 one-way); ride the **bus** (#111 from main stop in Villefranche, 6/day, 10 min; bus from Nice to Monaco also drops you at edge of the Cap—4/hr, 5 min, a 15-min walk to Villa Ephrussi); or **walk** (50 min from Villefranche). Walkers from Villefranche-sur-Mer go past the train station along the beach and climb the steps at the far end. Continue straight past the mansions (with gates more expensive than my house) and make the first right. You'll see signs to the Villa Ephrussi de Rothschild, then to Cap Ferrat's port.

SIGHTS AND ACTIVITIES

Villa Ephrussi de Rothschild—In what seems like the ultimate in Riviera extravagance, Venice, Versailles, and the Côte d'Azur come together in the pastel-pink Villa Ephrussi. Rising above Cap Ferrat, this 1905 mansion comes with territorial views east to Villefranche-sur-Mer and west to Beaulieu-sur-Mer.

Start with the well-furnished belle époque **interior** (helpful English handout provided). An 18-minute film (English subtitles) gives background on the life of rich and eccentric Beatrice, Baroness de Rothschild, who built and furnished the place. As you stroll the halls, you'll pass rooms of royal furnishings and personal possessions, including her bathroom case for cruises. A fancy tearoom serves drinks and lunch with a view.

But the gorgeous **gardens** are why most come here. Behind the mansion, stroll through the seven lush gardens recreated from different parts of the world. The sea views from here are lovely. Don't miss the Alhambra-like Spanish gardens, the rose garden at the far end, and the view back to the house from the "Temple of Love" gazebo.

Cost and Hours: Palace and gardens-€8.50, skippable tour of upstairs-€2 extra, combo-ticket with Villa Kérylos-€14.50; Feb–Oct daily 10:00–18:00, July–Aug until 19:00; Nov–Jan Mon–Fri 14:00–18:00, Sat–Sun 10:00–18:00; tel. 04 93 01 45 90, www.villa-ephrussi.com. Parking is tricky; a small turnaround is at the top.

Plage de Passable—Tucked away at the top of Cap Ferrat (a 5-min hike below the Villa Ephrussi), with a view of Villefranche, is this remarkably humble and peaceful beach. Half is public (free, with shower), and the other half is privately run by a small restaurant (€12/half day with changing locker, lounge chair, and shower; 14:00 is change-over time, reserve ahead as this is a prime spot, easy parking, tel. 04 93 76 06 17). If ever you were to do the French Riviera rent-a-beach ritual, this is the place.

St. Jean-Cap-Ferrat Village—This sophisticated port lies at Cap Ferrat's center (facing east), with yachts, boardwalks, views, and boutiques packaged in a "take your time, darling" atmosphere.

Walks Around Cap Ferrat—The Cap is an ideal place for a walk, as well-maintained foot trails follow most of its length. You have three easy, mostly level options (25 min, 40 min, or 3 hrs). The TIs in Villefranche and St. Jean-Cap-Ferrat have maps of Cap Ferrat with walking paths marked.

The 25-minute, 1.5-mile **stroll to the town of Beaulieu-sur-Mer** takes you past sumptuous views and ends near the Villa Kérylos (see below). Leave St. Jean-Cap-Ferrat's port with the water on your right and take avenue Denis Séméria to promenade Maurice Rouvier.

I also like the **40-minute trail** that leaves from near St. Jean-Cap-Ferrat, by plage Paloma (parking available at the port or on streets near plage Paloma). Do this walk counterclockwise, starting behind the phone booth just before plage Paloma. The trail is level and paved, yet uneven enough that good shoes are helpful. Benches offer ideal picnic sites over crashing waves, or eat at the café on plage Paloma at the end of the walk (sandwiches and salads).

Those interested in a **three-hour hike** should follow the signs below Villa Ephrussi to plage de Passable (10 min on foot from the villa, parking available). Walk down to the beach (great café, ideal for lunch), turn left, and cross the beach. Go along a paved road behind a big apartment building, and after 350 feet, take the steps down to a trail *(Sentier Touristique)* that circles the Cap. You'll pass by the port of Cap Ferrat near the end of the trail, where you can cross back to the Villa Ephrussi and plage de Passable.

Beaulieu-sur-Mer

In this village, on the Low Corniche just after Cap Ferrat, the main point of interest is the remarkable **Villa Kérylos.** In 1902, an eccentric millionaire modeled his new mansion on a Greek villa from the island of Delos from about 200 B.C. No expense was spared—from floor mosaics to Carrara marble columns to exquisite wood furnishings—as he recreated his Greek fantasy. The rain-powered shower is fun, and the included audioguide will increase your Greek IQ (€7.50, combo-ticket with Villa Ephrussi de Rothschild-€14.50, Feb–Oct daily 10:00–18:00, July–Aug daily 10:00–19:00, Nov–Jan Mon–Fri 14:00–18:00, Sat–Sun 10:00–18:00, tel. 04 93 01 01 44, www.villa-kerylos.com; park near Casino in Beaulieu, not on the Villa's access road).

Buses and trains leave from Beaulieu-sur-Mer to seafront destinations (by bus to Nice: 4/hr, 20 min; to Monaco: 4/hr, 20 min; by train to Nice: 2/hr, 10 min, Monaco 2/hr, 10 min).

Eze-le-Village

Floating high above the sea, flowery Eze-le-Village (don't confuse it with the seafront town of Eze-Bord-de-Mer) is entirely consumed by tourism. This *village d'art et de gastronomie* (as it calls itself) mixes perfume outlets, upscale boutiques, steep cobbled lanes, and magnificent views. Touristy as the place certainly Eze, its stony state of preservation and magnificent hilltop setting make a visit here worthwhile.

Bus stops and parking lots weld the town to the highway (Middle Corniche) that passes under its lowest wall. The **TI** is in the car park below the town (place de Gaulle, tel. 04 93 41 26 00, www.eze-riviera.com).

Getting to Eze-le-Village: There are two Ezes, namely Eze-le-Village (the spectacular hill town, your destination) and Eze-Bord-de-Mer (a dull beach town far below Eze-le-Village). Eze-le-Village is about 20 minutes east of Villefranche-sur-Mer on the Middle Corniche. There are six buses per day from Nice to Eze-le-Village (3 on Sun), or you can take the train to Eze-Bord-de-Mer and take the shuttle bus up to Eze-le-Village (€4, May–Oct only, daily 9:30–18:30, 8/day; or allow €22 one-way for a taxi between the two Ezes).

Eze Town Wander

From the TI and car park, wander uphill into the town. You'll pass an exclusive hotel and the start of a steep trail down to the beach marked *Eze-Bord-de-Mer*. (For a panoramic view and ideal picnic perch, walk 30 steps down this path.) If you continue up, you enter **place du Centenaire.** A town map here helps you get oriented. The monument celebrates the 100th anniversary of the 1860 plebiscite in which all 133 Eze residents voted to leave the Italian Duchy of Savoy and join France. Now pass through the once-formidable town gate (designed to keep the Turks out) and climb into the 14th-century village.

Wandering the narrow lanes—ever uphill—you'll come to the **Eze Château.** This was the winter getaway of the Swedish royal family from 1923 until 1953; today it's a hotel. The château's tea-room (Salon de Thé) offers the most scenic €4 tea or coffee break you'll ever enjoy, on a cliff overlooking the jagged Riviera and sea.

Eventually the town ends at its hilltop castle ruins—now the **Exotic Gardens,** a prickly festival of cactus (well-described in English, €3, covered by Riviera Carte Musées pass, open daily, hours change frequently but usually 9:00–18:30, tel. 04 93 41 10 30). Since 1949, these ruins have been home to 400 different plants 1,300 feet above the sea. At the top, you'll be treated to a commanding 360-degree view, with a helpful *table d'orientation*. (On a clear day, you can see Corsica.) The castle was demolished by Louis XIV in 1706. The French destroyed castles like this all over Europe (most notably along the Rhine), because they didn't want to risk having to do battle with them at some future date.

As you descend, drop by the Eze **church.** While built during Napoleonic times, it has an uncharacteristic Baroque fanciness—a reminder that 300 years of Savoy rule left the townsfolk with an Italian savoir faire and a sensibility for decor.

Before leaving town, consider visiting the Fragonard perfume outlet (see below).

Near Eze

Fragonard Perfume Factory—This factory, with its huge tour-bus parking lot, lies on the Middle Corniche 350 feet below Eze-le-Village. It's designed for tour groups and cranks them through all day long (you'll see the gravel littered with the color-coded "F" stickers that each tourist wears so that the salespeople know which guide gets the kickback). Drop in for a free 15-minute tour (daily 8:30–18:00, but best Mon–Fri 9:00–11:00 & 14:00–15:30, when the "factory" actually has people working, tel. 04 93 41 05 05). You'll see how the perfume and scented soaps are made and bottled before you're herded into the gift shop.

EATING

To enjoy Eze-le-Village in relative peace, visit at sunset and stay for dinner. You'll dine well at the stone-cozy **Le Troubador** (€30 *menu,* closed Sun–Mon, 4 rue du Brec, tel. 04 93 41 19 03), or for less, with better views, at the basic **Nid de L'Aigle** ("Eagle's Nest," closed Wed except in summer, tel. 04 93 41 19 08).

La Trophée des Alpes

High above Monaco, on the High Corniche in the village of La Turbie, lies one of this region's most evocative historic sights (with dramatic views over the entire country of Monaco as a bonus). This massive Roman monument, worth ▲▲, commemorates Augustus Caesar's conquest of the Alps and its 44 hostile tribes. It's exciting to think that, in a way, La Trophée des Alpes celebrates a victory that kicked off the Pax Romana—joining Gaul and Germania, freeing up the main artery of the Roman Empire, and lacing together Spain and Italy.

Walk around the monument and notice how the Romans built a fine quarried-stone exterior, filled in with rubble and coarse concrete. Flanked by the vanquished in chains, the towering inscription tells the story: It was erected "by the senate and the people to honor the emperor." The monument was restored in the 1930s and 1940s with money from the Tuck family of New Hampshire.

The one-room museum shows a reconstruction and translation of the dramatic inscription, listing all of the feisty alpine tribes that put up such a fight (€5, daily 9:30–11:30 & 13:00–18:30, tel. 04 93 41 20 84). Escorts from the museum take people up the monument, but it's not worth waiting for.

The charming village of **La Turbie** is less touristy than others around here, and has plenty of cafés and restaurants.

Getting to La Trophée des Alpes: By **car,** take the High Corniche to La Turbie (10 min east of, and above, Eze-le-Village). At La Regence Café in La Turbie, turn right for the gate to the monument and parking lot. You can also get here by **bus** from Nice or Monaco (from either: €3, 4/day, 45 min; last bus returning to Nice is at about 18:00).

Monaco

Despite overdevelopment, high prices, and wall-to-wall daytime tourists, Monaco (mah-nah-koh) is a Riviera must. Monaco is on the go. Since 1929, cars have raced around the port and in front of the casino in one of the world's most famous auto races, the Grand Prix of Monaco (May 19–22 in 2005; see page 257). The new breakwater—constructed elsewhere and towed in by sea—enables big cruise ships to actually dock here. The district of

Fontvieille, reclaimed from the sea, bristles with luxury high-rise condos. But don't look for anything too deep in this glittering tax haven. Two-thirds of its 30,000 residents live here because there is no income tax—leaving fewer than 10,000 true Monegasques.

This miniscule principality (.75 square mile) borders only France and the Mediterranean. The country has always been tiny, but it used to be...less tiny. In an 1860 plebiscite, Monaco lost two-thirds of its territory as the region of Menton voted to join France. To compensate, France suggested Monaco build a fancy casino and promised to connect it to the world with a road (the Low Corniche) and a train line. This started a high-class tourist boom that has yet to let up.

While "independent," Monaco is run as a piece of France. A French civil servant appointed by the French president—with the

Monaco

- **T** – ACCESS TO TRAIN STATION
- **P** – PARKING

300 YARDS
300 METERS

TO MENTON

TO MENTON

MIDDLE CORNICHE

FRANCE

BLVD. PRINCESSE CHARLOTTE

BLVD. MOULINS

LOEW'S SPEL. CASINO

AVE. SPEL.

JARDIN EXOTIQUE

AVE. COSTA

PLACE DU CASINO

CASINO

AVE. D'OSTENDE

PALAIS DES CONGRES & "LE CASINO"

TO NICE

BLVD. DU RAINIER III

RUE GRIMALDI

PORT LOTSA YACHTS!

MONTE-CARLO

JARDIN EXOTIQUE

R. PRIN CAR

PLACE D'ARMES

BLVD. ALBERT I

MONACO-VILLE

TO NICE

BLVD.

RAMPE MAJOR

AVE. DE LA PORTE NEUVE

POST

MONTE CARLO STORY & **P** "LE PALAIS"

PALACE & NAPOLEON COLLECTION

CATHEDRAL

COUSTEAU AQUARIUM

OLD TOWN

FONT-VIEILLE

BOTANICAL GARDEN

1. Hôtel de France
2. Pan Bagnat sandwiches at rue Basse #8
3. Local bus stops
4. Bus stops FROM Nice
5. Bus stops TO Nice

blessing of Monaco's Prince Rainier—serves as state minister and manages the place. Monaco's phone system, electricity, water, and so on, are all French.

Monaco is a business, and Prince Rainier is its CEO. While its famous casino provides only 5 percent of the state's revenue, its 43 banks—which offer an attractive way to hide your money—are hugely profitable. The prince also makes money with a value-added tax (19.6 percent, the same as in France), plus real estate and corporate taxes.

The glamorous romance and marriage of the American actress Grace Kelly to Prince Rainier added to Monaco's fairy-tale mystique. Grace Kelly first came to Monaco to star in the 1955

Hitchcock film *To Catch a Thief,* in which she was filmed racing along the Corniches. Later, she married her prince and adopted the country. Tragically, Monaco's much-loved Princess Grace died in a car wreck on that same Corniche in 1982.

It's a special place...there are more people in Prince Rainier's philharmonic orchestra (about 100) than in his army (about 80 guards). His princedom is well-guarded, with police and cameras on every corner. (They say you could win a million dollars at the casino and walk through the wee hours to the train station without a worry.) Stamps are so few, they increase in value almost as soon as they're printed. And collectors snapped up the rare Monaco versions of euro coins (with Prince Ranier's portrait) so quickly that many locals have never even seen one.

ORIENTATION

The principality of Monaco consists of three distinct tourist areas: Monaco-Ville, Monte Carlo, and La Condamine. Monaco-Ville fills the rock high above everything else. This is the oldest section, home to Prince Rainier's palace and all the sights except the casino. Monte Carlo is the area around the casino. And La Condamine is the port (which divides Monaco-Ville and Monte Carlo). You may also pass through a fourth, less-interesting area, Fontvieille.

Buses #1 and #2 link all areas (one ticket-€1.40, four tickets-€3.50, until 21:00, 10/hr, less on Sun). From the port (and train station), it's a 15-minute walk to the Prince's Palace or to the casino (40 min from palace to casino).

Telephone Tip: To call Monaco from France, dial 00, then 377 (Monaco's country code) and the eight-digit number. Within Monaco, simply dial the eight-digit number.

Tourist Information
The main TI is near the casino (2 boulevard des Moulins, Mon–Sat 9:00–19:00, Sun 10:00–12:00), but there's a handier branch in the train station (daily in summer 8:00–19:30, less off-season, tel. 00-377/92 16 61 16 or 00-377/92 16 61 66, www.monaco-tourisme .com). From June to September, you'll find information kiosks in the Monaco-Ville parking garage and on the port.

Arrival in Monaco
By Bus from Nice and Villefranche-sur-Mer: There are three stops in Monaco, in order from Nice: in front of a tunnel at the base of Monaco-Ville (place d'Armes), on the port, and below the casino (on avenue d'Ostende). The first stop is the best starting point. From there, you can walk up to Monaco-Ville and the palace (10 min straight up), or catch a local bus (lines #1 or #2). To reach the bus

stop and steps up to Monaco-Ville, cross the street right in front of the tunnel and walk with the rock on your right for about 200 feet.

Keep your receipt for the return ride to Nice or Villefranche (RCA buses run twice as often as Cars Broch). The bus stop back to Nice is across the major road from your arrival point, at the light. The last bus leaves Monaco for Nice at about 20:00 (last train leaves at about 23:30).

By Train from Nice: The train station is in central Monaco, about a 10-minute walk to the casino in Monte Carlo or the port, and 25 minutes to the palace in Monaco-Ville.

This is a long, underground station with many services. The TI, baggage check, and ticket windows are up the escalator at the Italy end of the station. There are three exits: two from the train platform level (one at each end) and one from above the platforms, up the escalator, past the TI. To walk to the casino, use this upper exit (go past TI, then up the elevator, then exit station and turn left on boulevard Princesse Charlotte and turn right on rue Iris; allow 10 min).

To reach Monaco-Ville and the palace from the station, take one of the two platform-level exits. The exit near the Italy end of the platform leads to the port and to the bus stop for city buses #1 and #2, serving Monaco-Ville and the casino (follow *Sortie la Condamine* and go down two escalators, then go left following *Accès Port* signs). The port is a few blocks downhill from this exit, from which you can walk another 20 minutes to the palace (or casino, though this is the longer way there). The other platform-level exit is at the Nice end of the tracks (signed *Sortie Fontvieille*), which takes you along a long tunnel (TI annex at end) to the foot of Monaco-Ville; from here, it's a 15-minute walk to the palace.

To take the short-but-sweet coastal **walking path** into Monaco's Fontvieille district, get off the train one station before Monaco, in Cap d'Ail. Turn left out of the little station and walk 50 yards up the road, then turn left, going downstairs and under the tracks. Turn left onto the coastal trail, and hike the 20 minutes to Fontvieille. Once you reach Fontvieille, it's a 15-minute uphill hike to Monaco's sights.

By Car: Follow *Centre-Ville* signs into Monaco, then follow the red-letter signs to parking garages at *Le Casino* (for Monte Carlo) or *Le Palais* (for Monaco-Ville). The first hour of parking is free; the next costs €3.50.

Getting Around Monaco

In addition to the city bus system (described under "Orientation," above), here are your other transportation options.

Tourist Train: "Azur Express" tourist trains begin at the aquarium and pass by the port, casino, and palace (€6, 30 min, 2/hr, 10:30–18:00 in summer, 11:00–17:00 in winter depending on weather, taped English commentary, tel. 00-377/92 05 64 38).

Taxis: If you've lost track of time at the casino, you can call the 24-hour taxi service (tel. 00-377/93 15 01 01)...provided you still have enough money to pay for the cab home.

SIGHTS

Monaco-Ville

All of Monaco's sights (except for the casino) are in Monaco-Ville, packed within a few Disney-esque blocks. To get from anywhere in Monaco to the palace square, place du Palais (Monaco-Ville's sight-seeing ground zero), take bus #1 or #2 to place de la Visitation (leave bus to the right and walk straight 5 min, passing a fountain). If you're walking up from the port, the well-marked lane leads directly to the *Palais.*

Palace Square (Place du Palais)—This square is the best place to get oriented to Monaco, as it offers views on both sides of the rock. Facing the palace, go to the right and look out over the city. This little, pastel Hong Kong look-alike was born on this rock in 1215 and has managed to remain an inde-pendent country for most of its nearly 800 years. Looking beyond the glitzy port, notice  the faded green roof above and to the right: the casino that put Monaco on the map.

Now walk to the statue of the monk grasping a sword near the palace. Meet **François Grimaldi,** a renegade Italian dressed as a monk, who captured Monaco in 1297 and began the dynasty that still rules the principality. Prince Rainier is his great-great-great...grandson, which makes Monaco's royal family Europe's longest-lasting dynasty.

Walk to the opposite side of the square and the Louis XIV **cannonballs.** Down below is Monaco's newest area, Fontvieille, where much of its post-WWII growth has been. Prince Rainier has continued (some say, been obsessed with) Monaco's economic growth, creating landfills (topped with homes, such as Fontvieille), flashy ports, new beaches, and the new rail station. Today, thanks to Prince Rainier's efforts, tiny Monaco is a member of the United Nations. The current buzz is about how soon he'll hand over the reign of the principality to his son, Albert.

You can buy Monaco stamps (popular collectibles, or mail from here) at the post office (PTT) a few blocks down rue Comte Félix Gastaldi.

Prince's Palace (Palais Princier)—A medieval castle sat where Monaco's palace is today. Its strategic setting has had a lot to do with Monaco's ability to resist attackers. Today, Prince Rainier and his son Albert live in the palace; princesses Stephanie and Caroline live just down the main street. The palace guards protect the prince 24/7, and still stage a Changing of the Guard ceremony with all the pageantry of an important nation (daily at 11:55, fun to watch but jam-packed). Automated and uninspired tours (in English) take you through part of the prince's lavish palace in 30 minutes. The rooms are well-furnished and impressive, but interesting only if you haven't seen a château lately (€6, daily June–Sept 9:30–18:00, Oct 10:00–17:00, closed Nov–May, tel. 00-377/93 25 18 31).

Napoleon Collection—Napoleon occupied Monaco after the French Revolution. This is the prince's private collection of what Napoleon left behind: military medals, swords, guns, letters, and, most interesting, his hat. I found this collection more appealing than the palace (€4, June–Sept daily 9:30–18:00, Oct daily 10:00–17:00, Dec–May Tue–Sun 10:30–12:30 & 14:00–17:00, closed Mon, next to palace entry).

Cathedral of Monaco (Cathédrale de Monaco)—The somber cathedral, rebuilt in 1878 to show Monaco cared for more than just its new casino, is where centuries of Grimaldis are buried. Circle behind the altar (counterclockwise). The last tomb—inscribed *"Gratia Patricia, MCMLXXXII"*—is where Princess Grace was buried in 1982 (daily 8:30–19:00, until 18:00 in winter).

As you leave the cathedral, step across the street and look down on the newly-reclaimed Fontvieille district and the fancy condos that contribute to the incredible population density of this miniscule country. The adjacent and immaculately maintained Jardin Botanique offer more fine views and a good place to picnic.

Cousteau Aquarium (Musée Océanographique)—Prince Albert I built this impressive cliff-hanging aquarium in 1910 as a monument to his enthusiasm for things from the sea. One wing features Mediterranean fish; tropical species swim around in the other (all well-described in English). Jacques Cousteau directed the aquarium for 17 years. The fancy Albert I Hall upstairs houses the museum (no English), featuring models of Albert and his beachcombers hard at work (aquarium and museum-€12, kids-€6, daily April–June and Sept 9:30–19:00, July–Aug 9:30–19:30, Oct–March 10:00–18:00, at opposite end of Monaco-Ville from palace, down the steps from Monaco-Ville bus stop, tel. 00-377/93 15 36 00, www.oceano.mc).

Monte Carlo Story—The informative 35-minute film gives a help-ful account of Monaco's history and offers a comfortable soft-chair break from all that walking (€6.50, usually on the hour, daily Jan–June and Sept–Oct 14:00–17:00, July–Aug 14:00–18:00, closed Nov–Dec, you can join frequent extra showings for groups, English headphones; from aquarium, take escalator into parking garage, then take elevator down and follow signs).

Monte Carlo

▲**Casino**—Monte Carlo, which means "Charles' Hill" in Spanish, is named for the local prince who presided over Monaco's 19th-century makeover. Begin your visit to Europe's most famous casino in the park above the traffic circle. In the mid-1800s, olive groves stood here. Then, with the construction of this casino, spas, and easy road and train access, one of Europe's poorest countries was on the Grand Tour map—*the* place for the vacationing aristocracy to play. Today, Monaco has the world's highest per-capita income.

The casino is designed to make the wealthy feel comfortable while losing money. Charles Garnier designed this casino (with an opera house inside) in 1878, in part to thank the prince for his financial help in completing Paris' Opéra Garnier (which Garnier also designed). The central doors provide access to slot machines, private gaming rooms, and the opera house. The private gaming rooms occupy the left wing of the building.

Count the counts and Rolls-Royces in front of Hôtel de Paris (built at the same time), then strut inside past the slots to the sumptuous atrium. This is the lobby for the opera house (open only for performances). There's a model of the opera at the end of the room, and marble WCs on the right. Anyone over 21 (even in shorts, if before 20:00) can get as far as the one-armed bandits (push button on slot machines to claim your winnings), though you'll need decent attire to go any further. After 20:00, shorts are off-limits anywhere.

The scene, flooded with camera-toting tourists during the day, is great at night—and downright James Bond–like in the private rooms. The park behind the casino offers a peaceful café and a good view of the casino's rear facade and of Monaco-Ville.

If paying an entrance fee to lose money is not your idea of fun, access to all games in the new, plebeian, American-style Loews Casino, adjacent to the old casino, is free.

Cost and Hours: The first rooms, Salons Européens, open at 12:00 and cost €10 to enter. The glamorous private game rooms—where you can rub elbows with high rollers—open at 16:00, others not until 21:00, and cost an additional €10 (and you must show your passport). A tie and jacket (necessary in the evening) can be rented at the bag check for €30, plus a €40 deposit. Dress standards for women are far more relaxed (only tennis shoes are a definite no-no, tel. 00377/92 16 20 00, www.casino-monte-carlo.com).

Take the Money and Run: The return bus stop to Nice is at the top of the park above the casino on avenue de la Costa. To

Le Grand Prix Automobile de Monaco

Each May (May 19–22 in 2005), the Grand Prix of Monaco focuses the world's attention on this little country. The car race started as an enthusiasts' car rally by the Automobile Club of Monaco (and is still run by the same group, 90 years later). Racers still consider this one of the most important races on their circuits. By Grand Prix standards, it's an unusual course, running through the streets of this tiny principality, sardined between

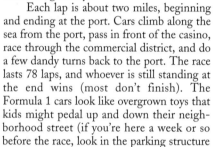

mountains and sea. The hilly landscape makes the streets of Monaco narrow, with tight curves, steep climbs, and extremely short straightaways.

Each lap is about two miles, beginning and ending at the port. Cars climb along the sea from the port, pass in front of the casino, race through the commercial district, and do a few dandy turns back to the port. The race lasts 78 laps, and whoever is still standing at the end wins (most don't finish). The Formula 1 cars look like overgrown toys that kids might pedal up and down their neighborhood street (if you're here a week or so before the race, look in the parking structure below Monaco-Ville where many are kept—you're free to browse). Time trials to establish pole position begin three days before race day, which is always a Sunday. In 2005, the time trials will take place May 19, 20, and 21, and the race itself will be on May 22. More than 150,000 people attend the gala event; like the nearby film festival in Cannes, it involves parties on yachts, in fine restaurants, and at four-star hotels.

return to the train station from the casino, walk up the parkway in front of the casino, turn left on boulevard des Moulins, turn right on impasse de la Fontaine, climb the steps, and turn left on boulevard Princesse Charlotte (entrance to train station is next to Parking de la Gare; look for *Gare SNCF* sign).

SLEEPING AND EATING

(€1 = about $1.20, country code: 377)
For many, Monaco is best after dark. The perfectly pleasant **$$ Hôtel de France**** is reasonable (Sb-€72, Db-€94, includes breakfast, 6 rue de la Turbie, near west exit from train station, tel. 00-377/93 30 24 64, fax 00-377/92 16 13 34, hotel-france@monte-carlo.mc).

Several cafés serve basic fare at reasonable prices (day and night) on the port, along the traffic-free rue Princesse Caroline. In

Monaco-Ville, you'll find good *pan bagnat* and other sandwiches at 8 rue Basse, just off the palace square.

TRANSPORTATION CONNECTIONS

From Monaco by train to: Nice (2/hr, 20 min), **Villefranche-sur-Mer** (2/hr, 10 min), **Antibes** (2/hr, 45 min).

By bus to: Nice (4/hr, 40 min), **Villefranche-sur-Mer** (4/hr, 25 min).

The last bus leaves Monaco for Villefranche-sur-Mer and Nice at about 20:00; the last train leaves Monaco for Villefranche-sur-Mer and Nice at about 23:30.

ANTIBES, CANNES, AND ST-TROPEZ

The Riviera opens up west of Nice with bigger, sandier beaches and cheap high-rise development. Ancient Antibes and glamorous Cannes buck the blue-collar, high-rise trend, each with thriving centers jammed with pedestrians and yachts. Trendy St-Tropez, a scenic hour's drive from Antibes, marks the western edge of the French Riviera.

Antibes

Antibes has a down-to-earth, easygoing ambience that's rare for this area. Its old town is postcard-perfect: a cluster of red-tiled roofs rising above the blue Mediterranean, watched over by twin medieval lookout towers and wrapped in a rampart. Visitors making the 30-minute trip from Nice browse Europe's biggest yacht harbor, snooze on a sandy beach, loiter through an enjoyable old town, stumble upon characteristic markets, and climb to a castle filled with Picassos.

Though it's much smaller than Nice, Antibes has a history that goes back just as far. Both towns were founded by Greek traders in the fifth century B.C. To the Greeks, Antibes was "Antipolis"—the town *(polis)* opposite *(anti)* Nice. For the next several centuries, Antibes remained in the shadow of its neighbor. By the turn of the 20th century, the town was a military base—so the rich and famous partied elsewhere. But when the army checked out after World War I, Antibes was "discovered" and enjoyed a particularly roaring '20s—with the help of party animals like Rudolph Valentino and the rowdy-yet-very-silent Charlie Chaplin. Fun-seekers even invented water skiing right here in the 1920s.

Antibes

① To Hôtel le Mas Djoliba
② Auberge Provençale
③ Modern Hôtel
④ Hôtel Relais du Postillon
⑤ To Hôtel Beau Site
⑥ Hôtel le Cameo
⑦ Restaurant le Vauban
⑧ Restaurant l'Ecureuil
⑨ Restaurant Chez Juliette
⑩ Restaurant les Vieux Murs
⑪ Le Café Jardin
⑫ Heidi's English Bookshop
⑬ Market Hall
⑭ Launderette

ORIENTATION

Antibes' old town lies between the port and boulevard Albert 1er and avenue Robert Soleau. Place Nationale is the old town's hub of activity. Lively rue Aubernon connects the port and the old town. Stroll along the sea between the Picasso Museum and square Albert 1er (where boulevard Albert 1er meets the water); the best beaches lie just beyond square Albert 1er, and the path is beautiful. Good play areas for children are on place des Martyrs de la Résistance (close to recommended Hôtel Relais du Postillon).

Tourist Information

There are two TIs. The most convenient is located in the old town, just inside the walls at 21 boulevard d'Aguillon (unpredictable hours, generally June–Aug daily 9:00–21:00, Sept–May Mon–Fri 10:00–12:00 & 14:00–17:00, closed Sat–Sun, tel. 04 93 34 65 65, www.antibes-ville.com). The big *Maison de Tourisme* is in the newer city, east of the old town where boulevard Albert 1er and rue de la République meet at 11 place Général de Gaulle (July–Aug daily 9:00–19:00, Sept–June Mon–Sat 9:00–12:30 & 13:30–18:00, closed Sun, tel. 04 92 90 53 00, www.antibes-juanlespins.com). At either TI, pick up the excellent city map and the interesting brochure with a walking tour of old Antibes (in English), and get details on the hikes described below. The Nice TI has Antibes maps; plan ahead.

Arrival in Antibes

By Train: To get to the port (5-min walk), cross the street in front of the station and follow avenue de la Libération downhill. To reach the main TI in the modern city (15-min walk), exit right from the station on avenue Robert Soleau; follow *Maison du Tourisme* signs to place Général de Gaulle. Or hop on the free minibus (see "Getting Around Antibes," below; exit station to the right and cross the street to the park).

By Bus: The bus station is at the edge of the old town on place Guynemer, a block below the TI (info desk open Mon–Sat 8:30–12:00 & 14:30–17:30, closed Sun, public WCs around back).

By Car: Day-trippers should follow *Centre-Ville* and *Vieux Port* signs, and park near the old town walls—as close to the beach as you can (first 30 min free, then about €4/3 hrs, €8/day). Enter the old town through the last arch on the right. If you're sleeping here, hotels are signed; get advice from your hotelier on where to park.

Getting Around Antibes

A free **minibus** (*Minibus Gratuit* or *Navette Gratuite*) circles Antibes (Mon–Sat 7:30–19:30, not on Sun). There are four different circuits, two of which are useful for tourists. Line #1 goes from Fort Carré to the old port, the old town, the ramparts, and back again (every 15 min). Line #2 connects the train station to the main TI at place de Gaulle and to the port every 25 mins. Stops are tricky to find—look for bus stop signs around town (the TI has a small map).

A **tourist train** offers several circuits around old Antibes, the port, and the ramparts (€6.50, departs from place de la Poste, ask about schedule, tel. 06 03 35 61 35). It even has daily departures to Juan-les-Pins (see page 265).

To call a **taxi,** dial 04 93 67 67 67.

Helpful Hints

Laundry: A full-service launderette is near the market hall on rue de la Pompe (Mon–Sat 9:00–12:00 & 14:30–19:00, closed Sun).

Bookstore: Heidi's English Bookshop has a great selection of new and used books (daily 10:00–19:00, 24 rue Aubernon).

Antibes Orientation Stroll

This quick walk will help you get your bearings. Begin at the train station (or harborside parking lot), and stroll the **harbor** along avenue de Verdun. Locals claim that this is Europe's biggest yacht harbor, with 1,600 stalls. At the end of the yachts (quai des Pêcheurs), you'll see the pathetic remains of a once-hearty fishing fleet. The Mediterranean is getting fished out. Most of the seafood you'll eat here comes from fish farms or the Atlantic.

Cross through the old gate under the ramparts to enter the **old town.** Because Antibes was the last fort before the Italian border, the French king made sure the ramparts were strong and well-defended. Today the town is the haunt of a large community of English, Irish, and Aussie boaters who help crew giant yachts of the rich and famous. (That explains the Irish pubs and English bookstores.) Drop by the cute shell-shaped **plage de la Gravette,** an adorable public beach tucked right in the middle of old Antibes.

Continue following the ramparts to the 16th-century, white-stone **Château Grimaldi.** The castle stands on prime real estate: This site has been home to the acropolis of the Greek city of Antipolis, a Roman fort, and a medieval bishop's palace. This château was the home of the Grimaldi family (who still rule Monaco), and today it houses the Picasso Museum (listed below; also see tour on page 273). The neighboring **cathedral** is built over a Greek temple.

Notice the two **towers.** They symbolized society's two dominant land-owning classes: the Church and the nobility. (In 1789, the Revolution changed all that.) From the bluff below the castle, you can see **Cap d'Antibes** crowned by its lighthouse and studded with mansions (see "Cap d'Antibes Hike," below).

The ramparts lead to the **History and Archaeology Museum** (see below). Just before that (at rue du Haut Castelet), hook inland and explore the charming, cobbled **pedestrian zone** around rue du Haut Castelet and rue du Bas Castelet. Poking around Antibes' peaceful back lanes, gradually work your way back to the entertaining covered **market hall** on cours Masséna.

SIGHTS AND ACTIVITIES

▲▲**Picasso Museum (Musée Picasso)**—The museum inside the Château Grimaldi features works from Picasso's prolific "Antibes period." The highlight is his lively, frolicking *La Joie de Vivre* painting (€5, covered by Riviera Carte Musées pass, June–Sept Tue–Sun 10:00–18:00, July–Aug Wed and Fri until 20:00; Oct–May Tue–Sun 10:00–12:00 & 14:00–18:00, always closed Mon; tel. 04 92 90 54 20). ✪ See Picasso Museum Tour on page 273.

History and Archaeology Museum (Musée d'Histoire et d'Archéologie)—Displaying Greek, Roman, and Etruscan odds and ends, this is the only place to get a sense of this city's ancient roots. I liked the 2,000-year-old lead anchors (€3, no English explanations, June–Sept Tue–Sun 10:00–18:00, July–Aug Wed and Fri until 20:00; Oct–May Tue–Sun 10:00–12:00 & 14:00–18:00, always closed Mon; on the water between Picasso Museum and place Albert 1er).

▲**Market Hall (Marché Provençal)**—The daily market bustles under a 19th-century canopy, with flowers, produce, Provençal products, and beach accessories (in old town behind Picasso Museum on cours Masséna). The market wears many appealing hats: produce daily except Monday until 13:00; handicrafts Thursday through Sunday in the afternoon; and romantic outdoor dining in the evenings.

Other Markets—Antibes' lively antique/flea market fills place Nationale and place Audiberti (next to the port) on Saturdays (7:00–18:00). Its clothing market winds through the streets around the post office (rue Lacan) on Thursdays (9:00–18:00).

Fort Carré—This impressively situated citadel, dating from 1487, was the last fort inside France. It protected Antibes from Nice, which until 1860 was part of Italy. You can tour this unusual four-pointed fort—at its height, it held 200 soldiers—but there's precious little to see inside. People visit for the stunning views (€3, covered by Riviera Carte Musées pass, includes tour, daily June–Sept 10:15–17:30, Oct–May 10:15–16:00).

Scenic footpaths link the fort to the port along the sea. It's a 30-minute portside walk from the old town to the fort (or taxi there and walk back). By foot or car, follow avenue du 11 Novembre around the port, stay on the main road (walkers can follow path by sports fields), then park on the beach just after the soccer field. A signed dirt path leads to Fort Carré. Keep following green-lettered signs to *Le Fort/Sens de la Visite.*

Beaches (Plages)—The best beaches  stretch between Antibes' port and Cap d'Antibes, and the very best (plage de la Salis and plage du Ponteil) are just south of square Albert 1er. All are golden and sandy. Plage de la Salis is busy in summer, but it's manageable, with snack stands every so often and views of the old town. The closest beach to the old town is at the port (plage de la Gravette) and remains relatively calm in any season.

Walks and Hikes

From square Albert 1er (where boulevard Albert 1er meets the beach), there's a great view of plage de la Salis and Cap d'Antibes. That tower on the hill is your destination for the first walk described below. The longer "Cap d'Antibes Hike" begins on the next beach, just over that hill.

▲▲**Chapelle et Phare de la Garoupe**—The sensational views (best at sunset) from this chapel and lighthouse more than make up for the 25-minute uphill climb from the far end of plage de la Salis (a block after Maupassant Apartments, follow pedestrian-only chemin du Calvaire up to lighthouse tower). An orientation table explains that you can see from Nice to Cannes and up to the Alps. By car, follow signs for Cap d'Antibes, then look for signs to Chapelle et Phare de la Garoupe.

▲**Cap d'Antibes Hike (Sentier Touristique Piétonnier de Tirepoil)**—At the end of the mattress-ridden plage de la Garoupe (over the hill from lighthouse) is a well-maintained trail around Cap d'Antibes. The beautiful path follows the rocky coast below exclusive mansions for about two miles, then heads inland, ending at the recommended Hôtel Beau-Site (and bus stop). You can walk as far as you'd like and then double back, or do the whole loop (allow 2 hrs, use the TI Antibes map). Locals call this the "Bay of Millionaires."

To get to the trail from Antibes, take **bus** #2A from the bus station to *La Fontaine* stop at the Hôtel Beau-Site (every 40 min, return stop is 50 yards down on opposite side, get return times at station, also posted at stop). Walk 10 minutes down to plage de la Garoupe and start from there. By **car,** follow signs to Cap d'Antibes, then plage de la Garoupe, and park there. The trail begins at the far-right end of plage de la Garoupe.

Near Antibes
Juan-les-Pins—This village, across the Cap d'Antibes isthmus from Antibes, is where the action is in the evenings. It's a modern beach resort with good beaches, plenty of lively bars and restaurants, and a popular jazz festival in July. Buses, trains, and even a tourist train (see "Getting around Antibes," above) make the 10-minute connection to and from Antibes constantly.

Marineland and Parc de la Mer—A few backstrokes from Antibes, Parc de la Mer is a massive waterworld of waterslides, miniature golf, exhibits, and more. Marineland anchors this sea park extravaganza with shows featuring dolphins, sea lions, and killer whales (Marineland only—adults-€32, kids-€23, prices €2 more in July–Aug and €6 less in winter; the whole shebang—adults-€39, kids-€30; various combo-tickets available for aquasplash waterslides, miniature golf, and other attractions; daily 10:00–19:00, until 22:00 July–Aug, tel. 04 93 33 49 49, www.marineland.fr). The park is five minutes on foot from the train station in Biot (between Nice and Antibes); exit Biot's station and walk toward Nice, following the signs. By car, the park is signed from RN-7, several miles from Antibes toward Nice.

More Day Trips from Antibes—Antibes is halfway between Nice and Cannes (easy train service to both), and close to the artsy pottery and glassblowing village of Biot, home of the Fernand Léger Museum (frequent buses, get details at TI).

SLEEPING

The best Antibes hotels require a car or taxi—central pickings are slim in this city, where most hoteliers seem more interested in their restaurants.

Outside the City Center
$$$ **Hôtel Pension le Mas Djoliba***** is a good splurge, but best for drivers (since it's a 15-min walk from the beach and old Antibes, and a 25-min walk from the train station). Reserve early for this tranquil, bird-chirping, flower-filled manor house where no two rooms are the same. After a busy day of sightseeing, dinner by the pool is a treat (they request that you dine here May–Sept). You'll be in good hands with sweet Stephanie serving and Sylvan cooking with market-fresh products (Db with breakfast and dinner-€80–96 per person, Db room only-€85–125, several good family rooms-€160–170, suite-€210, breakfast-€10, 29 avenue de Provence; from boulevard Albert 1er, look for blue signs and turn right up avenue

Sleep Code

(€1 = about $1.20, country code: 33)
S = Single, **D** = Double/Twin, **T** = Triple, **Q** = Quad,
b = bathroom, **s** = shower only, **no CC** = Credit Cards not
accepted, **SE** = Speaks English, **NSE** = No English, ***** = French
hotel rating (0–4 stars). Credit cards are accepted unless otherwise noted.

To help you sort easily through these listings, I've divided
the rooms into three categories based on the price for a standard
double room with bath:

$$$ **Higher Priced**—Most rooms €95 or more.
$$ **Moderately Priced**—Most rooms between €65–95.
$ **Lower Priced**—Most rooms €65 or less.

Gaston Bourgeois; tel. 04 93 34 02 48, fax 04 93 34 05 81, www
.hotel-djoliba.com, hotel.djoliba@wanadoo.fr).

$$ Hôtel Beau Site*** is my only listing on Cap d'Antibes, a
10-minute drive from the old town. It's a fine value if you want to
get away, but not *too* far away. This place is a sanctuary, with friendly
owners (Nathalie SE), a pool, a big patio, and easy parking. The 30
plush and well-cared-for rooms are priced fairly (standard Db-
€67–77, bigger Db-€87–92, extra bed-€25, bikes available, 141
boulevard Kennedy, tel. 04 93 61 53 43, fax 04 93 67 78 16,
www.hotelbeausite.net, hbeausit@club-internet.fr). From the hotel,
it's a 10-minute walk down to the crowded plage de la Garoupe and
a nearby hiking trail (see "Walks and Hikes," above).

In the City Center

$$ Modern Hôtel** this spick-and-span, well-run place is in the
pedestrian zone. The 17 standard-size rooms, each with air-condi-
tioning and pleasing decor, are an excellent value (Sb-€55–60, Db-
€64–76, €10 more in summer, 1 rue Fourmillière, tel. 04 92 90 59
05, fax 04 92 90 59 06).

$$ Hôtel Relais du Postillon**, on a thriving square, offers 15
small, tastefully designed rooms, all with names instead of numbers,
accordion bathrooms in need of TLC, and owners who take more
pride in their well-respected restaurant (Db-€46–84, price depends
on size and whether you're facing courtyard or park, *menus* from €32,
8 rue Championnet, tel. 04 93 34 20 77, fax 04 93 34 61 24, postillon
@atsat.com, SE).

$$ Auberge Provençale*, on charming place Nationale, has a
popular restaurant and seven Old World rooms (those on the square
get all the noise, day and night), with nonexistent management and

a couldn't-care-less-if-you-stayed-here attitude (Db-€63–85, Tb-€72–94, Qb-€110, reception in restaurant, 61 place Nationale, tel. 04 93 34 13 24, fax 04 93 34 89 88). Their huge loft room, named "Céline," faces the back and comes with a royal canopy bed and a dramatic open-timbered ceiling for no extra charge.

$ **Hôtel le Cameo**** is a rambling, refreshingly non-aggressive old place above a bustling bar (where you'll find what reception there is). The public areas are dark, but the nine very simple, linoleum-lined rooms are almost huggable. All open onto the delightful place Nationale, which means you don't sleep until the restaurants close (Ds-€50, Db-€60, Ts-€59, Tb-€69, 5 place Nationale, tel. 04 93 34 24 17, fax 04 93 34 35 80, NSE).

EATING

The old town is crawling with possibilities. Lively place Nationale is filled with tables and tourists (great ambience), while locals seem to prefer the restaurants along the market hall. Take a walk and judge for yourself, considering these suggestions. Romantics and those on a budget should buy a picnic dinner and head for the beach.

Le Vauban is near the port, with an appealing interior and rea-sonably- priced salads and *plats* (*menus* from €20, open daily, 7 rue Thuret, tel. 04 93 34 33 05).

Le Café Jardin, serves simple food and has a quiet, hidden garden terrace behind the café (look for *Jardin* sign pointing through a door in the back, left of café; open Mon–Sat for lunch only, also open for dinner July–Aug, always closed Sun, 8 rue James Close, tel. 04 93 34 42 66).

L'Ecureuil (or "Casa Amando" in Spanish) is a fun, inexpensive place to try paella in the traffic-free zone. Señor and Madame Carramal are the friendly owners—he's Spanish, which explains why the paella is so *bueno* (closed Sun-Mon, 17 rue Fourmillière, tel. 04 93 34 07 97).

The recommended hotels **Auberge Provençale** (seafood spe-cialties) and **Relais du Postillon** (cozier decor and an interior court-yard) both offer well-respected cuisine with *menus* from €30–35 (both open daily).

Chez Juliette, just off place Nationale, offers budget meals (*menus* from €14, closed for lunch and on Mon, rue Sade, tel. 04 93 34 67 37).

Les Vieux Murs is the place to splurge in Antibes for regional specialties. Its candlelit, red-tone, *très romantique* interior overlooks the sea (€40 *menu*, open daily June–mid-Sept, closed Tue off-season, along ramparts beyond Picasso Museum at 25 promenade Amiral de Grasse, tel. 04 93 34 06 73).

TRANSPORTATION CONNECTIONS

TGV and local trains serve Antibes' little station.

From Antibes by train to: Cannes (2/hr, 15 min), **Nice** (2/hr, 25 min), **Villefranche-sur-Mer** (2/hr, 40 min), **Monaco** (2/hr, 60 min), **Marseille** (16/day, 2.25 hrs).

By bus to: Cannes (3/hr, 25 min), **Nice Airport** (1/hr, 40 min), **Biot** (2/hr, 20 min).

Cannes

Cannes (pronounced kahn—think Madeline, not "can") is famous for its film festival. Its sister city is Beverly Hills. That really says it all. When I asked the TI for a list of museums and sights, they simply smiled. Cannes—with exclusive hotels lining mostly private stretches of perfect, sandy beach—is for strolling, shopping, dreaming of meeting a movie star, and lounging on the seafront. Money is what Cannes has always been about—wealthy people come here to make the scene, so there's always enough *scandale* to go around. The king of Saudi Arabia purchased a serious slice of waterfront just east of town and built his mecca with no regard to local zoning regulations. Money talks on the Riviera...always has, always will.

ORIENTATION

Don't sleep or drive in Cannes. Day-trip in by train. It's a breeze, as trains run frequently along the Riviera, and they all stop in Cannes (2/hr, 15 min from Antibes, 40 min from Nice).

From the train station, rue du 24 Août leads down to the **TI** (daily 9:00–19:00, July–Aug until 20:00, 1 boulevard de la Croisette, tel. 04 93 39 24 53, www.cannes.fr; there's also a TI branch at the train station).

The Film Festival Hall is next to the TI. From here, as you face the sea, Cannes' famous promenade (La Croisette) leaves to the left, and the harbor stretches to the right. Beyond and above the harbor, Cannes' old town (Le Suquet) caps a small hill with grand views. You can buy an ice cream cone at the train station and see everything before you've finished eating it.

SIGHTS AND ACTIVITIES

Film Festival and Hall—Cannes' film festival (Festival de Cannes), staged since 1939, completes the "Big Three" of Riviera events (with Monaco's Grand Prix and Nice's Carnival). But to get into this one, you have to be a star (or a photographer—some 3,000 paparazzi attended the gala event in 2004). Even though it's off-limits to us, it's still a big deal around here. Locals claim it's the world's third-biggest media event, after the Olympics and the World Cup. The festival prize is the Palme d'Or (like the Oscar for Best Picture). The French press can't cover the event enough, and the average Jean in France follows it as Joe would the World Series in the States. Jean lost to Joe in 2003 and 2004, as American films took the Palme d'Or both years (Gus Van Sant's *Elephant*, then Michael Moore's *Fahrenheit 9/11*). In 2005, the festival takes place from May 11–22.

The hall where the festival takes place sits like a plump movie star on the beach. It's a busy-but-nondescript convention center that the world tunes into each May. You'll recognize the formal grand entryway—but the red carpet won't be draped for your visit. Find the famous (Hollywood-style) handprints in the sidewalk—recognize anyone? (Around the other side is the Gare Maritime, with mega-yachts.)

Promenade (La Croisette)—Unlike Nice, Cannes was never part of Italy—so its architecture is more French-Provençal. You won't find the pastel oranges and reds that so define Nice and Villefranche-sur-Mer. Boulevard de la Croisette is Cannes' grand two-mile-long promenade. First popular with kings who wintered

here after Napoleon fell, the elite parade was later joined by British aristocracy. Today boulevard de la Croisette is fronted by some of the most expensive apartments in Europe. Even if you lack a poodle, stroll here to people-watch, admire the big apartments, and ponder huge yachts anchored beyond the reach of the normal world.

Shopping—Cannes is made for window-shopping (the best streets are between the station and the waterfront). Stroll rue d'Antibes for the trendiest boutiques. Rue Meynadier anchors a pedestrian zone with more affordable shops. To bring home a real surprise, consider cosmetic surgery. Cannes is well-known as *the* place on the Riviera to have your face realigned.

Hit the Beach—The majority of Cannes' beaches are private, run by the hotels. The "top of the top" is to cross over from your fancy hotel in a robe, settle your lounge chair into the sand just right under an umbrella, and while away a sunny afternoon. While you probably won't be doing the "fancy hotel and robe" part of this ritual, you can—for about €10—rent a chair and umbrella and make pretend. While Cannes has its few obligatory public beaches (open to the rabble for free), the real Cannes experience is paying to sunbathe without commoners mucking up your space. In July and August,

Handy Cannes Phrases

Where is a movie star?	*Où est une vedette?*
I am a movie star.	*Je suis une vedette.*
I am rich and single.	*Je suis riche et célibataire.*
Are you rich and single?	*Etes-vous riche et célibataire?*
How long is your yacht?	*Quelle est la longeur de votre yacht?*
How much did that cost?	*Combien coûtait-il?*
You can always dream...	*Vous pouvez toujours rêver...*

smart sunbathers reserve a spot on the beach.

Old Town (Le Suquet)—Cannes's oldest neighborhood is a 15-minute walk above the sophistication, with little of interest except the panoramic views from its ancient church, Notre-Dame de l'Espérance (Our Lady of Hope).

Yachters' Itinerary—If you're visiting Cannes on your private yacht, consider this suggested itinerary:

1. Take in the Festival de Cannes and the accompanying social scene. Organize an evening party on your boat.

2. Motor over to Monte Carlo for the Grand Prix, now scheduled—conveniently for yachters—just after the film festival.

3. Drop by Porto Chervo on Sardinia, one of the few places where your yacht is "just average."

4. Head west to Ibiza and Marbella in Spain, where your friends are moored for the big party scene.

TRANSPORTATION CONNECTIONS

TGV and local trains serve Cannes' station.

From Cannes by train to: Antibes (2/hr, 15 min), **Nice** (2/hr, 30 min).

By bus to: Nice Airport (1/hr, 60 min).

St-Tropez

St-Tropez is a sizable, charming, and traffic-free port town smothered with fashion boutiques, elegant restaurants, and luxury boats. If you came here for history or quaintness, you caught the wrong yacht. There are 5,700 year-round residents...and 100,000 visitors daily in the summer.

As with many seaside villages in southern France, the pastel beauty of St-Tropez was first discovered by artists. Paul Signac introduced several of his friends to St-Tropez in the late 1800s, giving the village its first notoriety. But it wasn't until Brigitte

Bardot made the scene here in the 1956 film *...And God Created Woman* that St-Tropez became synonymous with Riviera glamour.

Since then, it's the first place that comes to mind when people think of the jet set luxuriating on Mediterranean beaches. The true Riviera begins here and runs east to Menton, on the Italian border.

In St-Tropez, the village itself is the attraction, as the nearest beach is miles away. Wander the harborfront, where fancy yachts moor stern-in, their carefully coiffed captains and first mates enjoying *pu-pus* (snacks) for happy hour—they're seeing and being seen. Stroll the back streets while nibbling a chocolate-and-Grand Marnier crêpe.

ORIENTATION

St-Tropez lies between its famous port and the hilltop Citadelle (with good views). The network of lanes between the port and Citadelle are strollable in a Carmel-by-the-Sea sort of way.

Tourist Information: The TI is starboard on the port (to you landlubbers, that's to the right as you face the sea), where quai Suffren and quai Jean Jaurès meet (daily April–Oct 9:30–12:30 & 14:00–19:00, July–Aug until 20:00; Nov–March 9:30–12:30 & 14:00–18:00; tel. 04 94 97 45 21, www.saint-tropez.st). Pick up their good, free English walking-tour brochure, *St-Tropez: A Village in Provence.*

SIGHTS AND ACTIVITIES

Window-shopping, people-watching, tan maintenance, and enjoying slow meals fill people's days. People dress up, size up each other's yachts, and troll for a partner. While the only models you'll see are in the shop windows, Brigitte Bardot still hangs out on a bench in front of the TI signing autographs (Thu 15:00–17:30).

Museum of the Annonciade (Musée de l'Annonciade)— Generally ignored, this museum houses an enchanting collection of Post-Impressionist and Fauvist artists who came to this village before Brigitte did. Almost all canvases feature St-Tropez. You'll see colorful paintings by Paul Signac, Henri Matisse, Georges Braque, Pierre Bonnard, Maurice de Vlaminck, and more. Gaze out the windows and see how the port has changed since they were here (€5, Wed–Mon 10:00–12:00 & 14:00–18:00, closed Tue, place Grammont, tel. 04 94 97 04 01).

Boules—The vast *pétanque (boules)* court on place des Lices is worth your attention. Have a drink at the appropriately named Café des

Boules and take in the action. Study up on the sport (see page 156) and root for your hero. The cafés on quai Bouchard offer fine port views and quieter confines.

SLEEPING

(€1 = about $1.20, country code: 33)
$$$ Hôtel Sube***, opposite the TI, has the most central rooms in town (Db-€95–195, Db with port view costs an outrageous €260 in high season or €155 in low season, elevator, quai Suffren, tel. 04 94 97 30 04, fax 04 94 54 89 08). You'll find St-Tropez's best port-view seats on the small deck at the hotel's café.

TRANSPORTATION CONNECTIONS

From St-Tropez by public transportation: With no trains to St-Tropez, buses and boats are your only options. **Buses** serve St-Tropez from St-Raphaël's train station to the east (5/day, 80 min) and from Toulon to the west (7/day, 2 hrs). **Boats** make the one-hour trip from St-Raphaël to St-Tropez twice daily (morning and afternoon, one-way-€11, round-trip-€20, tel. 04 94 95 17 46, or call the TI).

By car: Prepare for traffic in any season—worse on weekends (forget leaving on Sun afternoons) and impossible during summer. It's a too-long, two-lane road with one way in, one way out, and too many people going exactly where you're going. You'll pay dearly to park—figure €4 per hour. The Parking du Vieux Port is marginally closer than Parking des Lices.

PICASSO
MUSEUM
TOUR

In Antibes

In the early 20th century, Antibes' castle (Château Grimaldi) was home to an obscure little museum that nobody cared about. Then its director had a brainstorm: Offer the castle to Pablo Picasso as a studio. Picasso lived in the castle for four months in 1946, where he cranked out an amazing amount of art—and the resulting collection put Antibes on the tourist map.

Sitting serenely where the old town meets the sea, this museum offers a remarkable collection of Picasso's work: paintings, sketches, and ceramics. Picasso said that if you want to see work from his Antibes period, you'll have to see it in Antibes. You'll understand why Picasso liked working here. Several photos of the artist and a movie of him hard at work (when making art, he said he was "working" rather than "painting") make this already intimate museum even more so. In his famous *La Joie de Vivre* (the museum's highlight), there's a new love in Picasso's life, and he's feelin' groovy.

ORIENTATION

Cost: €5, included in the Riviera Carte Musées pass.

Hours: June–Sept Tue–Sun 10:00–18:00, July–Aug Wed and Fri until 20:00; Oct–May Tue–Sun 10:00–12:00 & 14:00–18:00; always closed Mon.

Getting There: It's in Château Grimaldi, just inside the rampart in Antibes' old town. To reach the museum from the train station or harborside parking lot, walk along the harborfront on avenue de Verdun. Enter the old gate under the rampart, and follow the rampart to the white-stone château.

Information: Tel. 04 92 90 54 20.

Museum Tour: An English audioguide is available for €3.

Length of This Tour: One hour.

Museum Overview: There are three manageable floors; Picasso's paintings are on the top floor.

THE TOUR BEGINS

• *Start on the ground floor, where you'll find a good bookshop, ceramics by Picasso, paintings by Nicolas de Stael, and a dramatic seaside sculpture terrace.*

Picasso's Ceramics

A year after leaving Antibes (1947), Picasso discovered ceramics, and his passion for this new medium consumed him. Working in a small family-owned ceramics factory (just outside of Antibes, in Vallauris), he shaped the wet clay, painted it, and fired up a dozen or more pieces a day—2,000 in a single year. He created plates with faces, bird-shaped vases, woman-shaped bottles, bull-shaped statues, and colorful tiles. This timeless medium, reminiscent of the ancient Greeks who once lived here, was given new life in Pablo's playful hands.

Nicolas de Stael

The castle's ground floor displays works by another modern artist who found inspiration in Antibes. Nicolas de Stael (1914–1955), an exiled Russian noble, was raised in Brussels and went on to study art in Paris. He spent his final lonely winter in Antibes near the château, where he committed suicide by jumping out a window. These works depict barely-recognizable boats, seagulls, and seascapes done in a colorful abstract style. Scraping the paint on with a palette knife, he built his figures out of blocks of thick, bright colors.

The Sculpture Terrace

With the Bay of Antibes as the backdrop, see works by local artists (mostly Germaine Richier's Giacometti-like statues). Picasso's friend Joan Miró did the *Sea Goddess.* Arman's *Homage to Picasso* (found in the entrance courtyard) is a pile of bronze guitars reminiscent of Picasso's jumbled Cubist paintings of guitarists.

• *Skip the first floor (temporary exhibitions) and go directly to the second floor ("third floor" for Americans). It's dedicated to works Picasso produced while living on this floor in Antibes. The collection is still being arranged, so you may need to hunt a bit for the art described below, but the area is small.*

Picasso in Antibes

In the summer of 1946, 65-year-old Pablo Picasso was reborn. World War II was over, and Picasso could finally escape the gray skies and gray uniforms of Nazi-occupied Paris. Enjoying worldwide

Picasso in Wartime Paris

No wonder Picasso was so happy in Antibes after the war. Not only had he suffered in Paris from wartime shortages, condescending Nazis, and watching comrades die or be deported—he also had Girl Troubles. His beloved mother died, and he endured an endless, bitter divorce from his first wife—all the while juggling two longtime feuding mistresses (the jealous Marie-Thérèse Walter and the cynical Dora Maar), as well as the occasional extra-mistress fling. At war's end, he left that baggage behind, found fun in the Riviera sun, and dedicated himself to the love of young, beautiful, talented Françoise and a fresh start at fatherhood.

fame and the love of 23-year-old Françoise Gilot (who would soon have Picasso's babies Claude and Paloma), he moved to Antibes. He spent mornings swimming in the Mediterranean, days painting, evenings partying with friends, and late nights painting again, like a madman. Ever-restless Picasso had finally found his Garden of Eden and rediscovered his joie de vivre.

For four months, Picasso worked in a sun-bathed studio in the Château Grimaldi, with a wide-angle view of the Bay of Antibes. Dressed in rolled-up white pants and a striped sailor's shirt, bursting with pent-up creativity, he often cranked out more than a painting a day. Only when the chill and damp of winter set in did he abandon the studio. In a gesture of gratitude uncharacteristic of the stingy Spaniard, he donated all the work he'd done at the Château—nearly 200 paintings and drawings—to create the Picasso Museum we visit today.

These works set the tone for Picasso's postwar art: sunny, light-hearted, childlike, experimenting in new media, and using motifs of Greek mythology, the sea, and animals (such as birds and goats).
• *Find the museum's highlight...*

La Joie de Vivre

Everybody dance! In the center, a dark-haired, bare-breasted flower-child/woman (Gee, could it maybe be Françoise?) kicks up her heels and dances, surrounded by flute-playing satyrs, centaurs, and pronging fauns. They frolic across a wide seaside landscape with boats gliding by on the horizon, under a sky that puts the azure in Côte d'Azur. This large (4 feet by 8 feet) Greek bacchanal sums up the newfound freedom in a newly-liberated France, and sets the tone for the rest of the collection.

This is not oil on canvas—it's boat paint on fibro-cement, a cheap reinforced wallboard used in postwar construction. Other works are done on plywood. Picasso even painted over used canvases. From now on, Picasso was ready to take whatever he found, play with it, and transform it into something beautiful.

Satyr, Faun, and Centaur with Trident

Picasso often portrayed half-man, half-animal fantasies that represented rational man's (and Picasso's own) struggle with his irrational impulses. But these creatures from Greek mythology seem to have found the happy medium: They're smiling, frolicking, relaxed, confident...like Picasso in love. Always an excellent cartoonist and caricaturist, Picasso captures an image with the simplest of lines. His "pagan triptych" exudes an innocent, childlike playfulness.

Man Gulping Sea Urchins

Picasso found inspiration while walking among the fishermen in Antibes' old port. Here, a fisherman in a striped shirt and white pants hunches over to gobble the urchin. Watch out for the fingers.

More Paintings

Among the museum's collection, you'll likely see several Cubist-style nudes *(nus couchés)*, plus the *Antipolis Suite*—a series of 25 (mostly reclining) nudes, very simplified and stripped-down in style. Many of these were studies for his famous *La Joie de Vivre.*

While in Antibes, Picasso took inspiration from the beautiful and interesting surroundings, capturing it in several still lifes *(natures mortes)*. These paintings of fish, octopus, sea urchins, and fruit were likely done after a trip to Antibes' daily market.

INLAND
RIVIERA

For a verdant, rocky, fresh escape from the beaches, head inland and upward. Some of France's most perfectly-perched hill towns and splendid scenery are overlooked in this region more famous for beaches and bikinis. A short car or bus ride away from the Mediterranean reaps huge rewards: lush forests, dramatic canyons, and adorable hilltop villages. A longer drive brings you to Europe's greatest canyon, the Grand Canyon du Verdon.

Getting Around the Inland Riviera
Virtually all the sights mentioned in this chapter are covered on the recommended "Inland Riviera Drive" (see page 284).

Driving is the easiest way to navigate, though the bus gets you to many of the places described. Vence, St-Paul-de-Vence, and Grasse are well served by bus from Nice every 30 minutes (see "Getting Around the Riviera" on page 196). Buses to Tourrettes-sur-Loup, Le Bar-sur-Loup, and Grasse leave from Vence daily except Sunday (7/day, 15 min to Tourrettes, 35 min to Le Bar-sur-Loup, 50 min to Grasse, tel. 04 93 42 40 79). Buses do not enter the Gorges du Loup or Gourdon.

Vence

Vence is a well-discovered yet appealing hill town high above the Riviera. While growth has spread outside its old walls, the mountains are front and center and the breeze is fresh in this engaging town that bubbles with workaday life and ample tourist activity.

Tourist Information
Vence's fully loaded TI is at 8 place du Grand Jardin. They offer bus

Inland Riviera

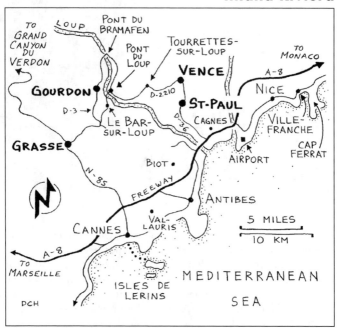

schedules, English-language brochures on the cathedral, and a city map with a well-devised self-guided walking tour (25 stops, incorporates informative English wall plaques). They also publish a list of Vence art galleries with English descriptions of the collections (May–Sept Mon–Sat 9:00–18:00, Sun 9:00–13:00; Oct–April Mon–Sat 9:00–13:00 & 14:00–17:00, closed Sun; tel. 04 93 58 06 38).

Market day in the Cité Historique is on Tuesday and Friday mornings. There's a big, day-long antique market on place du Grand Jardin every Wednesday.

Arrival in Vence

By Bus: The bus stop is on place du Grand Jardin, next to the TI (schedules are posted in the window).

By Car: Follow signs to *Cité Historique,* and park where you can. The most central pay lot is at place du Grand Jardin.

SIGHTS

Stroll the narrow lanes of the old town *(Cité Historique),* using the TI's self-guided tour map. Enjoy a drink on a quiet square, sample art galleries, and find the small cathedral with its Chagall mosaic.

Château de Villeneuve—This 17th-century mansion bills itself as "one of the Riviera's high temples of modern art," with a rotating collection. Check with the TI to see what's playing (€4, Tue–Sun 10:00–12:30 & 14:00–18:00, closed Mon, tel. 04 93 58 15 78).

Chapel of the Rosary (Chapelle du Rosaire)—The chapel, a 20-minute walk from town, was designed by Henri Matisse in thanks to the Dominican sister who had taken care of him (he was 81 when the chapel was completed—see Matisse sidebar, Nice chapter, page 206). The chapel is a simple collection of white walls, laced with yellow, green, and blue stained-glass windows and charcoal black-on-white tile sketches. The sunlight fil-

tered through glass does a cheery dance across the sketches. The experience may be a bit subtle for all but his fans, for whom this is a rich and rewarding pilgrimage (€2.50, Mon and Wed 14:00–17:30, Tue and Thu 10:00–11:30 & 14:00–17:30, Sun only open for Mass at 10:00 followed by tour of chapel, closed Fri–Sat and Nov, tel. 04 93 58 03 26). To reach the chapel from the Vence TI, turn right out of the TI and walk down avenue Henri Isnard, then right on avenue de Provence, following signs to *St. Jeannet*. Or take the little white train that runs to the chapel from in front of the TI (round-trip-€4, 1/hr).

SLEEPING

$$$ Hôtel la Villa Roseraie*** is a Provençal paradise with a pool, lovely garden, and 14 *charmantes* rooms on the fringe of the city (Db-€110–145, most about €125, parking, easy walk to Matisse's chapel and a 15-min walk to TI, along the road to Col de Vence at 128 avenue Henri Giraud, tel. 04 93 58 02 20, fax 04 93 58 99 31).

$$ L'Auberge des Seigneurs**, in the old city, has six appealing rooms with wood-accented character, red-tiled floors, and a low-key, friendly feel (spacious Sb-€48, Db-€65–72, no elevator, place du Frêne, tel. 04 93 58 04 24, fax 04 93 24 08 01). It's a short walk from the bus stop and TI: turn right out of the TI, then right again, then left.

Sleep Code

(€1 = about $1.20, country code: 33)
S = Single, **D** = Double/Twin, **T** = Triple, **Q** = Quad,
b = bathroom, **s** = shower only, **no CC** = Credit Cards not
accepted, **SE** = Speaks English, **NSE** = No English, ***** = French
hotel rating (0–4 stars). Credit cards are accepted unless otherwise noted.

To help you sort easily through these listings, I've divided
the rooms into three categories based on the price for a standard
double room with bath:

$$$ **Higher Priced**—Most rooms €95 or more.
  $$ **Moderately Priced**—Most rooms between €65–95.
    $ **Lower Priced**—Most rooms €65 or less.

EATING

Tempting outdoor places fill the old city; every place looks good
to me.

La Pêcheur de Soleil Pizzeria offers inexpensive meals on a
quiet square (daily July–Aug, otherwise closed Sun–Mon, 1 place
Godeau, tel. 04 93 58 32 56).

For an untouristy, full-blown dinner, try **L'Auberge des
Seigneurs,** and dine by the chimney in which your dinner is cooked
(*menus* from €29, closed Sun–Mon; see "Sleeping," above).

HILL TOWNS AND SIGHTS NEAR VENCE

The sights listed below are connected with a recommended driving
tour, "Inland Riviera Drive," on page 284.

St-Paul-de-Vence—The most famous
of Riviera hill towns, and the most-
visited village in France, feels that
way—like an overrun and over-
restored artist-shopping-mall. Wall-
to-wall upscale galleries and ice cream
shops compete for the attention of the
hordes of day-trippers. Avoid visiting

between 11:00 and 18:00 (I avoid it completely). If you must go,
meander deep into St-Paul-de-Vence's quieter streets and wander
far to enjoy the panoramic views (**TI,** at Maison Tour, rue Grande,
tel. 04 93 32 86 95).

▲**Fondation Maeght**—This inviting, pricey, and far-out private museum is situated above St-Paul-de-Vence. Fondation Maeght (fohn-dah-shown mahg) offers a fine introduction to modern

Mediterranean art by gathering many of the Riviera's most famous artists under one roof. The founder, Aimé Maeght, long envisioned an ideal exhibition space for the artists he supported and befriended as an art dealer. He purchased a dry piece of hilltop land, planted more than 35,000 plants, and hired an architect (José Luis Sert) with the same vision.

A sweeping lawn laced with amusing sculptures and bending pine trees greets visitors. On the right, a chapel designed by Georges Braque—in memory of the Maeghts' young son, who died of leukemia—features a moving purple stained glass over the altar. The unusual museum building is purposefully low-profile, to let its world-class modern-art collection take center stage. Works by Fernand Léger, Joan Miró, Alexander Calder, Georges Braque, and Marc Chagall are thoughtfully arranged in well-lit rooms. The backyard of the museum has views, a Gaudí-esque sculpture labyrinth by Miró, and a courtyard filled with wispy works of Alberto Giacometti. The only permanent collection in the museum consists of the sculptures, though the museum tries to keep a good selection of paintings by the famous artists here all year.

Cost and Hours: €11.50, €2.50 to take photos, not covered by Riviera Carte Musées pass, daily July–Sept 10:00–19:00, Oct–June 10:00–12:30 & 14:30–18:00, great gift shop and cafeteria, tel. 04 93 32 81 63, www.maeght.com.

Getting There: It's a steep (uphill) 15-minute walk from St-Paul-de-Vence; blue signs indicate the way (use St-Paul-de-Vence bus stop; parking is available at the top, though lot can be full).

Tourrettes-sur-Loup—The town, hemmed in by forests, looks ready to skid down its abrupt hill. Tourrettes-sur-Loup is small, with no sprawl. Wander its steep streets. You'll still find some arts and crafts, though much less than in the "Vence towns." Plunge deep to find good views, as well as Tom's ice cream. Known as the "Cité des Violettes," Tourrettes-sur-Loup produces more violets than anywhere else in France, most of which end up in bottles that make you smell better. Wednesday is market day on place de la Libération. Fabulous views of Tourrettes-sur-Loup await a minute away on the drive to Pont-du-Loup.

Sleeping and Eating: $$$ **L'Auberge de Tourettes*****, an exquisite restaurant at the western edge of town, produces new *menus* each day. It's ideal for lunch with a view (good *plats*-€16, dinner *menus* from €45, restaurant closed Tue–Wed). Its six thoughtfully-designed rooms—some with sea views and all with access to a view terrace—seem to go unnoticed (mountain-side Db-€115, grand-view-side Db-€135, buffet breakfast-€11, 11 route de Grasse, tel. 04 93 59 30 05, fax 04 93 59 28 66, www.aubergedetourrettes.fr, info@aubergedetourrettes.fr).

Le Bar-sur-Loup—This town is the yin of St-Paul-de-Vence's yang: It has almost no tourist shops and little to do except wander the peaceful brick-lined lanes and enjoy the view. Park at the lot by the Hôtel de Ville and Syndicat d'Initiative (TI).

Confiseries Florian—The candied-fruit factory hides between trees down in Pont-du-Loup (though their big, bright sign is hard to miss). Ten-minute tours of their factory leave regularly, covering the candied-fruit process and explaining the use of flower petals (like violets and jasmine) in their products. Everything they make is fruit-filled—even their chocolate (with oranges). The tour ends with a tasting of the *confiture* in the dazzling gift shop.

Cost and Hours: Free, request a tour with English commentary, daily 9:00–12:00 & 14:00–18:30, tel. 04 93 59 32 91.

Grasse

The historic and contemporary capital of perfume, Grasse offers a welcome contrast to the dolled-up hill towns above the Riviera. While famous for its spendy product, Grasse's urban center is a gritty yet appealing collection of walking lanes and vertical staircases. The place feels at once in need of a facelift, and yet refreshingly real. Its historic alliance with Genoa explains the Italianesque look of the old city. Still the only good reasons to visit Grasse are if you care about perfume, or if you're heading to or from the Grand Canyon du Verdon.

ORIENTATION

Tourist Information

All sights in Grasse cluster near the main TI in the Palais du Congrès on cours Honoré Cresp, sometimes referred to as place du Cours (summer Mon–Sat 9:00–19:00, off-season Mon–Sat 9:00–12:30 & 14:00–18:00, always closed Sun, tel. 04 93 36 66 66). There's a branch TI (Grasse Espace Accueil) on place de la Foux near the bus station. At either TI, pick up an English map with a self-guided tour of the old city (uses handy information plaques). If heading to the Grand Canyon du Verdon, get specifics here.

Fragrant Grasse

Grasse has been at the center of fragrance since the 1500s, when it was known for its scented leather gloves. The cultivation of aromatic plants around Grasse slowly evolved to soaps and perfumes, and by the 1800s, Grasse was recognized as the center for perfume (thanks largely to its flower-friendly climate), making it a wealthy city.

It can take a ton (roughly 10,000 flowers) of carefully picked petals like jasmine to make about two pounds of essence (a damaged flower petal is bad news). Today, perfumes are made from as many as 500 different scents; most are imported to Grasse from countries around the world. The "blender" of these scents and the perfume mastermind is called the "nose" (who knows best). The five master "noses" who work here have studied their profession longer than a medical student (7 years). They had to show that they had the gift before entering "nose school" (in Versailles) and cannot drink alcohol, ever.

Skip outlying perfumeries with French-only tours. Only three factories out of 40 open their doors to visitors, and only one is worth visiting: Fragonard Perfume.

Arrival in Grasse

By Bus: Buses let you off a five-minute downhill walk from the sights (from the bus station on place de la Buanderie, walk up to boulevard du Jeu de Ballon, and stroll downhill to cours Honoré Cresp). Buses run directly to Cannes in 30 minutes and to Nice in 50 minutes. There is no train station in Grasse.

By Car: Drivers should park at the underground lot near the TI, Parking du Cours (follow signs to *Centre-Ville,* then *Office de Tourisme,* then *Parking du Cours*).

SIGHTS

Fragonard Perfume—This well-run, functioning factory, located dead-center in Grasse, offers frequent, informative 20-minute tours and an interesting "museum" to explore while you wait. Pick up their English brochure describing what's in the museum cases, then drop down to where the fragrant tour begins. On your tour, you'll learn that the difference between perfume, eau de toilette, and cologne is only a matter of perfume-percentages. You'll also learn how the product is made today, as well as how they used to do it (I like the old way of pressing flowers in animal fat). The tour ends with a whiff in the elegant gift shop (tours run daily 9:00–17:30, just off cours Honoré Cresp at 20 boulevard Fragonard).

The same company runs a two-room museum (**Musée Provençal du Costume et du Bijou**), displaying traditional dresses and jewelry—a block above, on the pedestrian street (free, daily 10:00–13:00 & 14:00–18:00, 2 rue Jean Ossola). Upon leaving, you'll be given a card to be exchanged for a free gift at a shop next door.

International Museum of Perfume (Musée International de la Parfumerie)—This city museum, facing the main square, packages the best background on the historical production of perfume. Get the English handout and start with the informative video, then work your way up past exhibits describing the process from extraction to distillation to blending. The top floor is the highlight, with a balmy greenhouse and small garden plots showing key plants used for making perfume. Pull the stainless-steel cylinders to smell; don't miss the vanilla (€3, covered by Riviera Carte Musées pass, June–Sept daily 10:00–18:30; Oct and Dec–May Wed–Mon 10:00–12:30 & 14:00–17:30, closed Tue and all of Nov; 8 cours Honoré Cresp).

Old Grasse—The rue Jean Ossola leads into the labyrinth of ancient streets that form an intriguing if unpolished pedestrian area. Follow the TI's self-guided tour with your map (takes an hour at a speedy pace), or just read the information plaques when you see them. The Point de Vue gives a nice view over Grasse from the mountains to the sea.

Inland Riviera Drive

This drop-dead-beautiful loop drive connects the villages and sights near Vence (described above) and the Grand Canyon du Verdon (described below). It's best done as a day trip from the Nice area (allow all day). Each of the stops described is only minutes away from the next by car or bus, but allow 45 minutes to drive from Nice to the first stop, St-Paul-de-Vence (see map on page 278).

Start early if you want to see beautiful St-Paul-de-Vence without seeing mobs (consider breakfast here). Leave Nice along the promenade des Anglais, then follow Grasse signs until you see Vence and St-Paul-de-Vence. After sampling **St-Paul-de Vence**, visit the **Fondation Maeght** just above (page 281; park at the museum, or walk 20 min from St-Paul, following blue signs). After completing your course in contemporary art, find artsy **Vence**, a few miles above. You'll find many good lunch options in Vence, though if you want a special meal, wait for Tourrettes-sur-Loup. From Vence, visit Matisse's famous chapel (best views of Vence are a mile beyond the chapel, where there's a turnaround), then head for slippery-sloped **Tourrettes-sur-Loup** (which has a great restaurant, L'Auberge de Tourrettes—see page 281).

From Tourrettes-sur-Loup, follow Pont-du-Loup (fabulous views of Tourrettes-sur-Loup a mile after leaving, pullouts and a café available). Before long, you'll see views of Le Bar-sur-Loup, clinging to its hillside in the distance. When you arrive at the junction of Gourdon and Le Bar-sur-Loup, look way up to your destination, the tiny rock-top village of Gourdon. Candy addicts can detour quickly down to Pont-du-Loup and visit the small candied-fruit factory of **Confiseries Florian** (page 282). Follow Gourdon signs to the right and climb into the teeth of a rocky canyon, the **Gorges du Loup** (page 282). It's a mostly second-gear road that winds between intimidating rock faces above a surging stream (buses do not enter the gorges).

The drive passes all too fast to the pont de Bramafen bridge, where the road hooks back toward Gourdon. Climb above the canyon you just drove through and watch the world below turn to miniature. The sky-high (2,300 feet) village of **Gourdon** awaits at the top with grassy picnic areas, little, stone-to-stone tourist shops, and a few cafés (the château has French-only tours). Still, the views from the far side of the village are amazing, and the most appropriately named restaurant in France, the Eagle's Nest *(Le Nid de l'Aigle)*, tempts travelers with fine cuisine and a remarkable setting (daily July–Aug, otherwise closed Mon, tel. 04 93 77 52 02).

From Gourdon, slide downhill to **Grasse** with views down to (literally) overlooked Le Bar-sur-Loup. Follow signs to Grasse, then *Centre-Ville,* and park at the first underground lot you come to (by the Grasse TI—see page 282). After improving your body odor in Grasse, return to your Riviera home base (allow 45 min to Nice, via Cannes and the autoroute).

Le Grand Canyon du Verdon
(Les Gorges du Verdon)

Two hours north of Nice and three hours east of Avignon lies the Parc Naturel Grand Canyon du Verdon (a.k.a. Gorges du Verdon), an immense area of natural beauty (worth ▲▲▲, even to Arizonans).

The Grand Canyon of Verdon, Europe's greatest canyon, offers a dilly of a detour between Provence and the Riviera. If you start early, you can enjoy a round-trip drive from Nice (see "Inland Riviera Drive," above) or you could connect your home bases in the Riviera and Provence (figure 7 hrs with modest canyon time between Nice and Roussillon or Aix-en-Provence; allow 8 hrs to Avignon). But many visitors prefer to stop and smell the canyon, overnighting en route (suggestions listed below).

ORIENTATION

The Grand Canyon du Verdon is the heart of the park, where over-powering, white-rock slabs drop impossible distances to a snaking, turquoise river below. Roads run its length on both sides (*Rive Gauche* and *Rive Droite*); the *Rive Gauche* (left bank) works best for most, though both are spectacular. The Grand Canyon du Verdon, far more than just its famous canyon, is a huge area comprising sublime alpine scenery with misty villages, poster-child lakes, meandering streams, and miles of gentle meadows. Just the drive between Grasse and the park is spectacular; the jaw-numbing canyon was the icing on *le gâteau*. You need a car, patience, and a lack of vertigo to explore this area. If traveling in summer, go really early or skip it. Fill your tank before leaving Grasse or Moustiers-Ste-Marie, as gas is scarce.

The *Rive Gauche* (Left Bank) Route

The Grand Canyon du Verdon is located between Moustiers-Ste-Marie (description below) to the northwest (Provence end) and little Comps-sur-Artuby to the southeast (Riviera end).

Approaching from Nice: Coming from the Riviera, pass through Grasse (the A-8 autoroute from Nice to Cannes saves time), then follow signs for Digne, then Draguignan (for a short distance), then *Gorges du Verdon*. The climb from Grasse is magnificent (con-sider a stop at the ridge-top snack bar 10 min above the city). The scenery only gets better, and by the time you reach the actual canyon (described below), you've had more than your share of nature's bounty. Follow the road *Gorges du Verdon Rive Gauche* along the canyon rim for 15 miles from the Balcon de la Mescla to Aiguines (good overnight stop, listed below), then leave the canyon, heading for Moustiers-Ste-Marie. To continue to Provençal destinations from here, follow Riez, then Gréoux-les-Bains. From Gréoux, roads split toward Manosque (best for Luberon and Avignon) and Aix-en-Provence (best for Cassis, Marseille, and Arles).

Approaching from Provence: All roads pass through Gréoux, about an hour northeast of Aix-en-Provence. Those coming from Cassis, Aix-en-Provence, and Arles will find the A-51 autoroute from Aix the fastest path; those coming from the Luberon and Avignon should take N-100 via Apt and Manosque. From Gréoux, follow Riez, Moustiers-Ste-Marie, and Aiguines before entering the Grand Canyon du Verdon *(Rive Gauche)*. Leave the canyon after the Balcon de la Mescla following Comps-sur-Artuby (and Draguignan for a short distance), then Grasse and Nice for the Riviera. The fastest way from Grasse to Nice is via Cannes and the A-8 autoroute.

THE CANYON

The gorges drop 2,200 feet at their deepest points to the river that carved them. Down below, canyons can get as narrow as 26 feet across, and at the top they can be as far apart as 4,700 feet.

You'll drive at an escargot's pace, navigating hairpin turns along the *Corniche Sublime* with constant views of rocky masses and vanishing-point views up the canyon. The driver loses unless you stop frequently and get out. Hikes into the canyon are too long for most. You're better off walking along the road for a bit, or better, walking along sections of two-track dirt roads that lead away from the asphalt (plenty to choose from). There are many small pullouts along the route; one of the more impressive is at Balcon de la Mescla, the first pullout drivers reach as they approach from Nice. Nearby, walk across Europe's highest suspension bridge (pont d'Artuby) and imagine working on this construction crew.

About halfway through the canyon, you'll come to $$ **Hôtel-Restaurant Grand Canyon du Verdon****, which must have been grandfathered in to own its unbelievable location 2,500 feet high on the *Corniche Sublime.* This concrete, funky place looks slapped together, but the café terrace has a table for you with stupendous views. The hotel rents 15 modern and basic rooms, half on the canyon and a few with view decks. Its restaurant is closed on Wednesdays, so BYO on that evening; you don't want to drive to the nearest restaurant (open mid-April–mid-Oct, canyon-side Db-€80, non-canyon-side Db-€60, add €15 during summer and holidays, reasonably-priced meals, tel. 04 94 76 91 31, fax 04 94 76 92 29, hotel.gd.canyon@wanadoo.fr).

Aiguines, huddled at the western edge of the canyon, is a cute little village with a few hotels and cafés, and a 15th-century château (closed to the public). It's an outdoors-oriented place that most canyon visitors cruise right through. Stop for a drink by the fountain and consider a night at $ **Hôtel du Vieux Château****, which has been in business for 200 years. It has 12 pleasing rooms, with no two alike (Db-€62, extra bed-€14, cozy restaurant, place de la Fontaine, tel. 04 94 70 22 95, fax 04 94 84 22 36, www.hotelvieuxchateau.fr, contact@hotelvieuxchateau.fr, Frederick SE). $ **Hôtel Altitude 823**** has clean rooms but less character (Db-€55–60, tel. 04 98 10 22 17, fax 04 98 10 22 16, altitude823@aol.com).

Moustiers-Ste-Marie is a pretty village with an impressive setting between a rock and a hard place. It's sadly overrun with tourist boutiques selling the locally famous china, in addition to the usual Provençal kitsch. You can weather the crowds and climb 70 minutes on a remarkable switchback trail to the too-high Chapelle Notre-Dame de Beauvoir, or trust me that the view is exceptional—views are immediately good if you prefer a smaller sample of the trail. If you need to bed down, do so in the well-run **$$ La Bonne Auberge****, with a pool and modern comforts in all of its generously sized rooms (Db-€65–70, elevator, a few blocks outside village center, route de Castellane, tel. 04 92 74 66 18, fax 04 92 74 65 11, http://perso.club-internet.fr/lbauberg, labonneauberge@post.club -internet.fr).

TRAVELING WITH CHILDREN

This part of France is kid-friendly. Teenagers love the beach towns (Cassis is best), and they tend to prefer the hustle and bustle of cities like Avignon, Arles, Aix-en-Provence, and Nice. Younger kids usually prefer the rural areas with more swimming pools, open spaces, and parks. To make your trip fun for everyone in the family, mix heavy-duty sights with kids' activities, like playing miniature golf, renting bikes, and riding the little tourist trains popular in many towns. If you're in France near Bastille Day, remember that firecracker stands pop up everywhere on the days leading up to July 14. Putting on their own fireworks show can be a highlight for teenagers.

Minimize hotel changes by planning three-day stops. Aim for hotels with restaurants, so kids can go back to the room and play while you finish a pleasant dinner. We've listed public pools in many places, but be warned: Public pools in France commonly require a small, Speedo-like bathing suit for boys and men (American-style swim trunks won't do)—though they usually have these little suits to loan.

For breakfast, croissants are a hit. For lunch and dinner, it's easy to find fast-food places and restaurants with kids' menus, but it's more fun to find *crêperies,* which have plenty of stuffings for both savory and dessert crêpes. For food emergencies, we travel with a plastic container of peanut butter brought from home and smuggle small jars of jam from breakfast.

Kids homesick for friends can keep in touch with cheap international phone cards (a dollar buys 10 minutes of time for catching up). Hotel Internet stations and cybercafés are a godsend for parents with teenagers. Some parents find French mobile phones a worthwhile investment; adults can stay connected to teenagers while allowing them maximum independence (see "Telephones," page 30).

Kids like the French adventure comics Asterix and Tintin (both available in English, sold in bigger bookstores with English sections).

It's fun to take kids to movies (even if not in English) just to see how theaters work elsewhere. Movies shown in their original language—usually with subtitles—are listed as *v.o.* at the box office (one showing could be *v.o.* and the next could be dubbed in French, labeled *v.f.*). *Dessin animé* means "cartoon."

Swap babysitting duties with your partner if one of you wants to take in an extra sight. And for memories that will last long after the trip, keep a family journal. Pack a small diary and a glue stick. While relaxing at a café over a *citron pressé* (lemonade), take turns writing the day's events and include mementos such as ticket stubs from museums, postcards, or stalks of lavender.

Before You Go

- Get your kids into the spirit ahead of time. Pick up books at the library and rent videos. Watch or read the Madeline stories by Ludwig Bemelmans, *The Hunchback of Notre-Dame* by Victor Hugo, *The Three Musketeers* by Alexandre Dumas, or Dumas' *The Man in the Iron Mask. Anni's Diary of France* by Anni Axworthy is a fun, picture-filled book about a young girl's trip; it could inspire your children. *How Would You Survive in the Middle Ages* by Fiona MacDonald is an appealing "guide" for kids to the Middle Ages. Serious kid-historians will devour *The Kingfisher History Encyclopedia.* If your children are interested in art, get your hands on *The History of Art for Young People* by Anthony Janson and *Discovering Great Artists: Hands-On Art for Children in the Styles of the Great Masters* by MaryAnn Kohl. (Also see "Recommended Books and Movies," which has some good choices for teenagers, on page 10.)
- Get your kids involved in trip planning. Have them read about the places that you may include in your itinerary (even the hotels you're considering) and let them help in your decisions.
- Hotel selection is critical. In my recommendations, I've identified hotels that seem particularly kid-friendly (pools, ping-pong, grassy areas, easygoing owners, etc.). If you're staying for a week or more, rent a *gîte* (see "*Gîtes* and Apartments," page 38).

What to Bring

- Bring plenty of children's books; they're scarce and expensive in France. Our children read much more when traveling in Europe than while at home in the United States, so don't skimp here (see list above).
- Bring peanut butter (hard to find in France)...or help your kids acquire a taste for Nutella, the tasty hazelnut-chocolate spread available everywhere.

- For younger kids, Legos are easily packed and practical.
- Compact travel games and a deck of cards are airplane-, train-, and hotel room–friendly.
- If you have older kids, bring along a Walkman.
- For traveling with infants, car rental agencies usually have car seats for a small price, though you must reserve one ahead of time. And while most hotels have some sort of crib, we brought a portable crib and did not regret it.
- Cameras (even disposable ones) are a great investment to get your kids involved.
- For longer drives, books on tape or CD can be fun for the whole family (if carefully chosen). I recommend Peter Mayle's *A Year in Provence*, available on both cassette tape and CD.

Planning Your Time

- Don't overdo it. Tackle one key sight each day and mix in a healthy dose of fun activities.
- Follow this book's crowd-beating tips to a tee. Kids despise long lines more than you do.
- Eat dinner early (19:00–19:30 at restaurants, earlier at cafés). Skip romantic eateries. Try relaxed cafés (or fast-food restaurants) where kids can move around without bothering others. Picnics work well.
- The best and cheapest toy selection is in the department stores, like Monoprix and Galeries Lafayette (see the Shopping chapter, page 293).
- Let kids help choose daily activities, lead you through ancient sights, and so on.
- Keep an eye out for *mini-golfs* (miniature golf).

SIGHTS AND ACTIVITIES

These are listed in no particular order:
- The Pont du Gard. An entire wing of the museum is dedicated to kids, who can also swim or take a canoe trip on the river. See page 117.
- Cassis: Boat trip to the *calanques* or the port and beaches for teenagers
- Changing of the Guard in Monaco (11:55 daily). See page 255.
- Cousteau Aquarium in Monaco. See page 255.
- Pedal boats on the Mediterranean. See page 210.
- Les Baux's castle ruins, with medieval weaponry and great walls to climb. See page 75.
- Canoeing on the Ardèche River (page 133) or the Sorgue River (page 152).
- Biking on the Promenade des Anglais in Nice. See page 202.

- Marineland near Antibes in Biot. See page 265.
- Little white tourist trains (in nearly every city).

Honorable mention goes to Arles' Ancient History Museum (see page 59), horseback riding in the Camargue (page 87), Roman Arenas in Nîmes (page 108) and Arles (page 57), Cathedrale d'Images near Les Baux (page 79), City Segway Tours of Nice (see page 204), the beaches of Antibes (page 264), and the narrow-gauge train ride from Nice (see page 211).

SHOPPING

Provence and the Riviera offer France's best shopping outside of Paris, with a great range of reasonably-priced items ideal for souvenirs and gifts. If approached carefully, shopping in the south can be a culturally enlightening experience. There's no better way to mix shopping business with travel pleasure than at the weekly markets in towns and villages throughout the region. These traditional market days are much more than fresh produce and fish; in many cases, at least half the market is devoted to durable goods (like baskets, tablecloths, pottery, and local fabrics), ideal for gift-scavenging travelers. If you miss market day, most Provençal towns have more than enough small shops selling local products—and more than enough kitschy souvenirs. (They're often selling the same items you can find more cheaply at weekly markets.) The cities described in this book have unlimited boutique shopping for clothing. In this chapter, you'll find information on shopping for souvenirs, navigating market days, and browsing boutiques.

What to Buy

Here are some ideas of locally made goods to shop for in Provence and the Riviera. You'll find most of these items in tourist-oriented boutiques, though many of them can be had for less on market days. If you buy more expensive, non-perishable goods, most stores will work with you to send them home (see "Tips on VAT Refunds and Customs Regulations," below).

- **Jams** *(confiture)* containing lush and often exotic fruits, such as *fruits de passion* (passion fruit), *figues* (figs), or *pastèque* (a type of watermelon).
- **Honey** *(miel)*, particularly lavender- or thyme-infused. Stronger palates should try the chestnut- or even oak-flavored honey.

- Tins of **tapenade** (olive paste) and all kinds of olives: black, green, and pricked with garlic or anchovies.
- **Olive-wood products** such as utensils and bowls. Olives are not just for nibbling; in Provence, the entire tree is used.
- Canned **pâtés,** including the buttery, rich *fois gras* (its "home" is Périgord, but you'll also find it in the markets of Provence).
- Packets of **herbs** (including the famous *herbes de Provence*), **salt** from the Camargue (look for *Fleur de Sel* for the best, and use sparingly), and bottles or tins of **olive oil** from local trees (Nyons is France's olive capital). Most of these items can be found in attractive packaging that can be saved and enjoyed long after the product itself is gone.
- Sweets, including the famous *nougat de Montélimar* (a rich, chewy confection made with nuts and honey and sometimes flavored with lavender or other fragrances), *calissons* (orange-and-almond-flavored candy, shaped like the nut and originally from Aix-en-Provence), and **chocolates** from the Provençal producer Puyricard.
- **Soaps and lotions,** particularly those "perfumed" with local plants such as lavender, rosemary *(romarin),* or linden *(tilleul).* You'll also find colorful **sachets** containing the same fragrances.
- **Table linens,** brightly colored. Souleiado and Les Olivades are the most famous local manufacturers, but good-quality knock-offs can be found in most any market or store.
- Local **pottery** (*poterie*; *faïence* is hand-painted *poterie*). Terre Provence is a well-known (and pricey) brand, but many other producers offer excellent quality, usually for less.
- *Santons,* the tiny, brightly-adorned clay or wood Provençal fig-urines. Originally designed for traditional Christmas crèche scenes, today's *santons* represent all walks of life—from the local *boulanger* to the woman sewing bright Provençal cloth to the village doctor. The most famous *santon* makers are in Séguret and Aubagne.

Market Day (Jour du Marché)

Market days are a big deal throughout France, and in no other region are they celebrated more than in Provence and the Riviera. Markets have been a central feature of life in rural areas since the Middle Ages. No single event better symbolizes the French pre-occupation with fresh products and their strong ties to the small farmer than the weekly market. Many locals mark their calendars with the arrival of the new season's produce.

Provence is France's melting pot, where Italy, Spain, and North Africa intersect with France to do business. Notice the ethnic mix of the vendors (and the products they sell). Spices from Morocco and Tunisia, fresh pasta from Italy, saffron from Spain, and tapenade from Provence compete for your attention at Provence's *marchés.*

There are two kinds of weekly, open-air markets: *les marchés* and *les marchés brocantes*. *Les marchés* are more general in scope, more common, and more colorful, featuring products of local farmers and artisans. *Les marchés brocantes* specialize in quasi-antiques and flea-market bric-a-brac. *Brocantes* markets began in the Middle Ages, when middlemen would gather to set up small stalls and sell old, flea-infested clothes and discarded possessions of the wealthy at bargain prices to eager peasants. Buyers were allowed to rummage through piles of aristocratic garbage.

Several general *marchés* have good selections of both produce and *brocantes*. The best of all market worlds may rest in the picturesque town of Isle-sur-la-Sorgue, where, on Sunday mornings, a brilliant food *marché* joins forces with an active flea market and a polished antiques enterprise.

I've listed days and locations for both market types throughout this book. Notice the signs as you enter towns indicating the *jours du marché* (essential information to any civilized soul and a reminder to non-locals not to park on the streets the night before). Most *marchés* take place once a week in the town's main square, and, if large enough, spill into nearby streets. Markets can offer a mind-boggling array of products from the perishable (produce, meats, cheeses, breads, and pastries) to the non-perishable (kitchen wares, inexpensive clothing, brightly-colored linens, and pottery).

The bigger the market, the greater the overall selection, particularly for nonperishable goods. Bigger towns (like Arles) may have two weekly markets, one for produce and another for nonperishable goods; in other towns, the second weekly market may simply be a smaller version of the main market day (as in Isle-sur-la-Sorgue). The biggest market days are usually on weekends, so that everyone can go. In the largest cities (like Avignon and Nîmes), market halls have been established with produce stands and meat counters selling fresh goods daily.

Market day is as important socially as commercially—it's a weekly chance for locals to resume friendships and get the current gossip. Here, neighbors can catch up on Henri's barn renovation, see photos of Jacqueline's new grandchild, and relax over *un café*. Dogs are tethered to café tables while friends exchange kisses. Tether yourself to a café table and observe: three cheek-kisses for good friends (left–right–left), a fourth for friends you haven't seen in a while. (The appropriate number of kisses varies by region—Paris, Lyon, and Provence each have separate standards.)

Markets typically begin at about 8:00, with set-up commencing in the pre-dawn hours (a reason not to stay in a main-square hotel the night before market day). They usually end by 13:00. Most perishable items are sold directly from the producers—no middle-men, no Visa cards, just really fresh produce (*du pays* means "grown locally"). Sometimes, you'll meet a widow selling a dozen eggs, two rabbits, and a wad of herbs tied with string. But most vendors typi-cally follow a weekly circuit of markets they feel works best for them, showing up in the same spot every week, year in and year out. At a favorite market, my family has done business with the same olive vendor and "cookie man" for 15 years.

It's bad form to be in a hurry on market day. Allow the crowd to set your pace. Observe the interaction between vendor and client. Notice the joy they can find in chatting each other up. Wares are dis-played with pride. Generally the rule is "don't touch"—instead, point and let them serve you. If self-serve is the norm, the seller will hand you a bag. Remember, they use metric weight. Ask for *un kilo* (to get two pounds), *un demi-kilo* (about one pound), or *un quart-kilo* ("car-kilo," about half a pound). Many vendors speak enough English to assist you in your selection. Your total price will be hand-tallied on small scraps of paper and given to you. Vendors are normally honest. If you're struggling to find the correct change, just hold out your hand and they will take only what is needed. (Still, you're wise to double-check the amount you just paid for that olive tree.)

At the root of a good market experience is a sturdy shopping basket or bag. Find the vendor selling baskets and other wicker items and go local (*osier* is the French name for wicker, *cade* is the Provençal name—from the basket-making Luberon village of Cadenet); you can also find plastic and nylon versions. Most baskets are inexpensive, make fun and colorful souvenirs, and can come in handy for odd-shaped or breakable carry-ons for the plane trip home. With basket in hand, shop for your heaviest items first. (You don't want to put a kilo of fresh apples on top of the bread you bought for your picnic).

Markets change seasonally. In May, look for asparagus (green, purple, or the prized white—after being cooked, these are dipped in vinegar and eaten by hand). In early summer, shop for strawberries, including the best: *fraises des bois* (wild strawberries). Soon after, you'll see cherries and other stone fruits, plus the famously sweet Cavaillon melons (looking like tiny cantaloupes, often served cut in half with a spoonful or two of the sweet Rhône white wine Beaumes-de-Venise). In late summer, watch for figs *(figues)* and the critical vegetables for the Provençal dish ratatouille—including egg-plant, tomatoes, zucchinis, and peppers. In the fall, you'll see stands selling game birds and other beasts of the hunt.

After November and throughout the winter, look for little (or big, depending on your wallet size) black truffles. Truffles, preserved and sealed in jars, can safely be brought back to the United States. The

Key Phrases

Just looking.	*Je regarde.*	zhuh ruh-gar
How much is it?	*Combien?*	kohm-bee-ehn
Too big/small/	*Trop grand/*	troh grahn/
expensive	*petit/cher.*	puh-tee/sher
May I try it on?	*Je peux l'essayer?*	zhuh puh luh-say-yay
Can I see more?	*Puis-je en voir*	pweezh'en vwahr
	d'autres?	doh-truh
I'll think about it.	*Je vais y penser.*	zhuh vayz-ee pahn-say
I'd like this.	*Je voudrais ça.*	zhuh voo-dray sah
On sale	*Solde*	sold-ay
Discounted price	*Prix réduit*	pree ray-dwee
Big discounts	*Prix choc*	pree shock

Luberon is one of Provence's largest truffle-producing areas, and the town of Carpentras hosts a truffles-only market in season (in winter). Richerenches, Northern Provence's truffle capital, holds its own winter truffle market; during its annual truffle-themed Mass, many parishoners would give a truffle as a small offering, instead of money.

For more immediate consumption, look for local cheeses (cow, sheep, or the Provençal favorite—goat cheese, or *chèvre,* named *picodons*). Cheeses range from very fresh (aged one day) to aged for weeks. The older the cheese, the more dried and shrunken. Some may even be speckled with edible mold. Cheeses come in many shapes (round, logs, pyramids) and various sizes (from single-bite mouthfuls to wheels that will feed you for several meals). Some are sprinkled with herbs or spices. Others are more adorned, such as those rolled in ash *(à la cendre)* or wrapped in leaves *(banon).* Watch for the locally-produced *banon à la feuille,* a goat (or sometimes cow) cheese soaked in *eau-de-vie* (the highly alcoholic "water of life"), then wrapped in a chestnut leaf and tied with string.

Next, move on to the sausages (many also rolled in herbs or spices). Samples are usually freely offered—try the *sanglier* (boar). Usually you can also taste locally produced wines or ciders. Look also for samples of *fois gras* (available in take-it-home tins), good with the sweet white wine of Beaumes-de-Venise. These items make perfect picnic fare when teamed with a crusty baguette.

Throughout Provence, you'll see vendors selling paella made *sur place* (on the spot) in huge, traditional round pans. Paella varies by area and by chef, but most recipes include the traditional ingredients of fresh shellfish, chicken, and sausages mixed into saffron-infused rice. And throughout France, you'll see vans selling sizzling, spit-roasted chicken (perfectly bagged for carrying-out) or pizza (made to your liking on the spot). *Bon appétit!*

Clothing Boutiques

Those preferring fashion to food will be pleased to learn that they don't have to go to Paris to enjoy the latest trends. The stylish boutiques lining the shopping streets of Avignon, Nîmes, Aix-en-Provence, and Nice offer more than sufficient selection and style for the fashion-conscious. The expression for window-shopping in French is *faire du lèche-vitrines* (literally "window-licking"). While hardly as freewheeling and relaxed as *les marchés,* you're a long way from the intimidating clerks of Paris. Still, they play by a different set of rules in France, and the better knowledge you have of the rules, the better player you'll be. Consider these tips to get you off on the right track:

- In small stores, always say *"Bonjour, Madame/Mademoiselle/ Monsieur"* when entering and *"Au revoir, Madame/Mademoiselle/ Monsieur"* when leaving.
- Except in department stores, it's not normal for the customer to handle clothing. Ask first if you can look at an item.
- Forget returns (and don't count on exchanges).
- The customer is not always right; some clerks figure they're doing you a favor by waiting on you.
- Saturdays are busiest.
- Observe French shoppers, then imitate.

Getting a VAT Refund

Wrapped into the purchase price of your Provençal souvenirs is a Value Added Tax (VAT) that's generally about 19.6 percent. If you make a purchase in France of more than €175 at a store that participates in the VAT refund scheme, you're entitled to get most of that tax back. Personally, I've never felt that VAT refunds are worth the hassle, but if you do, here's the scoop.

You must be over 15 and if you're lucky, the merchant will subtract the tax when you make your purchase; this is more likely if the store ships the goods to your home. If not, follow these steps:

Get the paperwork. Have the merchant completely fill out the necessary refund document (*Bordereau de Vente à l'Exportation*—also called a "cheque"). You'll have to present your passport at the store.

Get your stamp at the border. Process your cheque(s) at your last stop in the EU by the customs agent who deals with VAT refunds. It's best to keep your purchases in your carry-on for viewing, but if they're too large or considered too dangerous (such as knives) to carry on, then track down the proper customs agent to inspect them before you check your bag. You're not supposed to use your purchased goods before you leave. If you show up at customs wearing your chic new French ensemble, officials might look the other way—or deny you a refund.

Collect your refund. You'll need to return your stamped document to the retailer or its representative. Many merchants work with a service, such as Global Refund or Premier Tax Free, which have offices at major airports, ports, or border crossings. These services, which extract a 4 percent fee, can refund your money immediately in your currency of choice or credit your card (within two billing cycles). If you have to deal directly with the retailer, mail the store your stamped documents and wait. It could take months.

Customs

You can take home $800 in souvenirs per person duty-free. The next $1,000 is taxed at a flat 3 percent. After that, you pay the individual item's duty rate. You can also bring in duty-free a liter of alcohol (slightly more than a standard-sized bottle of wine), a carton of cigarettes, and up to 100 cigars. As for food, anything in sealed jars or cans (such as foie gras or meat products) is acceptable. Skip cheeses, dried meats, and fresh fruit and vegetables. To check customs rules and duty rates, visit www.customs.gov.

APPENDIX

Let's Talk Telephones

Here are general instructions for making phone calls. For information specific to France, see "Telephones" in the Introduction.

Making Calls within a European Country: About half of all European countries use area codes (like we do); the other half uses a direct-dial system without area codes.

To make calls within a country that uses a direct-dial system (France, Belgium, Czech Republic, Denmark, Italy, Portugal, Norway, Spain, and Switzerland), you dial the same number whether you're calling across the country or across the street.

In countries that use area codes (such as Austria, Britain, Finland, Germany, Ireland, Netherlands, and Sweden), you dial the local number when calling within a city, and you add the area code if calling long-distance within the country.

Making International Calls: You always start with the international access code (011 if you're calling from America or Canada, or 00 from anywhere in Europe), then dial the country code of the country you're calling (see chart below).

What you dial next depends on the phone system of the country you're calling. If the country uses area codes, drop the initial 0 of the area code, then dial the rest of the number.

Countries that use direct-dial systems (no area codes) vary in how they're accessed internationally by phone. For instance, if you're making an international call to the Czech Republic, Denmark, Italy, Norway, Portugal, or Spain, simply dial the international access code, country code, and phone number. But if you're calling France, Belgium, or Switzerland, drop the initial 0 of the phone number.

European Calling Chart

Just smile and dial, using this key:
AC = Area Code, LN = Local Number.

European Country	Calling long distance within...	Calling from the U.S.A./ Canada to...	Calling from a European country to...
Austria	AC + LN	011 + 43 + AC (without the initial zero) + LN	00 + 43 + AC (without the initial zero) + LN
Belgium	LN	011 + 32 + LN (without initial zero)	00 + 32 + LN (without initial zero)
Britain	AC + LN	011 + 44 + AC (without initial zero) + LN	00 + 44 + AC (without initial zero) + LN
Czech Republic	LN	011 + 420 + LN	00 + 420 + LN
Denmark	LN	011 + 45 + LN	00 + 45 + LN
Estonia	LN	011 + 372 + LN	00 + 372 + LN
Finland	AC + LN	011 + 358 + AC (without initial zero) + LN	00 + 358 + AC (without initial zero) + LN
France	LN	011 + 33 + LN (without initial zero)	00 + 33 + LN (without initial zero)
Germany	AC + LN	011 + 49 + AC (without initial zero) + LN	00 + 49 + AC (without initial zero) + LN
Gibraltar	LN	011 + 350 + LN	00 + 350 + LN From Spain: 9567 + LN
Greece	LN	011 + 30 + LN	00 + 30 + LN

European Country	Calling long distance within ...	Calling from the U.S.A./ Canada to ...	Calling from a European country to ...
Ireland	AC + LN	011 + 353 + AC (without initial zero) + LN	00 + 353 + AC (without initial zero) + LN
Italy	LN	011 + 39 + LN	00 + 39 + LN
Morocco	LN	011 + 212 + LN (without initial zero)	00 + 212 + LN (without initial zero)
Netherlands	AC + LN	011 + 31 + AC (without initial zero) + LN	00 + 31 + AC (without initial zero) + LN
Norway	LN	011 + 47 + LN	00 + 47 + LN
Portugal	LN	011 + 351 + LN	00 + 351 + LN
Spain	LN	011 + 34 + LN	00 + 34 + LN
Sweden	AC + LN	011 + 46 + AC (without initial zero) + LN	00 + 46 + AC (without initial zero) + LN
Switzerland	LN	011 + 41 + LN (without initial zero)	00 + 41 + LN (without initial zero)
Turkey	AC (if no initial zero is included, add one) + LN	011 + 90 + AC (without initial zero) + LN	00 + 90 + AC (without initial zero) + LN

- The instructions above apply whether you're calling a fixed phone or cell phone.

- The international access codes (the first numbers you dial when making an international call) are 011 if you're calling from the U.S.A./Canada, or 00 if you're calling from anywhere in Europe.

- To call the U.S.A. or Canada from Europe, dial 00, then 1 (the country code for the U.S.A. and Canada), then the area code and number. In short, 00 + 1 + AC + LN = Hi, Mom!

Country Codes

After you've dialed the international access code (00 if calling from Europe, 011 if calling from the United States or Canada), then dial the code of the country you're calling.

Austria—43	Ireland—353
Belgium—32	Italy—39
Britain—44	Morocco—212
Canada—1	Netherlands—31
Croatia—385	Norway—47
Czech Rep.—420	Poland—48
Denmark—45	Portugal—351
Estonia—372	Slovenia—386
Finland—358	Spain—34
France—33	Sweden—46
Germany—49	Switzerland—41
Gibraltar—350	Turkey—90
Greece—30	U.S.A.—1

Useful French Phone Numbers

Note that calls made to numbers starting with 08 are billed by the minute (about €.30/min).

Directory Assistance for France (some English spoken): tel. 12
Collect Calls to the U.S.: tel. 00 00 11

Embassies and Consulates

U.S. Consulate in Nice: 7 avenue Gustave V, tel. 04 93 88 89 55, fax 04 93 87 07 38 (the Consular Agency, does *not* provide visa services—Paris is the nearest office for these services).
Canadian Consulate in Nice: 10 rue Lamartine, tel 04 93 92 93 22.
U.S. Consulate in Marseille: place Varian Fry, 13006 Marseille, tel. 04 91 54 92 00, fax 04 91 55 09 47.
U.S. Consulate in Paris: Open Mon–Fri 9:00–12:30 & 13:00–15:00, 2 rue St. Florentin, Mo: Concorde, tel. 01 43 12 22 22.
U.S. Embassy in Paris: 2 avenue Gabriel (to the left as you face Hôtel Crillon), Mo: Concorde, tel. 01 43 12 22 22.
Canadian Consulate and Embassy in Paris: 35 avenue Montaigne, Mo: Franklin D. Roosevelt, tel. 01 44 43 29 00.

Emergency/Medical Needs

Police: tel. 17
Emergency Medical Assistance: tel. 15
Riviera Medical Services: tel. 04 93 26 12 70. They have a list of English-speaking physicians and can help you make an appointment or call an ambulance.

Lost or Stolen Credit Cards
Visa: tel. 08 00 90 11 79 or U.S. tel. 410/581-9994
MasterCard: tel. 08 00 90 13 87 or U.S. tel. 636/722-7111
American Express: tel. 01 47 77 72 00 or U.S. tel. 336/393-1111
Diner's Club: Call U.S. collect 00-1-702-797-5532.

Travel Advisories
U.S. Department of State: tel. 202/647-5225, www.travel.state.gov
Canadian Department of Foreign Affairs: Canadian tel. 800-267-6788, www.dfait-maeci.gc.ca
Centers for Disease Control and Prevention: U.S. tel. 877-FYI-TRIP, www.cdc.gov/travel

Travel Companies
American Express (in Nice): 11 promenade des Anglais, tel. 04 93 16 53 53.
Train (SNCF) Reservations and Information: tel. 3635.

Cheap Flights
These companies offer inexpensive flights to Provence and/or the Riviera from other European cities.
easyJet: www.easyjet.com
Ryanair: www.ryanair.ie
Virgin Express: www.virgin-express.com

Airports
Nice: Aéroport de Nice—tel. 04 93 21 30 30, www.nice.aeroport.fr
Marseille: Aéroport Marseille-Provence—tel. 04 42 14 14 14, www.marseille.aeroport.fr
Paris: Aéroport Charles de Gaulle—tel. 01 48 62 22 80, Aéroport d'Orly—tel. 01 49 75 15 15, www.adp.fr

Airlines
Aer Lingus: tel. 01 70 20 00 72
Air Canada: tel. 08 25 88 08 81
Air France: tel. 08 20 82 08 20
Alitalia: tel. 08 02 31 53 15
American Airlines: tel. 08 10 87 28 72
British Airways: tel. 08 25 82 54 00
bmi (British Midland Airways): tel. 01 41 91 87 04
Continental: tel. 01 42 99 09 09
Delta: tel. 08 00 35 40 80
Iberia: tel. 08 02 07 50 75
Icelandair: tel. 01 44 51 60 51
KLM: tel. 08 90 71 07 10
Lufthansa: tel. 08 20 02 00 30

Northwest: tel. 08 90 71 07 10
Olympic: tel. 01 44 94 58 58
SAS: tel. 08 25 32 53 35
Swiss: tel. 08 20 04 05 06
United: tel. 08 10 72 72 72
US Airways: tel. 08 10 63 22 22

Car Leasing in France
Europe by Car: U.S. tel. 800-223-1516, www.europebycar.com
Auto France: U.S. tel. 800-572-9655, U.S. fax 201/934-7501, www.autofrance.net

Hotel Chains
Huge Chain of Hotels: www.accorhotels.com (handles Ibis, Mercure, and Novotel hotels)
Ibis Hotels: tel. 08 92 68 66 86; from United States, dial 011 33 8 92 68 66 86, www.ibishotel.com
Mercure Hotels: toll tel. 08 25 88 33 33, www.mercure.com
Kyriad Hotels: tel. 08 25 00 30 03; from United States, dial 011 33 1 64 62 46 46, www.kyriad.com
Country Home Rental: www.gites-de-france.fr/eng or www.gite .com

Youth Hostels
Hostelling International-U.S.A.: tel. 202/783-6161, www.hiayh .org
Hostelling International-Canada: tel. 800-663-5777, www .hostellingintl.ca

Cooking Classes
Sylvie Lallemand: Sylvie offers excellent small-group cooking classes in her beautiful stone home near Gordes. For about €1,000 per week, the price includes accommodations (tel. 04 90 72 23 41, www.taste-of-europe.com/luberon).
Maison d'Hôtes de Provence: In central Arles, you can take educational and convivial courses, either for several days or for a full week, offered by a Franco-American team (see listing under "Helpful Hints" in the Arles chapter, page 59).

Public Holidays and Festivals
This list includes major festivals in the Provence and French Riviera region, plus national holidays observed throughout France. Many sights close down on national holidays, and weekends around those holidays are often wildly crowded with vacationers (book your hotel room for the entire holiday weekend well in advance). Note that this isn't a complete list; holidays often strike without warning.

2005

JANUARY

S	M	T	W	T	F	S
						1
2	3	4	5	6	7	8
9	10	11	12	13	14	15
16	17	18	19	20	21	22
23/30	24/31	25	26	27	28	29

FEBRUARY

S	M	T	W	T	F	S
		1	2	3	4	5
6	7	8	9	10	11	12
13	14	15	16	17	18	19
20	21	22	23	24	25	26
27	28					

MARCH

S	M	T	W	T	F	S
		1	2	3	4	5
6	7	8	9	10	11	12
13	14	15	16	17	18	19
20	21	22	23	24	25	26
27	28	29	30	31		

APRIL

S	M	T	W	T	F	S
					1	2
3	4	5	6	7	8	9
10	11	12	13	14	15	16
17	18	19	20	21	22	23
24	25	26	27	28	29	30

MAY

S	M	T	W	T	F	S
1	2	3	4	5	6	7
8	9	10	11	12	13	14
15	16	17	18	19	20	21
22	23	24	25	26	27	28
29	30	31				

JUNE

S	M	T	W	T	F	S
			1	2	3	4
5	6	7	8	9	10	11
12	13	14	15	16	17	18
19	20	21	22	23	24	25
26	27	28	29	30		

JULY

S	M	T	W	T	F	S
					1	2
3	4	5	6	7	8	9
10	11	12	13	14	15	16
17	18	19	20	21	22	23
24/31	25	26	27	28	29	30

AUGUST

S	M	T	W	T	F	S
	1	2	3	4	5	6
7	8	9	10	11	12	13
14	15	16	17	18	19	20
21	22	23	24	25	26	27
28	29	30	31			

SEPTEMBER

S	M	T	W	T	F	S
				1	2	3
4	5	6	7	8	9	10
11	12	13	14	15	16	17
18	19	20	21	22	23	24
25	26	27	28	29	30	

OCTOBER

S	M	T	W	T	F	S
						1
2	3	4	5	6	7	8
9	10	11	12	13	14	15
16	17	18	19	20	21	22
23/30	24/31	25	26	27	28	29

NOVEMBER

S	M	T	W	T	F	S
		1	2	3	4	5
6	7	8	9	10	11	12
13	14	15	16	17	18	19
20	21	22	23	24	25	26
27	28	29	30			

DECEMBER

S	M	T	W	T	F	S
				1	2	3
4	5	6	7	8	9	10
11	12	13	14	15	16	17
18	19	20	21	22	23	24
25	26	27	28	29	30	31

For specifics and a more comprehensive list of festivals, contact the French tourist information office in the U.S. (see page 7) and visit www.whatsonwhen.com, www.franceguide.com, and www .festivals.com.

Jan 1:	New Year's Day
Jan 6:	Epiphany
Feb 11–27:	Carnival (Mardi Gras, parades, fire-works), Nice
March 27:	Easter Sunday
March 28:	Easter Monday
April 30–May 2:	Labor Day weekend
May 5–8:	Ascension Weekend
May 8:	VE Day
May 11–22:	Cannes Film Festival, in Cannes
May 15:	Pentecost
May 19–22:	Monaco Grand Prix (auto race), in Monaco, as well as Ascension weekend

June 21:	Music festival (Fête de la Musique), concerts and dancing in the streets throughout France
July:	Tour de France, the national bicycle race that begins and ends in Paris (www.letour.fr)
July:	International Music and Opera Festival (www.festival-aix.com), Aix-en-Provence
July:	Avignon Festival (theater, dance, music, www.festival-avignon.com), Avignon
Early July:	Classical Music Festival, Cannes
July 14:	Bastille Day (fireworks, dancing, and revelry)
Mid-July:	Chorégies d'Orange Music and Opera Festival (performed in a Roman theater, www.choregies.asso.fr), Orange
Mid-July:	"Jazz at Juan" International Jazz Festival, Antibes/Juan-les-Pins.
Late July:	Jazz Festival (www.nicejazzfest.com), Nice
August:	International Fireworks Festival, Cannes
Aug 15:	Assumption of Mary
Oct 29–Nov 1:	All Saints' Day weekend
Nov 11–13:	Armistice Day weekend
Dec 17–Jan 3:	Winter holidays
Dec 25:	Christmas Day

Nice's Climate

First line, average daily low; second line, average daily high; third line, days of no rain.

J	F	M	A	M	J	J	A	S	O	N	D
35°	36°	41°	46°	52°	58°	63°	63°	58°	51°	43°	37°
50°	53°	59°	64°	71°	79°	84°	83°	77°	68°	58°	52°
23	22	24	23	23	26	29	26	24	23	21	21

Numbers and Stumblers

- Europeans write a few of their numbers differently than we do. 1 = 𝟣 , 4 = 𝟦 , 7 = 𝟩 . Learn the difference or miss your train.
- In Europe, dates appear as day/month/year, so Christmas is 25/12/05.
- Commas are decimal points and decimals commas. A dollar and a half is $1,50, and there are 5.280 feet in a mile.
- When pointing, use your whole hand, palm down.
- When counting with fingers, start with your thumb. If you hold up your first finger to request one item, you'll probably get two.

- What Americans call the second floor of a building is the first floor in Europe.
- When using escalators and moving sidewalks, Europeans keep the left "lane" open for passing. Keep to the right.

Metric Conversion (approximate)

1 inch = 25 millimeters
1 foot = 0.3 meter
1 yard = 0.9 meter
1 mile = 1.6 kilometers
1 centimeter = 0.4 inch
1 meter = 39.4 inches
1 kilometer = 0.62 mile

32 degrees F = 0 degrees C
82 degrees F = about 28 degrees C
1 ounce = 28 grams
1 kilogram = 2.2 pounds
1 quart = 0.95 liter
1 square yard = 0.8 square meter
1 acre = 0.4 hectare

Converting Temperatures: Fahrenheit and Celsius

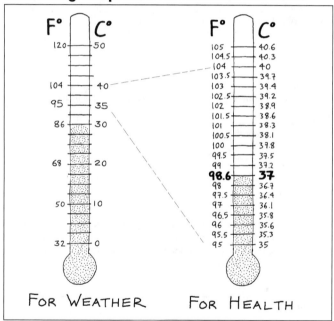

Making Your Hotel Reservation

Most hotel managers know basic "hotel English." Faxing or e-mailing are the preferred methods for reserving a room. They're more accurate than telephoning and much faster than writing a letter. Use this handy form for your fax or find it online at www.ricksteves.com/reservation. Photocopy and fax away.

One-Page Fax

To: _____ @ _____
            hotel   **fax**

From: _____ @ _____
            name   **fax**

Today's date: _____ / _____ / _____
            day   month   year

Dear Hotel _____ ,
Please make this reservation for me:

Name: _____

Total # of people: _____ # of rooms: _____ # of nights: _____

Arriving: _____ / ____ / ____   My time of arrival (24-hr clock): _____
            day   month year   (I will telephone if I will be late)

Departing: ____ / ____ / ____
            day   month year

Room(s): Single _____ Double ____ Twin _____ Triple ____ Quad _____

With: Toilet _____ Shower _____ Bath _____ Sink only _____

Special needs: View ____ Quiet ____ Cheapest ____ Ground Floor ____

Please fax, mail, or e-mail confirmation of my reservation, along with the type of room reserved and the price. Please also inform me of your cancellation policy. After I hear from you, I will quickly send my credit-card information as a deposit to hold the room. Thank you.

_____
Signature

_____
Name

_____
Address

_____
City   **State**   **Zip Code   Country**

_____
E-mail Address

French Survival Phrases

When using the phonetics, try to nasalize the n̲ sound.

English	French	Phonetics
Good day.	Bonjour.	bohn̲-zhoor
Mrs. / Mr.	Madame / Monsieur	mah-dahm / muhs-yur
Do you speak English?	Parlez-vous anglais?	par-lay-voo ahn̲-glay
Yes. / No.	Oui. / Non.	wee / nohn̲
I understand.	Je comprends.	zhuh kohn̲-prahn̲
I don't understand.	Je ne comprends pas.	zhuh nuh kohn̲-prahn̲ pah
Please.	S'il vous plaît.	see voo play
Thank you.	Merci.	mehr-see
I'm sorry.	Désolé.	day-zoh-lay
Excuse me.	Pardon.	par-dohn̲
(No) problem.	(Pas de) problème.	(pah duh) proh-blehm
It's good.	C'est bon.	say bohn̲
Goodbye.	Au revoir.	oh vwahr
one / two	un / deux	uhn̲ / duh
three / four	trois / quatre	twah / kah-truh
five / six	cinq / six	san̲k / sees
seven / eight	sept / huit	seht / weet
nine / ten	neuf / dix	nuhf / dees
How much is it?	Combien?	kohn̲-bee-an̲
Write it?	Ecrivez?	ay-kree-vay
Is it free?	C'est gratuit?	say grah-twee
Included?	Inclus?	an̲-klew
Where can I buy / find...?	Où puis-je acheter / trouver...?	oo pwee-zhuh ah-shuh-tay / troo-vay
I'd like / We'd like...	Je voudrais / Nous voudrions...	zhuh voo-dray / noo voo-dree-ohn̲
...a room.	...une chambre.	ewn shahn̲-bruh
...a ticket to ___.	...un billet pour ___.	uhn̲ bee-yay poor
Is it possible?	C'est possible?	say poh-see-bluh
Where is...?	Où est...?	oo ay
...the train station	...la gare	lah gar
...the bus station	...la gare routière	lah gar root-yehr
...tourist information	...l'office du tourisme	loh-fees dew too-reez-muh
Where are the toilets?	Où sont les toilettes?	oo sohn̲ lay twah-leht
men	hommes	ohm
women	dames	dahm
left / right	à gauche / à droite	ah gohsh / ah dwaht
straight	tout droit	too dwah
When does this open / close?	Ça ouvre / ferme à quelle heure?	sah oo-vruh / fehrm ah kehl ur
At what time?	À quelle heure?	ah kehl ur
Just a moment.	Un moment.	uhn̲ moh-mahn̲
now / soon / later	maintenant / bientôt / plus tard	man̲-tuh-nahn̲ / bee-an̲-toh / plew tar
today / tomorrow	aujourd'hui / demain	oh-zhoor-dwee / duh-man̲

In the Restaurant

I'd like / We'd like...	**Je voudrais / Nous voudrions...**	zhuh voo-dray / noo voo-dree-oh<u>n</u>
...to reserve...	**...réserver...**	ray-zehr-vay
...a table for one / two.	**...une table pour un / deux.**	ewn tah-bluh poor uh<u>n</u> / duh
Non-smoking.	**Non fumeur.**	noh<u>n</u> few-mur
Is this seat free?	**C'est libre?**	say lee-bruh
The menu (in English), please.	**La carte (en anglais), s'il vous plaît.**	lah kart (ah<u>n</u> ah<u>n</u>-glay) see voo play
service (not) included	**service (non) compris**	sehr-vees (noh<u>n</u>) koh<u>n</u>-pree
to go	**à emporter**	ah ah<u>n</u>-por-tay
with / without	**avec / sans**	ah-vehk / sah<u>n</u>
and / or	**et / ou**	ay / oo
special of the day	**plat du jour**	plah dew zhoor
specialty of the house	**spécialité de la maison**	spay-see-ah-lee-tay duh lah may-zoh<u>n</u>
appetizers	**hors-d'oeuvre**	or-duh-vruh
first course (soup, salad)	**entrée**	ah<u>n</u>-tray
main course (meat, fish)	**plat principal**	plah pra<u>n</u>-see-pahl
bread	**pain**	pa<u>n</u>
cheese	**fromage**	froh-mahzh
sandwich	**sandwich**	sah<u>n</u>d-weech
soup	**soupe**	soop
salad	**salade**	sah-lahd
meat	**viande**	vee-ah<u>n</u>d
chicken	**poulet**	poo-lay
fish	**poisson**	pwah-soh<u>n</u>
seafood	**fruits de mer**	frwee duh mehr
fruit	**fruit**	frwee
vegetables	**légumes**	lay-gewm
dessert	**dessert**	duh-sehr
mineral water	**eau minérale**	oh mee-nay-rahl
tap water	**l'eau du robinet**	loh dew roh-bee-nay
milk	**lait**	lay
(orange) juice	**jus (d'orange)**	zhew (doh-rah<u>n</u>zh)
coffee	**café**	kah-fay
tea	**thé**	tay
wine	**vin**	va<u>n</u>
red / white	**rouge / blanc**	roozh / blah<u>n</u>
glass / bottle	**verre / bouteille**	vehr / boo-teh-ee
beer	**bière**	bee-ehr
Cheers!	**Santé!**	sah<u>n</u>-tay
More. / Another.	**Plus. / Un autre.**	plew / uh<u>n</u> oh-truh
The same.	**La même chose.**	lah mehm shohz
The bill, please.	**L'addition, s'il vous plaît.**	lah-dee-see-oh<u>n</u> see voo play
tip	**pourboire**	poor-bwar
Delicious!	**Délicieux!**	day-lee-see-uh

For more user-friendly French phrases, check out *Rick Steves' French Phrase Book and Dictionary* or *Rick Steves' French, Italian & German Phrase Book*.

INDEX

RESEARCHER

KRISTEN KUSNIC

Kristen Kusnic, lover of all things French, leads tours and researches guidebooks for Rick Steves. She lived for a year each in the south of France and in Berlin, becoming fluent in French, German, and red wine. When she's not in Europe, Kristen calls Seattle home.

Start your trip at
www.ricksteves.com

Rick Steves' website is packed with over 3,000 pages of timely travel information. It's also your gateway to getting FREE monthly travel news from Rick — and more!

Free Monthly European Travel News

Fresh articles on Europe's most interesting destinations and happenings. Rick will even send you an e-mail every month (often direct from Europe) with his latest discoveries!

Timely Travel Tips

Rick Steves' best money-and-stress-saving tips on trip planning, packing, transportation, hotels, health, safety, finances, hurdling the language barrier...and more.

Travelers' Graffiti Wall

Candid advice and opinions from thousands of travelers on everything listed above, plus whatever topics are hot at the moment (discount flights, packing tips, scams...you name it).

Rick's Annual Guide to European Railpasses

The clearest, most comprehensive guide to the confusing array of railpass options out there, and how to choo-choose the railpass that best fits your itinerary and budget. Then you can order your railpass (and get a bunch of great freebies) online from us!

Great Gear at the Rick Steves Travel Store

Enjoy bargains on Rick's guidebooks, planning maps and TV series DVDs—and on his custom-designed carry-on bags, wheeled bags, day bags and light-packing accessories.

Rick Steves Tours

Every year more than 5,000 lucky travelers explore Europe on a Rick Steves tour. Learn more about our 26 different one-to-three-week itineraries, read uncensored feedback from our tour alums, and sign up for your dream trip online!

Rick on TV

Read the scripts and see video clips from the popular Rick Steves' Europe TV series, and get an inside look at Rick's 13 newest shows.

Respect for Your Privacy

Ordering online from us is secure. When you buy something from us, join a tour, or subscribe to Rick's free monthly travel news e-mails, we promise to never share your name, information, or e-mail address with anyone else. You won't be spammed!

Have fun raising your Travel I.Q. at
www.ricksteves.com

Travel smart…carry on!

The latest generation of Rick Steves' carry-on travel bags is easily the best—benefiting from two decades of on-the-road attention to what really matters: maximum quality and strength; practical, flexible features; and no unnecessary frills. You won't find a better value anywhere!

Convertible, expandable, and carry-on-size:

Rick Steves' Back Door Bag $99

This is the same bag that Rick Steves lives out of for three months every summer. It's made of rugged water-resistant 1000 denier Cordura nylon, and best of all, it converts easily from a smart-looking suitcase to a handy backpack with comfortably-curved shoulder straps and a padded waistbelt.

This roomy, versatile 9" x 21" x 14" bag has a large 2600 cubic-inch main compartment, plus three outside pockets (small, medium and huge) that are perfect for often-used items. And the cinch-tight compression straps will keep your load compact and close to your back—not sagging like a sack of potatoes.

Wishing you had even more room to bring home souvenirs? Pull open the full-perimeter expando-zipper and its capacity jumps from 2600 to 3000 cubic inches. When you want to use it as a suitcase or check it as luggage (required when "expanded"), the straps and belt hide away in a zippered compartment in the back.

Attention travelers under 5'4" tall: This bag also comes in an inch-shorter version, for a compact-friendlier fit between the waistbelt and shoulder straps.

Convenient, durable, and carry-on-size:

Rick Steves' Wheeled Bag $119

At 9" x 21" x 14" our sturdy Rick Steves' Wheeled Bag is rucksack-soft in front, but the rest is lined with a hard ABS-lexan shell to give maximum protection to your belongings. We've spared no expense on moving parts, splurging on an extra-long button-release handle and big, tough inline skate wheels for easy rolling on rough surfaces.

This bag is not convertible! Our research tells us that travelers who've bought convertible wheeled bags never put them on their backs anyway, so we've eliminated the extra weight and expense.

Rick Steves' Wheeled Bag has exactly the same three-outside-pocket configuration as our Back Door Bag, plus a handy "add-a-bag" strap and full lining.

Our Back Door Bags and Wheeled Bags come in black, navy, blue spruce, evergreen and merlot.

For great deals on a wide selection of travel goodies, begin your next trip at the Rick Steves Travel Store!

Visit the Rick Steves Travel Store at
www.ricksteves.com

Rick Steves

COUNTRY GUIDES 2005

France
Germany & Austria
Great Britain
Greece
Ireland
Italy
Portugal
Scandinavia
Spain
Switzerland

CITY GUIDES 2005

Amsterdam, Bruges & Brussels
Florence & Tuscany
London
Paris
Prague & The Czech Republic
Provence & The French Riviera
Rome
Venice

BEST OF GUIDES

Best European City Walks & Museums
Best of Eastern Europe
Best of Europe

More *Savvy.* More *Surprising.* More *Fun.*

PHRASE BOOKS & DICTIONARIES

French
French, Italian & German
German
Italian
Portuguese
Spanish

MORE EUROPE FROM RICK STEVES

Easy Access Europe
Europe 101
Europe Through the Back Door
Postcards from Europe

DVD
RICK STEVES' EUROPE

Rick Steves' Europe All Thirty
   Shows 2000–2003
Britain & Ireland
Exotic Europe
Germany, The Swiss Alps
   & Travel Skills
Italy

For a complete list of Rick Steves' guidebooks, see page 8.

Avalon Travel Publishing
1400 65th Street, Suite 250
Emeryville, CA 94608

Avalon Travel Publishing
An Imprint of Avalon Publishing Group, Inc.

AVALON
publishing group incorporated

Text © 2004 by Rick Steves
Maps © 2004 by Europe Through the Back Door
Printed in the U.S.A. by Worzalla

Portions of this book were originally published in *Rick Steves' France, Belgium & the Netherlands* © 2002, 2001, 2000, 1999, 1998 by Rick Steves and Steve Smith; and in *Rick Steves' France* © 2004 by Rick Steves and Steve Smith.

ISBN 1-56691-787-5
ISSN 1546-2749

For the latest on Rick's lectures, guidebooks, tours, and public-television series, contact Europe Through the Back Door, Box 2009, Edmonds, WA 98020, tel. 425/771-8303, fax 425/771-0833, www.ricksteves.com, rick@ricksteves.com.

Europe Through the Back Door Managing Editor: Risa Laib
ETBD Editors: Cameron Hewitt, Jennifer Hauseman, Christine Grabowski
Avalon Travel Publishing Series Manager: Roxanna Font
Avalon Travel Publishing Project Editor: Patrick Collins
Research Assistance: Kristen Kusnic, Gene Openshaw (sidebars on art), Karen Lewis Smith (food, wine, and shopping)
Production & Typesetting: Patrick David Barber
Copy Editor: Matthew Reed Baker
Indexer: Stephen Callahan
Cover Design: Kari Gim, Laura Mazer
Interior Design: Jane Musser, Laura Mazer, Amber Pirker
Maps & Graphics: David C. Hoerlein, Zoey Platt, Lauren Mills, Mike Morgenfeld
Photography: Steve Smith, Rick Steves
Front cover photos: Front: Villefranche-sur-Mer © Paul Thompson/Folio; Back: © Pont du Gard © Rick Steves
Front matter color photos: page i © Europe Through the Back Door; page iv © Dominic Bonuccelli
Avalon Travel Publishing Graphics Coordinator: Susan Snyder